THE DYSFUNCTIONAL ALLIANCE

Emotion and Reason in Justice Administration

by

Daniel B. Kennedy

University of Detroit

 anderson publishing co./cincinnati

Copyright © 1977 by Anderson Publishing Co.

Library of Congress Catalog Card Number: 77-73529
ISBN: 0-87084-483-0

Dedicated to Kelley

CONTENTS

(Articles reprinted by permission)

Acknowledgments

Foreword

PART I: ARREST, DELIBERATION, AND JUDGMENT

ACKNOWLEDGMENTS

Many individuals have made valuable contributions during the preparation of this volume.

Thanks, as always, go to the McLean family and to Marilyn MacRae. Much of the thought concerning the legal aspects of criminological studies was offered by Dennis J. Grifka and many ideas regarding the social sciences originated with Dr. Thomas Kelley. Dr. Terry Myers is also to be appreciated for his constant and incisive guidance. Certainly, many thanks are due to my students, both here on the mainland and at the College of the Virgin Islands, St. Thomas, U.S. Virgin Islands.

A special debt is owed to the administration of the University of Detroit for providing a supportive atmosphere in which to work and, especially to my two colleagues at the Center for Criminal Justice Studies, Dr. Jerome J. Rozycki and Dr. Joseph D. Macri.

Two excellent editors at the Anderson Publishing Company, Candice Piaget and Mark Hineline, are to be congratulated for their expertise and thanked for their efforts on my behalf.

FOREWORD

The original intention of this collection was to present various sociopsychological perspectives of the criminal justice system; it was to be a general introductory sourcebook. However, as the articles were reviewed and evaluated, it was noted that, regardless of the immediate subject at hand, they had something in common; each addressed a peculiarity of administering justice, usually based on something like human frailty, and each concluded on a note of regret that the peculiarity exists and would not easily be remedied. With this in mind, it was realized that the manuscript could serve a very definite purpose—that its potential in instruction could extend beyond the general niceties of an introductory reader. At this point, we entitled this collection of articles CRIMINAL JUSTICE: POLEMICS AND APOLOGIES. Hence began efforts to reorganize the articles so that they would reveal a specific progression of interrelated ideas.

That the cover reads THE DYSFUNCTIONAL ALLIANCE: EMOTION AND REASON IN JUSTICE ADMINISTRATION instead of POLEMICS AND APOLOGIES results not from a change of intent but rather as a mark of respect. Many people, among them the authors of the articles included herein, have spent a great deal of time and effort trying to improve a system which has been called, alternatively, a "non-system." No one who has worked so hard in order to right so many wrongs will appreciate being called an apologist. Yet, as the criminal justice system now exists, little more than apologies, can be had from its researchers. The purpose of this volume, very simply, is to explain why.

The controversies that are discussed in THE DYSFUNCTIONAL ALLIANCE reflect critical philosophical divisions—traditional policing v. professionalism; individual v. equal justice; the punitive v. the rehabilitative function of incarceration; and the controlling v. the reintegrative function of probation.

The natural tendency of criminal justice reformists is to resolve these issues so that the system can function more effectively. Yet, at the root of all these controversies is the question of the obligations of democratic justice and whether efficacy is, or should be, the ultimate goal.

In a totalitarian state, emotional concern for one who has transgressed is inappropriate. Rules are regarded as absolute, the consequences of crime are understood. In a democracy, on the other hand, emotional concern for not only the victim but for the criminal as well makes formulaic justice an impossibility. Yet, emotion must be tempered by reason and reason must be mitigated by emotion. Unfortunately, it is also the tendency of criminal justice reformists and critics in their search for solutions to the issues mentioned above either to attempt an objectivity that is deadly in its blind application or to embrace humanistic ideals that ignore the social necessity for artificial order. These camps of sentiment and reason are strong. They reflect what L. H. DeWolf terms in his book *CRIME and JUSTICE in AMERICA,* "a paradox of conscience."

What must be recognized by criminal justice professionals as well as the public is that this confusion as to the obligations of democratic justice is unavoidable, criminal justice controversy equally inevitable. Apologies are not so much in order as a common recognition that there are no absolute solutions to the obvious philosophical difficulties that arise in the administration of justice. It will always be as difficult to punish as it is to ignore the necessity for order. Emotion and reason are permanently allied in our system of justice; they provide the basis for controversy that ironically preserves, rather than prevents, democratic justice.

Mark Hineline   Candice Piaget

Editors, Anderson Publishing Company

PART I:

ARREST, DELIBERATION, AND JUDGMENT

1. Dramatic Aspects of Policing: Selected Propositions, *Peter Manning*

2. A Sketch of the Policeman's "Working Personality", *Jerome Skolnick*

3. The Police Personality: Fact or Fiction, *Robert Balch*

4. Toward an Understanding of Police Anomie, *Rodney Lewis*

5. The Informal Code of Police Deviancy: A Group Approach to "Blue-Coat Crime," *Ellwyn Stoddard*

6. Command, Control, and Charisma: Reflections on Police Bureaucracy, *David Bordua and Albert Reiss, Jr.*

7. Two Police Departments: The Influence of Structure on Operation, *James Wilson*

8. Criminal Sentencing in the United States: An Historical and Conceptual Overview, *Alan Dershowitz*

9. Individualized Judges, *Marvin Frankel*

10. The Psychology of Judges, *Charles Winick, Israel Gerver, and Abraham Blumberg*

11. Trial by Combat, *David Dressler*

12. Informal Relations in the Practice of Criminal Law, *Arthur Wood*

13. The Behavior of Grand Juries: Acquiescence or Justice? *Robert Carp*

1. *Innumerable studies of the police personality have indicated that policemen occupy an ambiguous position in society. Peter Manning, in "Dramatic Aspects of Policing: Selected Propositions," explains the dramatic effects this fact has on police and community relations. This article provides the foundation for more detailed analyses of the psychological and sociological difficulties arising from the police profession today.*

The dramatic aspects of policing, according to Dr. Manning, are the ways in which the police seek to reinforce their identity. For instance, "The police tend to seize on aspects of their work that can be publicly underscored and highlighted." If proof of their social importance dwindles to "Policemen Collect Garbage While Trash Collectors Strike," police become repressive and belligerent in order to prove, if nothing else, that they represent sanctified force.

In a society that is based on an unquestionable value system representing a strong moral code, the Law is sanctified and force, or the overt expression of authority, is merely a necessary tool for the maintenance of order. In a society that becomes incredulous of its government, however, force alone allows the policeman to powerfully assert himself; he cannot maintain a viable social identity if the laws he represents have lost a crucial sense of mystic definitude. Force becomes sanctified, in the policeman's mind, because it provides a raison d'etre and law becomes merely a prop in the maintenance of public acquiescence.

Manning is not implying that American police are becoming increasingly brutal and indiscriminately forceful. Instead, he concludes that the function of police must be regarded as symbolic—that regardless of their motivations, as long as the "appearance of consensual constraining moral order" is maintained, the policeman's existence in our society is justified and necessary.

DRAMATIC ASPECTS OF POLICING: SELECTED PROPOSITIONS

PETER MANNING

Introduction

Social control, defined as "social reactions to behavior defined as deviant, including over-conformity to, as well as violation of, norms" (Clark and Gibbs, 1965: 401), can be seen as having a set of *instrumental* (deterrence, education, prevention, treatment, punishment) and *expressive* functions. The enforcement of a norm, or reaction to a behavioral event, may result not only in a set of intended consequences, but also in unanticipated consequences (cf. Selznick, 1966), some of which can be considered expressive in character.[2] Social control agents occupying an organizationally defined role emit unintended messages ("expressive meaning") while engaged in rule enforcement.[3]

This paper presents a *dramaturgical view of policing* based upon six orienting propositions. "Dramaturgical" in this context refers to a perspective on conduct that is sensitive to the functions of selective public presentation of behaviors and the symbolizations and meanings attached to them.[4] Examples are drawn from urban police departments employing a professional model (Wilson, 1968) where differing conceptions of appropriate public order are encountered (given an altered structure of policing,

1

2 / THE DYSFUNCTIONAL ALLIANCE

different behavioral and social consequences would occur).

1. *To the degree that police agencies lack a legitimated mandate on which there is widespread consensus, they will tend to direct energy either into dramatization of their effectiveness or into repressive actions in attempts to expand their mandate* (cf. Hughes, in Becker, ed., 1963; Manning, 1971). Operating with a symbolic screen of legitimacy, government agencies can supply a canopy of meanings within which distant, ambiguous events where people have little or no factual or empirical knowledge are to be defined (Edelman, 1972). The case for a governmental monopoly of meanings so long as they fit the cognitions and perceptions of a public (or segment "target group" in case of an agency) that attends to the messages is less persuasive at the local government level. There are some 45,000 police agencies in the United States, including federal, state, county, and municipal forces, employing some 450,000 people. Local police agencies seeking to mobilize power will in the process create the possibilities of a specific set of political meanings will be attached to their action by their target audience that will in turn serve to legitimate (or alternatively de-legitimate) their perspectives.[5]

Local social control agencies compete for resources, clientele, self-esteem, and prestige. These agencies engage in minimal cooperation. They compete and overlap, and owe allegiance to different levels of government, industry and locally bounded communities. Between social control agencies at this level, competition for resources, clientele, self-esteem, and prestige is typical. No single overlapping moral authority in an urban community governs all agency-agency relationships. Minimal pragmatic rules govern the content and dynamics of their competitive relationships: these might include tacit agreements to compete, cooperate, or segmentaize areas of control, etc. (cf. Long, 1958: Bailey, 1969).

Let us simply indicate some of the conditions under which one or the other of these two polar dramatic tendencies occur. Typically, in this country at least, the police tend to dramatize by indirect or symbolic means efficient control and capture of criminals. Most police work is administrative (50% of police time) and is not publically visible. The police tend to seize on aspects of their work that can be publicly underscored and highlighted. They utilize the official crime rate as a symbolic indication of their effectiveness (consequently, they claim effectiveness when the rate drops or remains low, while justifying their importance when it rises!). The rate is used to persuade the public that the police protect life and property, and the validity of police claims to public trust or a *mandate*. On the other hand, where public disagreement is high, where the laws are numerous and under direct public criticism (e.g., crimes without victims, especially drug laws), where local government is under question, and the linkage between the local government and the police is directly and mutually agreed upon, repressive action will tend to occur. Examples are: communities in the South seeking control of racial demonstrations, in Chicago during the Democratic National Convention of 1968, and in local communities where police brutality has been reported as common. It would appear that actions of the Chicago police over the last ten or more years represent a paradigm case of a demonstrated repressive tendency among police departments.

2. *To the degree that dramatic aspects of policing become the dominant concern of the police and the public, then ceremony replaces instrumentalism; police work becomes redundant; it simply reaffirms other modes and forms of social control.*

Messages inherent in the communicational order and content of a ceremony are sanctified, or given a truth value by the "unquestionable truthfulness imputed by the faithful to unverifiable propositions." (Rappaport, 1971: 69). For example, the statements "you have broken a law;" "policemen represent the law," come to possess power because they are imbedded in a context (police-citizen encounters) that is conventionally defined and displayed. The sanctification of social behavior creates orderliness and predictability. When a variety of actions, informal and associational, as well as formal, refer to and recreate the *same* set messages for persons, formal control is but a single instance of an ineluctable patterning of human meaning and resultant human action. Thus, the English police are defined as no more than citizens in uniform predisposed to offer assistance to others; insofar as this definition is affirmed in belief and action by policemen, they do indeed act in ways designed to affirm in the reality of their imputed role.

Policing as miscellaneous and unspecialized services is thus *redundant* (in communication theory terms); it adds no further information to the system of human relations. By this token, the ceremony of policing replicates the banality of everyday life. On the other hand, following the above points, we can assert that

> "In modern society, a multiplicity of ways can be used to create a context and the most important of these is coercive force."

instrumental behavior is that for which meaning must be assigned, or designated. It is a matter of empirical discovery. Empirical variation then is a matter of relative contrast, a matter of standing out, and pattern can be supplied then from a variety of frames or contexts. In modern society, a multiplicity of ways can be used to create context and the most important of these is coercive *force* "In such societies authority is no longer contingent upon sanctity; the sacred, or discourse for which sanctity is claimed, has become contingent upon authority." (Rappaport, 1971: 73). The appearance of force thus creates the artifice of sanctity, thus reducing the viability of sanctity itself. Instrumental social control, where the law is an isolated and foreign force, or where legal norms are virtually always enacted by means of force, tends to create *schismogenesis,* or differentiation of meaning, decreased redundancy, and reduced moral consensus. The implications of this can be most readily detected by an examination of what functions as an alternative source of meaning for organizations employing force under the rubric of sanctity (Props. 4. and 5.).

3. *To the degree that instrumentalism replaces the ceremonial features of policework, the degree of sanctity of moral rules that they convey will be*

reduced. In time, coercion replaces consensus on the police mandate and its legitimation.

Much has been written on the problematic features of the police situation, and the parallel police problem of maintaining control while appearing to be fair, and maintaining self-esteem in the face of adversary relations (cf. Westley, 1953). Where the law is not technically involved (questions of order maintenance e.g., domestic disputes, crowds, public use of streets and level of noise, etc.), the policeman is "stripped" of his legal sanctioning authority.[6] In these contexts, lying, brusque statements, disattention to others, and the use of force are common.[7] Reiss (1971) found that 50% of all arrests involved physical force, and 9% involved gross force. Chevigny (1968) argued in selected cases that he was able to prove in court, that New York police, faced with non-compliance to their "requests," tended to respond with violence, and a recovering charge (e.g., assaulting an officer).

American policemen see human service or order maintenance as not being "real police work" as "shit work," and therefore morally degrading to them as protectors of the public safety, i.e., enforcers of the law. Thus, non-adversary, morally binding, interactions are *avoided* or treated with disdain. The tendency to assert a controlling force in interaction, and to create adversary relationships even where the initial situation involves conflict between two others, sets policemen apart interactionally from those they are meant to serve. Their claims to authority and for deference when insufficiently reciprocated as is often the case, create conditions where disagreements over the *locus* of authority are likely.

4. *If the conceptions of policing* provided by the police themselves (*i.e., "the secondary reality of polic-ing"*) are legitimated, then police action frees itself from the community in which it is rooted and may establish its own norms and values.

The police, in following a line of action, build up understandings which filter conduct, are read off by others, and their responses, in turn, are responded to by the police (cf. Parsons, 1951: 252-256ff; Glaser, 1970, 42-46). They do not simply "respond" to citizen demands.

Citizen calls for assistance in themselves as behavioral events do not provide either the necessary or sufficient basis for police action.[8] What occurs in a given incident cannot be understood by simply counting behavioral outcomes. One must give attention to what is "out of sight" or the "preconstituted typifications" of normal and routine encounters employed by the police (Chatterton, 1973). It should be emphasized that (1) police patrolmen develop *prospective understandings* of the police-relevant meanings of calls (e.g., what problems and arrest will make for constables in the reserve room of the station at particular times or how an arrest and associated paperwork might affect personal time). This issue is especially critical at the end of a shift, but may also be relevant because of the court time that may be required. (2) Calls are set within a "reasonable" context of understandings of *types* of events that predetermine how events will be handled in advance (e.g. the availability of detective investigators, the possibility that an arrest will be considered a "good pinch"). The police thus create by their own defintions of "crime," and "criminals" a system of typifications and assumptions that might be called an "occupational culture." (Manning,

1971: 1974) which guides, directs, channels and controls what it is possible to read from their actions.

"The most significant police product is symbolic..."

The messages conveyed, read, and reflected thus create a *secondary reality* (Young, 1971), or alternative system of typification, normal procedures, and common-sense theories of policing which in time become a reality confronting everyone.

5. *To the degree that formally constituted control agencies are faced with a paradox between what is formally expected of them in the community and what is possible, they will tend to retreat from a collective defintion of morality, the law, and social order* (Westley, 1953; Skolnick, 1966; Chevigny, 1968; Manning, 1971; Cain, 1973).

In most towns and cities of America, and in England, the middle-class- property- owner- head- of- the-household is seen by the police as the most significant police audience. Positing a *consensual other* seems to be a significant part of the police ideology.

> Policemen need to believe in a largely consensual populace whose values and standards they represent and enforce. It is by reference to this that they legitimate their activities. They are intermediaries who bring forth for punishment whom 'most people' deem to deserve it (Cain, 1973: 69).

The police are in an adversary relationship with the public on many occasions; they tend to adopt a symbolic rationale for their "enemy."

This *evil* "out there" stands as a polar symbolic representation to that of the *public,* the middle-class property owner. First, this enemy is more significant as a symbol for the administrators of the department for they lack the face to face contact with the public which would reduce their stereotype. This collective representation facilitates and mobilizes their policy decisions—it provides the *qui bonum.* Policemen, although they are in greater contact with evil, and are therefore more polluted by this relationship, at the same time can rationalize their activities as the essence of good policework.

The patrolmen tend to control information on their activities in order to protect themselves from arbitrary administration action, thus further isolating the administrator who sets policies in the pursuit of the criminal from the actual criminal and criminality. This secrecy binds together the lower participants, separating them from the administrators. Police secrecy, as Bittner points out, integrates the police organization *vis a vis* the public, and is the grounds which form the symbolization of evil, but it internally divides the organization (Bittner, 1970: 63). Solidarity *symbolized outside* is converted inwardly as dissensus. The contact with evil, i.e., with informants, with criminals and ex-criminals, with the demi-monde of large cities, makes moral pollution inevitable for the lower participants, while freeing the higher participants to symbolize and dramatize their distance from the very thing they are expected to "destroy," "control," or "prevent." What is expected externally by the public as a result of the publicity of the police cannot be realized internally and a schizoid existence is established.

Actions that affirm the police role as

the police believe it should be defined by the middle classes in actuality separate the police from these very middle classes. The police rarely deal with "crime," and "criminals"; they deal for the most part with requests for service that are not imbedded in a legal context, but in a framework of 24-hour availability. Among the actual contacts that involve the law, surprisingly few eventuate in arrest (Reiss, 1971: Chapter 1). Of course, police knowledge of crimes is almost exclusively dependent upon citizen information. Arrest possibilities for a given crime are exceedingly low; only in the case of homicide or serious assault does the arrest and charge rate approach a reasonable level. Even then, the crime may be cleared only by a guilty plea, or by plea bargaining, rather than by police action or evidence. Cain's (1973) enthnography of police in two English towns, suggests that arrests of drunks and other public order offenders are used to inflate the clearance rate. Thus emphasis upon making visible crime-fighting activities leads to (a) futile attempts to elevate arrest rates by the arrest of "innocuous offenders" (who in turn, clog jails and courts and occupy inordinate amounts of police time); (b) a relative loss of public service activities that might benefit the middle class audience; (c) because of the belief in the crime-stopper/crime-catcher role, moral drops when it is not possible, and affect is withdrawn from the very public service demanded structurally.

Organizations and occupations, failing to "win" public support within the international or everyday sphere, tend to move to the political or legal sphere to gain the authority they desire over job, working conditions, pay, public deference and the like (e.g., unionization campaigns, legal suits, strikes, etc.). In the case of the police, these campaigns have taken the character of emphasis upon the symbolic threat to the public of "crime," the isolation of this symbol from everyday life, and the consequent rationale for violation of procedural rules in the control of crime. After the events in Washington, this hardly requires emphasis. Stan Cohen's FOLK DEVILS AND MORAL PANICS (1973: 87-143) beautifully illustrates what he calls "innovation" in social control, an excess in enforcement of rules which results from the stripping and dehumanization of the criminal and uncontrolled controllers.

6. *The greater the gap between the moral standards of the community (i.e., their behavior), and the police culture, the greater the growth of cynicism among the police and the greater number of internal disciplinary violations and corruption.*

Since policemen see individuals in a significant portion of time in adversary relationships, where citizens are likely to have violated conventional standards, i.e., where they have threatened to harm or harmed others, or where they have violated property rights, policemen come to expect the worst of people. Their stereotypes of people are cynical (Neiderhoffer, 1967): they are distrustful, and they share a "rotten apple" view of collective social life (Knapp, 1972; Stark, 1972). When persons viewed as discredited do not defer to the police, the self of the controller is threatened, or perceived as violated. The police view themselves collectively as "failures," as "dirty workers," as a minority without honor.

The pattern of respect-seeking and self-violation, when coupled with the attribution of risk to citizen-police encounters, has further consequences. Policemen withdraw *affect.*

from moral restraints symbolized by commitment to departmental rules and legal controls.[9] If recent research is representative of the behavior of policemen in large cities, where moral and political diversity is the rule, then one must conclude that police malfeasance is very common indeed. In Boston, Washington and Chicago, Reiss estimated that 40% of the men observed violated departmental rules (sleeping or drinking on the job, falsification of reports, or other "serious" infractions); 60% received reports (Reiss, 1971: 164). Two recent studies of the New York City Department reveal a similar pattern. Of the 2,000 officers joining the force in 1957, nearly 60% had received one allegation of misconduct and a total of 2,137 complaints had been filed: 9.5% involved criminal charges: 25.3% accused an officer of abusing a citizen, and 64.2% cited violation of departmental rules. The pattern of corruption, the acceptance of bribes, pay-offs, or "considerations" is apparently well-established in New York City. The *Knapp Commission Report* concluded: "corruption is widespread ...not all policemen are corrupt. ...Yet, with extremely rare exceptions, even those who themselves engage in no corrupt activities are involved in corruption in the sense that they take no steps to prevent what they know or suspect to be going on about them." (Knapp, 1972: 1;3). The variety of types of corruption included pay-offs in gambling, prostitution, bars, construction and narcotics. (The situation in narcotics, from all indications, made distinctions between pushers, agents, users, and organized crime essentially moot. Accepting money, protecting informants, received regular pay-offs and even dealing in drugs themselves was the rule rather than the exception). *Reiss'*

(1971: 169) *conclusion from his three-city work can be generalized perhaps "... during any year a substantial minority of all police officers violate the criminal, a majority misbehave* towards citizens in an encounter, and most engage in serious violations of the rules and regulations of the department."

Conclusion

What are the police for? Rejecting administrative accounts based on systems theory of the nature of police aims and activities (cf. Wilson and McClaren, 1973) should not lead us to assume that the police are ineffectual. The principal consequence of the development of a bureaucratically organized police is that the presence of the state is symbolized in the everyday lives of the citizenry; the police, a bureaucratic mobilization of manpower and resources, represent the virtual and potential penetration of civil authority into mundane events (Silver, 1967: 14-15 ff).

The police deal in a significant way with materials and situations taken to be symbolic of social order itself. Their arrest rates and their actual activities in the arrest and charge of "serious crime" cannot be set aside; these functions must be carried out and the law applied with some degree of certainty. However, index crimes, although highly significant to the public, do not seem to be prevented by present measures (Wilson, 1967). Nor are they likely to be prevented by what is now the prevalent pattern of allocation of police manpower and resources: "preventive" or proactive patrol to seek crimes (cf. Reiss, 1971: 99-100). The most significant police product is *symbolic:* their distinctive uniforms, their displays of police presence in public crowd situations, at important crimes (what is called "showing the flag" by the English police); their almost random encounters with the everyday world of the citizen, *all ritualize and create in everyday life the appearance of a consensual constraining moral order.*

Notes

[1]Presented as a working paper to a faculty seminar at the Department of Sociology and Anthropology, Manchester University, Manchester, England, May, 1973. The essay is a segment of a longer working paper tentatively entitled, "The Drama of Social Control: Some Propositions."

[2]The focus of this paper is narrow, aimed at the development of a dramaturgical perspective of policing. However, two important implications of a concept of social control which included expressive elements are: a) it can be sensitive to the *situational* interpretations of rules and norms, rather than seeing social control as a pervasive reaction to a set of broadly agreed upon normative standards (cf. Bittner, 1970; Gibbs, 1966); b) it suggests conditions under which announcing a norm not only provides a rational legitimization of social control activities (as in the case of legal norms where the law is a means of control claims to apply equally to all members of a politically defined community), but serves also the education function: sets boundaries, clarifies moral hierarchies and highlights the significance of the moral order within which the conduct is thereby located. (Erickson, 1966).

[3]This conception of social control is based upon the following symbolic interactionist assumptions.

(A) Social objects and processes take on meaning and significance from the frame of reference within which they are placed. (B) Interaction is patterned because persons selectively attend to and attribute symbolic elements to a behavioral display. Through awareness of interactional contingencies, persons can strategically employ interactional control. (C) Social order is created, maintained and kept selective through symbolically highlighted displayed symbols which large segments of the population are pre-disposed or prepared to accept as legitimate. These displays are ceremonies, expressive rejuvenations of a community's moral values. Furthermore:..."in so far as the expressive bias of performances come to be accepted as reality, then that which is at the moment defined as reality will have some of the characteristics of a celebration" (Goffman, 1959: 35-36). (D) The capacity to control the selection and dissemination of symbols, and hence to limit the *range* of meanings attributed to social action, is a function of power (Goode, 1969). (E) Organizations operating in an environment where they must negotiate for power in order to survive, can be seen as seizing upon particular aspects of their activities to dramatize their effectiveness, efficacy and utility vis-a-vis their stated goals. In so doing, they *evoke* a version of social reality which can be as much mystification as *revelation.*

[4]The term "the drama of control" is itself metaphoric. A persistent problem in the use of metaphor is that such ambiguity fails to note whether the perspective adopted is one mirroring, reflecting, or replicating the *subject's* or the *observer's* point of view (cf. Pitt-Rovers, 1967). In this analysis, the perspective is the *observer's.* The observer makes the distinctions which are possible readings of the behavior; whether the actors themselves are actually aware of the consequences of what they are doing is problematic and varies from situation to situation. There is no assumption that social life *is* scripted, staged, directed or that roles are parcelled out according to a single underlying structure. It is neither a necessary nor sufficient part of the argument. Activities guided by highly moral premises and sanctioned in the process by organizational *dicta* can have quite pernicious effects or be seen as illegal or immoral. Conversely, quite immorally intended action can be read as a "defense of national liberties" or as being in the public interest, yet can create social havoc. Machiavelli and some contemporary politicians provide a catalog of such techniques. These anomalies are not of concern here. Individual intentions are not at issue; what is of concern are the expressive elements of and unanticipated consequences of rational forms of active social control.

[5]There are nearly a half million persons employed in law enforcement in this country. However, they work for agencies located at five separate levels of governmental responsibility. In addition to federal agencies, including the FBI, Bureau of Narcotics, Post Office, IRS, Customs, the Alcohol, Firearms and Tobacco Unit of the Treasury, the Immigration-Border Patrol and U.S. Marshalls, there are agents of the 50 states, including state police forces and criminal investigation agencies, county sheriffs and deputy sheriffs in over 3,000 counties; police of a thousand cities and over 20,000 townships and New England towns; and the police of 15,000 villages, boroughs, and incorporated towns, together with a small number of special purpose forces serving public quasi-corporations and ad hoc districts. Finally, within certain county or metropolitan areas, there are "ad hoc squads" to deal with organized crime, drugs, or riots which are composed of members of a number of police forces and are

commanded by officers from several departments. The number of private police agencies such as Pinkerton's (an agency now employing over 30,000 persons) and other protective and detective agencies is presently over 3,000 and growing. The amount spent on legally constituted private forces is over 3 billion dollars. Finally, an unknown number of more than ad hoc "vigilante" groups (which do continue to appear to conduct voluntary searches, patrol neighborhoods, and make inquiries in communities), exist such as the Maccabbees in Brooklyn, and Black Protectors in large urban areas. There are no accurate estimates of the numbers of people involved on an ad hoc basis or on a semi-official capacity such as these, but they form a type of quasi-legal social control even though they normally do not arrest persons.

[6]In these situations, Reiss found, citizens mobilize the police about 90% of the time, more citizens than police are present when the policemen arrive in the scene (54½ of encounters involved 3 plus citizens to the single policeman), and in 70% of these cases, the scene takes place in a private place where arrest powers are significantly reduced or controlled, i.e., they depend on the citizen's willingness to make a civil complaint.

[7]Several studies of police interactions with juveniles have underscored the import of situational violations of etiquette in the dispositions of suspects (cf. Westley, 1953; Piliavin & Briar, 1964; Black, 1968, 1970; and Black & Reiss, 1970). (Differential dispositions are made at the juvenile bureau level and above: McEachern & Bauzer, 1967; Terry, 1967; Goldman, 1953; and Cicourel, 1968). Such variables as race, previous record, probation status, age, department and officers all pattern dispositions when offenses hold constant, i.e., for the same offense categories, different outcomes may be predicted using other criteria. See Bordua, 1965 for a useful review of these studies and Black, 1968. Piliavin & Briar (1964),

for example, found that in 66 cases of police/juvenile encounters, demeanor was significant in 90% of the cases other than those leading to a felony charge. Those that did not manifest the appropriate signs of respect tended to receive the more severe dispositions: 67% of the "uncooperative" juveniles were arrested, while only 4% of those labeled "cooperative" were arrested. Ferdinand and Lutcher Hand (1970), in a large study of teenagers randomly sampled from inner city neighborhoods, (N = 1,525) found that although black teenagers were *less* "anti-social and aggressive" than whites, those blacks who came in contact with the police were given more severe dispositions, "largely in terms of their superficial attitudes toward and demeanor toward the police, whereas white offenders are judged by different and more basic criteria." (517-518) Black & Reiss (1970), on the other hand, using trained observers in 3 departments, found the arrest rates for participants in encounters characterized as follows: "antagonistic" 22%; "civil" 16%; "very deferential" 22%. This pattern held true when only serious misdemeanors, rowdiness and felonies were combined. Black (1968), analyzing those 10% of the encounters where arrest did eventuate, found a number of social variables were at work (social status of the complainant, his preference for arrest/non-arrest: the availability of evidence and the race of the alleged offender). Although the evidence is somewhat scattered, it is fair to conclude that particularly with "minor crimes" (those where the police are likely to intervene on their own initiative), deference and demeanor of the suspect play an important role in the determination of the arrest and charge.

[8]I am indebted to Chatterton's (1973) incisive analysis in the material presented here.

[9]I have considered some of these consequences in a paper dealing with police lying tentatively entitled, "Paradoxes of Police Lying."

2. *The three major characteristics of the police task, according to Skolnick, are danger, authority, and efficiency. These elements of the police task have three very definite personality correlatives—the policeman's "working personality" can be characterized as suspicious (as a response to the possibilities of danger), alienated (as the result of transcending public life in order to protect it), and solidaristic (as a reaction to social isolation). What must be emphasized in Skolnicks article is that the policeman responds to the contradictory demands of his task in ways that are not incongruous to a "conventional personality." However, the elements of danger, authority and efficiency lead to certain cognitive responses—a "working personality" that disguises the policeman's "conventionality" and leads to an assumption that the policeman is inherently authoritarian, hence, reprehensible.*

The policeman from this point of view, is a somewhat tragic figure. Consider Robert Balch's rather poignant description of the policeman's dilemma.

> *On the one hand [policemen] regard themselves as competent craftsmen performing a vital task; on the other, they are condemned and degraded by the very people they have sworn to protect.* *

*See Robert Balch, "The Police Personality" (Article 3).

A SKETCH OF THE POLICEMAN'S "WORKING PERSONALITY"

JEROME H. SKOLNICK

A recurrent theme of the sociology of occupations is the effect of a man's work on his outlook on the world.[1] Doctors, janitors, lawyers, and industrial workers develop distinctive ways of perceiving and responding to their environment. Here we shall concentrate on analyzing certain outstanding elements in the police milieu, danger, authority, and efficiency, as they combine to generate distinctive cognitive and behavioral responses in police: a "working personality." Such an analysis does not suggest that all police are alike in "working personality," but that there are distinctive cognitive tendencies in police as an occupational grouping. Some of these may be found in other occupations sharing similar problems. So far as exposure to danger is concerned, the policeman may be likened to the soldier. His problems as an authority bear a certain similarity to those of the schoolteacher, and the pressures he feels to prove himself efficient are not unlike those felt by the industrial worker. The combination of these elements, however, is unique to the policeman. Thus, the police, as a result of combined features of their social situation, tend to develop ways of looking at the world distinctive to themselves, cognitive lenses through which to see situations and events. The strength of the lenses may be weaker or stronger depending on certain conditions, but they are ground on a similar axis.

Analysis of the policeman's cognitive propensities is necessary to understand the practical dilemma faced by police required to maintain order under a democratic rule of law. A conception of order is essential to the resolution of this dilemma. It is suggested that the paramilitary character of police organization naturally leads to a high evaluation of similarity, routine, and predictability. Our intention is to emphasize features of the policeman's environment interacting with the paramilitary police organization to generate a "working personality." Such an intervening concept should aid in explaining how the social environment of police affects their capacity to respond to the rule of law.

We also stated earlier that emphasis would be placed on the division of labor in the police department, that "operational law enforcement" could not be understood outside these special work assignments. It is therefore important to explain how the hypothesis emphasizing the generalizability of the policeman's "working personality" is compatible with the idea that police division of labor is an important analytic dimension for understanding "operational law enforcement." Compatibility is evident when one considers the different levels of analysis at which the hypotheses are being developed. Janowitz states, for example, that the military profession is more than an occupation; it is a "style of life" because the occupational claims over one's daily existence extend well beyond official duties. He is quick to point out that any profession performing a crucial "life and death" task, such as medicine, the ministry, or the police, develops such claims.[2] A conception like "working personality" of police should be understood to suggest an analytic breadth similar to that of "style of life." That is, just as the professional behavior of military officers with similar "styles of life" may differ drastically depending upon whether they command an infantry battalion or participate in the work of an intelligence unit, so too does the professional behavior of police officers with similar "working personalities" vary with their assignments.

The policeman's "working personality" is most highly developed in his constabulary role of the man on the beat. For analytical purposes that role is sometimes regarded as an enforcement speciality, but in this general discussion of policemen as they comport themselves while working, the uniformed "cop" is seen as the foundation for the policeman's "work-

---

"the police... tend to develop ways of looking at the world distinctive to themselves, cognitive lenses through which to see situations and events."

---

ing personality." There is a sound organizational basis for making this assumption. The police, unlike the military, draw no caste distinction in socialization, even though their order of ranked titles approximates the military's. Thus, one cannot join a local police department as, for instance, a lieutenant, as a West Point graduate joins the army. Every officer of rank must serve an apprenticeship as a patrolman. This feature of police organization means that the constabulary role is the primary one for all police officers, and that whatever the special requirements of roles in enforcement specialties, they are carried out with a common background of constabulary experience.

The process by which this "personality" is developed may be summarized: the policeman's role contains two principal variables, danger and authority, which should be interpreted in the light of a "constant" pressure to appear efficient.[3] The element of danger seems to make the policeman especially attentive to signs indicating a potential for violence and lawbreaking. As a result, the policeman is generally a "suspicious" person. Furthermore, the character of the policeman's work makes him less desirable as a friend, since norms of friendship implicate others in his work. Accordingly, the element of danger isolates the policeman socially from that segment of the citizenry which he regards as symbolically dangerous and also from the conventional citizenry with whom he identifies.

The element of authority reinforces the element of danger in isolating the policeman. Typically, the policeman is required to enforce laws representing puritanical morality, such as those prohibiting drunkenness, and also laws regulating the flow of public activity, such as traffic laws. In these situations the policeman directs the citizenry, whose typical response denies recognition of his authority, and stresses his obligation to respond to danger. The kind of man who responds well to danger, however, does not normally subscribe to codes of puritanical morality. As a result, the policeman is unusually liable to the charge of hypocrisy. That the whole civilian world is an audience for the policeman further promotes police isolation and, in consequence, solidarity. Finally, danger undermines the judicious use of authority. Where danger, as in Britain, is relatively less, the judicious application of authority is facilitated. Hence, British police may appear to be somewhat more attached to the rule of law, when, in fact, they may appear so because they face less danger, and they are as a rule better skilled than American police in creating the appearance of conformity to procedural regulations.

The Symbolic Assailant and Police Culture

In attempting to understand the policeman's view of the world, it is useful to raise a more general question: What are the conditions under which police, as authorities, may be threatened?[4] To answer this, we must look to the situation of the policeman in the community. One attribute of many characterizing the policeman's role stands out: the policeman is required to respond to assaults against persons and property. When a radio call reports an armed robbery and gives a description of the man involved, every policeman, regardless of assignment, is responsible for the criminal's apprehension. The *raison d'etre* of the policeman and the criminal law, the underlying collectively held moral sentiments which justify penal sanctions, arises ultimately and most clearly from the threat of violence and the possibility of danger to the community. Police who "lobby" for severe narcotics laws, for instance, justify their position on grounds that the addict is a harbinger of danger since, it is maintained, he requires one hundred dollars a day to support his habit, and he must steal to get it. Even though the addict is not typically a violent criminal, criminal penalties for addiction are supported on grounds that he may become one.

The policeman, because his work requires him to be occupied continually with potential violence, develops a perceptual shorthand to identify certain kinds of people as symbolic assailants, that is, as persons who use gesture, language, and attire that the policeman has come to recognize as a prelude to violence. This does not mean that violence by the symbolic assailant is necessarily predictable. On the contrary, the policeman responds to the vague indication of danger suggested by appearance.[5] Like the animals of the experimental psychologist, the policeman finds the threat of random damage more compelling than a predetermined and inevitable punishment.

Nor, to qualify for the status of symbolic assailant, need an individual ever have used violence. A man backing out of a jewelry store with a gun in one hand and jewelry in the other would qualify even if the gun were a toy and he had never in his life fired a real pistol. To the policeman in the situation, the man's personal history is momentarily immaterial. There is only one relevant sign: a gun signifying danger. Similarly, a young man may suggest the threat of violence to the policeman by his manner of walking or "strutting," the insolence in the demeanor being registered by the policeman as a possible preamble to later attack.[6] Signs vary from area to area, but a youth dressed in a black leather jacket and motorcycle boots is sure to draw at least a suspicious glance from a policeman.

Policemen themselves do not necessarily emphasize the peril associated with their work when questioned directly, and may even have well-developed strategies of denial. The element of danger is so integral to the policeman's work that explicit recognition might induce emotional barriers to work performance. Thus, one patrol officer observed that more police have been killed and injured in automobile accidents in the past ten years than from gunfire. Although his assertion is true, he neglected to mention that the police are the only peacetime occupational group with a systematic record of death and injury from gunfire and other weaponry. Along these lines, it is interesting that of the two hundred and twenty-four working Westville policemen (not including the sixteen juvenile policemen) responding to a question about which assignment they would like most to have in the police department,[7] 50 percent selected the job of detective, an assignment combining elements of apparent danger and initiative. The next category was adult street work, that is, patrol and traffic (37 percent). Eight percent selected the juvenile squad,[8] and only 4 percent selected administrative work. Not a single policeman chose the job of jail guard. Although these findings do not control for such factors as prestige, they suggest that confining and routine jobs are rated low on the hierarchy of police preferences, even though such jobs are least dangerous. Thus, the policeman may well, as a personality, enjoy the possibility of danger, especially its associated excitement, even though he may at the same time be fearful of it. Such "inconsistency" is easily understood. Freud has by now made it an axiom of personality theory that logical and emotional consistency are by no means the same phenomenon.

However complex the motives aroused by the element of danger, its consequences for sustaining police culture are unambiguous. This element requires him, like the combat soldier, the European Jew, the South African (white or black), to live in a world straining toward duality, and suggesting danger when "they" are perceived. Consequently, it is in the nature of the policeman's situation that his conception of order emphasize regularity and predictability. It is, therefore, a conception shaped by persistent *suspicion*. The English "copper," often portrayed as a courteous, easy-going, rather jolly sort of chap, on the one hand, or as a devil-may-care adventurer, on the other, is differently described by Colin MacInnes:

> The true copper's dominant characteristic, if the truth be known, is neither those daring nor vicious qualities that are sometimes attributed to him by friend or enemy, but an ingrained conservatism, and almost desperate love of the conventional. It is untidiness, disorder, the unusual, that a copper disapproves of most of all: far more, even than of crime which is merely a professional matter. Hence his profound dislike of people loitering in streets, dressing extravagantly, speaking with exotic accents, being strange, weak, eccentric, or simply any rare minority—of their doing, in fact, anything that cannot be safely predicted.[9]

Policemen are indeed specifically *trained* to be suspicious, to perceive events or changes in the physical surroundings that indicate the occurrence or probability of disorder. A former student who worked as a patrolman in a suburban New York police department describes this aspect of the policeman's assessment of the unusual:

> The time spent cruising one's sector or walking one's beat is not wasted time, though it can become quite routine. During this time, the most important thing for the officer to do is notice the *normal*. He must come to know the people in his area, their habits, their automobiles and their friends. He must learn what time the various shops close, how much money is kept on hand on different nights, what lights are usually left on, which houses are vacant... only then can he decide what persons or cars under what circumstances warrant the appellation "suspicious."[10]

The individual policeman's "suspiciousness" does not hang on whether he has personally undergone an experience that could objectively be described as hazardous. Personal experience of this sort is not the key to the psychological importance of exceptionality. Each, as he routinely carries out his work, will experience situations that threaten to become dangerous. Like the American Jew who contributes to "defense" organizations such as the Anti-Defamation League in response to Nazi brutalities he has never experienced personally, the policeman identifies with his fellow cop who has been beaten, perhaps fatally, by a gang of young thugs.

Social Isolation

The patrolman in Westville, and probably in most communities, has come to identify the black man with danger. James Baldwin vividly expresses the isolation of the ghetto policeman:

> The only way to police a ghetto is to be oppressive. None of the police commissioner's men, even with the best will in the world, have any way of understanding the lives led by the people they swagger about in twos and threes controlling. Their very presence is an insult, and it would be, even if they spent their entire day feeding gumdrops to children. They represent the force of the white world, and that world's criminal profit and ease, to keep the black man corraled up here, in his place. The badge, the gun in the holster, and the swinging club make vivid what will happen should his rebellion become overt....
>
> It is hard, on the other hand, to blame the policeman, blank, good-natured, thoughtless, and insuperably innocent, for being such a perfect representative of the people he serves. He, too, believes in good intentions and is astounded and offended when they are not taken for the deed. He has never, himself, done anything for which to be hated—which of us has? and yet he is facing, daily and nightly, people who would gladly see him dead, and

he knows it. There is no way for him not to know it: there are few things under heaven more unnerving than the silent, accumulating contempt and hatred of a people. He moves through Harlem, therefore, like an occupying soldier in a bitterly hostile country; which is precisely what, and where he is, and is the reason he walks in twos and threes.[11]

While Baldwin's observations on police-Negro relations cannot be disputed seriously, there is greater social distance between police and "civilians" in general, regardless of their color, than Baldwin considers. Thus, Colin MacInnes has his English hero, Mr. Justice, explaining:

...The story is all coppers are just civilians like anyone else, living among them not in barracks like on the Continent, but you and I know that's just a legend for mugs. We *are* cut off: we're *not* like everyone else. Some civilians fear us and play up to us, some dislike us and keep out of our way but no one—well, very few indeed—accepts us as just ordinary like them. In one sense, dear, we're just like hostile troops occupying an enemy country. And say what you like, at times that makes us lonely.[12]

MacInnes' observation suggests that by not introducing a white control group, Baldwin has failed to see that the policeman may not get on well with anybody regardless (to use the hackneyed phrase) of race, creed, or national origin. Policemen whom one knows well often express their sense of isolation from the public as a whole, not just from those who fail to share their color. Westville police were asked, for example, to rank the most serious problems police have. The category most frequently selected was not racial problems, but some form of public relations: lack of respect for the police, lack of cooperation in enforcement of law, lack of understanding of the requirements of police work.[13] One respondent answered:

As a policeman my most serious problem is impressing on the general public just how difficult and necessary police service is to all. There seems to be an attitude of "law is important, but it applies to my neighbor—not to me."

Of the two hundred and eighty-two Westville policemen who rated the prestige police work receives from others, 70 percent ranked it as only fair or poor, while less than 2 percent ranked it as "excellent" and another 29 percent as "good." Similarly, in Britain, two-thirds of a sample of policemen interviewed by a Royal Commission stated difficulties in making friends outside the force; of those interviewed 58 percent thought members of the public to be reserved, suspicious, and constrained in conversation; and 12 percent attributed such difficulties to the requirement that policemen be selective in associations and behave circumspectly.[14]

A Westville policeman related the following incident:

Several months after I joined the force, my wife and I used to be socially active with a crowd of young people, mostly married, who gave a lot of parties where there was drinking and dancing, and we enjoyed it. I've never forgotten, though, an incident that happened on one Fourth of July party. Everybody had been drinking, there was a lot of talking, people were feeling boisterous, and some kid there—he must have been twenty or twenty-two—threw a firecracker that hit my wife in the leg and burned her. I didn't know exactly what to do—punch the guy in the nose, bawl him out, or just forget it. Anyway, I couldn't let it pass, so I walked over to him and told him he ought to be careful. He began to rise up at me, and when he did, somebody yelled, "Better watch out, he's a cop." I saw everybody standing there, and I could feel they were all against me and for the kid, even though he had thrown the firecracker at my wife. I went over to the host and said it was probably better if my wife and I left because a fight would put a damper on the party. Actually, I'd hoped he would ask the kid to leave, since the kid had thrown the firecracker. But he didn't so we left. After that incident, my wife and I stopped going around with that crowd, and decided that if we were going to go to parties where there was to be drinking and boisterousness, we weren't going to be the only police people there.

Another reported that he seeks to overcome his feelings of isolation by concealing his police identity:

> I try not to bring my work home with me, and that includes my social life. I like the men I work with, but I think it's better that my family doesn't become a police family. I try to put my police work into the background, and try not to let people know I'm a policeman. Once you do, you can't have normal relations with them.[15]

Although the policeman serves a people who are, as Baldwin says, the established society, the white society, these people do not make him feel accepted. As a result, he develops resources within his own world to combat social rejection.

Police Solidarity

All occupational groups share a measure of inclusiveness and identification. People are brought together simply by doing the same work and having similar career and salary problems. As several writers have noted, however, police show an unusually high degree of occupational solidarity.[16] It is true that the police have a common employer and wear a uniform at work, but so do doctors, milkmen, and bus drivers. Yet it is doubtful that these workers have so close knit an occupation or so similar an outlook on the world as do police.

Set apart from the conventional world, the policemen experiences an exceptionally strong tendency to find his social identity within his occupational milieu.

Compare the police with another skilled craft. In a study of the International Typographical Union, the authors asked printers the first names and jobs of their three closest friends. Of the 1,236 friends named by the 412 men in their sample, 35 percent were printers.[17] Similarly, among the Westville police, of 700 friends listed by 250 respondents, 35 percent were policemen. The policemen, however, were far more active than printers in occupational social activities. Of the printers, more than half (54 percent) had never participated in any union clubs, benefit societies, teams, or organizations composed mostly of printers, or attended any printers' social affairs in the past 5 years. Of the Westville police, only 16 percent had failed to attend a single police banquet or dinner in the past *year* (as contrasted with the printers' 5 *years*); and of the 234 men answering this question, 54 percent had attended 3 or more such affairs *during the past year.*

These findings are striking in light of the interpretation made of the data on printers. Lipset, Trow, and Coleman do not, as a result of their findings, see printers as an unintegrated occupational group. On the contrary, they ascribe the democratic character of the union in good part to the active social and political participation of the membership. The point is not to question their interpretation, since it is doubtlessly correct when printers are held up against other manual workers. However, when seen in comparison to police, printers appear a minimally participating group; put positively, police emerge as an exceptionally socially active occupational group.

Police Solidarity and Danger

There is still a question, however, as to the process through which danger and authority influence police solidarity. The effect of danger on police solidarity is revealed when we examine a chief complaint of police: lack of public support and public apathy. The complaint may have several referents including police pay, police prestige, and support from the legislature. But the repeatedly voiced broader meaning of the complaint is resentment at being taken for granted. The policeman does not believe that his status as civil servant should relieve the public of responsibility for law enforcement. He feels, however, that payment out of public coffers somehow obscures his humanity and, therefore, his need for help.[18] As one put it:

> Jerry, a cop, can get into a fight with three or four tough kids, and there will be citizens passing by, and maybe they'll look, but they'll never lend a hand. It's their country too, but you'd never know it the way some of them act. They forget that we're made of flesh and blood too. They don't care what happens to the cop so long as they don't get a little dirty.

Although the policeman sees himself as a specialist in dealing with violence, he does not want to fight alone. He does not believe that his specialization relieves the general public of citizenship duties. Indeed, if possible, he would prefer to be the foreman rather than the workingman in the battle against criminals.

The general public, of course, does withdraw from the workaday world of the policeman. The policeman's responsibility for controlling dangerous and sometimes violent persons alienates the average citizen perhaps as much as does his authority over the average citizen. If the policeman's job is to insure that public order is maintained, the citizen's inclination is to shrink from the dangers of maintaining it. The citizen prefers to see the policeman as an automation, because once the policeman's humanity is recognized, the citizen necessarily becomes implicated in the policeman's work, which is, after all, sometimes dirty and dangerous. What the policeman typically fails to realize is the extent he becomes tainted by the character of the work he performs. The dangers of their work not only draws policemen together as a group but separates them from the rest of the population. Banton, for instance, comments:

> ...patrolmen may support their fellows over what they regard as minor infractions in order to demonstrate to them that they will be loyal in situations that make the greatest demands upon their fidelity....
> In the American departments I visited it seemed as if the supervisors shared many of the patrolmen's sentiments about solidarity. They too wanted their colleagues to back them up in an emergency, and they shared similar frustrations with the public.[19]

Thus, the element of danger contains seeds of isolation which may grow in two directions. In one, a stereotyping perceptual shorthand is formed through which the police come to see certain signs as symbols of potential violence. The police probably differ in this respect from the general middle-class white population only in degree. This difference, however, may take on enormous significance in practice. Thus, the policeman works at identifying and possibly apprehending the symbolic assailant; the ordinary citizen does not. As a result, the ordinary citizen does not assume the responsibility to implicate himself in the policeman's required response to danger. The element of danger in the policeman's role alienates him not only from populations with a potential for crime but also from the conventionally respectable (white) citizenry, in short, from that segment of the population from which friends would ordinarily be drawn. As Janowitz has noted in a paragraph suggesting similarities between the police and the military, "...any profession which is continually preoccupied with the threat of danger requires a strong sense of solidarity if it is to operate effectively. Detailed regulation of the military style of life is expected to enhance group cohesion, professional loyalty, and maintain the martial spirit."[20]

Social Isolation and Authority

The element of authority also helps to account for the policeman's social isolation. Policemen themselves are aware of their isolation from the community, and are apt to weight authority heavily as a causal factor. When considering how authority influences rejection, the policeman typically singles out his responsibility for enforcement of traffic violations.[21] Resentment, even hostility, is generated in those receiving citations, in part because such contact is often the only one citizens have with police, and in part because municipal administrations and courts have been known to utilize police authority primarily to meet budgetary requirements, rather than those of public order. Thus, when a municipality engages in "speed trapping" by changing limits so quickly that drivers cannot realistically slow down to the prescribed speed or, while keeping the limits reasonable, charging high fines primarily to generate revenue, the policeman carries the brunt of public resentment.

That the policeman dislikes writing traffic tickets is suggested by the quota system police departments typically employ. In Westville, each traffic policeman has what is euphemistically described as a working "norm." A motorcyclist is supposed to write two tickets an hour for moving violations. It is doubtful that "norms" are needed because policemen are lazy. Rather, employment of quotas most likely springs from the reluctance of policemen to expose themselves to what they know to be public hostility. As a result, as one traffic policeman said:

> You learn to sniff out the places where you can catch violators when you're running behind. Of course, the department gets to know that you hang around one place, and they sometimes try to repair the situation there. But a lot of the time it would be too expensive to fix up the engineering fault, so we keep making our norm.

When meeting "production" pressures, the policeman inadvertently gives a false impression of patrolling ability to the average citizen. The traffic cyclist waits in hiding for moving violators near a tricky intersection, and is reasonably sure that such violations will occur with regularity. The violator believes he has observed a policeman displaying exceptional detection capacities and may have two thoughts, each apt to generate hostility toward the policeman: "I have been trapped," or "They can catch me; why can't they catch crooks as easily?" or The answer, of course, lies in the different behavior patterns of motorists and "crooks." The latter do not act with either the frequency or predictability of motorists at poorly engineered intersections.

While traffic patrol plays a major

role in separating the policemen from the respectable community, other of his tasks also have this consequence. Traffic patrol is only the most obvious illustration of the policeman's general responsibility for maintaining public order, which also includes keeping order at public accidents, sporting events, and political rallies. These activities share one feature: the policeman is called upon to *direct* ordinary citizens, and therefore to restrain their freedom of action. Resenting the restraint, the average citizen in such a situation typically thinks something along the lines of "He is supposed to catch crooks; why is he bothering me?" Thus, the citizen stresses the "dangerous" portion of the policeman's role while belittling his authority.

Closely related to the policeman's authority-based problems as *director* of the citizenry are difficulties associated with his injunction to *regulate public morality*. For instance, the policeman is obliged to investigate "lovers' lanes," and to enforce laws pertaining to gambling, prostitution, and drunkenness. His responsibility in these matters allows him much administrative discretion since he may not actually enforce the law by making an arrest, but instead merely interfere with continuation of the objectionable activity.[22] Thus, he may put the drunk in a taxi, tell the lovers to remove themselves from the back seat, and advise a man soliciting a prostitute to leave the area.

Such admonitions are in the interest of maintaining the proprieties of public order. At the same time, the policeman invites the hostility of the citizen so directed in two respects: he is likely to encourage the sort of response mentioned earlier (that is, an antagonistic reformulation of the policeman's role) and the policeman is

apt to cause resentment because of the suspicion that policemen do not themselves strictly conform to the moral norms they are enforcing. Thus, the policeman, faced with enforcing a law against fornication, drunkenness, or gambling, is easily liable to a charge of hypocrisy. Even when the policeman is called on to enforce the laws relating to overt homosexuality, a form of sexual activity for which police are not especially noted, he may encounter the charge of hypocrisy on grounds that he does not adhere strictly to prescribed heterosexual codes. The policeman's difficulty in this respect is shared by all authorities responsible for maintenance of disciplined activity, including industrial foremen, political leaders, elementary schoolteachers, and college professors. All are expected to conform rigidly to the entire range of norms they espouse.[23] The policeman, however, as a result of the unique combination of the elements of danger and authority, experiences a special predicament. It is difficult to develop qualities enabling him to stand up to danger, and to conform to standards of puritanical morality. The element of danger demands that the policeman be able to carry out efforts that are in their nature overtly masculine. Police work, like soldiering, requires an exceptional caliber of physical fitness, agility, toughness, and the like. The man who ranks high on these masculine characteristics is, again like the soldier, not usually disposed to be puritanical about sex, drinking, and gambling.

On the basis of observations, policemen do not subscribe to moralistic standards for conduct. For example, the morals squad of the police department, when questioned, was unanimously against the statutory rape age limit, on grounds that as late teen-agers they themselves might not have refused an attractive offer from a seventeen-year-old girl.[24] Neither, from observations, are policemen by any means total abstainers from the use of alcoholic beverages. The policeman who is arresting a drunk has probably been drunk himself; he knows it and the drunk knows it.

More than that, a portion of the social isolation of the policeman can be attributed to the discrepancy between moral regulation and the norms and behavior of policeman in these areas. We have presented data indicating that police engage in a comparatively active occupational social life. One interpretation might attribute this attendance to a basic interest in such affairs; another might explain the policeman's occupational social activity as a measure of restraint in publicly violating norms he enforces. The interest in attending police affairs may grow as much out of security in "letting oneself go" in the presence of police, and a corresponding feeling of insecurity with civilians, as an authentic preference for police social affairs. Much alcohol is usually consumed at police banquets with all the melancholy and boisterousness accompanying such occasions. As Horace Cayton reports on his experience as a policeman:

> Deputy sheriffs and policemen don't know much about organized recreation; all they usually do when celebrating is get drunk and pound each other on the back, exchanging loud insults which under ordinary circumstances would result in a fight.[25]

To some degree the reason for the behavior exhibited on these occasions is the company, since the policeman would feel uncomfortable exhibiting insobriety before civilians. The police-

man may be likened to other authorities who prefer to violate moralistic norms away from onlookers for whom they are routinely supposed to appear as normative models. College professors, for instance, also get drunk on occasion, but prefer to do so where students are not present. Unfortunately for the policeman, such setings are harder for him to come by than they are for the college professor. The whole civilian world watches the policeman. As a result, he tends to be limited to the company of other policemen for whom his police identity is not a stimulus to carping normative criticism.

Correlates of Social Isolation

The element of authority, like the element of danger, is thus seen to contribute to the solidarity of policemen. To the extent that policemen share the experience of receiving hostility from the public, they are also drawn together and become dependent upon one another. Trends in the degree to which police may exercise authority are also important considerations in understanding the dynamics of the relation between authority and solidarity. It is not simply a question of how much absolute authority police are given, but how much authority they have relative to what they had, or think they had, before. If, as Westley concludes, police violence is frequently a response to a challenge to the policeman's authority, so too may a perceived reduction in authority result in greater solidarity. Whitaker comments on the British police as follows:

> As they feel their authority decline, internal solidarity has become increasingly important to the police. Despite the individual responsibility of each police officer to pursue justice, there is sometimes a tendency to close ranks and to form a

square when they themselves are concerned.[26]

These inclinations may have positive consequences for the effectiveness of police work, since notions of professional courtesy or colleagueship seem unusually high among police.[27] When the nature of the policing enterprise requires much joint activity, as in robbery and narcotics enforcement, the impression is received that cooperation is high and genuine. Policemen do not appear to cooperate with one another merely because such is the policy of the chief, but because they sincerely attach a high value to teamwork. For instance, there is a norm among detectives that two who work together will protect each other when a dangerous situation arises. During one investigation, a detective stepped out of a car to question a suspect who became belligerent. The second detective, who had remained overly long in the back seat of the police car, apologized indirectly to his partner by explaining how wrong it had been of him to permit his partner to encounter a suspect alone on the street. He later repeated this explanation privately, in genuine consternation at having committed the breach (and possibly at having been culpable in the presence of an observer). Strong feelings of empathy and cooperation, indeed almost of "clannishness," a term several policemen themselves used to describe the attitude of police toward one another, may be seen in the daily activities of police. Analytically, these feelings can be traced to the elements of danger and shared experiences of hostility in the policeman's role.

Finally, to round out the sketch, policemen are notably conservative, emotionally and politically. If the element of danger in the policeman's role tends to make the policeman suspicious, and therefore emotionally attached to the status quo, a similar consequence may be attributed to the element of authority. The fact that a man is engaged in enforcing a set of rules implies that he also becomes implicated in *affirming* them. Labor disputes provide the commonest example of conditions inclining the policeman to support the status quo. In these situations, the police are necessarily pushed on the side of the defense of property. Their responsibilities thus lead them to see the striking and sometimes angry workers as their enemy and, therefore, to be cool, if not antagonistic, toward the whole conception of labor militancy.[28] If a policeman did not believe in the system of laws he was responsible for enforcing, he would have to go on living in a state of conflicting cognitions, a condition which a number of social psychologists agree is painful.[29]

> "[The policeman] develops resources within his own world to combat social rejection."

This hypothetical issue of not believing in the laws they are enforcing simply does not arise for most policemen. In the course of the research, however, there was one example. A Negro civil rights advocate (member of CORE) became a policeman with the conviction that by so doing he would be aiding the cause of impartial administration of law for Negroes. For him, however, this outside rationale was not enough to sustain him in administering a system of laws that depends for its impartiality upon a reasonable measure of social and economic equality among the citizenry. Because this recruit identified so much with the Negro community as to be unable to meet the enforcement requirements of the Westville Police Department, his efficiency was impaired, and he resigned in his rookie year.

Police are understandably reluctant to appear to be anything but impartial politically. The police are forbidden from publicly campaigning for political candidates. The London police are similarly prohibited, and before 1887 were not allowed to vote in parliamentary elections, or in local ones until 1893.[30] It was not surprising that the Westville Chief of Police forbade questions on the questionnaire that would have measured political attitudes.[31] One policeman, however, explained the chief's refusal on grounds that, "A couple of jerks here would probably cut up, and come out looking like Commies."

During the course of administering the questionnaire over a three-day period, I talked with approximately fifteen officers and sergeants in the Westville department, discussing political attitudes of police. In addition, during the course of the research itself, approximately fifty were interviewed for varying periods of time. Of these, at least twenty were interviewed more than once, some over time periods of several weeks. Furthermore, twenty police were interviewed in Eastville, several for periods ranging from several hours to several days. Most of the time was *not* spent on investigating political attitudes, but I made a point of raising the question, if possible making it part of a discussion centered around the contents of a

right-wing newsletter to which one of the detectives subscribed. One discussion included a group of eight detectives. From these observations, interviews, and discussions, it was clear that a Goldwater type of conservatism was the dominant political and emotional persuasion of police. I encountered only three policemen who claimed to be politically "liberal," at the same time asserting that they were decidedly exceptional.

Whether or not the policeman is an "authoritarian personality" is a related issue, beyond the scope of this discussion partly because of the many questions raised about this concept. Thus, in the course of discussing the concept of "normality" in mental health, two psychologists make the point that many conventional people were high scorers on the California F scale and similar tests. The great mass of the people, according to these authors, is not much further along the scale of ego development than the typical adolescent who, as they describe him, is "rigid, prone to think in sterotypes, intolerant of deviations, punitive and anit-psychological—in short, what has been called an authoritarian personality."[32] Therefore it is preferable to call the policeman's a conventional personality.

Writing about the New York police force, Thomas R. Brooks suggests a similar interpretation. He writes:

> Cops are conventional people. . . . All a cop can swing in a milieu of marijuana smokers, interracial dates, and homosexuals is the night stick. A policeman who passed a Lower East Side art gallery filled with paintings of what appeared to be female genitalia could think of doing only one thing—step in and make an arrest.[33]

Notes

[1]For previous contributions in this area, see the following: Ely Chinoy, *Automobile Workers and the American Dream* (Garden City: Doubleday & Co., Inc., 1955); Charles R. Walker & Robert H. Guest, *The Man on the Assembly Line* (Cambridge: Harvard Univ. Press, 1952); Everett C. Hughes, "Work and the Self," in his *Men and Their Work* (Glencoe, Ill.: The Free Press, 1958), pp. 42-55; Harold L. Wilensky, *Intellectuals in Labor Unions: Organizational Pressures on Professional Roles* (Glencoe, Ill.: The Free Press, 1956); Wilensky, "Varieties of Work Experience," in Henry Borow, ed., *Man in a World at Work* (Boston: Houghton Mifflin Co., 1964), pp. 125-154; L. Kriesberg, "The Retail Furrier: Concepts of Security and Success," *Amer. J. Sociology* 57 (Mar. 1952), 478-485; W. Burchard, "Role Conflicts of Military Chaplains," *Amer. Sociological Rev.* 19 (Oct. 1954), 528-535; H. S. Becker & B. Geer, "The Fate of Idealism in Medical School," *Amer. Sociological Rev.* 23 (1958), 50-56; H. S. Becker & A.L. Strauss, "Careers, Personality, and Adult Socialization," *Amer. J. Sociology* 62 (Nov. 1956), 253-363.

[2]Morris Janowitz, *The Professional Soldier: A social and Political Portrait* (New York: The Free Press of Glencoe, 1964), p. 175.

[3]By no means does such an analysis suggest there are no individual or group differences among police. On the contrary, most of this study emphasizes differences, endeavoring to relate these to occupational specialities in police departments. This chapter, however, explores similarities rather than differences, attempting to account for the policeman's general disposition to perceive and to behave in certain ways.

[4]William Westley was the first to raise such questions about the police, when he inquired into the conditions under which police are violent. Whatever merit this analysis has, it owes much to his prior insights, as all subsequent sociological studies of the police must. See his "Violence and the Police," *Amer. J. Sociology* 59 (July 1953), 34-41; also his "The Police: A Sociological Study of Law, Custom, and Morality" (unpubl. Ph.D. diss., Univ. of Chicago, Dept. of Sociology, 1951).

[5]Something of the flavor of the policeman's attitude toward the symbolic assailant comes across in a recent article by a police expert. T.F. Adams, "Field Interrogation," *Police* (Mar.-Apr. 1963), p. 28. In discussing the problem of selecting subjects for field interrogation, the author writes:

A. Be suspicious. This is a healthy police attitude, but it should be controlled and not too obvious.
B. Look for the unusual.
1. Persons who do not "belong" where they are observed.
2. Automobiles which do not "look right."
3. Businesses opened at odd hours, or not according to routine or custom.

C. Subjects who should be subjected to field interrogations.
1. Suspicious persons known to the officer from previous arrests, field interrogations, and observations.
2. Emaciated appearing alcoholics and narcotics users who invariably turn to crime to pay for cost of habit.
3. Person who fits description of wanted suspect as described by radio, teletype, daily bulletins.
4. Any person observed in the immediate vicinity of a crime very recently committed or reported as "in progress."
5. Known trouble-makers near large gatherings.
6. Persons who attempt to avoid or evade the officer.
7. Exaggerated unconcern over contact with the officer.
8. Visibly "rattled" when near the policeman.
9. Unescorted women or young girls in such places as cafes, bars, bus and train depots, or street corners.
10. "Lovers" in an industrial area (make good lookouts).
11. Persons who loiter about places where children play.
12. Solicitors or peddlers in a residential neighborhood.
13. Loiterers around public rest rooms.
14. Lone male sitting in car adjacent to schoolground with newspaper or book in his lap.
15. Lone male sitting in car near shopping center who pays unusual amount of attention to women, sometimes continuously manipulating rearview mirror to avoid direct eye contact.
16. Hitchhikers.
17. Person wearing coat on hot days.
18. Car with mismatched hub caps, or dirty car with clean license plate (or vice versa).
19. Uniformed "deliverymen" with no merchandise or truck.
20. Many others. How about your own personal experiences?

[6]See I. Piliavin & S. Briar, "Police Encounters with Juveniles," *Amer. J. Sociology* 70 (Sept. 1964), 206-214.

[7]A questionnaire was given to all policemen in operating divisions of the police force: patrol, traffic, vice control, and all detectives. The questionnaire was administered at police lineups, over a period of three days, mainly by the author but also by some of the police personnel themselves. Before the questionnaire was administered, it was circulated to and approved by the policemen's welfare association.

[8]Indeed, the journalist Paul Jacobs, who has ridden with the Westville juvenile police as part of his own work on poverty, observed in a personal communication that juvenile police

appear curiously drawn to seek out dangerous situations, as if juvenile work without danger is degrading.

[9]Colin MacInnes, *Mister Love and Justice* (London: New English Library, 1962), p. 74.

[10]Peter J. Connell, "Handling of Complaints by Police" (unpubl. paper, Criminal Procedure course, Yale Law School, Fall 1961).

[11]James Baldwin, *Nobody Knows My Name* (New York: Dell Publishing Co., 1962), pp. 65-67.

[12]MacInnes, *supra* note 9, p. 20.

[13]Respondents were asked "Anybody who knows anything about police work knows that police face a number of problems. Would you please state—in order—what you consider to be the two most serious problems police have." On the basis of a number of answers, the writer and J. Richard Woodworth devised a set of categories. Then Woodworth classified each response into one of the categories (see table below). When a response did not seem clear, he consulted with the writer. No attempt was made to independently check Woodworth's classification because the results are used impressionistically, and do not test a hypothesis. It may be, for instance, that "relations with public" is sometimes used to indicate racial problems, and vice versa. "Racial problems" include only those answers having specific reference to race. The categories and results were as follows:

WESTVILLE POLICE RANKING OF NUMBER ONE PROBLEM FACED BY POLICE

	Number	Percent
Relations with public	74	26
Racial problems and demonstrations	66	23
Juvenile delinquents and delinquency	23	8
Unpleasant police tasks	23	8
Lack of cooperation from authorities (DA, legislature, courts)	20	7
Internal departmental problems	17	6
Irregular life of policeman	5	2
No answer or other answer	56	20
	284	100

[14]Royal Commission on the Police, 1962, App. IV to *Minutes of Evidence,* cited in Michael Banton, *The Policeman in the Community* (London: Tavistock Publications, 1964), p. 198.

[15]Similarly, Banton found Scottish police officers attempting to conceal their occupation when on holiday. He quotes one as saying: "If someone asks my wife, 'What does your husband do?,' I've told her to say, 'He's a clerk,'" and that's the way it went because she found that being a policeman's wife—well, it wasn't quite a stigma, she didn't feel cut off, but that a sort of invisible wall was up for conversation purposes when a policeman was there." (p. 198).

[16]In addition to Banton, William Westley and James Q. Wilson have noted this characteristic of police. See Westley, *supra* note 4, p. 294; Wilson, "The Police and Their Problems: A Theory," *Public Policy* 12 (1963), 189-216.

[17]S.M. Lipset, Martin H. Trow & James S. Coleman, *Union Democracy* (New York: Anchor Books, 1962), p. 123. A complete comparison is as follows:

CLOSEST FRIENDS OF PRINTERS AND POLICE, BY OCCUPATION

	Printers N = 1236 (%)	Police N = 700 (%)
Same occupation	35	35
Professionals, business executives, and independent business owners	21	30
White-collar or sales employees	20	12
Manual workers	25	22

[18]On this issue there was no variation. The statement "the policeman feels" means that there was no instance of a negative opinion expressed by the police studied.

[19]Banton, *supra* note 14, p. 114.

[20]Janowitz, *supra* note 2.

[21]O.W. Wilson, for example, mentions this factor as a primary source of antagonism toward police. See his "Police Authority in a Free Society," *J. Crim. Law, Criminology & Police Science* 54 (June 1964), 175-177. In the current study, in addition to the police themselves, other people interviewed, such as attorneys in the system, also attribute the isolation of police

to their authority. Similarly, Arthur L. Stinch-combe, in an as yet unpublished manuscript, "The Control of Citizen Resentment in Police Work," provides a stimulating analysis, to which I am indebted, of the ways police authority generates resentment.

[22]See Wayne R. LaFave, "The Police and Nonenforcement of the Law," *Wisconsin Law Rev.* (1962), pp. 104-137, 179-239.

[23]For a theoretical discussion of the problems of leadership, see George Homans, *The Human Group* (New York: Harcourt, Brace & Co., 1950), esp. ch.: "The Job of the Leader," pp. 415-440.

[24]The work of the Westville morals squad is analyzed in detail by J. Richard Woodworth, "The Administration of Statutory Rape Complaints: A Sociological Study" unpubl. master's thesis, (Berkeley: Univ. of California, 1964).

[25]Horace R. Cayton, *Long Old Road* (New York: Trident Press, 1965), p. 154.

[26]Ben Whitaker, *The Police* (Middlesex, Eng.: Penguin Books, 1964), p. 137.

[27]It would be difficult to compare this factor across occupations, since the indicators could hardly be controlled. Nevertheless, I felt that the sense of responsibility to policemen in other departments was on the whole quite strong.

[28]In light of this, the most carefully drawn lesson plan in the "professionalized" Westville police department, according to the officer in charge of training, is the one dealing with the policeman's demeanor in labor disputes. A comparable concern is now being evidenced in teaching policemen appropriate demeanor in civil rights demonstrations. See, e.g., Juby E. Towler, *The Police Role In Racial Conflicts* (Springfield: Charles C. Thomas, 1964).

[29]Indeed, one school of social psychology asserts that there is a basic "drive," a fundamental tendency of human nature, to reduce the degree of discrepancy between conflicting cognitions. For the policeman, this tenet implies that he would have to do something to reduce the discrepancy between his beliefs and his behavior. He would have to modify his behavior, his beliefs, or introduce some outside factor to justify the discrepancy. If he were to modify his behavior, so as not to enforce the law in which he disbelieves, he would not hold his position for long. Practically, then, his alternatives are to introduce some outside factor, or to modify his beliefs. However, the outside factor would have to be compelling in order to reduce the pain resulting from the dissonance between his cognitions. For example, he would have to be able to convince himself that the only way he could possibly make a living was by being a policeman. Or he would have to modify his beliefs. See Leon Festinger, *A Theory of Cognitive Dissonance* (Evanston, Ill.: Row-Peterson, 1957). A brief explanation of Festinger's theory is reprinted in Edward E. Sampson, ed., *Approaches, Contexts, and Problems of Social Psychology* (Englewood Cliffs, N.J.: Prentice-Hall, 1964), pp. 9-15.

[30]Whitaker, *supra* note 26, p. 26.

[31]The questions submitted to the chief of police were directly analogous to those asked of printers in the study of the I.T.U. See Lipset et al., *supra* note 17, "App. II—Interview Schedule," pp. 493-503.

[32]J. Loevinger & A. Ossorio, "Evaluation of Therapy by Self-Report: A Paradox," *J. Abnormal & Social Psych.* 58 (May 1959), 392; see also Edward A. Shils, "Authoritarianism: 'Right' and 'Left'," in R. Christie & M. Jahoda, ed., *Studies in Scope and Method of "The Authoritarian Personality"* (Glencoe, Ill.: The Free Press, 1954), pp. 24-49.

[33]T.R. Brooks, "New York's Finest," *Commentary* 40 (Aug. 1965), 29-30.

3. Skolnick implies that to define the police personality as "authoritarian" is too simplistic—that the label "authoritarian" connotes specific characteristics which are predictable and immutable. Balch states, "...authoritarianism... is one of those labels that allows us to make sense of police behavior and to discredit it at the same time."

The problem of identifying a specific police personality, from Balch's perspective, can be reduced to this simple statement: We have people —some agressive, some meek, some insecure, some complacent, some cynical, some idealistic—all of them individuals who are attempting, by entering the police profession, to adjust themselves to the ideal role of "Protector of Society." At the same time, the task demands the development of certain attitudes (the emergence of a "working personality") which almost inevitably lead to social isolation. The ways in which police acclimate themselves to their precarious social position, then, are complex, and, as Skolnick indicated, often self-defeating.

Not only do visions of the "Ideal Cop" thwart a realistic understanding of police work, but, and herein lies the prime justification for Skolnick's and Balch's obvious refusal to recognize a definite "police personality," the concept of the ideal role of the policeman within our society has changed radically within the past two decades. Hopping from images of the happy Irish Cop to either a Superhero or "Pig" of the late '60s, to a typically human and fallible arm of the government in post Watergate days, the police cadet may find himself attempting to adjust to a role that is no longer valid or desirable. Until the position of the police officer in our society is clarified, until the discrepancy between public expectations, private beliefs, and social realities are lessened, Balch succinctly concludes that "[improvement] in police work...may simply mean that college graduates will be 'busting' heads instead of high school graduates."

THE POLICE PERSONALITY: FACT OR FICTION

ROBERT BALCH

In the last few years a great deal has been written about the police mentality. If we can believe everything we read in magazines, journals, and sociology books, the typical policeman is cynical, suspicious, conservative, and thoroughly bigoted. This is not a flattering picture to be sure, but it recurs again and again in the popular and "scientific" literature on the police. Perhaps there is something about the police system itself that generates a suspicious, conservative world-view. Or perhaps certain personality types are inadvertently recruited for police work. Either explanation is plausible, and both may be correct. Unfortunately only a few writers have bothered with the most basic question of all: Is there really a model police personality? At one time most white Americans thought blacks were superstitious tap dancers who preferred watermelon to work. Could it be that we have stereotyped policemen in the same way? The following pages will examine the controversy over the police mentality and suggest a sociological alternative to current speculation about the nature of police personalities.

The Police Personality As It Appears in the Literature

Although authors vary in emphasis, there is remarkable agreement on the characteristics believed to make up the police mentality. The cluster of traits that consistently emerges includes suspicion, conventionality, cynicism, prejudice, and distrust of the unusual. The traits are poorly defined and the names vary, but the syndrome is always the same.

Policemen are supposed to be very suspicious characters. A good policeman is always on the lookout for the unusual: persons visibly rattled in the presence of policemen, people wearing coats on hot days, cars with mismatched hubcaps, and so on.[1] A good policeman presumably suspects evil wherever he goes. As Buckner put it, "Once the commonplace is suspect, no aspect of interaction is safe, on or off duty."[2]

According to Colin MacInnes suspicion is simply a manifestation of deep-seated political and emotional conservatism.

The true copper's dominant characteristic, if the truth be known, is neither those daring nor vicious qualities that are sometimes attributed to him by friend or enemy, but an ingrained conservatism, an almost desperate love of the conventional. It is untidiness, disorder, the unusual, that a copper disapproves of most of all: far more, even than of crime which is merely a professional matter. Hence his profound dislike of people loitering in streets, dressing extravagantly, speaking with exotic accents, being strange, weak, eccentric, or simply any rare minority—of their doing, in fact, anything that cannot be safely predicted.[3]

Furthermore, policemen supposedly have no faith in their fellow man. Most are firmly convinced that only the police stand between a tenuous social order and utter chaos.

The people I see in the streets and in trouble are the same people who just a little while before that were in their nice homes and not involved in trouble. You can't fool me. I see people in the raw, the way they really are. Underneath their fine, civilized manners and clothes they're animals.[4]

If people in general are no good, then "coons" and "spics" are worse. All they like to do is drink, make love, and collect their welfare checks: "These scum aren't people; they're animals in a jungle...Hitler had the right idea."[5] Even many black officers share this outlook:

There have always been jobs for Negroes, but the f----- people are too stupid to go out and get an education. They all want the easy way out. Civil Rights has gotten them nothin' they didn't have before.[6]

Several other traits are frequently but less consistently used to describe the typical policeman. Police officers supposedly distrust ivory-tower intellectuals and bleeding-heart humanitarians. A good policeman is a realist who learns by experience and not by reading books. He respects authority and knows how to take orders. He likes to give orders too, and he demands respect from juveniles, criminals, and minorities. If necessary he will use force to see that he gets it. Brutality is perhaps the most infamous feature of the policeman's reputation:

A common thread of inhumanity runs through policemen in every city across the land. The potential for brutality is always there. Some psychologists say that this is the character trait that draws them to police work in the first place.... In too many cops the beast still slumbers, ready to enjoy another bout of sadism....[7]

Interestingly enough, the cluster of traits that apparently make up the police personality also defines authoritarianism.[8] Consider the parallels between the so-called police mentality and the following dimensions of the F-Scale:

a. Conventionalism: rigid adherence to conventional, middle-class values.
b. Authoritarian Submission: submissive, uncritical attitude toward idealized moral authorities of the ingroup.
c. Authoritarian Aggression: tendency to be on the lookout for, and to condemn, reject, and punish people who violate conventional values.
d. Anti-intraception: opposition to the subjective, the imaginative, the tender-minded.
e. Superstition and Stereotypy: the the belief in mystical determinants of the individual's fate; the disposition to think in rigid categories.
f. Power and "Toughness": preoccupation with the dominance-submission, strong-weak, leader-follower dimension; identification with power figures; overemphasis upon the conventionalized attributes of the ego; exaggerated assertion of strength and toughness.
g. Destructiveness and Cynicism: generalized hostility, vilification of the human.
h. Projectivity: the disposition to believe that wild and dangerous things go on in the world; the projection outwards of unconscious emotional impulses.
i. Sex: exaggerated concern with sexual "goings-on."

Only superstition, apparently, has never been used to describe policemen. Otherwise the dimensions of authoritarianism seem to describe police officers very well. In fact, the typical policeman, as he is portrayed in the literature, is almost a classic example of the authoritarian personality.

Is There Really a Police Personality?

While many writers assume as a matter of course that there is a police personality, the empirical evidence is less than convincing. Unfortunately good data are hard to come by. In one study the authors compared the authoritarianism of policemen with a partially matched sample of nonpolice students.[9] Both police and nonpolice subjects were attending the John Jay College of Criminal Justice at the time. Using Rokeach and Piven scales, they found the policemen were considerably *less* authoritarian than the other students. At a glance these results cast doubt on the so-called police personality, but in fact they cannot be interpreted so easily. In the first place, the nonpolice students cannot be equated with the general population because as many as 25 percent of them said they were "completely committed" to a career in police work. Second, the nonpolice students were still less authoritarian than a sample of noncollege policemen in a previous study by the same authors.[10]

The preliminary results of a recent study[11] using the Edwards Personal Preference Schedule indicate there are significant differences between police recruits and nonpolice college students, but the differences are not necessarily consistent with the authoritarian stereotype of policemen. The recruits were more likely to believe in the value of punishment, and they received significantly higher scores on the dimensions of deference and orderliness. They also appeared to be far less independent than the college students, and they were less likely to prefer new experiences. On the other hand, the recruits did not differ from the college students on three dimensions which are closely related to authoritarianism: aggression, nurturance, and intraception. The recruits also scored lower on the dimension of heterosexuality which belies Niederhoffer's claim that policemen are preoccupied with sexual matters.[12]

Another study undertook extensive psychiatric assessment of 116 applicants for the Portland Police Department.[13] All the applicants had passed their mental and physical exams, so, before the program of psychological testing began, they would have become officers as vacancies occurred. The authors administered a variety of psychological tests including the Edwards Personal Preference Schedule, Strong Vocational Interest Blank, and the Minnesota Multiphasic Personality Inventory. They concluded that the typical police applicant was very similar to the average male college student. Of course it is entirely possible that a unique police personality develops *after* recruits have spent some time on the job. Unfortunately there has been no follow-up study of the Portland recruits.

There are studies of experienced policemen in other cities, but they have not used the same personality scales. Bayley and Mendelsohn,[14] for example, administered an extensive questionnaire to a sample of Denver policemen. The questionnaire included items designed to measure anomia, authoritarianism, prejudice, and social distance. Using Srole's five-item F-Scale as their measure of authoritarianism, they found that Denver policemen scored lower than control populations sampled in previous studies. Their conclusion is worth repeating. Since their sample consisted of experienced policemen, the evidence also does not support the belief that a particular personality develops after joining the force.

In a study of the New York Police Department, McNamara used the original F-Scale to measure the authoritarianism of recruits in the police academy.[15] The recruits' mean F-score was virtually the same as the mean for working-class males found by Adorno and his colleagues. If we define "working class" as skilled, semi-skilled, and service work, then between 60 and 70 percent of the recruits in the New York Police Department come from working-class homes.[16] Therefore, McNamara's findings suggest that police recruits are typical of the class from which they are drawn. But since socio-economic status is inversely related to authoritarianism,[17] it is also true that working-class men, and therefore policemen, are more authoritarian than most. The McNamara study has to be taken with a grain of salt, however, because McNamara did not compare his recruits with a contemporary sample of working-class men in New York. Not only had many years elapsed since Adorno and his colleagues completed their study, but their working-class sample was selected on the West Coast.

McNamara also found evidence of increasing authoritarianism over time. He re-tested the recruits at the end of their first year and discovered a slight increase in their mean F-score. He also compared the recruits with men who had served on the force for two years. The more experienced police-men and the highest authoritarianism scores of all. A very liberal interpreta-tion of McNamara's data suggests the following conclusion: Police depart-ments do not attract particular person-alities, but instead tend to recruit members from a relatively authoritar-ian class of people. Furthermore, the police experience itself intensifies authoritarianism. It must be empha-sized, however, that this conclusion is tenuous, and certainly is not consis-tent with Bayley and Mendelsohn's findings.

Although not concerned with per-sonality *per se,* a study by Toch and Schulte suggests that policemen may perceive violence more readily than others.[18] They compared a group of advanced police administration stu-dents with two control groups—one consisting of introductory psychology students and the other of first year police administration students. All subjects were shown nine stereo-grams for a half second each. One figure in each stereogram depicted an act of violence of crime, while the other, matched in size and outline, showed some nonviolent "neutral" activity. The average number of violent percepts was the same for the two control groups, but the advanced police administration students per-ceived roughly twice as many violent scenes. Because the first year police administration students did not differ significantly from the psychology students, the authors concluded that police training increases one's readi-ness to perceive violence.

It is widely believed that policemen are prejudiced against minority groups. For example, Black and Reiss concluded[19] that 72 percent of the policemen they observed in Boston, Chicago, and Washington, D.C., were prejudiced against Negroes. Obser-vers rode or walked with officers for eight hours a day, six days a week, for seven weeks in 1966. Officers were classified as "highly prejudiced" when they "referred to Negroes as sub-human, suggested an extreme solu-tion to the 'Negro problem,' expressed dislike to the point of hatred, or used very pejorative nicknames when speaking of Negroes."[20] Officers were classified as "prejudiced" if they "simply showed general dislike for Negroes as a group." On the other hand, Black and Reiss did not find that verbal expressions of prejudice were translated into discriminatory behavior. Police behavior was "obvi-ously prejudiced" in only 2 percent of the cases and showed "some signs" of prejudice in only 6 percent. Moreover, whites were targets of police discrim-ination more often than blacks. Apparently, aggressive discriminatory police behavior was a response to the citizen's demeanor rather than his race. Skolnick[21] came to a similar conclusion when he observed the behavior of warrant officers on the Oakland police force.

The Black and Reiss data are not easy to interpret, however. Their "highly prejudiced" category could have been inflated by including offi-cers who used "pejorative nick-names." As Skolnick points out, many officers use derogatory nicknames even when they are not extremely prejudiced:

> The policeman's culture is that of the masculine workingman. It is of the docks, the barracks, the ballfield —Joe Di Maggio was a helluva good 'wop' centerfielder, not an athlete of 'Italian extraction,' and similarly, the black man is a 'nigger,' not a member of an 'underprivileged minority.'[22]

Black and Reiss also failed to employ a control group, so there is no way of assessing what their percentages mean. Skolnick, for instance, admits that policemen are prejudiced, but he does not believe they are any more so than the average white workingman.

In their study of the Denver Police Department, Bayley and Mendelsohn[23] also concluded that policemen simply share the prejudices of the community as a whole. Responses to simple prejudice and social distance scales were not greatly different from those given by a sample of white Denver citizens. In fact, neither the police nor the citizens scored highly on either scale. Similarly, Preiss and Ehrlich[24] found that 71 percent of their respondents in a Midwestern state police department were unprejudiced and tolerant on Srole's "anti-minorities" scale. However, there was no control group in their study.

The picture that emerges from these studies is not easy to interpret. Portland police applicants are like ordinary college males. Recruits in New York are somewhat authoritarian, but not as much as experienced policeman. Denver police are less authoritarian than the general public. In Boston, Chicago, and Washington police are prejudiced against Negroes, but their prejudice is not reflected in their behavior. In Denver and a Midwestern department, the police do not even appear to be prejudiced.

The picture is further complicated by methodological problems. The studies have been conducted in different cities in different parts of the country. What is true of Portland need not be true of New York, and what holds for a big-city force like Chicago's need not hold for a state or rural department. Even within departments there can be a tremendous amount of variation. Preiss and Ehrlich, for example, found that policies, standards, and procedures varied consid-erably from one post to the next in the state department they studied.

Only a few studies used adequate control groups and some did not use a control group at all. While it is very impressive to learn that 72 percent of the policemen in one study were prejudiced—or that 71 percent were unprejudiced in another—these figures are meaningless until we know how they compare to some nonpolice control group.

In addition, the methods of study and measuring instruments may not be comparable. In the studies mentioned above, three different measures of authoritarianism were employed. Prejudice has been "measured" by the subjective accounts of participant observers as well as by paper-and-pencil tests. These divergent methods may account for some of the apparently inconsistent results.

Finally, most of the results are subject to a "social desirability" interpretation. Niederhoffer[25] has commented on the policeman's transition "from station house to glass house." In other words, policemen are being watched and studied as never before. Liberals, minorities, and intellectuals are clamoring for greater civilian control over the police. The public has been sensitized to police brutality and prejudice, and police administrators are desperately trying to upgrade the quality of men in their departments. Furthermore, many policemen have had a smattering of social sciences somewhere along the line, so it is not surprising that they should know how to respond to an "anti-minorities" or authoritarianism scale in order to present themselves in the most favorable light.

In short, the evidence—by its very inconsistency, if nothing else—does not indicate the existence of a police personality, authoritarian or otherwise. With approximately 40,000 police departments in the United States, the chances of finding a single dominant personality type appear to be slim, to put it mildly. Obviously, however, none of the evidence so far is good enough to draw any firm conclusions. Writers who believe in a police mentality may not have a strong case, but they have yet to be disproved. Therefore it may be worthwhile to review some of the current hypotheses about the origin of police authoritarianism. Popular explanations generally fall into two broad categories. Some writers believe that police work itself develops an authoritarian world-view, while others believe that authoritarian personalities are selected for police work in the first place.

The Consequences of Police Work

According to the first point of view, authoritarianism is an unavoidable by-product of police work, i.e., the formal responsibilities, informal expectations, and everyday experiences of police patrolmen. The word "patrolmen" is used deliberately. The police mentality, as described in the literature, does not develop at the top of the police hierarchy and filter down to the underlings. Instead it develops at the bottom of the ladder as men patrol their beats and is carried to the top as they work their way up. Since virtually all police administrators begin their careers as patrolmen, it would not be surprising to find symptoms of the police mentality throughout the organization.[26] Most writers only deal with patrolmen, however, and so will this writer.

Suspiciousness

Danger is a recurrent theme in police work. Stories are told of

policemen shot and killed while trying to settle a family dispute or write a simple speeding ticket. Danger is part of the folklore to be sure, but even the most bizarre legends may have some basis in fact. Statistically speaking, police work is one of the most dangerous jobs in the country,[27] and policemen are aware of that fact. Sterling[28] found that policemen were more likely to perceive danger in 20 different situations the longer they had served on the force. No one can deny the widespread and often violent hostility policemen encounter in minority-group neighborhoods. At Christmastime the Black Panthers even sell greeting cards featuring uniformed pigs with knives in their bellies. Skolnick coined the term "symbolic assailant" to describe the policeman's psychological response to the continual threat of violence.

> The policeman, because his work requires him to be occupied continually with potential violence, develops a perceptual shorthand to identify certain kinds of people as symbolic assailants, that is, as persons who use gesture, language, and attire that the policeman has come to recognize as a prelude to violence.[29]

Although many policemen try to minimize the dangerous aspects of their work, Skolnick believes their "strategies of denial" are defense mechanisms that enable them to perform their job effectively. He concludes that the "unambiguous" consequence of danger in police work is a suspicious outlook on life.

Policemen are also *trained* to be suspicious. According to Skolnick, a good policeman has an intuitive ability to sense the unusual. He pays close attention to normal everyday routines so he can spot anything out of the ordinary. He notices when stores open and close, which houses are vacant, which lights are left on. He has to be suspicious or he will overlook tell-tale signs of criminal activity. Toch and Schulte's[30] study of the perception of violence indicates that police training has a very significant effect on one's perceptual processes. Suspicion, therefore, may be an occupational requirement. Unsuspecting cops do not make "good pinches."

Unfortunately most writers have not distinguished between suspicious-ness as a specific or generic trait. While many of them imply that suspiciousness pervades all aspects of the policeman's life, it may well be confined to his working hours, and even then to only certain aspects of his job. Because black ghettos are high-risk areas where crime and delinquency are commonplace, the men who patrol the ghettos are understandably suspicious of the local residents. But will their suspiciousness carry over during their off-duty hours? Will they be equally suspicious when they patrol "respectable" middle-class neighborhoods? If not, we ought to be cautious about treating suspiciousness as if it were a pervasive feature of the policeman's personality. In all fairness it should be added that Skolnick may have coined the term "working personality" to avoid treating suspiciousness as a generic trait. Nevertheless, other writers have not been so careful, and even Skolnick refuses to rule out the possibility that policemen are authoritarian personalities in the generic sense of the term.

Cynicism

One of the outstanding features of the police mentality is supposed to be cynicism—a deep-seated distrust of basic human goodness. The police-man's subjective world is full of savagery and hypocrisy: police officers are assaulted every day; respectable housewives try to fix their traffic tickets; and businessmen uphold the law only when it is in their interest to do so. Everyone, it seems, is "on the take" in one way or another.

One of the most common explanations for police cynicism is public antipathy toward the police. Westley found that 73 percent of the policemen he interviewed believed the average citizen dislikes police officers.[31] As Westley points out, the policeman's image of the public is shaped by the people he deals with every day on the job. To many, perhaps most of these people, the policeman is an intruder. Nowhere is the policeman's status as an outsider better illustrated than in the case of the family quarrel. The police officer is most apt to be called to settle a family dispute in a low-income neighborhood, the very place he is most likely to be defined as an outsider. Even if he has been called by one of the parties to the dispute, there is a good chance that everyone will turn on him before he leaves. The following comment by a police officer illustrates the policeman's predicament:

> Her husband was drunk and ugly when we got there... I started to grab him and struggled with him and the first thing I know I felt an aluminum pan pounding on my head and there is the little woman who ten seconds ago was standing there trembling at what the husband would do when we left, beating me on the head with an aluminum pan and saying, 'You are not supposed to hurt him. Let him alone.'[32]

The policeman's social identity as a law enforcement officer, and therefore as an intruder, is a "master status." It overrides all other aspects of his public identity. Whatever else the policeman may be, he is still a cop who can arrest you if he sees fit. The exclamation, "Better watch out, he's a cop," underscores the policeman's marginal identity. Presumably the policeman withdraws into his own circle of friends and defines the public in deviant terms just as he is so defined by them.

Public hostility toward the police takes many forms, some direct, others not. One kind of hostility is the abuse the policeman absorbs day after day as he patrols his beat. Another takes the form of biased reporting and editorial attacks in the newspapers. Niederhoffer found that 72 percent of a large sample of New York police officers believed that newspapers "seem to enjoy giving an unfavorable slant to the news concerning the police...."[33] In a less direct way, public hostility is reflected in the low prestige of his police work generally. The police officer's pariah feelings are intensified by his low occupational status. McNamara found[34] that 75 percent of the experienced policemen he studied in the New York Police Department believed that police work should be ranked as high as medicine and law. Yet he and Reiss have found that policemen believe their prestige has actually been declining in recent years[35] Skolnick discovered that 70 percent of the officers in a large Western city ranked the prestige of police work as "only fair or poor," while Westley found that 70 percent of the policemen he interviewed in an Eastern department said they would not want their sons to become police officers. According to Watson and Sterling,

> [I]t appears that many of these officers exhibit characteristics similar to those shown by a persecuted minority. They are very sensitive about criticism. They seem to fear that everyone is against them including their own commanding officers. They are hypersensitive and touchy about their status and their prerogatives[36]

As usual, however, the evidence is not completely consistent. Bayley and Mendelsohn found that Denver policemen believed they had higher-than-average respect in the eyes of the public[37] Preiss and Ehrlich found that the state police department they studied also enjoyed relatively high prestige.[38] In a nationwide survey of police opinions,[39] only 50 percent of the experienced officers believed that "public support for the police seems to be growing." But surprisingly the more experience an officer had, the more likely he was to endorse this statement. Furthermore, only three percent of the officers said the "gradual drifting away of nonpolice friends" was the most important personal problem they faced as policemen.[40] The Denver police also displayed little evidence of social isolation. Only 12 percent said they had difficulty making friends with non-police families, and less than 25 percent complained of difficulties in their social relationships because of their job. As many as 68 percent even said they associated primarily with nonpolice people. Banton has also criticized the assumption that American policemen are isolated from the public.[41] He contends that American policemen, unlike their British counterparts, are able to segregate police work from the rest of their lives. In fact many of his American respondents ridiculed those who played the policeman's role in their off-duty hours. Banton found that 67 percent of his Scottish respondents said their job affected their private lives. This is considerably higher than the 40 percent found in three Illinois cities by

Clark who asked the very same question.[42] Yet 40 percent is still a sizeable figure and is difficult to interpret—fully 40 percent or only 40 percent? Banton himself adds in passing that relative to other *American* occupations, policemen in this country really can be considered socially isolated.

Of course police isolation may be myth created by policemen themselves in order to make their job easier. Ronald Tauber agrees with Banton that American policemen are not as isolated as many have claimed.[43] However, he says that policemen *need* a sense of isolation if they are going to function effectively. The greater the social distance between the policeman and the public, the less cognitive strain there is in enforcing the law. According to Niederhoffer, the most successful policemen are the most cynical.[44]

Another commonly mentioned source of police cynicism is the judicial system. Policemen believe they have been hamstrung by the courts. The police officer is not just paid to enforce the law—the public *demands* that he do so. The blame for rising crime rates invariably falls on the police department, yet policemen are frustrated at every turn in their efforts to win convictions.

Because of the defense attorney's interrogations, [the police officer] often feels that he is being tried rather than the culprit. He is made to play the part of the fool. He is often frustrated in his attempt to make a pinch stick by the political machinations of the courts and the existence of the fix. He tends to lose faith in the course of justice and in obtaining the support of the courts for his judgments. He may feel that the only way in which the guilty are going to be punished is by the police. He has anxieties about the results of court action, for if the prisoner is declared innocent, he, the policeman, may be subject to a suit for false arrest.[45]

As this quotation illustrates, police officers are not just frustrated by fast-talking attorneys and bleeding-hearts on the bench. They are frustrated by the "fix," the back-stage deals against which they are helpless. Not even the courtroom is immune to the corruption which the policemen believe pervades our society.

A persistent theme in discussions of police cynicism is the police officer's continual exposure to the very worst in life.[46] While it is true that policemen spend more time rescuing cats and giving directions than they do fighting crime, one could argue that they still have more contact with the seamy side of life than most people. The very nature of their position makes them constant targets for bribes and payoffs by "respectable" and disreputable citizens alike. Of course policemen are not the only ones who see the "dark side" of human nature. Ghetto dwellers see crime and violence every day. But the policeman sees these things from a unique point of view. As a law enforcement officer the fact of *deviance* is foremost in his mind. Not surprisingly, Niederhoffer found that cynicism in the New York Police Department was directly related to the length of time an officer spent on the force.

Bigotry

Police cynicism supposedly finds its strongest expression in racial prejudice. Prejudice, after all, is really a kind of "directed cynicism." There is some indirect evidence that anti-minority sentiment among policemen is directly related to the amount of contact with members of minority groups. Black and Reiss found that a larger proportion of officers made "highly prejudiced" statements in Negro precincts than they did in racially mixed or white areas.[47] Of course the crime rate is higher in black neighborhoods; the poverty is greater; and the values are different. According to Johnson,[48] many policemen suffer from cultural shock in the ghettos, so it would not be surprising to find a high degree of prejudice among them. Kephart found a similar relationship between the arrest rate in black neighborhoods and the negative attitudes of white policemen who patrolled there.[49] The high crime rate might have contributed to the officers' prejudice, but the causal arrow could point the other way as well. The officers could have arrested more blacks because they were prejudiced in the first place. Not only that, but Kephart failed to find any relationship between anti-Negro feelings and length of service on the police force. As Skolnick points out, it is wise to keep police prejudice in the proper perspective: "the policeman may not get on well with anybody regardless (to use the hackneyed phrase) of race, creed, or national origin."[50]

Anti-intraception

Policemen have been accused of anti-intraception. They are supposedly opposed to tender-minded, sympathetic visionaries who insist on complicating "reality" with unworkable idealism.

> Police tend to be pragmatists, a characteristic related, no doubt, to the exigencies of their calling. Much of a policeman's work calls for action—now. He frequently handles emergencies in which time is precious. He has to make decisions in situations where facts are hard to come by and guidelines are uncertain. Small wonder, then, that he values 'common sense' more than

theory, successes more than ideals.[51]

According to Watson and Sterling,[52] the policeman's hard-bitten pragmatism is closely tied to his cynical outlook on life. Deterministic theories which, from the policeman's point of view, excuse the criminal from responsibility for his actions are inconsistent with a cynical, misanthropic worldview. Nevertheless, Watson and Sterling found that most officers *disagreed* with the view that social science is unrelated to the "everyday realities" of police work.

Violence

Critics also accuse the police of being overly fond of violence as a problem-solving technique. Police cynicism supposedly forms a background against which police brutality is understandable: Policemen need not have compunctions about splitting the heads of vile degenerate men. The police officer's reaction to the sex offender is a prime example: "If I saw a guy beat up a sex criminal I'd figure the guy had a good reason for it. If the guy is no Goddam good...I think it's all right to rough him up."[53]

Westley[54] believes that the root of police brutality is the public's definition of the police officer as a pariah. Policemen simply spend too much time dealing with the public to escape its opinions. They are ambivalent about their status. On the one hand, they regard themselves as competent craftsmen performing a vital task; yet on the other, they are condemned and degraded by the very people they have sworn to protect. Because their status is insecure, because they are not even sure if they respect themselves, policemen feel compelled to demand respect from the public. Significantly, Westley found that disrespect for the

> *"Police simply spend too much time dealing with the public to escape its opinions."*

police was the greatest single reason officers gave for "roughing a man up." Likewise Black and Reiss concluded that a "disproportionate part of 'unprofessional' or negative police conduct is oriented toward citizens who extend no deference to them."[55]

According to Banton[56] and Tauber,[57] American policemen cannot rely on the authority vested in their uniform to gain compliance. Instead they feel compelled to assert their *personal* authority. The citizen may take offense at the policeman's intimidating manner, and the stage is set for a violent confrontation in which each party is struggling to maintain his self-respect in the face of a perceived threat by the other. Westley adds that the lower the status of the citizen, the greater the threat he poses to the officer's uncertain self-esteem. In this context police brutality is indeed understandable.

Conventionalism

One of the policeman's outstanding characteristics, we are told, is his rigid adherence to middle-class values. By and large, policemen are recruited from the working class, but they are required to display middle-class values. Mustaches and long side-burns are prohibited, and hair must be trimmed in a conservative style.[58] In their study of a Midwestern police department, Preiss and Ehrlich found[59] that over a ten-year period

most of the cases to come before the department's trial board were for social offenses—intoxication, sexual promiscuity, financial negligence, and so on. A police department is a paramilitary organization. Strict discipline is required at all times, and conformity to the rules can become an end in itself. When in doubt, the safest course of action is to follow the rules, even if it means ineffective law enforcement.[60] The policemen's suspiciousness could also contribute to his conventionality. Things out of the ordinary indicate criminal activity.

In addition policemen are politically conservative and seem to be heavily represented in the John Birch Society.[61] In the 1964 Presidential election, Denver policemen not only voted for Goldwater in far greater proportion than the general public, but in greater proportion than white Denver citizens with the same educational and economic backgrounds as policemen. Watson and Sterling found that respondents in a nation-wide survey of police opinions tended to "side with" a sample of "civilian conservatives" more often than a sample of "civilian liberals."[62] The conservatives included several Klansmen and members of the John Birch Society. However, the police officers were not as extreme in their views as the conservatives, and Watson and Sterling caution us against "the mistaken impression that the police are 'all of a mind'—that they are a monolithic group so far as their views, opinions, and attitudes are concerned. This is definitely not the case...."

Skolnick has suggested that Festinger's theory of cognitive dissonance may explain why policemen are conservative and support the laws they enforce. Unless they were tough law-and-order conservatives when they joined the force, they are apt to experience some cognitive strain since they are required to enforce the law whether they believe in it or not. Their dissonance can be reduced in one of two ways. They can either modify their behavior—and risk losing their job—or they can decide that the laws are pretty good after all.

Policemen, then, seem to have good reason to be suspicious, cynical, conventional, and so on. There seem to be powerful forces at work in the policeman's role that could generate an authoritarian outlook on life. Recall that McNamara[63] found that more experienced policemen were more authoritarian than recruits in the police academy. However, policemen do not confront their problems alone. They are submerged in a subculture which provides a ready-made set of solutions. When police recruits leave their sheltered academies, experienced patrolmen begin to re-socialize them. Preiss and Ehrlich[64] found that police supervisors took special delight in debunking what rookies had learned in school—in fact, they considered it an important part of their job. Authoritarianism may not be an individual reaction which, incidentally, happens to be shared by others. It may be an attitude that is conveyed from one generation of policemen to the next. Niederhoffer is quite explicit about the system's ability to create authoritarian personalities. He goes so far as to say the system is a failure if it does *not* develop authoritarianism.

The Selection of Authoritarian Personalities

An alternative explanation of police authoritarianism is that authoritarian individuals are recruited for police work in the first place. Three kinds of selection are possible: 1) self-selection, 2) the weeding-out of "liberals," and 3) recruitment from an authoritarian class of people.

Self-Selection

Authoritarian individuals may deliberately choose police work because it is compatible with their personality needs. It is easy to see how an authoritarian might be drawn to police work. The police are a paramilitary organization whose job is to uncover suspicious activities and protect conventional moral standards. McNamara[65] found that police recruits did not object to the rigorous discipline of the police academy. He points out that this is what we should expect, given their relatively high F-scores. However, even if high F-scores are compatible with a militaristic organization, we cannot conclude that members have been self-selected. McNamara also believed that his recruits were no more authoritarian than the average working-class male. Similarly the authors of the Portland study of police applicants concluded that their subjects were very much like the typical male college students[66] Bayley and Mendelsohn also concluded that policemen were "absolutely average people." [67]

The evidence that particular personalities are selected for different occupations is not at all clear. According to Donald Super,[68] the more narrowly and specifically defined the occupation, the better the chance certain personalities will be attracted. But the problem with police work is that it defies easy description. the average policeman is a social worker, watchman, detective, guide, and so on.

The Elimination of "Liberal" Recruits

Even if authoritarian personalities do not deliberately seek out police work, a second selective factor may be operating. Liberals simply may not apply for police work. This is a much more parsimonious explanation of police conservatism than the theory of cognitive dissonance. Bayley and Mendelsohn not only found that Denver policemen were considerably more conservative than the general public, but that age was unrelated to political beliefs. If police work really develops a conservative outlook, then the older, more experienced policemen should have been more conservative than the younger ones. Of course, police selection procedures are geared to weed out unconventional applicants if they do apply. Applicants are subjected to rigorous character investigations, and any tinge of radicalism in one's background may be grounds for disqualification.[69]

Even when liberals do become policemen, they are not apt to last on the job.[70] The police force is already a conservative organization when the liberal arrives—he will not find much social support there for his beliefs. Even if he is not ostracized by other policemen, the job itself may be antithetical to his values. The police organization is a paramilitary bureaucracy which rewards conformity and discourages innovation. The liberal will have to enforce many laws he finds personally objectionable, and law itself may be subordinated to order-maintenance. The liberal has three alternatives. He can develop an "underlife" by seeking alternative sources of support for his values and self-esteem. He might, for instance, find a compatible niche in the community relations division. He could also change his belief system, and this is what we might predict from dissonance theory. But if the change is too radical and would require a complete realignment of the self-

concept, it may be easier to opt for the third alternative and drop out of the system altogether. It seems reasonable to assume, then, that liberals are unlikely to apply for police work, and, even if they do, they are unlikely to survive.

Working-Class Authoritarianism[71]

The third kind of selection has already been mentioned: The police recruit their members from a relatively authoritarian segment of the population.[72] It does not follow, however, that policemen themselves are authoritarian. The working class, the family background of many police officers, comprises a large portion of our population, and within that class there is room for a tremendous range of variation. While the mean level of authoritarianism may be very high, policemen could be selected from the lower end of the distribution. Bayley and Mendelsohn[73] found that Denver policemen were *less* authoritarian than their nonpolice control populations. On the other hand, McNamara's finding that police recruits scored as high on the F-Scale as Adorno's working-class sample does not support this interpretation.[74] In other respects policemen seem to be very much like the general public, which, unfortunately is never well defined. One study found substantial agreement between the police and the general public when they were asked to judge the rightness or wrongness of various actions.[75] Matarazzo, *et al.*,[76] and Bayley and Mendelsohn also found strong similarities between policemen and the public. Once more, the same inconsistencies prevent us from drawing any firm conclusions.

Many writers believe that police work is a "natural" choice for working-class men. It offers reasonably good pay, security, and adventure for young men without a college education or any special training.[77] For many, securing a job on the force represents an advance in social status. Studies show that Denver policemen and recruits at the New York Police Academy are upwardly mobile in relation to their fathers.[78]

Although most policemen come from working-class homes, they share typical middle-class values such as "looking toward the future and getting ahead, owning a home and a new car, being on time, and assuming responsibility."[79] Many, however, feel insecure precisely because they are new to the middle class. In a sense they are marginal men and seem to have profound doubts about their social standing.[80] In the absence of tangible social rewards like high pay and prestige, they cling to respectability to verify their middle-class status. As Chwast put it, the "police are more middle-classy than the average...."[81] It may be significant that 52 percent of

---

> "In a sense they are marginal men and seem to have profound doubts about their social standing."

---

the police applicants in the Portland study arrived for their interviews wearing a suit and tie.[82] The researchers were also interviewing potential firemen, but only 15 percent of them wore ties to their interviews. Yet all the applicants had working-class backgrounds. Perhaps the policeman's upward mobility accounts for

his authoritarian predilections.

> The police officer of lower class background may be insecure in his new status position and consequently may cling tenaciously to middle-class values while suppressing all traces of his previous class identification. To him, 'lower-class-ness' in others may be intolerable.[83]

The policeman's uncertainty is aggravated by his ambiguous standing in the eyes of the public. Many policemen believe they are not given the recognition or prestige they deserve. Some even believe the prestige of police work has been declining. Policemen also believe they are being "handcuffed" by the courts, civil rights groups, and local government. Not only is their social standing marginal, but their effectiveness as a law enforcement agency is being threatened. Studies indicate that a large proportion of police officers join the force in search of job security.[84] For these men especially, the uncertain status of police work must be very hard to bear.

Declining status and influence have been implicated in the growth of fascism.[85] The Nazi Party was supported initially and primarily by small business and property owners who were being squeezed out of existence by labor unions and big business. They felt powerless to cope with the changes occurring in Germany and seized on Nazism to restore their former social and economic security. Although the word fascism has been over-used and misused, and parallels should not be drawn too closely, a similar status-anxiety explanation might explain the policeman's apparent authoritarianism, especially his conventionality and conservatism.

In spite of the uncertainties inherent in police work, status-anxiety may characterize lower middle- and working-class people in general. There is some evidence that today's "silent majority" shares the policeman's feelings of insecurity. A recent Gallup Poll of the "forgotten man," the white middle-class American, reveals that middle-class whites are increasingly pessimistic about America's future.[86] Almost 50 percent believe that the United States has changed for the worse in the last ten years, and a majority believe things are going to get even worse in the next ten. They decry the decline of community spirit and religious and moral standards. They worry about runaway crime rates and believe the world is becoming a dangerous place. What we need, they say, is to take the handcuffs off the police: "To most people, the possibility of added police power offers no conceivable threat to anyone but wrongdoers. 'Behave yourself and there's no problem.' "[87] The forgotten Americans are also feeling the economic squeeze. Blacks are unfairly getting the biggest slice of the pie—they should have to work for what they get like everyone else.

Apparently the frustration and resentment are greatest in the working class—"families whose breadwinners have at most a high-school education, hold blue-collar jobs and bring home incomes of $5,000 to $10,000 a year."[88] They too, worry about crime, racial violence, rising prices, and crumbling values, but they worry more and their opinions are more extreme. Marginal socioeconomic status becomes intolerable in an age of affluence.

What has been described is the white middle- and working-class American, but one could easily substitute the word "policeman" in all the appropriate places and still be reasonably correct. Members of the "silent majority" are certainly not fascists,

any more than policemen are, but they seem to have many authoritarian characteristics: conventionalism, authoritarian aggression, stereotypy, cynicism, and projectivity. From this point of view, policemen appear to be good representatives of white middle- or working-class America.

Toward a Sociological Model of Police Behavior

Unfortunately, only one firm conclusion can be drawn from this review: The evidence is inconclusive. We began with the assumption that policemen are very unusual people, set apart from the rest of the population by virtue of their authoritarian mentality. Now it looks like policemen may be rather ordinary people, not greatly unlike other Middle-Americans. We cannot even be sure there is such a thing as a police personality, however loosely we define it.

According to Howard Becker,[89] everyone has deviant impulses and practically everyone violates social norms at one time or another. Yet only a few are publicly labeled deviant. The same reasoning may apply to the police. Authoritarianism, as a personality syndrome, is widespread in this country, and policemen may not be any more authoritarian than other people from similar socioeconomic backgrounds. Bigotry is hardly unusual in the United States. Nor is conservatism, cynicism, or any other authoritarian trait. From a sociological point of view, the important question is not, "Why are policemen authoritarian?" but "Why are they singled out for special attention?"

The police might have escaped the authoritarian label if they were not so visible. If the average workingman is bigoted, that is his business, but if a policeman is bigoted, that is everyone's business. Policemen may simply be very ordinary people who happen to be extraordinarily visible. Police behavior is public behavior, not just because police work involves members of public, or because it often

---

"Policemen may simply be very ordinary people who happen to be extraordinarily visible."

---

occurs in public places, but because the police are being subjected to public scrutiny as never before—in news stories, editorial columns, scholarly journals, radical tirades, and everyday conversation.

However, not all aspects of police behavior are equally visible to the public. A great deal of police work is only peripherally related to law enforcement. Patrolmen spend most of their time giving directions, writing reports, breaking up family quarrels, and the like, but we hardly notice these activities because they do not conform to our popular cops-and-robbers stereotype of police work. On the other hand, we are outraged by police brutality and discrimination. We pay attention when innocent citizens are stopped and frisked, when blacks are harassed and demonstrators beaten. Law enforcement may be only a small part of police work, but it is certainly the part that attracts the most attention and criticism. Police behavior often *appears* to be authoritarian simply because the public only pays attention to certain aspects of the policeman's job.

Cummins[90] has drawn some interesting parallels between the study of the police and early attempts by social scientists to come to grips with the problem of criminality. At one time most American criminologists were preoccupied with the nature of the "criminal mind." Cummins suspects that these early criminologists were driven by an "ideological need" to separate criminals from noncriminals. Today the evidence indicates that the personality characteristics of criminals are not appreciably different from those of people generally. But as the attention of criminologists has shifted away from criminals to the agents of social control, the need to psychologize and dichotomize has reasserted itself.

> Even though the earlier researches on criminality had wandered unsatisfactorily through the thicket of psychological distinctiveness, the same basic elements of the old framework cropped up again when the sociologists turned to analyzing the police side of deviance. True to form, the sociological studies emphasize the importance of some distinguishing psychological trait structure of police officers, particularly some undesirable feature. Perhaps once again, the ideological need for separation underlies the analyses.[91]

As Cummins points out, discussions of the police mentality have strong moral overtones. The use of labels like "cynical" and "suspicious" is "implicitly unfavorable, for it is, after all, a long stretch of the imagination to portray suspiciousness as a virtue."[92] He adds that more positive adjectives like "realistic" or "analytical" might be equally appropriate. While none of the authors cited in this paper have been openly hostile to the police, their studies provide ammunition for those who are. One of the favorite means of discrediting an undesirable character is to pin a psychiatric label on him. Authoritarianism, like mental illness or any number of more specific terms, is one of those convenient labels that allows us to make sense of police behavior and to discredit it at the same time.

Perhaps, considering the unproductiveness of the personality model, we need an alternative approach to the study of police behavior. An undue emphasis on personality diverts our attention from a far more important issue: the structure of police work itself. In his remarks about the suspiciousness of policemen, Cummins points out that our concern with the police mentality overlooks the sociological aspects of police work.[93]

Police brutality in minority-group neighborhoods is often cited as evidence of authoritarianism, reflecting bigotry and authoritarian aggression. As we have seen, there are many explanations for police violence, but the most parsimonious comes from the police themselves. They will tell you that they have to be tough, especially in the ghettos, or they will lose control of difficult situations.[94] As James Baldwin put it, "...the only way to police a ghetto is to be oppressive."[95] In this sense, being tough is a matter of survival. Bayley and Mendelsohn[96] found that 98 percent of their police respondents claimed to have been physically or verbally abused. Under these circumstances policemen become alert to cues signaling criminal activity and trouble—the symbolic assailant. The greater their anxiety, the less likely they are to take chances and the quicker they are to try to forestall injury to themselves. Policemen are most anxious in minority-group neighborhoods, and it is there that most police brutality is said to occur. In white middle-class neighborhoods the

police are less apt to worry about their well-being, and therefore they can be more relaxed in their encounters with citizens. Force, then, is not just an expression of personal prejudice or a fondness for violence. It may simply be a way of forestalling injury to oneself. Likewise, if policemen stop Negroes for suspicious activities more often than whites, it does not necessarily mean they are prejudiced. Rather the officers have learned that Negroes belong to a high-risk category and are more likely to have committed a crime.[97]

A great deal of significant police behavior can be explained solely in terms of the organizational characteristics of police departments. Wilson's study of the effect of professionalization on juvenile arrests is an excellent example.[98] When Wilson compared delinquency rates in two cities, he discovered that the city with the "professionalized" police force had a much higher juvenile arrest rate than the city with a nonprofessional force. Yet the rates of juvenile offenses known to the police in the two cities were remarkably similar. He attributed the differences to the organizational characteristics of the two departments. In the "professional" department precincts had been eliminated and the force had been centralized. Because the department had been plagued by scandals in the past, new regulations had been introduced, old ones had been made more stringent, and supervision had been tightened. Officers believed their behavior was constantly being monitored and their productivity measured. In order to "play it safe" they began to treat juveniles in strict accordance with the rules, without regard to personal characteristics or extenuating circumstances. On the other hand, the nonprofessional department was decentralized and run at the precinct level. Regulations were few, supervision lax, and individual officers had broad discretionary powers in juvenile matters. In cases where the "professional" officer would be likely to arrest, the officer in the nonprofessional department might simply give the juvenile a "kick in the pants" and send him home. In this case, police behavior can be explained without recourse to the psychological characteristics of individual policemen.

These remarks are not intended to deny the validity or usefulness of personality as an explanatory construct. Instead, they are meant to keep personality in the proper perspective. Personality and social structure *interact* with each other. For example, Watson and Sterling have argued persuasively that personality patterns acquired in childhood have varying degrees of influence on police behavior *depending on the nature of departmental organization.*

> If a police department is loosely organized, if the men get little in the way of training, if leadership is nonexistent, if supervision is lax, if there are few rules and regulations, which actually govern the conduct of the men, if the men don't see themselves as part of the law enforcement profession, if they think of their job as just another job, and if they don't feel a sense of dedication to their work, then the social class values of their childhood will probably come into play in their occupational role. To the

contrary, if a department is well organized, if the men are thoroughly trained in all aspects of their work, if those in command of the department show strong leadership and direction, if supervision is constant and effective, if rules and regulations are both known and followed by the men, and if the men feel they are strongly dedicated to the law enforcement profession, then there will probably be little relationship between social class upbringing and adult occupational performance. For example, the patrolman from a working-class background would not be inclined to use rough language or show a gruff manner in the latter kind of department.[99]

Presumably the effects of social class background would be minimal in a highly professionalized police force.

Conclusion

The controversy over the police mentality will probably persist for some time to come. There is simply not enough good evidence to support or refute any side of the controversy. Even the existence of modal personality characteristics among policemen is open to serious question. The devotion of social scientists to the personality model has obscured the important role that organizational factors play in shaping police behavior. Attracting better people to the same old job is not necessarily an improvement. In the case of police work, it may simply mean that college graduates will be "busting heads" instead of high school drop-outs.

Notes

[1]Adams, "Field Interrogation," *Police* (Mar.-Apr. 1963), p. 28.
[2]H. T. Buckner, "The Police: The Culture of a Social Control Agency," p. 190 (unpubl. Ph.D. diss., Univ. of Calif., Berkeley, 1967).
[3]Quoted in J. Skolnick, *Justice Without Trial: Law Enforcement in Democratic Society* (1967), p. 48.
[4]A. Black, *The People and the Police* (1968), pp. 6-7.

[5]Black & Reiss, "Patterns of Behavior in Police and Citizen Transactions," in *Studies of Crime and Law Enforcement in Major Metro. Areas 2* (1967), 113.
[6]*Ibid.*, p. 137.
[7]J. W. Sterling, "Changes in Role Concepts of Police Officers During Recruit Training: A Progress Report," p. 31 (mimeo., 1969), quoting Harriet Van Horne.
[8]J. Adorno, E. Frenkel-Brunswich, D. Leven-

son & R. Sanford, *The Authoritarian Personality* (1955), pp. 255-57.

[9]Smith, Locke, & Walker, "Authoritarianism in Police College Students and Non-Police College Students," *J. Crim. Law, Criminology & Police Science* (1968), p. 440.

[10]Smith, Locke, & Walker, "Authoritarianism in College and Non-College Oriented Students," *J. Crim. Law, Criminology & Police Science* 58 (1967), 128.

[11]Sterling, *supra* note 7.

[12]A. Niederhoffer, *Behind the Shield: The Police in Urban Society* (1967).

[13]Matarazzo Allen, Saslow & Wiens, "Characteristics of Successful Policemen and Firemen Applicants," *J. Applied Psychology* 48 (1964), 123.

[14]D. Bayley & H. Mendelsohn, *Minorities and the Police* (1969).

[15]McNamara, "Uncertainties in Police Work: The Relevance of Police Recruits' Backgrounds and Training," in *The Police: Six Sociological Essays,* D. Bordua, ed. (1967), p. 163.

[16]*Ibid.;* Niederhoffer, *supra* note 12.

[17]R. Brown, *Social Psychology* (1965).

[18]Toch & Schulte, "Readiness to Perceive Violence as a Result of Police Training," *Br. J. Psychology* 52 (1961), 389.

[19]Black & Reiss, *supra* note 5.

[20]*Ibid.,* p. 133.

[21]Skolnick, *supra* note 3.

[22]*Ibid.,* p. 82

[23]Bayley & Mendelsohn, *supra* note 14.

[24]J. Preiss & H. Ehrlich, *An Examination of Role Theory: The Case of the State Police* (1966).

[25]Niederhoffer, *supra* note 12.

[26]Significantly, the President's Commission on Law Enforcement and the Administration of Justice recommends increasing the amount of lateral entry into police administrative positions. *President's Commission on Law Enforcement and the Administration of Justice, Task Force Report: The police* (1967).

[27]W. Wirtz, quoted in "Copsules," *The Police Chief* (January 1969).

[28]Sterling, *supra* note 7.

[29]Skolnick, *supra* note 3.

[30]Toch & Schulte, *supra* note 18.

[31]W. Westley, *Violence and the Police* (1970).

[32]*Ibid.,* p. 61.

[33]Niederhoffer, *supra* note 12, p. 234.

[34]McNamara, *supra* note 15.

[35]Reiss, "Career Orientations, Job Satisfaction, and the Assessment of Law Enforcement Problems by Police Officers," in *Studies of Crime and Law Enforcement in Major Metropolitan Areas* 2 (1967).

[36]N. Watson & J. Sterling, *Police and Their Opinions* (1969), p. 9.

[37]Bayley & Mendelsohn, *supra* note 14.

[38]Preiss & Ehrlich, *supra* note 24.

[39]Watson & Sterling, *supra* note 36, p. 55.

[40]*Ibid.,* p. 101.

[41]M. Banton, *The Policeman in the Community* (1964).

[42]Clark, "Isolation of the Police: A comparison of the British and American Situations," *J. Crim. Law, Criminology & Police Science,* 56 (1965), 307.

[43]Tauber, "Danger and the Police: A theoretical Analysis," in *Issues in Criminology* 3 (1967), 69.

[44]Niederhoffer, *supra* note 12, p. 76.

[45]Westley, *supra* note 31, p. 82.

[46]Black, *supra* note 4; Niederhoffer, *supra* note 12; Westley, *supra* note 31.

[47]Black & Reiss, *supra* note 5.

[48]Johnson, "Police Community Relations: Attitudes and Defense Mechanisms," in *Issues in Criminology* 4 (1968), 69.

[49]W. Kephart, *Racial Factors and Urban Law Enforcement* (1957).

[50]Skolnick, *supra* note 3, pp. 49-50.

[51]Watson & Sterling, *supra* note 36, p. 6.

[52]*Ibid.*

[53]Quoted in Westley, *supra* note 31, p. 135.

[54]*Ibid.*

[55]Black & Reiss, *supra* note 5, p. 37.

[56]Banton, *supra* note 41.

[57]Tauber, *supra* note 43.

[58]Niederhoffer, *supra* note 12.

[59]Preiss & Ehrlich, *supra* note 24.

[60]McNamara, *supra* note 15.

[61]Niederhoffer, *supra* note 12.

[62]Watson & Sterling, *supra* note 36.

[63]McNamara, *supra* note 15.

[64]Preiss & Ehrlich, *supra* note 24.

[65]McNamara, *supra* note 15

[66]Matarazzo, et al., *supra* note 13.

[67]Bayley & Mendelsohn, *supra* note 14.

[68]D. Super, *The Psychology of Careers* (1957).

[69]Niederhoffer, *supra* note 12.

[70]Vego, "The Liberal Policeman: A contradiction in Terms?" in *Issues in Criminology* 4 (1968), 15.

[71]Watson & Sterling, *supra* note 36, have challenged the assumption that most policemen come from lower middle- and working-class families. However, their data seem to support the very assumption they wish to challenge:

> [T]oday's police officers have come from the families of craftsmen and foremen, and service workers (including police) in larger proportion than is true for the general adult work force. Conversely, the data shows [*sic*] that proportionately fewer police officers than other adults are children of professional, technical and managerial workers; clerical and sales workers; operatives; farmers; and laborers. (119).

[72]J. Wilson, *Varieties of Police Behavior: The Management of Law and Order in Eight Communities* (1970).

[73]Bayley & Mendelsohn, *supra* note 14.

[74]McNamara, *supra* note 15.

[75]Clark, *supra* note 42.

[76]Matarazzo, et al., *supra* note 13.

[77]Although the President's Commission on Law Enforcement and the Administration of Justice has recommended that police officers have at least two years of college, very few departments require any amount of college preparation. See note 26 *supra*.

[78]Bayley & Mendelsohn, *supra* note 14; McNamara, *supra* note 15.

[79]Chwast, "Value Conflicts in Law Enforcement" in *Crime and Delinquency* (1965), pp. 151, 154

[80]Bayley & Mendelsohn, *supra* note 14.

[81]Chwast, *supra* note 79, p. 154.

[82]Matarazzo, et al., *supra* note 13.

[83]Watson & Sterling, *supra* note 36, p. 121.

[84]Niederhoffer, *supra* note 12; Preiss & Ehrlich, *supra* note 24; Reiss, *supra* note 35.

[85]S. Lipset, *Political Man: The Social Bases of Politics* (1960).

[86]*Newsweek* (Oct. 6, 1969), p. 46

[87]*Ibid.*

[88]*Ibid.*

[89]H. Becker, *Outsiders: Studies in the Sociology of Deviance* (1963).

[90]M. J. Cummins, "The Problem of Police Minds" (m.d. unpubl.).

[91]*Ibid.*, p. 3.

[92]*Ibid.*, p. 7.

[93]*Ibid.*, p. 9.

[94]Niederhoffer, *supra* note 12; Skolnick, *supra* note 3; McNamara, *supra* note 15.

[95]J. Baldwin, *Nobody Knows My Name* (1962), p. 61.

[96]Bayley & Mendelsohn, *supra* note 14.

[97]Wilson, "The Police and Their Problems: A Theory," *Public Policy* 12 (1963), 189.

[98]Wilson, "The Police and the Delinquent in Two Cities," in *Controlling Delinquents*, S. Wheeler, ed. (1968), p. 9.

[99]Watson & Sterling, *supra* note 36, p. 109.

4. Balch states that "a great deal of significant police behavior can be explained in terms of organizational characteristics." However, in his statement that "the effects of a social background would be minimized in a highly organized police force," Balch ignores one important factor—human reaction to change. A common tenet of modern philosophy is that man is often unable to adapt to change—that change is often regarded as a threat in an otherwise comfortable, if somewhat rote, existence. It follows, then, that if police behavior is affected by organizational structure and the move toward increased professionalism may be regarded by many as a threat, certain police behavior patterns will emerge. These personality patterns, according to Lewis and the social scientist Niederhoffer, are characterized by feelings of anomie and cynicism (as a response to feelings of isolation as explained by Skolnick).

Both Skolnick and Lewis agree that the police officer "form[s] a self-image based on his perception of how others view him." The policeman was initially regarded, according to Jim Munro, * as a "superhuman"—as one who daily encounters danger and is thus separate from the ordinary masses. This image necessarily isolates the policeman from the general citizenry. He must transcend the public if he is to discern and act upon criminal behavior efficiently. This isolation reinforces his image as a "superhuman" and thus can be justified in the policeman's mind. However, police are now finding that they are divided among themselves because of the disruptive forces of change—in this case, the move toward professionalism. Anomie, therefore, becomes a very real threat to the policeman who finds himself isolated within his own ranks.

*See Jim Munro, ADMINISTRATIVE BEHAVIOR & POLICE ORGANIZATION (Cincinnati: Anderson Publishing Company), Chapter 10.

TOWARD AN UNDERSTANDING OF POLICE ANOMIE

RODNEY LEWIS

When one undertakes a critique of law enforcement, one invariably crosses paths with the conceptual relationship of professionalism, anomie, and cynicism as proposed by Arthur Niederhoffer in his analysis of law enforcement, *Behind The Shield*[1]. This work and the theory advanced in it are currently in vogue in law enforcement circles and appear to be widely accepted. Niederhoffer's thesis, in its most concise form, consists of three interacting elements: professionalism, anomie, and cynicism. The interaction of these factors is proposed to explain many of the ills afflicting the modern policeman.

Professionalism, says Niederhoffer, is the result of an influx of middle-class, college-trained men into law enforcement in the 1930s and 1940s. "These middle-class college men formed the nucleus of the future elite group: before long they began to try to raise the prestige of the police occupation to match their own middle-class ideologies and attainments: to transform it into a profession." This influx of middle-class men was in contrast to the fact that "the bulk of police condidates has been upper lower class with a sprinkling of lower middle class."

Niederhoffer examines, at considerable length, the problems of the various levels of police personnel, the attempts of members of these strata to obtain more desirable positions, and their frustration at being unable to do so. The catalyst for advancement is seen as professionalism: the professional patrolman will advance; the patrolman who cannot adopt professionalism will stagnate. This emphasis on professionalism has created a split in the workings of law enforcement. Niederhoffer states, "Within the ranks many of the less educated, tradition-directed members of the force continue to fight to preserve their hegemony. Dissension has reached serious proportions, verging on internecine class conflict between the lower-class conservatives and the upwardly mobile middle-class radicals."

Much of this conflict results from the dichotomy between the ideal of professionalism and the reality of the job. As Niederhoffer states, "The codes of ethics and the ideals that are not consistent with the force's sense of reality may actually impede professionalism. For example, professionals advocate higher education for policemen, to whom school represents at best a waste of time. Professionals support respect for the civil rights of minority groups, which the average policeman considers a concession to 'the other side.' Professionals want policemen to be active and involved in their duties, whereas many patrolmen are content to drift along doing as little as possible. The members of the force feel threatened by the proposed changes. In self-defense they join the opposition to professionalism and become part of the subculture of cynicism." The result is that "the split in the department along the lines of professionalism and education has created a new and more abrasive type of social tension."

This social tension, according to Niederhoffer, is anomie, "a morbid condition of society characterized by the absence of standards, by apathy, confusion, frustration, alienation, and despair." Niederhoffer's use of the word "anomie" appears to be in accordance with the classic sociological theory of Emile Durkheim and Robert Merton. Durkheim introduced the theory of anomie, applying it primarily to desire and achievement and its application to suicide incidence,[2] while Merton enlarged on the idea in a relationship that stresses success and establishes alternatives of reaction by an individual who finds himself suffering "anomia."[3] Niederhoffer claims a relationship between anomie and professionalism: "Anomie occurs particularly when the old values of a social system are being supplanted by a new code—exactly the case in the police organization. Seeking to wrest control from the old regime, the professionals are introducing a new ethic into the modern police force which is undermining old norms and loyalties. Caught between these contending forces, the policeman in the lower ranks feels uncertain of his position."

The relationship between anomie and cynicism is not pursued by Niederhoffer in as much detail as is the relationship between professionalism and anomie. While acknowledging cynicism directed "against life, the world, and people in general," Niederhoffer devotes his attention primarily to the "diffuse feelings of hate and envy, impotent hostility, and the sour-grapes pattern [that are] used in this study to refer to the state of mind in which the anomie of the police organization as a whole is reflected in the individual policeman." Niederhoffer appears to argue that, given the pressure for professionalism by middle-class professional administrators on working-class patrolmen, a condition of anomie is created in which the patrolmen react with rebellion and adopt a philosophy of cynicism. Although acknowledging that it may develop elsewhere, cynicism is primarily seen by Niederhoffer as a direct and inescapable result of professionalism.

A premise upon which Niederhoffer constructs his thesis is the lower-class origin of the police. Niederhoffer is not alone in this premise, however unique he may be in applying it to the professionalism conflict. The literature of police study is replete with inferences that the police have a blue-collar background which somehow interferes with their ability to function in a world which is primarily middle-class. Niederhoffer bases his statement of lower class origin on a study of the occupations of the fathers of 1,200 New York Police Department recruits to the effect that the background of those recruits was 85 percent working class. In contrast, the International Association of Chiefs of Police in 1969 published an exhaustive study of nationwide scope entitled *Police And Their Opinions.*⁴ As could be expected, this study was highly critical of the allegation that police were predominately lower class in origin. However, the points raised in support of this criticism are persuasive, particularly when it is understood that this study involved a nationwide polling of police. While acknowledging, as does Niederhoffer, that certain lower-class attitudes may be beneficial, particularly those involving fight-or-flight situations faced by the police, the study comes to the conclusion that police are basically middle-class in nature. This conclusion is supported empirically by investigation of the employment of police recruits' fathers and recruits'

prior employment, as well as secondary employment of police officers.

To whatever extent the foregoing findings serve to discredit Niederhoffer's reasoning in developing class conflict as a cause for anomie, those associated with law enforcement, and particularly the ones involved in police departments undergoing modernization and professionalism, will acknowledge the existence of conflict between those advocating professionalism and those advocating the status quo. It is tempting to view this conflict as something unique to law enforcement. However, when the conflict is viewed from the prospective of labor-management relations, it can be established that the police are not alone with their problems. Studies show that a large percentage of the total labor force is disgruntled for one reason or another. A recent study released by the United States Department of Labor showed that out of a total national work force of 82,854,-000, better than 60 percent of workers are dissatisfied with their position and feel that their management-labor relations are unsatisfactory. A recent trend by labor organizations to emphasize the influence of managerial decisions rather than monetary gain in collective bargaining is an indicator of the importance labor places on its supervision. When viewed as a management attempt to increase productivity and the quality of its product, professionalism may be seen in a new prospective. It is entirely possible that professionalism is not a basic conflict of classes, and that the absence of standards, apathy, confusion, frustration, alienation, and despair of anomie have their roots elsewhere.

The empirical evidence establishing the existence of anomie as a condition of police is sound and Niederhoffer shows it succinctly. It is patterned after the investigation of suicide as a measure of anomie by Emile Durkheim and states, "The suicide rate for males in the general New York City population is about 15 per 100,000. The average police rate of 22.7 is almost 50 percent more than this." However, examination of the New York Police suicide statistics for information other than a high level of anomie poses interesting questions.[5] For example, when these statistics are broken into groups of five years, the trend seems to be toward a decreasing number of suicides at the same time that the middle-class professionals of the 1930s and 1940s would be reaching the peak of their 20-year careers. It appears that considerable study of the suicide statistics for police should be undertaken before these statistics are used in support of any fact other than the comparatively high rate of police anomie.

Beyond this categorical examination of police suicide, however, is the feeling prevalent among police officers that they are indeed facing something unique. Many officers frequently feel one or all of the symptoms, although they may experience difficulty defining their symptoms as anomie. As one police officer commented in a study to be examined later, being a police officer will "age you beyond your years."

If professionalism can be ruled out as a cause for law enforcement anomie, how is it that the police find themselves in this unfortunate condition? At best, one can only hypothesize in an attempt to establish the cause of anomie among policemen. The alternate hypothesis proposed here has its base in the primary instinctual drives of self-preservation and fear, drives which psychologists acknowledge exist in all manner of men.

Psychologists differ substantially on the relative ranking of drives in the establishment of the total individual, but few of them deny that self-preservation and fear are among the strongest. The physical effects of fear have been well studied. When confronted by a situation which stimulates the instinct of self-preservation, the autonomic nervous system creates an internal condition which puts the entire body in a state of emergency. This sensation of a fluttering heart, rapid breathing, disrupted digestion and elimination, is one which many have experienced over the course of their lifetimes.[6]

Fear is common in combat situations, and the largest mass of information on it would presumably have been accumulated by the military, yet little current data can be obtained, possibly due to the military system of classification. Older data from military sources show that fear can stimulate temporary reactions which might otherwise be considered neurotic or abnormal. However, military research has found that group support, effective leadership, intensive indoctrination and training can minimize the undesirable effects of fear.[7]

Research into the effects of fear on the policeman is almost nonexistent. A recent study on the fear of death among patrolmen was all that could be located.[8] This study of 17 policemen and control groups of 15 mail carriers and 23 male college undergraduates showed that patrolmen did not differ significantly from the control groups, and that the "greater cooperation shown by the patrolmen in taking the test suggests less defensiveness about death and the probability they may have worked through death anxiety in part." The study concludes that on "a conscious verbal level," the policemen "resemble other adult males." It is interesting to note that the authors of the above study hinted that the police subjects somehow differed from the control groups on an unconscious level. Furthermore, it can be intimated that death and fear of death have many manifestations which may not have exhibited themselves in this study.

There is little doubt that law enforcement is a hazardous occupation. This can be borne out by examination of statistics published by yearly by the Federal Bureau of Investigation.[9] However, these statistics do not begin to establish the magnitude of the problem, as they show only a small part of the violence and injury the police officer encounters. To illustrate the situation more accurately, a questionnaire was distributed to all personnel actively engaged in law enforcement in the Charlottesville, Va. Police Department. When questioned regarding potentially unpleasant situations encountered, the respondents, who included patrolmen, detectives, and their supervisors, indicated that they observed minor bleeding three times a month, life-threatening bleeding once every three months, an injured adult three times a month, an injured child once every two months, the victim of severe assault slightly more than once every two months, and a dead person about once every three months. In the month studied, seven officers were involved in violent or potentially violent activity, two of whom were assaulted, and four of whom had to strike someone. However, the study showed that in the average 10 years of employment, an average officer was injured only twice, with only one of these injuries requiring time off from work to recover. These figures show that, while the officer frequently observes injury and violence, he is himself injured somewhat less than might be expected.

It is proposed that police anomie, to a large extent, is a result of a unique type of stress placed on the police by the physically dangerous and often violent nature of their employment, and, more importantly, by their conceptualization of this hazard. This stress and its conceptualization by the police is labeled danger-stress and an attempt is made to establish danger-stress as a prime force in the anomia of police. Further, it is proposed that danger-stress anomia is subject to influence by police socialization, which is in turn subject to influence by other outside factors, not the least of which is professionalism.

The existence of danger-stress begins with the existence of hazard in police employment. Although the degree of hazard is subject to discussion and is to some degree determined by location, it cannot be denied that the hazard is greater than in many other fields of endeavor. This amount of hazard involved in the profession is the subject of voluminous literature in the field of police training. From the day a police recruit enters the academy to the day the seasoned officer retires, he is bombarded with admonitions to "be careful" and is repeatedly assured that he runs a substantial risk of injury, even while performing the most innocuous tasks. The officer is assured he will daily confront the depraved, the criminal, and the average citizen, all of whom may harm him if provoked or given the opportunity.

To be sure, policemen face dangerous situations and it is unfair to criticize those who attempt to prepare themselves for this danger. All such attempts are in preparation for the time when quick thought and instant action will extract a policeman from a potentially fatal situation. Yet no-where in police literature can be found an accurate guide for the police officer which statistically details his probability of injury or which attempts to reassure him that his life is not constantly in danger. And, indeed, those inside law enforcement are hardly more responsible for instilling this attitude in the police than are his friends and neighbors and the mass media. What police officer has not heard someone say he would never be a police officer because of "all that danger"? Nothing, moreover, can be more distorted than the image the policeman sees of himself in the mass media. From friends and family, from cohorts and strangers, from training material to the mass media, the policeman receives repeated reminders of the hazards of his profession.

The conceptualization of hazard by police can perhaps be shown to be divergent from reality, but the self-image the police officer obtains from this conceptualization is nonetheless existent and personal. The police officer seems to have formed a self-image based on his perception of how others view him. While this point itself is subject to further investigation, it appears to be in line with the analysis of the self by Charles H. Cooley and others, who have established self-image as a "looking glass"—our interpretation of the way others see us.[10]

Consciousness of being in a hazardous occupation, however, is only part of the establishment of danger-stress as a possible police ailment. It must be realized that by placing himself in a position of danger, even if it is only imagined, the police officer is putting himself in a position contrary to human instincts. It is possible to view this conflict of hazard and instinct, continually reinforced by the observa-tion of incidents of bleeding, injury and death over an extended period of time, as a prime cause of the intense danger-stress feelings of policemen.

When one moves from this establishment of the danger-stress state and attempts to determine the nature and effect of stress on the individual, a problem of immense complexity develops. Medicine, psychology, and sociology look at stress from different perspectives and consequently define it in different ways.[11]

Sociology has made most of its contributions to the study of the effect of group relationships on the formation and intensity of stress. Groups identified by sociologists as principal generators of stress are the family, work and organizations, and class and race. A large body of work on stress has revolved around its relationship to Durkheim's concepts of suicide. It is at this point that the concept of danger-stress and anomie begin to merge.

In the study of suicide, Durkheim made a conceptual distinction between anomic suicide and egoistic suicide. Durkheim stated with regard to egoistic suicide that "suicide varies inversely with the degree of integration of the social groups of which the individual forms a part." The work of others in dealing with a frustrating (stressful) situation and suicide has also emphasized the importance of the group.[12]

The hypothesis of danger-stress places emphasis on the group as being a mitigating factor on this condition. The existence of danger-stress drives the police officer to seek relief from his condition of fear and tension in group relations, primarily relationships with those who also suffer danger-stress to varying degrees. Many police officers feel that one result of law enforcement employment is the loss of previous friends, and this is frequently seen as a form of criticism. However, this loss of previous friends and the police officer's withdrawal from previous primary groups can be seen as an action instigated by the police officer himself. The previous primary groups do not perform a new basic function for the policeman—that of helping him deal with danger-stress. It is for this reason that the new officer often rejects his friends and shifts to a position where he associates almost exclusively with fellow police officers.

At this point the phenomenon of professionalism as seen by Niederhoffer is injected as a catalyst. In years past, promotion and other choice assignments were based entirely upon seniority. The policeman could bear no ill will for associates seeking promotion, because promotion could not be seen as an event which was controllable either by the ability of the promoted officer or the observer's lack of it. Group relations could be maintained with no strain, and danger-stress could be counterbalanced by group cohesiveness. However, the advent of professionalism has disrupted the cycle by placing individual officers at odds with each other, to some extent disrupting the primary group relations and allowing the

> *"[The police officer] finds himself in a groupless, normless situation where the symptoms of danger-stress are unrestrained."*

expression of danger-stress to manifest itself in other ways, such as increased cynicism.

To see the manifestation of danger-stress as anomie in the sense in which Durkheim and Merton developed the term and in which Niederhoffer utilizes it, that of an economic nature, is difficult. However, many modern sociologists have simplified the concept of anomie to mean "loss of confidence in social norms"[13] or "a situation of complete normlessness."[14] Utilizing this definition of anomie, it is possible to see the police in a situation of anomie, for the police officer, having rejected civilian primary groups and finding his work-oriented primary group disrupted by professionalization and other factors, finds himself in a groupless, normless situation where the symptoms of danger-stress are unrestrained.

The result of danger-stress cannot be determined as a constant factor, as the degree of stress exhibited by an organism is mitigated by many factors. However, danger-stress can be seen in all police officers, ranging from an unconscious feeling to a state of total paranoia.

The implications of the danger-stress proposal are broad for both the sociologist and the police administrator. For the sociologist, it should be noted that the concept which has been advanced here is simply that—a concept. It is in need of specific empirical evaluation to determine its validity, and the sociologist has the tools and training to make this test. However, the implications for the police administrator are far greater, for if it can be established that danger-stress is a reality, the police officer is caught between the disruptive effects of professionalism on the one hand and danger-stress on the other. As neither professionalism nor the danger of police work appears to be on the verge of disappearing, the administrator may be faced with the possibility of meeting danger-stress head on. The administrator should consider the possibility of increased training in this area. An obvious solution would be increased on-the-job safety training. But to really attack the problem, the administrator may be required to instigate training which realistically and statistically attempts to show the police officer the actual amount of danger faced by an officer in his particular locale. Perhaps more importantly, the police administrator may be required to join forces with the sociologist and establish training programs which will help the officer face danger-stress on an individual basis and which will help the police work force achieve increased group cohesiveness.

Notes

[1]Niederhoffer, *Behind the Shield* (1969).
[2]Durkheim, *Suicide: A Study in Sociology,* ed. George Simpson (1951).
[3]Merton, *Social Theory and Social Structure* (1968).
[4]International Association of Chiefs of Police, *Police and Their Opinions* (1969).

[6]Pinard, Willem: *Mind: Psychological Re-orientation* (1959).
[7]U.S. Defense Dept., *Report of Working Group on Human Behavior Under Conditions of Military Service* (1951).
[8]Ford, Alexander & Lester, *Psychological Reports,* (State Univ. of N.Y. 1971).
[9]FBI, *Uniform Crime Reports* (1971).
[10]Cooley, *Human Nature and the Social Order* (1956).
[11]Torrence, *Constructive Behavior: Stress, Personality and Mental Health* (1965).
[12]Levine & Scotch, *Social Stress* (1970).
[13]Caplow, *Elementary Sociology* (1971).
[14]Bierstedt, *The Social Order* (1967).

[5]SUICIDES IN THE NEW YORK CITY POLICE DEPARTMENT

Year	Number of Suicides	Size of Force Jan. 1 ea. yr.	Rate Per 100,000	Five Year Variation
1950	11	18,563	58	
1951	3	19,016	16	
1952	3	18,451	16	
1953	6	18,762	31	
1954	4	19,840	20	141
1955	8	20,080	37	
1956	3	22,460	13	
1957	4	23,193	17	
1958	1	24,112	4	
1959	8	23,636	34	105
1960	6	23,805	25	
1961	5	22,515	20	
1962	5	24,374	20	
1963	3	24,837	11	
1964	4	25,432	16	92
1965	7	25,897	26	
Average Number of Suicides Per Year	5.0	Average Rate Per 100,000	22.7	

5. In the preceding articles, the "Police Personality," or, more accurately, the "working personality of police," has been viewed from several perspectives—it has been described as a response to:

Stereotyped notions of the police role (Skolnick)

Interaction between personality characteristics and social structure (Balch)

Authority and danger (Lewis)

Stoddard, in "The Informal Code of Police Deviancy: A Group Approach to 'Blue Coat Crime,'" maintains that deviant behavior can be attributed to interaction between personality traits (traits that tend to be "conventional") and organizational structure. Although Stoddard is mainly concerned with a description of police graft and its causes, his contention that "the social structure in which law enforcement is maintained has a definite bearing on what is considered normal and deviant behavior" reinforces the assertion that specific personality characteristics are created by, and not specifically attracted to, the profession. Police graft, Stoddard avers, exists not because deviant types are attracted to the police profession but because the organization itself creates a need for stealthy actions.

This author's emphasis on the importance of group cohesion in maintaining the informal code of deviancy takes Lewis' point one step further—if police solidarity suffers because of the tension created by some members of the force for increased professionalism and if police are more insecure because their "superhuman" image is threatened, it is inevitable that they will band together under the security of more informal codes. The attraction of these informal codes is that they not only promise a sense of camaraderie but are conveniently perpetuated by a reliance on "professional" ethnics:

> ...these same procedures which would effectively reduce the continuation of the [deviancy] "code" would also prove disfunctional to the maintenance of the ethics which are the core of the police profession itself.

Police, in other words, can gain the comfort of group companionship, of "belonging" by engaging in deviant behavior and still maintain a sense of professionalism (if, by nothing else) by not "squealing"—by not demeaning the police image.

THE INFORMAL CODE OF POLICE DEVIANCY: A GROUP APPROACH TO "BLUE COAT CRIME"

ELLWYN R. STODDARD

It has been asserted by various writers of criminology, deviant behavior, and police science that unlawful activity by a policeman is a manifestation of personal moral weakness, a symptom of personality defects, or the recruitment of individuals unqualified for police work. In contrast to the traditional orientation, this paper is a sociological examination of "blue-coat crime" as a functioning informal social system whose norms and practices are at variance with legal statutes. Within the police group itself, this pattern of illicit behavior is referred to as the "code".

Following an examination of these contrasting viewpoints this case study will provide data to ascertain the existence of the "code", its limitations and range of deviancy, and the processes through which it is maintained and sanctioned within the group.

The guiding hypothesis of this study is that illegal practices of police personnel are socially prescribed and patterned through the informal "code" rather than being a function of individual aberration or personal inadequacies of the policeman himself.

The Individualistic Approach

Three decades ago August Vollmer emphasized that the individual being suited to police work was the factor responsible for subsequent deviancy among officers. This approach implicitly assumes inherent personality characteristics to be the determinant which makes a police recruit into a good officer or a bad one. A current text of police personnel management by German reaffirms the individualistic orientation of Vollmer, and suggests that the quality of police service is ultimately dependent upon the individual police officer. There is no evidence of an awareness of group pressures within his analysis.

A modified version of this individualistic approach is the view that perhaps the individual chosen had already become "contaminated" prior to being hired as a member of the force, and when presented with chances for bribery or favoritism, the "hard core guy, the one who is a thief already, steps in".

A third factor, stressed by Tappan, is the poor screening method at the recruitment stage. Such an officer might have had inadequate training, insufficient supervision, and poor pay

and is ripe for any opportunity to participate in lucrative illicit enterprises. This author then goes into great detail to show the low intelligence and educational level of police officers. Another author adds that improved selection and personality evaluation have improved the quality of the police considerably over the past 20 years, thereby attacking this problem directly. One recent author wrote that low salaries make more difficult the attraction of applicants with the moral strength to withstand temptations of "handouts" and eventual corruption, Sutherland and Cressey, although aware that graft is a characteristic of the entire police system rather than of isolated patrolman, stress the unqualified appointments of police officials by corrupt politicians as the source of police deviancy. They state:

> Another consequence of the fact that police departments often are organized for the welfare of corrupt politicians, rathr than of society, is inefficient and unqualified personnel. This is unquestionably linked with police dishonesty, since only police officers who are "right" can be employed by those in political control. Persons of low intelligence and with criminal records sometimes are employed.

The Group Approach

In contrast to the individualistic approach of these foregoing authors, the emphasis on the social context in which police deviancy flourishes has preoccupied the sociological criminologists. The present case study would clearly reflect this latter orientation.

Barnes and Teeters mention police deviancy in conjunction with organized syndicated crime. Korn and McCorkle, Cloward, and Merton see political and police corruption as a natural consequence of societal demands for illegal services. When these desired services are not provided through legal structures, they are attained through illegal means. However, documentation in support of these theoretical explanations is sketchy and limited in scope. Bell suggests that "crime is an American way of life." In the American temper there exists a feeling that "somewhere, somebody is pulling all the complicated strings to which this jumbled world dances." Stereotypes of big crime syndicates project the feeling that laws are just for "the little guys." Consequently, while "Americans have made such things as gambling illegal, they don't really in their hearts think of it as wicked." Likewise, the routine discovery of an average citizen in overt unlawful activity rarely inflames the public conscience to the degree that it does when this same deviant behavior is exhibited by a police officer. Thus, the societal double standard demands that those in positions of trust must exhibit an artifically high standard of morality which is not required of the average citizen.

A measure of role ambivalence is an inevitable part of the policeman occupation in a democratic society. While he is responsible to protect the members of his society from those who would do them harm, the corre- sponding powers for carrying out this mandate are not delegated. To perform his designated duties, the conscientious policeman often must violate the very laws he is trying to enforce. This poses a serious dilemma for the police officer since his attempt to effectively discourage violation of the law among the general public is often hinged to extra-legal short-cut techniques which are in common practice by his law enforcement cohorts. For example, the use of "illegal" violence by policemen is justified by them as a necessary means to locate and harass the most vicious criminals and the Organized Syndicates. These procedures are reinforced through coordinated group action.

> The officer needs the support of his fellow officers in dangerous situations and when he resorts to practices of questionable legality. Therefore, the rookie must pass the test of loyalty to the code of secrecy. Sometimes his loyalty of colleagues has the effect of protecting the law-violating, unethical officer.

Such illegal practices which are traditionally used to carry out a policeman's assigned tasks might well be readily converted to the aims of personal gain.

In these tight informal cliques within the larger police force, certain "exploratory gestures" involving the acceptance of small bribes and favors can occur. This is a hazy boundary between grateful citizens paying their respects to a proud profession, and "good" citizens involved in corruption wishing to buy future favors. Once begun, however, these practices can become "norms" or informal standards of cliques of policemen. A new recruit can be socialized into accepting these illegal practices by mild, informal negative sanctions such as

> ## "Thus, the societal double standard demands that those in positions of trust must exhibit an artificially high standard of morality."

the withholding of group acceptance. If these unlawful practices are embraced, the recruits membership group—the police force—and his reference group—the clique involved in illegal behavior—are no longer one and the same. In such circumstances the norms of the reference group (the illegal-oriented clique) would clearly take precedence over either the formal requisites of the membership group (police department regulations) or the formalized norms (legal statutes) of the larger society. When such conflicts are apparent a person can:

> a. Conform to one, take the consequences of non-conformity to the other.
> b. He can seek a compromise position by which he attempts to conform in part, though not wholly, to one or more sets of role expectations, in the hope that sanctions applied will be minimal.

If these reference group norms involving illegal activity become routinized with use they become an identifiable informal "code" such as that found in the present study. Such codes are not unique to the police profession. A fully documented case study of training at a military academy in which an informal pattern of behavior was assimilated along with the formal standards clearly outlined the function of the informal norms, their dominance when in conflict with formal regulations, and the secretive nature of their existence to facilitate their effectiveness and subsequent preservation. The revelation of their existence to those outside the cadet group would destroy their integrative force and neutralize their utility.

This same secrecy would be demanded of a police "code" to insure its preservation. Although within the clique the code must be well defined, the ignorance of the lay public to even

its existence would be a requisite to its continuous and effective use. Through participation in activity regimented by the "code" an increased group identity and cohesion among "code" practitioners would emerge.

> Group identity requires winning of acceptance as a member of the inner group and, thereby, gaining access to the secrets of the occupation which are acquired through informal contacts with colleagues.

Lack of this acceptance not only bars the neophyte from the inner secrets of the profession, but may isolate him socially and professionally from his colleagues and even his superiors. There is the added fear that, in some circumstance in which he would need their support, they would avoid becoming involved, forcing him to face personal danger or public ridicule alone.

The social structure in which law enforcement is maintained has a definite bearing on what is considered normal and what is deviant behavior. The pattern of "Blue-Coat Crime" (i.e., the "code") seems far more deviant when compared to the dominant middle-class norms of our society as when compared to lower class values. Whyte maintains that in the Italian slum of Cornerville, the primary function of the police department is not the enforcement of the law, but the regulation of illegal activities:

> ...an outbreak of violence arouses the "good people" to make demands for law enforcement...even when they disturb police racketeer relations. Therefore, it is in the interest of the departments to help maintain a peaceful racket organization... By regulating the racket and keeping peace, the officer can satisfy the demands for law enforcement with a number of token arrests and be free to make his adjustment to the local situation.

Since an adjustment to the local situation might well involve adopting some of the "code" practices, the successful police rookie is he who can delicately temper three sets of uncomplementary standards: (1) the "code" practices adopted for group acceptance, (2) the societal standards regulating the duties and responsibilities of the police profession and (3) his own system of morality gained from prior socialization in family, religious, educational and peer-group interaction.

Methodological Considerations

The difficulties connected with any intensive investigation into the "code" are self-evident. The binding secrecy which provides the source of its power would be disrupted if the "code" were revealed to an "outsider." Thus, standard sociological research methods were ineffective in this type of investigation. The traditional ethnographic technique of using an informant familiar with the "code" and its related practices made available the empirical data within this study. Obviously, data from a single informant do not begin to meet the stringent scientific criteria of reliability for the purpose of applying the conclusions from this case to police agencies in general. It is assumed that subsequent research will establish whether this is a unique episode or more of a universal phenomenon. However, the decision to enrich the literature with this present study in spite of its methodological deficiencies was felt to be justified inasmuch as an intensive search through the professional literature revealed no empirical accounts dealing directly with deviant policemen.

Because of the explosive nature of such materials on the social, political and economic life of the persons involved, the use of pseudonyms to maintain complete anonymity is a precaution not without precedent, and was a guarantee given by the director of this study in return for complete cooperation of the informant. The informant was a police officer for 3-½ years before he was implicated in charges of Robbery and Grand Larceny. He was subsequently tried and convicted, serving the better part of a year in prison. At the time of these interviews, he had been released from prison about three years.

The initial design of this study attempted to correlate these empirical data with two journalistic accounts but the subjective handling of those stories neutralized any advantage gained from an increased number of informants. The present design is based exclusively on the single informant.

The Code and Its Practices

Some of these terms used to describe police deviancy are widely used, but because of possible variations in meaning they are defined below. These practices are ordered so that those listed first would generally elicit the least fear of legal prosecution and those listed last would invoke major legal sanctions for their perpetration.

Mooching—An act of receiving free coffee, cigarettes, meals, liquor, groceries, or other items either as a consequence of being in an underpaid, undercompensated profession *or* for the possible future acts of favoritism which might be received by the donor.

Chiseling—An activity involving police demands for free admission to entertainment whether connected to police duty or not, price discounts, etc.

Favoritism—The practice of using license tabs, window stickers or courtesy cards to gain immunity from traffic arrest or citation (sometimes extended to wives, families and friends of recipient).

Prejudice—Situations in which minority groups receive less than impartial, neutral, objective attention, especially those who are less likely to have "influence" in City Hall to cause the arresting officer trouble.

Shopping—The practice of picking up small items such as candy bars, gum, or cigarettes at a store where the door has been accidentally unlocked after business hours.

Extortion—The demands made for advertisements in police magazines or purchase of tickets to police functions, or the "street courts" where minor traffic tickets can be avoided by the payment of cash bail to the arresting officer with no receipt required.

Bribery—The payments of cash or "gifts" for past or future assistance to avoid prosecution; such reciprocity might be made in terms of being unable to make a positive identification of a criminal, or being in the wrong place at a given time when a crime is to occur, both of which might be excused as carelessness but no proof as to deliberate miscarriage of justice. Differs from mooching in the higher value of a gift and in the mutual *understanding* regarding services to be performed upon the acceptance of the gift.

Shakedown—The practice of appropriating expensive items for personal use and attributing it to criminal activity when investigating a break in, burglary, or an unlocked door. Differs from shopping in the cost of the items and the ease by which former ownership of items can be determined if the officer is "caught" in the act of procurement.

Perjury—The sanction of the "code" which demands that fellow officers lie to provide an alibi for fellow officers apprehended in unlawful activity covered by the "code."

Pre-meditated Theft—Planned burglary, involving the use of tools, keys, etc. to gain forced entry or a pre-arranged plan of unlawful acquisition of property which cannot be explained as a "spur of the moment" theft. Differs from shakedown only in the previous arrangements surrounding the theft, not in the value of the items taken.

Mooching, chiseling, favoritism and *prejudice* do not have rigid interpretations in the "code." Their presence appears to be accepted by the general public as a real fact of life. Since the employment of one of these practices can be done while in the normal routine of one's duties, such practices are often ignored as being "deviant" in any way. Ex-Officer Smith sees it in this light:

...the policeman having a free cup of coffee? I have never thought of this as being corrupt or illegal because this thing is just a courtesy thing. A cup of coffee or the old one—the cop on the beat grabbing the apple off the cart—these things I don't think shock too many people because they know that they're pretty well accepted.

But when asked about the practice of *mooching* by name, it assumed a different character of increased importance to Smith!

> I thing mooching is accepted by the police and the public is aware of it. My opinion now, as an ex-policeman, is that mooching is one of the underlying factors in the larger problems that come...it is one of the most basic things. It's the easiest thing to accept and to take in stride because it's so petty. I think that it is the turning point a lot of times.

The "Sunday Comics" stereotype of a policeman initiating mooching, bribery and favoritism is incorrect according to Smith's experience:

> Generally, the policeman doesn't have to ask for things, he just finds out about them. Take for example the theaters. I know the Roxy theaters would let the policeman in on his badge, just about anytime. It's good business because it puts the owner in a closer relationship with the policeman, and the policeman is obligated to him. If they had a break-in, a fire, or a little favor such as double parking out front to unload something, they'd expect special consideration from the policeman.
>
> When I walked the east side beat the normal thing was for bartenders to greet me and offer me a pack of cigarettes or a drink. When I walked the beat I was pretty straight laced, there were a few bartenders that I felt were just trying to get along with me, and I loosened up a little with those people. One bartender gave me cigars when he found out that I didn't smoke cigarettes. I always accepted them; he always pointed out there wasn't any obligation. Some of the beat men accepted cigarettes, some cigars, some took cash, and these men know when they're dealing with bootleggers, and why they're being paid. Different businessmen in the loop area give policemen Christmas presents every year.

Shoping and *shakedown, extortion* and *bribery* are all clearly unlawful, but in these practices the manner in which they are carried out contains a measure of safety to the policeman should his presence or behavior be questioned. A policeman's investigative powers allow him entry into an open building in which a "suspected robbery" has occurred, and various types of articles such as cigarettes and the like cannot be traced to any given retail outlet. Hence, his presence on such occasions is not *suspected;* rather, it is *expected!* Also, should a clumsy job of *shopping* or *shakedown* result in witnesses reporting these unlawful practices, the "code" requires that participating officers must commit *perjury* to furnish an alibi for those colleagues observed in illegal activities. This is both for the protection of the deviant officer and to preclude public disclosure of the widespread involvement of fellow officers in "code" practices. How extensive is *shopping* and *shakedown* as practiced by a department?

> As far as the Mid-City department is concerned I would say that 10 percent of the department would go along with anything, including deliberate forced entries or felonies. But about 50 percent of them would openly go along with just about anything. If they found a place open or if there had been a break-in or if they found anything they could use and it was laying there, they'd help themselves to it.
>
> Whenever there's an open door or window, they call for all the cars and they shake the whole building down—loot it!

Would those policemen involved in shopping and shakedown participate in something more serious? According to ex-officer Smith, they would.

> Most of the policemen who shop or go along with shopping would go

along with major theft, if it just happened. I think where you've got to draw the line is when you get into premeditated, deliberate thefts. I think this is where the big division comes.

In shopping, the theft just happens. Premeditated theft is a cold, deliberate, planned thing.

Here Smith points out the limits of the "code" which, through condoning any level of theft that "just happens," cannot fully support *premeditated theft.*

I think in premeditated theft that the general police attitude is against it, if for no other reason just for the matter of self-preservation, and survival. When you get to a premeditated, deliberate thing, then I think your police backing becomes pretty thin.

At the time when Smith was engaged in the practice of *premeditated theft* in Mid-City, it looked somewhat differently to him than it did later. When he took an objective look, he was aware of just how little this extreme deviancy *actually was practiced.*

When I was involved in it, it seemed like all the people around me were involved in it, and participating in it. It looked more to me like the generally accepted thing then, than it does now, because actually the clique that I was in that did this sort of thing was a small one. I'm not discounting the fact that there may have been a lot of other small cliques just like this.

Looking at his behavior as an outsider, after his expulsion, Smith saw it in this light:

After taking a long, hard look at my case and being real honest about it, I'd have to say that this (premeditated theft like mine) is the exception. The longer I'm away from this thing the more it looks like this.

In Mid-City, *extortion* was not generally practiced and the "code" prescribed "street courts" (i.e., bribery for minor traffic offenses) as outside the acceptable pattern.

(Extortion is) something that I would classify as completely outside the law (here in Mid-City), something that in certain areas has been accepted well on the side of both the public and the police. There's a long standing practice that in Chicago if you are stopped for a traffic violation if you had a five dollar bill slipped in your plastic holder, or your billfold, the patrolman then asks for your license, and if that's in there you'll very rarely be issued a summons. Now this thing was something that was well known by truck-drivers and people who travel through that area.

Smith maintains that the "code" is widespread, although from the above analysis of extortion it can be clearly seen that specific practices have been traditionally practiced and accepted in certain areas, yet not found acceptable in another community. Would this mean that the bulk of these "code" practices occur in police departments other than the one in which Smith served his "apprenticeship" in "Blue-Coat Crime"? Our informant says "yes" and offers the following to substantiate his answer:

I thing generally the Mid-City police department is like every police department in the world. I think the exceptions are probably in small towns or in a few cities that have never been touched by corrupt politics, if there are any. But I think that generally they are the same everywhere, because I have talked to policemen from other cities. I know policemen in other cities that I've had contact with that were in those things. I've discussed open things, or out and out felonies, with policemen from Kansas City on. And I know that at least in that city that it happens, and it's a matter of record that it happens in Denver and Chicago. And I think that this happens in all cities.

From a scientific point of view, other than the incidence of police scandals from time to time, there is no evidence to confirm or deny this one ex-officer's opinion regarding the universal existence of the "code."

The Recruit's Initiation into the "Code" Clique

Bucher describes a profession as a relatively homogeneous community whose members share identity, values, definitions of role, and interest. Socialization of recruits consists of inducting them into the "common core." This occurs on two levels: the formal, or membership group, and the informal, or the reference group.

In the Mid-City police department the failure to socialize most of the new recruits into the "code" would constitute a threat to those who presently practice it. Thus, all "code" practitioners have the responsibility of screening new recruits at various times to determine whether they are "alright guys," and to teach by example and mutual involvement the limitations of "code" practices. If the recruit accepts such training, he is welcomed into the group and given the rights and privileges commensurate with his new status. If he does not, he is classified as a "goof" and avoided by the rest.

In a journalistic account of police deviancy, it was argued that if corruption exists in the political structures controlling police department appointments, this "socialization" into deviancy begins at the point of paying for the privilege of making an application or of buying an appointment. Although Smith did not "buy" his appointment, he cited the existence of factions having influence in recruit appointments, even within the structure of a Civil Service Commission.

"the breakdown of each new recruit's morale is an important step in gaining his acceptance of the [deviancy] code."

There are four different requirements to the whole thing. One is your written test, one is your agility, one is your physical examination, and the fourth is the oral examination which is given by the civil service commission. I really crammed before I took the test. When I took the test it was a natural for me, it was snap. I scored a 94 on my test for the police department. With my soldiers preference, which gives you 5 points, I scored a 99. I passed my agility test and my physical. I could have had a 100 score, I could have been a gymnast, gone through the agility test and made everyone else look silly and still I could have failed in the oral exam. And this is the kicker where politics comes in.

There are three old men that are aligned with different factions, different people on and off the department, different businessmen that have power, different groups, different lodges and organizations and all these things influence these men, these three people that make up the civil service board.

The existence of the "code" had hurt the level of morale generally in the Mid-City department. In fact, the breakdown of each new recruit's morale is an important step in gaining his acceptance of the "code."

The thing that hurt the morale was

the fact that a large percentage of the people on the department were involved in illegal practices to some degree. And actually you take a man that has just joined the department, has good intentions and is basically honest, and in this, to a man that's never been dishonest and hasn't stepped over the line, there aren't degrees. It's all either black or white. And the illegal activity I know shocks a lot of these young men... because it was the thing to do. It's a way to be accepted by the other people. It's a terrible thing the way one policeman will talk about another. Say an old timer will have a new man working with him and he'll tell you, "You've got to watch him, because *he's honest!*"

For a recruit to be accepted in the Mid-City police department he must accept the informal practices occurring in the department. Illegal activity is pursued within the police force as the dominant "norm" or standard.

To illustrate the group pressure on each policeman who dares to enforce the law as prescribed in the legal statutes, the following account is typical.

We'll take a classic example—Mr. Sam Paisano. Now when I was on the force I knew that whenever I worked in the downtown area, I could go into Sam's restaurant and order my meal and never have to pay a dime. I think that just about every patrolman on the force knew that. If I had run across Sam doing anything short of murder, I think I would have treaded very lightly. Even if I hadn't accepted his free meals. Say I had turned it down; still, if I stopped this man for a minor traffic violation, say I caught him dead to rights, I'd be very reluctant to write this man a ticket because I'd suffer the wrath of the other men on the force. I'd be goofing up their meal ticket. Now he in turn knows this. The rest of the officers wouldn't waste any words about it, they'd tell you right off—"You sure fouled up our meal ticket." The old timers would give

you a cold shoulder. If it came to the attention of the gold braid, your immediate superiors, they'd make sure you had a little extra duty or something. In most cases if you did this just to be honest, just to be right, it would go badly for you.

This special treatment of Mr. Paisano wasn't something that you concealed, or that you were ashamed of because it was the normal accepted thing to do. I'd have been more ashamed, and I'd have kept it quiet if I'd stopped such a man as this, because I'd have felt like some kind of an oddball. I would have been bucking the tide, I'd been out of step.

Yet, such general practices must be converted to individual participation at some point, and to be effective this involvement must be on a primary group relationship basis. Smith's account of his introduction to the "code" follows the first steps of the assimilating process.

The first thing that I can recall seeing done [which was illegal] was on the night shift when I first went on patrol. The old timers were shaking buildings down and helping themselves to whatever was in the building. The first time I saw it happen I remember filing through the check-out counter at a supermarket, seeing all the officers grabbing their cigarettes or candy bars, or whatever they wanted and I passed through without anything.

I got in the car and this old timer had, of all the petty things, two of these 25 or 30 cent candy bars and he sat them down in the seat and told me to have some. I told him I really didn't want any. And he asked me if "that shook me up" or something. And I told him, "Well, it sort of surprised me." He said that everybody did it and that I should get used to that.

And as it went on it progressed more. Well, in fact, he justified it at the time by telling me he had seen the same market one time, when there had been a legitimate break-in and one particular detective had been so busy loading the back seat of his car full of hams and big pieces of beef that he was stumbling and falling down back and forth from the cooler to the alley, and he didn't even know who was around him he was so busy carrying things out. And he named this officer and I don't doubt it because I've seen the same officer do things in that same nature.

And this was the first direct contact I had with anything like this.

The old timers would test the new recruits with activities which could be laughed off if they were reported, such as the 30 cent candy bar taken from the supermarket in the above account.

> The old timers would nose around 'til they found out whether a young guy was going to work with them and "be right" as far as they were concerned, or whether he was going to resist it and be straight as far as the rest of the world was concerned.

If the recruit cooperated, the practices were extended and the rookie became involved. Once he was involved there was no "squealing" on fellow policemen breaking the law. Then he could have some personal choice as to how far he personally wished to go. However, those who were straightlaced and wanted to stay honest had their problems too. Social isolation appears to be a powerful sanction as can be seen from Smith's information.

> There are a few policemen that are straightlaced all the way. I can remember one policeman who might have made an issue of another policeman taking somethng. He had that attitude for the first six months that he was on the force but by that time, he had been brow beaten so bad, he saw the writing on the wall. He knew better than to tell anything. In addition to brow beating, this man in very short order was put in a position where they had him on the

information desk, or kicked around from one department to another, 'cause nobody wanted to work with him. This kind of a man they called "wormy," because anything that would happen he'd run to the braid.

> This fellow, I knew, wanted to be one of the boys, but he wanted to be honest, too. As it turned out, this guy was finally dismissed from the force for having an affair with a woman in his squad car. Just a couple of years before that he would have had a fit if he thought that somebody was going to take a drink on duty, or fool around with a woman, or steal anything. For this reason this man spent a lot of time on the information desk, working inside, and by himself in the squad car.

Negative sanctions were applied against "goofs" who advocated following the legitimate police ethic. Group acceptance by senior officers was the reward to a recruit accepting the "code," and the "code" was presented to the recruit as the police way of life having precedence over legal responsibilities.

> This small fraction that...are honest and would report illegal activity, are ostracized. Nobody will work with them. They look at them like they're a freak, talk about them like they're a freak, and they are a freak.

> The goofs that would talk about doing things the way they should be done, they had to be ignored or put down. There were older policemen that as they found out I would go along with certain things, pressed to see how much further I would go. And showed me that they went farther, whether I cared or not. So naturally I went along quite a ways with some of them. And I don't really remember how we first became aware of how far the other person would go. I think this is just a gradual thing.

The existence of a social system of an informal nature working quietly under the facade of the formal police department regulations has been clearly demonstrated in Mid-City. One further note in explaining the motivations of policemen toward illegal activities involves the condition of low salaries. Smith's department pay scale and working conditions would suggest that economic pressures were a factor in condoning or rationalizing "code" practices.

> The pay wasn't good. I went on the department and earned $292 a month. The morale of the force was as low as that of any group that I've ever been around. There was constant complaining from all of them about everything.

> The training programs were set up so that you would have to come in on your own time and weren't compensated for it....They dictated to you how you lived your whole life, not only what you did during the eight hours you were a policeman but how you'd live your whole life. This as much as anything hurt the morale.

But when Smith was asked directly, "With the policeman's low salary, do illegal activities become necessary to keep up financially?" he discounted it as a major factor.

> I don't thing this is the case. I don't think there are very many policeman that I knew, and I knew all of them, that were social climbers or that tried to keep up with the Joneses, by illegal activities anyway.

> Actually most of the police officers think that they are even above those people that have money, because they have power. Those people with money are pretty well forced to cater to a policeman. And you'll find that very few people ever tell a policeman what they think of him, whether they like him or not. They know that a policeman will do him harm. The businessmen, especially the bigger businessmen, pamper the policemen. They will treat

them with respect when they face them.

Sanctions for Preservation of the "Code"

Normally, practitioners of the "code" would consist of a united group working to protect all fellow patrolmen from prosecution. However, Smith had exceeded the "code" limits by committing *premeditated theft,* and in order to protect the "code" from being exposed during the scandal involving Smith and two accomplices, the "clique" socially and spatially isolated themselves from the three accused policemen.

> Everybody ran for cover, when the thing hit the front page of the newspapers. I've never seen panic like there was at that time. These people were all ready to sell out their mother to save their own butts. They knew there was no holding back, that it was a tidal wave. They were grabbing just anything to hang on. The other policemen were ordered to stay away from us, myself and the other men involved. They were ordered to stay away from the trials. They were told to keep their noses out of this thing, that it would be handled.

> There were a few policemen who came around during this time. Strangely the ones who came around were the ones who didn't go in for any of the illegal activity. They didn't have anything to worry about. Everybody else ran and hid.

During a time like this, group consensus is required to preserve the "code." A certain amount of rationalization is necessary to mollify past illicit activity in light of present public exposure. Smith continues:

> I think if they had really gone by the book during the police scandal, that 25 percent of the policemen would have lost their jobs. I've talked to some of them since, and the worst violators all now have them-

selves convinced that they weren't guilty of a thing.

I've never referred to myself as this before, but I was their goat, their scapegoat. The others stuck together and had support. I got what I deserved, but if I compare myself with the others, I got a real raw deal.

Preservation of the "code" occurs when policemen work with another person who has similar intentions and begin to "trust" one another in illegal activities without fear of the authorities being informed. A suggestion of rotating young officers from shift to shift to weaken the "code" had been given public discussion. To this, Smith reacted thusly:

I think that the practice of rotating young officers will serve a purpose. It will eliminate a lot of things because you just can't take a chance with somebody that you don't know. If you don't know but what the next person they throw you with might be a CID...short for Criminal Investigation Department. They're spies! Say there are just 10 percent of the men on the department that wouldn't go along with anything, and they are switching around with the new system, you don't know when you're going to catch one of them, and if you do you're a cooked goose. The old system you were 90 percent sure of the people you were with.

This same process used to preserve the illegal "code" as a group phenomenon is also the same process used to develop and promote the acceptable professional ethics of the police. A situation in which it is "normal" for a policeman to "squeal on his fellow patrolmen," would undermine professional ethics. Personal insecurity would mount with the constant fear of just being accused with or without supporting evidence. Such an anarchical system lends itself to intrigue, suspicion and an increased possibility of each officer being "framed." Thus,

these same procedures which would effectively reduce the continuation of the "code" would also prove dysfunctional to the maintenance of the ethics which are the core of the police profession itself. These concurrent processes reflect the dual standards extant in society at large.

Difficulties Involved in Breaking the "Code"

If a "code" does exist in a law enforcement agency, one of the major factors which protects it from attack is secrecy. This factor is compounded by public acceptance of the traditional view of illegal behavior as only an individualistic, moral problem.

Another shield of the "code" from attack is the apathy resulting from the myriad of complex demands and responsibilities placed upon the average citizen. So many things touch him with which he *must* become involved that he does not pursue problems which do not directly concern him. Inextricably connected with this is the realistic fear of retaliation, either through direct harassment by the police or indirectly through informal censures.

Smith says that only a real big issue will provoke an apathetic public to action.

Everybody's looking out for number one. And the policeman can do you harm. It's such a complex thing, there are so many ways, so many different people are affected by the police—Most people will back off. Most people are afraid to do anything, if it looks like it's going to affect them adversely.

If the police have carefully practiced *prejudice,* in their day-to-day operations, the chances are slim that the persons against whom these illegal practices were committed possess either the social or political power to break the "code" before the system could retaliate. Knowing this fact keeps most of the persons with any knowledge of the "code's" operation silent indeed.

The rigid procedures of obtaining legal evidence and the dangers of committing a *false arrest* are gigantic deterrents to bringing accusations against any suspicious person, especially a policeman. Ex-Officer Smith discusses the realistic problems involved in attempting to enforce legal statutes against *shopping* or other aspects of the "code":

> I think that any law against *shopping* would be hard to enforce against a police officer. You'd really have to have the evidence against him and really make it public, 'cause it would be soft pedaled all the way otherwise. Let's say you see a police officer in a restaurant taking a pack of cigarettes or let's say it's something other than a pack of cigarettes, something that you can prove came from the restaurant. And along comes a radio news unit and you stop the unit and say you just saw a policeman steal a pack of cigarettes or something bigger. When other police arrive on the scene the newsman would probably pull the other policemen off to the side and tell them that their buddy just took a pack of cigarettes and that goofball (the informer) wants to make trouble about it. You insist that they shake down the policeman and they find the item. Here you're in pretty good shape. In this case you'd have a policeman in a little bit of trouble. I don't think he'd lose his job or do any time over it, but I'd say there would be some scandal about it. Unless you were real hard headed they'd soft pedal it.
>
> Let's back up a little and say the policeman threw the item back into the restaurant, and then you made your accusation. Then you're in trouble 'cause when they shake him down and he doesn't have a thing. Now you're a marked man, because

every policeman in town will know that you tried to foul up one of their boys. Even the honest policemen aren't going to like what you did. In other words, they are tightly knit, and they police this city by fear to a certain extent.

In Mid-City only those who are involved in practicing the "code" are equipped with the necessary information to expose its operations. Whether one *can* inform on his fellow officers is directly connected with the degree of his illegal involvement prior to the situation involving the unlawful event.

> It all depends upon how deeply you are involved. If you've been a guy who has gone along with a free cup of coffee, the gratuities, the real petty things and you'd happen to drive up on a major theft, drive up on another policeman with his shoulder against the door, then you might take action. However, if you had gone a little farther, say you'd done some shopping, then you're forced to look the other way. It's like a spider spinning a web, you're drawn in toward the center.

It appears obvious that those who are involved in the "code" will be the least useful instruments for alleviating the problem. Only the professionally naive would expect a "code" practitioner to disclose the "code's" existence, much less reveal its method of operation, since his own position is so vulnerable.

Conclusion

From data furnished by a participant informant, an informal "code" of illegal activities within one police department was documented. The group processes which encouraged and maintained the "code" were identified. It was found that the new recruits were socialized into "code" participation by "old timers" and group acceptance was withheld from those who attempted to remain completely honest and not be implicated. When formal police regulations were in conflict with "code" demands among its practitioners, the latter took precedence. Since the "code" operates under conditions of secrecy, only those who participate in it have access to evidence enough to reveal its method of operation. By their very participation they are implicated and this binds them to secrecy as well. In this study the public indignation of a police scandal temporarily suspended the "code" but it flourished again when public apathy returned.

Although some individual factors must be considered in explaining police deviancy, in the present study the sanction of group acceptance was paramount. This study clearly demonstrates the social genesis of the "code," the breeding ground for individual unlawful behavior. From evidence contained herein, an individualistic orientation to police deviancy may discover the "spoiled fruit" but

only when the "code" is rooted out can the "seedbed" of deviancy be destroyed.

From related research in group deviancy, it can be stated that the social organization of a given community (including its respectable citizens), is the milieu in which a "code" flourishes. Thus, a police department is an integral element of that complex community structure, and deviancy found in an enforcement agency is a reflection of values which are habitually practiced and accepted within that community. This was found to be true in the present study.

The findings of this case study should not be interpreted as applicable to all police departments nor should it be a rationalization for the existence of an illicit "code" anywhere. Rather, it is a very limited effort to probe the very sensitive area of "Blue-Coat Crime" and describe its operation and method of perpetuation in one enforcement agency.

6. *If police experience a sense of anomie, if they lack a clear sense of social identity, how can they effectively satisfy the requirements of their job? On what principles can they rely to guide their actions?*

According to Bordua and Reiss, the principle of command "legitimates orders, instructions, or rules." It gives form to a profession characterized by ambiguities and contradictory tasks. Command is a controlling principle because it exacts obedience and careful obedience allows for a feeling of honor that is necessary for a sense of human dignity. The command-obedience-honor chain "provides the irreplaceable minimum structural conditions for at least the basic elements of status honor" and creates "a relatively closed, secure community of functionaries who can elaborate and apply honor-conferring criteria."

However, the major point in this article is that increased professionalism (characterized by centralized control and technological advancements) tends to obscure the chief's ultimate role as "Commander." He is able to control his force but his charismatic aura is somewhat diluted. At the same time, increased professionalism allows the police officer to act in accordance to very definite prescriptions, "orders, instructions and rules," but these are no longer obviously legitimated by the "command principle." Commands are viewed as specific orders but because of increasingly sophisticated bureaucratic methods of dispersion, their relation to the "Hero-Chief," to the command principle, in other words, is unclear. Hence, a sense of honor is no longer concomitant with obedience. Obedience becomes rote and as the authors state "Police organizations become 'professionalized,' not their members."

The authors' belief that the commander must not only assert himself but direct his force in a way to maximize efficiency and simultaneously maintain a sense of an "occupationally based community of honor" leads one to carefully reconsider Manning's rather pessimistic conclusion that the police task is, and should be, largely symbolic (Article 1). In other words, one cannot help but wonder whether a policeman who feels occupational pride and a commander with just the right amount of mystique will be able to deal more effectively with the complexities inherent in crime control and prevention.

COMMAND, CONTROL, AND CHARISMA: REFLECTIONS ON POLICE BUREAUCRACY

DAVID J. BORDUA and ALBERT J. REISS, JR.

Bureaucratization can be regarded as an organizational technique whereby civic pressures are neutralized from the standpoint of the governing regime. In the development of the modern police, bureaucratization has been a major device to commit members to the occupational organization, to the occupational community, and to its norms of subordination and service to a degree where these commitments take precedence over extra-occupational ones to family and community.

The political neutrality and legal reliability of the police in modern societies are less a matter of the social sources of their recruitment than of the nature of internal organization, training, and control. While this, of course, is true for all government organizations under a civil service or tenure system, it is true for the police not primarily because they are civil servants in the restricted sense but because of their allegiance to an occupationally organized community that sets itself apart. The situation is particularly crucial for the police since they often are called upon to enforce laws that are unpopular with the public or for which they have no personal sympathy, while at the same time they are armed and organized. Perhaps this fundamental significance of police bureaucratization can be seen by the fact that given a well-organized, well-disciplined, and internally well-regulated police, civil authorities can count on the police if they are assured of the political loyalty or neutrality of the commander. Indeed, the modern police emerged under conditions whereby they were an organized source of stability between the elites and the masses, serving to draw hostility from the elites to themselves and thereby permitting more orderly relations among the elites and the masses.[1]

Command Systems

To our knowledge, there is no detailed empirical description of command processes in a police department. It is necessary, therefore, to rely largely on published discourses that give information on the rhetoric of command and control and that are of variable and unknown validity as descriptions of behavior.[2]

Police literature emphasizes the quasi-military nature of police-command relations, and casual observation in metropolitan police depart-ments indicates that police officials are highly sensitive to "orders from above" and to probabilities of official disapproval of behavior. In principle and in rhetoric, a police organization is one characterized by strict subordination, by a rigid chain of command, by accountability of command, and more doubtfully, by a lack of formal provision for consultation between ranks.

Before accepting this description of its structure uncritically, it is necessary to say that such statements are meaningful only by comparison. We have relatively little data comparing the operating as opposed to the rhetorical nature of command in different types of organizations. In many ways, policing is a highly decentralized operation involving the deployment of large numbers of men alone or in small units where control by actual command, that is, by issuing orders, is difficult. This problem is generally recognized by top police administrators, leading to their stressing the importance of accountability of command to achieve control. O.W. Wilson puts it this way:

> Authority is delegated by some form of command; responsibility is effectively placed by some form of control. . . . The effective placing of responsibility or the act of holding accountable involves an evaluation of the manner in which the authority was exercised, hence the rule of control: He who gives an order must ascertain that it has been properly executed.
>
> It is relatively easy to delegate authority by giving a command, but to ascertain the manner in which the order was carried out so that the subordinate may be held responsible is often difficult.[3]

Other evidence from the police literature suggests that the description is overdrawn, that both internal and external transactions structure the effective range of command and control. Moreover, as J.Q. Wilson points out, it seems clear that the variations between "system-oriented" as opposed to "professionalized" departments includes fundamental differences in styles of control.[4]

Historical changes in the nature of police work and organization have increased the importance of more subtle and perhaps more important developments in methods of control. In the dialectic of dispersion versus centralization of command, every development in the technology for police control of the population is accompanied by changes in the capacity of the organization to control its members. Originally the bell, creaker, or rattle watches were limited in summoning help to the effective range of their "noise"; the addition of "calling the hours" served to monitor the behavior of the patrol (quite generally open to question).[5] Here we see evidence of a classic and continuing dilemma in organizations—that to control subordinates they must be required to make themselves visible. For the police, this means that when they become visible they likewise become more calculable to potential violators. Control of the dispersed police was really difficult before the call box that simultaneously enabled patrolmen to summon help and enabled commanders to issue calls and require periodic reporting.[6] The cruising car with two-way radio enabled still greater dispersion and flexibility in the allocation of patrols, while at the same time bringing the patrolman or team more nearly within the range of constant control. It is now a fundamental duty of the radio patrol officer to remain "in contact," that is, controllable.

More important, perhaps, is the fact that a centralized radio communication system, where telephoned complaints are received and commands given, makes it possible for top management to have independent knowledge of complaints and of who is assigned to them before either subordinate commanders or the patrol team does. A minimum of centralized control is available, then, not simply by the direct issuance of commands from superior to subordinate but by means of a paper-matching process whereby the complaint board's written record can be matched with the written record the patrolman is required to generate. This pattern of control by centralized communication and internal organizational audit is highly dependent upon the distribution of telephones in the population. The citizen's telephone enables the police commander to enlist the complainant—on a routine basis—as part of the apparatus for control of the policeman. A citizen's opportunity to mobilize the police is intricately balanced with that of the commander.

Added to these matters of task organization, in large police departments, the chief's power to command and control is limited by a complex system of "due process" that protects subordinates. This, of course, is true of all civil service organizations. The strong interest in keeping the police "out of politics" coupled with the interest of the rank and file in job security, however, creates a situation where, formally, the department head must contend with legally empowered authorities in the selection, promotion, and discharge of personnel. Even in matters of internal assignment and definition of task, decisions may impinge on the civil service classification system. Police employee organizations, likewise, are quite effective in seeing to it that the system of "due process" continues to protect them. The individual officer, furthermore, when accused of wrongdoing or a crime, demands all the legal safeguards he may deny to those whom he accuses of committing a crime.

Not all police operations are constituted in the fashion of this highly oversimplified picture of so-called routine patrol. Detectives, for example, are less subject to such control. But these considerations of due-process barriers to centralized command and historical changes in control procedures that rely less on actual command as a form of control are intended to raise questions about the sociological meaning of the stress generally placed on command and to lay the ground for a somewhat more systematic analysis of it.

Forms of Legitimation

Thus far, "command" has been used in two senses. In one, "command" refers to a technique of control in organizations that consists of "giving commands." The directive communication between superior and subordinate may be called "a command," or, if more impersonally clothed, "an order." In another sense, however, "command" means neither a specific technique of control nor an instance of its use, but something more general— a principle that legitimates orders, instructions, or rules. Orders, then, are obeyed *because* they are "commanded."

Sociologists are familiar with discussions of this type ever since Weber.[7] In Weberian terms, the police department "as an order" is legitimated by the principle of command. Each form of legitimation, however, as Weber so clearly saw, has a correlative requirement of "attitude" on the part of those subject to its sway. In the case of "an order" legitimated by a rhetoric of command, the correlative expectation is "obedience"—again not as a situational expectation in the case of a given specific command but as a principle relating member to organization. To be "obedient" in this sense carries the same general sense of principle as in the "poverty, chastity, and obedience" of the monk's vow. In a system so legitimated, we can expect that commitment to obedience will be displayed as a sign of membership.

It is not surprising, then, that social scientists who are based in organizations where independence is legitimated, rehabilitation workers based in those where professional discretion and supportiveness are legitimated, and police who are based in organizations where obedience is legitimated so often fail to communicate with one another when they are engaged in exchanges of ideologies.

We may point out as well that in orders legitimated by command and exacting obedience, the classic status reward is "honor." The moral and public-relations problems of the American police can be more clearly understood as an attempt to substitute public prestige sought in an occupational performance market for the Weberian status regard sought and validated in the "honor market." The American police are denied both, for the public seems unwilling to accord the police status either in the European sense of status honor as representatives of the State or in the more typically American sense of prestige based on a claim to occupational competence.

Command as a basis for legitimacy can be located under any of the three basic types of legitimation discussed by Weber—the rational-legal, the traditional, and the charismatic. Inherently, however, command as a principle focuses on the commander, and the exact nature of the concrete "order" legitimated by the principle of command will depend on the role of the specific commander. Because of this commander focus, the command principle is likely to lead to a mystique of the personal commander and an organizational stress on legitimating specific orders or even general rules as emanating from him.

Command and Task Organization

To regard a metropolitan police system solely in terms of the classic features of the hierarchically oriented command bureaucracy would be mistaken, however. Although the more

---

"the command principle is likely to lead to a mystique of the personal commander and an organizational stress on legitimating specific orders or even general rules as emanating from them."

---

traditional police departments in American cities are organized on quasi-military command principles, modernized ones display features of other control systems, particularly those of centralized and professional control structures.

The core of the modern metropolitan police system is the communications center, linking as it does by radio dispatch the telephoned demands of a dispersed population with a dispersed police in mobile units. The technology of the radio, the telephone, the recorder, and the computer permits a high degree of central control of operating units in the field. The more modern police departments, for example, have tape records of all citizen phone complaints, the response of dispatch to them, and the action of mobile units. This technology also makes possible reporting directly to a centralized records unit. Indeed, the more rationalized police-command systems make extensive use of the computer as a centralized intelligence system to which mobile units can make virtually direct inquiry, as a "decision-maker" about which units are to be dispersed for what service, and as a source of intelligence on the output of personnel and units in the department. Such a centralized and direct system of command and control makes it possible to bypass many positions in the hierarchical command structure, particularly those in the station command. More and more, those in the line of authority assume work supervision or informal adjudicatory rather than strictly command roles.

There undeniably is considerable variability among internal units of a police department in the degree to which they are centrally commanded such that routine patrol is more subject to central command than are tactical or investigation units. Yet, all in all, there is a growing tendency for all internal units to operate under programmed operations of a central command rather than under local commanders. Orders not only originate with the central command but pass directly from it.

The centralization of command and

control is one of the major ways that American police chiefs have for coping with the tendency toward corruption inherent in traditional hierarchically organized departments. Chiefs no longer need rely to the same extent upon the station commander to implement the goals of the department through the exercise of command. Indeed, a major way that corrupt departments are reformed these days is to reduce the command operations of local commanders, replacing them with centralized command and control. Yet it is precisely in those operations where corruption is most likely to occur, namely, the control of vice, that a centralized command is least effective. The main reason for this is that a centralized command lends itself best to a reactive strategy, whereas a professionalized or hierarchically organized command lends itself to a proactive strategy. Vice requires an essentially proactive strategy of policing in the modern metropolis, whereas the citizens' command for service demands an essentially reactive strategy and tactics.

A central command not only bypasses traditional hierarchical command relations but, like the hierarchical command, creates problems for the developing professionalized control in police systems. A professionalized model of control respects a more or less decentralized decision-making system where the central bureaucracy, at best, sets general policy and principles that guide the professional. Indeed, many police tasks and decisions would appear to lend themselves to a professional as well as technical role relationship with the client.

Yet, the institutionalized and legally defined role of the police formally denies professional discretion to them in decisions of prosecution and adjudication, granting them to professional lawyers. The "professionalizing" police, therefore, are formally left only with certain decisions regarding public order, safety, service, and arrest. These formal prohibitions coupled with the new technology and centralized command (developed under the banner of professionalization of the police) both serve to decrease rather than enhance discretionary decision-making by subordinates. Police organizations become "professionalized," not their members.

Command and Occupational Culture

The internal organizational life of American police departments displays features which distinguish the police from other organizations and which have important implications for the nature of organizational command. These features are the familial and/or ethnic inheritance of occupation, the almost exclusive practice of promotion from within, the large number of formal voluntary organizations that cut across organizational membership, and, finally, the existence of legal protections for tenure which inhere in civil service regulations.

Specific police jobs differ; yet it is quite important to recognize that, fundamentally, police status overrides these differentiations. Not only does the basic status override lateral differentiations, but it also tends to override differences in rank. Police occupational culture, unlike the situation in industry, unites rather than divides ranks.

This is perhaps the most fundamental significance of the practice of promoting from within. The fact that all police-command personnel came up through the ranks means not only that there is relatively little class distinction among police but that the sharp differences between managers and workers in industry is less apparent for the police.[8]

In addition to the vertical spread of police occupational culture due to promotion from within, local recruitment tends to entrench any specific department's version of the more general occupational culture. This combination of occupational culture and organizational culture produces what J.Q. Wilson referred to as "system-oriented" departments.[9]

Interlinked with the features of local recruitment and internal promotion is the factor of familial and ethnic inheritance of the police occupation. Many occupations are strongly based in ethnicity, and many organizations have widespread kinship bonds; indeed, some companies advertise the fact. The consequences, however, are more exaggerated in the police, partly because police culture emphasizes distance between the occupation and the general community but, more importantly we suspect, because of the relative lack of vertical differentiation. Thus, police corruption can become spread up precisely because of this lack of differentiation.

Finally, the development of civil service can mean that a rather rigid formal, legal shell is erected around occupational and organizational cultures in a way that makes the exercise of command from the top even more difficult than it would otherwise be. The reform chief must choose his command from among those who began tenure under his predecessors. And except for retirement, "resignation," or formal dismissal proceedings, he is left with the cadre of the "old department."

It should be noted, however, that occupational and organizational cultures and the reinforcing solidarities provided by formal organizations like the Fraternal Order of Police and by the legal protections of civil service have another side. They make possible the existence of police systems which function at least moderately well over long periods in a society notoriously inhospitable to police; indeed, they are partially a defensive response to that inhospitability. While they may inhibit modernization and reform, they do insure that the job will get done somehow. More importantly, they provide the irreplaceable minimum structural conditions for at least the basic elements of status honor. They provide the essential precondition for a sense of honor—a relatively closed, secure community (not just organization) of functionaries who can elaborate and apply honor-conferring criteria.

These internal solidarities create special barriers to the effective exercise of command over and above the features of task organization previously discussed. They become particularly significant in attempts at modernization or reform. The police commander ignores this internal culture at his peril. It can confront him with an opposition united from top to bottom.

The modernizing chief is constrained, therefore, to make at least symbolic obeisance to police solidarity by demonstrating that he is a "cop's cop" as well as a devotee of systems analysis and psychological screening of applicants. One of the ways he does so is by emphasis in his dress and bearing—the policeman's chief social tool—the ability to command personal respect.[10] At least during a period of change, personal charisma and "presence" are of particular significance. He must also make his orders stick, of course.

The reform chief's charisma is of special significance because of the objective uncertainty of obedience but also because reform depends on the co-operation of a cadre of immediate subordinates whose careers may depend upon the chief's success. His certainty becomes their hope.

Command and Civil Accountability

The structure of command is affected not only by elements of task organization and technology and by the features of occupational and organizational culture discussed above but also by the relationship between the chief and his civil superiors. In the case of the American municipality, police chiefs, at least traditionally, both at law and in practice, are politically accountable officials who ordinarily stand or fall with the fortunes of their civilian superiors (who are lodged in external systems). Given the often controversial nature of police work, and the often "irrational" and unpredictable nature of political fortunes in municipal government, the American police chief who is responsible to a politically elected official comes close to the position of a "patrimonial bureaucrat" in Weber's terms. His tenure as chief, though not necessarily his tenure in the department, depends on continuing acceptability to the elected official(s).

We have alluded to some of the dimensions along which police departments and their command processes seem to vary—using terms like "modernized," "rationalized," "reformed." It would be possible to indicate other dimensions which intersect these by referring to department age, growth rate, and other variables as well as environmental context variables such as variations in civic culture—comparing, for example, Los Angeles and San Francisco. It is not our intention, however, to attempt a systematic comparative scheme. In the case of the problem of civic accountability, however, it is possible to use some of the material presented thus far to begin development of such a scheme.

The relations of police commanders to civil superiors are actually more varied and complex than those depicted above. We shall discuss briefly only the two most important dimensions of variation: the security of tenure of the chief commander and the degree to which he is held strictly accountable by a mayor. Given strict accountability plus insecurity of tenure, we can expect a kind of obsession with command and a seemingly "irrational" emphasis on the twinned symbols of the visibility of the commander and the obedience of the force. Some of the rhetoric of command in the police literature likely arises from an attempt to "protect" the chief by the compulsive effort to "overcontrol" subordinates, almost any of whom can get him fired. This amounts to saying that as civil superiors increase the formal accountability of the police chief *without changing* the tenure features of the role, the increasing bureaucratization of the American municipal police stressed by J.Q. Wilson leads to the development of an organization animated by a principle of the commanding person.[11] This "personalized subordination" to the "Hero Chief" can become an operating, if not a formal, principle of organization.[12]

Increased professionalization can be another accommodative strategy in such a situation, but this time aimed not at control of the force but at control of the mayor by changing the grounds of accountability. One of the first jobs of the "professionalizing" police chief often is to convince his civil superior that "you can't win 'em

---

"This 'personalized subordination' to the 'Hero Chief' can become an operating, if not formal, principle of organization."

---

all" and that it is irrational and "unprofessional" to dismiss a police chief or commissioner because of failure to solve some particularly crime. Perhaps, in the long run, it is hard to have a professionalized police without a professionalized mayor. Perhaps also, this would lead us to expect different kinds of command styles where a professional city manager intervenes between the chief and the mayor.

If the civil superior, for whatever reason, does not demand accountability from the chief, the quasi-formalized obsession with "command" as a principle of control may be replaced by a complex system of feudal loyalties. In this situation, ties of personal political fealty between chief and mayor—or between chief and the local "powers"—may become prominent and "keep your nose clean" the principle of subordination. When this trend goes beyond a certain point, the department is commonly described as politically corrupt. Finally, to the degree that the chief is secure in his tenure, we would expect the obsession with command and the emphasis on personalized subordination to

decrease.

On the basis of this analysis of command and the position of the chief we may distinguish the four types of departments (Table 1).

We have consciously chosen words such as "feudality" with outrageously large quotas of surplus meaning since the concern here is to direct attention to features of police organization that receive relatively little attention and to questions of fundamental differences in the consequences of organizational membership between police and other organizations.[13]

A word about two of these types seems in order. The command-feudality type seems a contradiction in terms (and indeed derives from the cross-classification itself). Some small municipal and sheriff's departments, where the tenure of the chief in the local "feudal political structure" is secure, may fall here. Because everyone is secure in a relatively non-bureaucratic system, the operating principle of subordination can be command. Such an arrangement possibly characterizes the exceptionally long-tenure chiefs discovered in Lunden's study in Iowa.[14]

The "personalized command bureaucracy" seems likely to occur where an insecure reform head is in office. To reform successfully he must bureaucratize and rationalize administrative operations. To do this against the inevitable internal resistance he must emphasize the principle of command. To make clear that status quo-oriented commanders have been superseded he must emphasize *his* command and his *capacity* to command. In *short,* he must exercise what Selznick defines as one of the crucial functions of leadership in administration. He must define the emerging character of the institution.[15]

TABLE 1

Types of Police Departments

RELATION TO MAYOR	TENURE OF CHIEF	
	SECURE	INSECURE
Strictly accountable......	Command bureaucracy	Personalized command bureaucracy
Feudal allegiance........	Command feudality	Personalized "political" feudality

Conclusion

We have discussed features of American police systems that may account for variations in and possible changes in command structures and also features that account for both a rhetorical and behavioral emphasis not on one or the other formal command system but on something which seemingly appears as alien and contradictory—the personal charisma of the chief and the emphasis on personalized command as a symbolic, if not actual, principle of order.

Command, obedience, and honor ring strangely in analysis of organizational life in America except, perhaps, for the military. Yet it seems to us that meaningful analysis of the police must touch upon them as well as upon duty, courage, and restraint. The self-image of the police is different because of them. We have already alluded to the fact that the status reward for obedience is honor and that the maintenance of honor requires a status community—not simply a formal organization.[16]

The significance of honor is that it lies at the heart of the necessary police virtues—courage, devotion to duty, restraint, and honesty. In the absence of ritually symbolic auspices such as the European State or the English Crown, the personal charisma of chiefs is a necessary transitional step to an occupationally based community of honor. In the long run, such status honor, not only occupational prestige, is one fundamental answer to police corruption.[17] In the short run, it means that successful police commanders must attempt not to have the police reflect the society but transcend it.

Notes

[1] Alan Silver, "On the Demand for Order in Civil Society: A Review of Some Themes in the History of Urban Crime, Police and Riot in England" in David J. Bordua, ed., *The Police* (New York: John Wiley & Sons, 1966), p. 11.

[2] See e.g., Bruce Smith, *Police Systems in the United States,* 2d rev. ed.; New York: Harper & Brothers, 1960, esp. chs. vii-ix.

[3] O. W. Wilson, *Police Administration* (New York: McGraw-Hill Book Co., 1950), p. 59.

[4] James Q. Wilson, "The Police and Their Problems: A Theory," in Carl J. Friedrich & Seymour E. Harris, eds., *Public Policy,* 12 (Cambridge, Mass.: Harvard Univ. Press, 1963), pp. 12, 189-216.

[5] Selden D. Bacon, "The Early Development of American Municipal Police: A Study of the Evolution of Formal Controls in a Changing

Society" (unpubl. Ph.D. diss., Yale Univ., 1939).

[6]The innovation of the police patrol and signal service in Chicago in 1880 brought forth considerable resistance and indignation from the police patrol precisely because it made possible closer supervision of the patrol. See John Joseph Flynn, *History of the Chicago Police: From the Settlement of the Community to the Present Time* (Chicago: Police Book Fund, 1887), ch. xx.

[7]Talcott Parsons, ed., *Max Weber: The Theory of Social and Economic Organization* (New York: Oxford Univ. Press, 1947), pp. 324 ff.

[8]The more professionalized a police department, however, the more it displays manager-worker differences common in industry. The police in the line symbolize this by referring to those on the staff as "empty holster_____." The occupational culture holds, nevertheless, for police personnel in staff and line versus the non-sworn personnel, the latter commonly being referred to as "civilians."

[9]James Q. Wilson, *supra* note 4.

[10]The ability to command respect personally is more necessary in America than in Britain where police command more respect officially. See Michael Banton, *The Policeman in the Community* (New York: Basic Books, 1965).

[11]James Q. Wilson, *supra* note 4.

[12]One study reports that, as compared with welfare workers and school teachers, policemen were more likely to personalize authority. Robert L. Peabody, "Perceptions of Organizational Authority: A Comparative Analysis," *Administrative Science Q.*, 6 Mar. 1962, 477-80; see also Elaine Cumming, Ian M. Cumming, Laura Edell, "Policeman as Philosopher, Guide and Friend," *Social Problems*, 12 Winter 1965, 276-97.

[13]This typology owes much to the analysis of labor unions in Harold L. Wilensky, *Intellectuals in Labor Unions* (Glencoe, Ill.: Free Press, 1956).

[14]Walter A. Lunden, "The Mobility of Chiefs of Police," *Crim. Law, Criminology & Police Science*, 49 (1958), 178-83.

[15]Philip Selznick, *Leadership in Administration* (New York: Row, Peterson & Co., 1957).

[16]Military honor is similarly communal and not just organizational. Morris Janowitz, *The Professional Soldier* (Glencoe, Ill.: Free Press, 1960), esp. ch. iv and v.

[17]M. McMullen, "A Theory of Corruption," *Sociological Rev.* 9 (1961), 181-201.

7. *This article, through the presentation of two police departments from different areas, reinforces the major points raised in the preceding essays. Specifically, it touches on the effects of professionalism on job efficiency and the occupational milieu, on police deviancy, and on the possibility of anomistic reactions. Most significantly, however, Wilson clearly proves the necessity to recognize in a realistic analysis of the police profession that "police officers [are] products of their police organizations just as police departments themselves [are] products of their community."*

TWO POLICE DEPARTMENTS: THE INFLUENCE OF STRUCTURE ON OPERATION

Adapted from "The Police and the Delinquent in Two Cities" by James Q. Wilson in CONTROLLING DELINQUENTS by Stanton Wheeler, ed. (New York: John Wiley & Sons, 1968).

Headquarters for Ted Marek is an impressive multi-storied building of modern design in the downtown area of a large West Coast city. Within this complex Ted has a small but pleasant office on the sixth floor, secretarial help, the most modern technical facilities, and, for business purposes, use of one of the many shiny new cars parked immediately outside the building. Tall, trim, and efficient-looking, 36-year-old Ted might be any rising young businessman—except for his smart gray-green uniform and badge which stamp him as a member of the city's police force.

Like many of his fellow officers, Ted has not always lived in this city. He grew up in the Midwest and attended junior college in his hometown after military service in Korea. Then, deciding to make "detective work" his career, Ted entered the school of police administration of a nearby university. It was from this school, where he graduated at the head of his class, that Ted was recruited by a West Coast team of law enforcement officials prospecting for "top talent." The team accepted him into the recently reorganized and modernized police department of one of the major American cities.

Ted was glad to join a force which recruited and promoted on the basis of personal achievement, rather than "connections" or seniority, and he was further impressed by the department's generally high moral and educational standards. Officers here were drilled in the highest principles of law enforcement. That is, they were taught to apply the law equally to all persons at all times regardless of the suspect's race, religion, or social background and to be guided in the performance of their duties by impartial rules rather than by private prejudices or sudden intuition. In short, the police were trained to adhere to a professional code of ethics in the pursuit of specific professional goals.

Ted's job was also rewarding because it gave him an opportunity to specialize. Assigned to the juvenile bureau after his first 18 months on the force, he had been required to take department-financed graduate courses in psychology, sociology, and penology to help him with his case work. In the process he became something of an expert on the problems of youthful offenders and was promoted to lieutenant.

Ted was sympathetic toward the

young boys and girls he interviewed in the course of his work. Though, for the most part, they were quite unlike the stable middle-class adolescents he had been brought up with, he felt no personal dislike for them. He was primarily concerned with remedying the delinquent's behavior to the best of his ability, that is, with saving both the delinquent and society from suffering again. This is known as the "therapeutic" (or healing) approach.

He knew from his studies as well as from his field experience that delinquency had many causes. He knew that the root of the problem could be traced to the family setting, or to the maladjustment of the individual, or to the impoverishment of the youth's cultural and social environment, or even to the overall structure of society itself. He tried always to be objective and scientific when speaking about "delinquency" and the "delinquent personality." But his conduct on the job, of course, was limited by the necessity of adhering strictly and impartially to the law.

Like Ted Marek, Chick Donnelly is also a police officer who is involved in juvenile work. But there the similarity ends. Though not in as responsible a position as Marek, Donnelly, at the age of 47, has actually been with the police department of his native city in the Northeast for far longer—nearly 28 years. For him, joining the force a year after high school had been a natural step: at that time, two of his uncles were with the department and Captain (Big Jim) Grogan, especially, had assured him that police work would provide him with a "comfortable berth."

Chick felt completely at home on the force. He had known many of his fellow officers since boyhood, and,

furthermore, he liked working in neighborhoods which were familiar to him, where people of his "own kind" could be counted on to contribute to the annual policeman's benefit. Staff work at the precinct level gave him satisfaction. True, the building was old and dilapidated, patrol cars scarce and shabby, and official records hopelessly messy and imcomplete. But, on the other hand, the atmosphere at the station house was warm and personal and frequently lively; you could wear an unpressed uniform, and "big shots" were not always "breathing down your neck."

Donnelly believed the police force of his city served a very useful purpose in keeping order and in putting "real troublemakers" and hardened criminals behind bars. He had not received much formal training, but early in the game he had learned "the ropes" and how to get along on the force from some of his older colleagues.

His friends on the force had, for instance, warned him that no matter what the books said about enforcing the law without respect to persons or about the equality of all before the law, some people were more equal than others. Therefore, it was worthwhile to "fix" traffic tickets every so often and to investigate who a kid's father was—whether he was rich or " a power in City Hall"—before arresting him. It was not just a matter of showing favoritism, however. Donnelly sincerely believed that it was only proper to take into account personal circumstances and to treat each new case on its individual merits, not just blindly or according to the rules.

Donnelly thought this informal philosophy was particularly suited to his work with young people. He had not liked being assigned this job to begin with—he had sole responsibility in his precinct for handling all juvenile delinquents and was often ribbed by

What is the quality of for juvenile delinquents under these two distinct kinds of police force.

his brother officers for "picking on the kids." Nevertheless, he tried to do his best both by the job *and* his charges.

Chick did not think that most adolescents were "really bad." He liked kids (had five of his own) and never forgot that he had been "no angel" when he was young. But he knew delinquency was on the rise and had developed some pretty definite ideas about it. He felt, for instance, that some kids, particularly the blacks who had recently moved into the old Irish and Italian neighborhood on his beat, simply had "no respect for authority," that what they really wanted was to tear everything down and destroy the whole society. According to him, most of the worst cases came from broken or "immoral" homes, where there was no father around to set a good example. In general, he believed that modern teenagers were "too permissively brought up," and had life "too easy." Teenagers' freedom, he felt, should be restricted and they should be punished when they stepped out of line. Sergeant Donnelly, in fact, could cite chapter and verse when it came to discussing the shortcomings of the younger generation and had a hundred anecdotes to bear him out.

These two officers are fairly typical examples of their respective police forces—one on the West Coast, the other on the eastern seaboard. And, according to the Harvard political scientist, James Q. Wilson, these two police departments are in turn representative of two distinct types of American police force—what he calls the "professional," or modern, as compared with the "fraternal," or traditional. As we have seen, the two systems recruit, train, and promote very different sorts of officers. Officers Marek and Donnelly, for example, are miles apart in background, education, work habits, and philosophy of law enforcement.

What primarily interests Wilson, however, is whether these differences affect what the department does, especially in an area like juvenile delinquency. For the law gives the authorities considerable latitude in the handling of individual delinquents— that is, the officers have power of discretion and can decide themselves whether to arrest an offender, warn him, or refer him to parents or welfare agencies. In other words, what is the quality of justice for juvenile delinquents under these two distinct kinds of police force?

To study the question, Wilson interviewed officers in both forces and also compared the records kept by each city.

The Record

To his surprise, Wilson found that in most respects the behavior of Western City and Eastern City officers tended to be the very opposite of what might have been expected from the way they talked. For instance, Western City's officers, as typified by Ted

TABLE 1

PROCESSING AND ARREST RATES OF JUVENILES IN TWO CITIES

	WESTERN CITY	EASTERN CITY
Total juveniles processed (all offenses)............	8,331	6,384
Rate per 100,000 children*.....................	14,000	6,000
Number of juveniles arrested or cited (all offenses)...	3,869	1,911
Percent arrested or cited......................	47%	30%
Total juveniles processed, less those charged with		
loitering..	6,685	6,384
Rate per 100,000 children.....................	11,000	6,000
Number of juveniles arrested or cited, less loiterers ..	3,446	1,911
Percent arrested or cited......................	52%	30%

*Rate is based on number of children, ages six through 16, in population of city according to the 1960 census of population.

Marek, had much more complex views on juvenile delinquents than did Eastern City officers. And foremost in Ted's mind was the question: What should be done to save this boy from further offenses? Nevertheless, Western City police were much more likely to use their powers of discretion to restrict the youth's freedom. Western City's Police Department processed a larger proportion of that city's juvenile population as suspected offenders than did Eastern City's Police Department. Of those it processed, the Western City Police arrested a larger proportion than did Eastern City.

The table shows the processing and arrest rates of juveniles in both cities in one year. (By "processed" is meant that the youth came in contact with the police in a manner that required the latter to make an official report; by "arrested or cited" is meant a more serious step. This meant that the police brought formal action against the juvenile. They either turned him over to the courts, to the probation officers, or issued an order for him to appear before a court or the probation department.) By comparing them, one can see that the rate of juveniles processed for all offenses by Western City's police was more than twice as great as the rate in Eastern City (14,000 per 100,000 as opposed to 6,000 per 100,000). Of those processed, the proportion arrested or cited was more than 50 percent greater in Western City than in Eastern City (47 percent versus 30 percent). In short, the juvenile in Western City is one and one-half to two times more likely to come in contact with the police. After that, he is one and one-half times more likely to be arrested or cited than reprimanded or referred.

These two different styles in law enforcement. . . are supported by the dominant community values in each community.

Whereas Western City's rate of arrest of *adults* was 50 percent higher than Eastern City's, it was over 100 percent higher than the rate of *juvenile* arrests in Eastern City. Thus, Western City police arrested three times as many suspected burglars, three times as many suspected robbers, and 17 times as many murder suspects. In fact, Western City's rates of arrest of juveniles were generally one to three times greater than Eastern City's. These statistics mean that a delinquent in Eastern city was far more likely to be let off by the police with a reprimand than was a juvenile in Western City.

The Contradiction Between Ethos and Behavior

Of the two departments, the "professionalized" Western City police officers had more sophisticated, lenient, and therapeutic *attitudes.* Yet they actually exposed a higher proportion of juveniles to the possibility of court action than did the more old-fashioned punishment-minded Eastern City police force. Wilson saw in this a contradiction between ideology and behavior which, he reasoned, could be explained by the different structures of the two departments.

Wilson thought that certain differences in procedures might account for some of the differences in arrests. For example, in Eastern City the juvenile officer on the police force was also the prosecuting officer. He must personally prepare and present the case in court against the juvenile. But in Western City the juvenile officer referred each case to an independent probation department and this routine cost him very little effort. It may be that the Western City police processed a higher proportion of young offenders than the Eastern City force simply because it was easier under their system.

But why should the arresting officer (who in both departments is distinct from the juvenile officer) be less likely to make an arrest in one city than the other? It was certainly not because the police in the two cities were soft-hearted; in fact, they all considered the court and the probation authorities as excessively lenient. They justified this opinion by the facts: in Eastern City only 2 percent of juvenile first offenders were actually placed in a correctional institution and in Western City it was not quite 3 percent.

Wilson found the answer to his question in the differences between the organizational arrangements, community attachments, and institutionalized patterns which governed the daily lives of police officers in each city. He calls this the "ethos" (that is, the spirit) of each police force. In Western City this was the ethos of a "professional" force; in Eastern City, the ethos of a "fraternal" force.

To begin with, Western City's police officers worked in a highly centralized and specialized setting. Each officer had to account for every minute of his time on duty and to record all contacts with citizens. All juvenile offenders were processed in the office of the headquarters' juvenile bureau. There their disposition was determined by officers specially trained in this area.

Eastern City's police force, in contrast, was highly decentralized. Officers were assigned to, and sometimes spent their entire careers in, one precinct. Juvenile suspects were brought to the local station house and turned over to the officer of the juvenile bureau who worked there. Whatever records he kept or whatever dispositions he made were largely his own business.

There were other grounds for differences between the two forces besides ethos. To stop corruption and police brutality, Western City's reform-minded police chief had abolished the precinct system and had centralized control of the police force in his own hands. At the same time he reformed the rules and reporting procedures and tightened supervision on all levels. The net effect of the chief's measures was not only the intended outcome of making his officers behave properly in non-discretionary matters, such as taking bribes. The reforms also caused them to behave differently in areas over which they *did* have discretion. More precisely the new measures led officers to treat juveniles according to the rules and without regard to them as persons.

In contrast, Eastern City's officers used their discretionary powers to treat juveniles on the basis primarily of personal judgment and only secondarily on the basis of formal rules.

In Western City the work of juvenile officers had a marked professional stamp. Juvenile officers worked as a unit; they met daily for briefing; they worked out of a common headquarters; they had their own patrol cars; and field officers scouted together in pairs. Their primary contacts were with fellow officers who were serving identical interests and upholding the same values, and their behavior was likely to be guided by the practices and comments of their "professional" colleagues.

But in Eastern City the typical juvenile officer worked alone in his precinct. He had no car of his own; he rarely met with other juvenile officers; and there was practically no training for his job or systematic briefing while on it. His associates were usually patrolmen and detectives who had no understanding of his work and very little sympathy for it. In fact, they tended to look down upon juvenile law enforcement duties as "kid stuff," not worth taking seriously. And because they were reluctant to bring in adolescents themselves, they often dumped even the preliminary investigation and arrest procedures in the lap of the juvenile officer, thereby increasing his work load.

Thus, in spite of the more punitive attitudes of all members of Eastern City's police force, in practice, the juvenile officer, as influenced by his precinct associates, was likely to show greater permissiveness. In contrast, in Western City, neither juvenile officers nor arresting patrolmen were as exposed to the opinions of associates or as dependent upon them.

A further reason for the greater punitiveness of Western City's officers, Wilson believes, is that they were largely recruited from backgrounds which would not cause them to identify themselves strongly with delinquents in general. Moreover, they were organized in a way that prevented them from developing any personal ties with delinquents in particular. Like Ted Marek, most were out-of-towners who had spent their youth in solid middle-class neighborhoods free from violence, troubles with the police, or gang behavior. And, once on the force, the "professionalized" officer working through a centralized system has no chance to build up familiarity with or an affection for any particular precinct and its residents.

In contrast, the majority of Eastern City's officers were local residents from lower- or lower-middle-class backgrounds. Like Chick Donnelly, they grew up in tough neighborhoods where brushes with the law were a common occurrence. Though many alumni of the old street-corner gangs graduated into the Police or Fire Departments, quite a few also wound up in state prison. Delinquency, to these officers, therefore, was not a world apart but an everyday fact of life.

Wilson summarizes these differences in style between the two police departments by saying that in Western City the officer had a *generalized* knowledge of juveniles and of delinquency and that this theoretical knowledge provided the basis of his decisions. He was under less pressure to make exceptions, or to *particularize* than was his Eastern City counterpart. Therefore, he was less likely to behave in an arbitrary, inconsistent, or prejudiced fashion.

In Eastern City, the officer's knowledge (or what he took to be his knowledge) about delinquency, crime, and neighborhood affairs was *particular* and, above all, personal. Eastern City police tended to be authoritarian, old-fashioned, and narrow-minded when they were talking about delinquency. However, when they were dealing with delinquents, they applied not their expressed general beliefs but their particular knowledge of the case in question and some rough standard of personal justice. Thus, prejudice combined with personal experience may actually have induced them to indulge those very "over-indulged" youth of whom they complained. At the same time, a lack of understanding or of particular knowledge about blacks or other "alien" groups may have led them to conform to their rigid attitudes about the problem of delinquency as a whole.

By the same token, because they consistently acted according to general principles, Western City's officers tended to treat all juveniles with greater severity—but, at the same time, without making exceptions of race or class.

These two different styles in law enforcement, Wilson concludes, are supported by the dominant community values in each city. Western City has a modern, efficient, nonpartisan, municipal administration and a larger middle-class population. Eastern City, in contrast, has been governed for decades by old-style politics in which personal loyalties, neighborhood interests, and party preferment play a leading role. Besides, Eastern City is less prosperous and more "foreign" than its Western counterpart. A professional police force intent on vigorous law enforcement is in keeping with the demands of the one city, while a fraternal force operating in the traditional way is in keeping with the expectations of the other. In sum, in both cities the police officers were products of their police organizations, just as the police departments themselves were products of their communities.

8. *Social notions of justice and punishment reflect the emotional as well as the national ethos of the specific historical period. Nevertheless, it is widely agreed upon that criminal justice procedures be based on rationalistic motives if the criminal justice system is to maintain public respect. Alan Dershowitz, the author of the next article, states:*

> The difficult question facing a concerned people in contemporary America is not whether considerations of justice and punishment should play any role in sentencing decisions but rather what kind and how much a role these age-old factors be accorded in a rational sentencing system.

These "age-old factors," regardless of the emphasis on objectivity in planning and implementing criminal justice goals, cannot be ignored. Unfortunately, they are both volatile concepts that easily accommodate opposing camps of sentiment and reason.

Dershowitz recognizes in his argument that there is no operational "absolute justice" that will be eventually discovered and thus supply the answer to social consternation about the relationship of punishment to democratic ideals. This existential situation is an obvious tenet in realistic evaluations of criminal justice.

In the concluding sentence of the article, we are given an idea of the inevitability of a pendulum swing between individual justice and social justice. As courts and legislatures tend toward an emphasis in the practicality of social justice, "a reaction may again set in: complaints will be voiced against too much conformity and rigidity; a need for flexibility

will be noted. . . .And the cycle will turn once again." (emphasis added). He demonstrates this by relating the history of criminal sentencing to the vascillation of social concepts of justice and punishment.

There have been three prime social motives for incarceration—isolation, punishment, and reformation. If society justifies imprisonment as a social defense and simply isolates the criminal, the roles of the judge, lawyer, jury, and prison are clear. Their roles, however, become ambiguous because society itself cannot be objective in its reaction to crime; it demands ostracism, punishment in other words (not isolation), and prison conditions conducive to eventual reformation of the criminal's character. The courts and prisons operate, then, under a "confusion generated by [the] coalescence of functions." Neither are able to satisfy public demands. By using discretion in deciding the social culpability of a criminal act, the courts are frequently denounced as unfair. Through the use of indeterminate sentencing, thus recognizing the delicacy of deciding whether or not a criminal is "reformed," the courts are accused of "producing more cruelty and injustice than the benefits its supporters envisage."

The judge, the prosecutor, and, to a certain extent, prison officials, would shield themselves from social criticism by attaining and maintaining a high level of objectivity were such a level not inconsistent with a paired recognition that (1) current laws upon which they would solely base their judgments are not always in keeping with the current morality and (2) that each case contains certain human issues which cannot be ignored.

CRIMINAL SENTENCING IN THE UNITED STATES: AN HISTORICAL AND CONCEPTUAL OVERVIEW

ALAN M. DERSHOWITZ

The history of criminal sentencing in the United States has been a history of shifts in institutional responsibility for determining the sentence to be served by the convicted criminal. At different stages, this decision has been allocated in varying ways among the legislature, courts, parole agencies, and prosecutors. Although the primary object of the criminal sentence—to reduce the frequency and severity of crimes—has remained fairly consistent over time, different mechanisms of crime reduction have been emphasized at different periods in our history.

The Mechanisms of the Criminal Sentence

The mechanisms of the criminal sentence include the following: (1) *isolating* the convicted criminal from the rest of the population so that he is unable to commit crimes during the period of his enforced isolation; (2) *punishing* the convicted prisoner so that he—and others contemplating crime—will be deterred by the prospect of a painful response if convicted; (3) *rehabilitating* the convicted criminal so that his desire or need to commit future crimes will be diminished.

Isolation

The mechanism of isolation oper-ates directly to remove the criminal from the general population. It has been used throughout history, against all manner of "dangerous" beings. During the period of removal, the isolated criminal cannot generally commit crimes against the rest of the population. Imprisonment is not the only instrument of enforced isolation; banishment, exile, deportation, hospitalization, house arrest, and enforced enlistment in the military are other instruments of isolation that have been employed throughout history. In order to operate effectively, the removal of the convicted offender need not be accompanied by any pain other than that inherent in the isolation itself. Theoretically, isolation could be accomplished at any escape-proof area isolated from the law-abiding population.

Although the mechanism of isolation operates simply and directly, it does rest on a superstructure of complex assumptions, some of which are more easily demonstrable than others. It assumes that the population to be isolated includes a significant number of persons who, if permitted to remain in the general population, would commit crimes against that population. The actual number and seriousness of the crimes that would be committed by the population of those currently isolated is, of course, unknowable. Moreover, even if it could be determined how many crimes were ultimately prevented by isolating the prison population, that would still not tell us what percentage of the total serious crime is being prevented by isolating that population. For example, even if a large percentage of the prison population of a given jurisdiction would have committed several serious crimes had they been released rather than imprisoned, it may still turn out that these "prevented" crimes

order physical and/or financial punishment over and above that inherent in the confinement; or could he conclude that the confinement satisfied both purposes? What if the judge concluded that a defendant met the standard of dangerousness and also needed rehabilitation; could he then compel rehabilitative efforts during the period of confinement; or would such efforts have to await the convict's release? Once sentencing functions are permitted to be combined—as they surely would be in real life—analytic confusions would be generated.

Another advantage of such a system would be that the expensive resource of imprisonment—expensive both in liberty and in material costs—would be reserved for those convicted defendants whose imprisonment produced the most immediate and demonstrable results.

The disadvantages of a system under which imprisonment would be used only against dangerous convicts are also obvious. It would deny society a major deterrent weapon against crimes committed by "nondangerous" and "nonrecidivating" offenders—white-collar, governmental, and political criminals—who are uniquely deterred by the threat of being imprisoned along with "common" criminals. It would also deprive us of the important education and symbolic message that certain crimes committed by the wealthy and powerful are as serious and as destructive of important values as are crimes of violence.

Another problem with the "model" system is that, by denying society the use of imprisonment as a punishment, it requires the creation and employment of other forms of punishment which may be deemed less "civilized." Whether whipping should indeed be considered less civilized than imprisonment is a debatable question, but the "cruel and unusual punishment" of our state and federal constitutions— such as currently interpreted—may impose serious constraints upon the employment of physical punishments other than imprisonment. In order to replace imprisonment, alternate punishments would have to be severe. Otherwise, nondangerous criminals convicted of serious crimes would be treated with undue leniency in comparison with dangerous criminals convicted of less serious crimes; and the seriousness of nonviolent, nonrecidivating crimes would be unduly diminished.

Consider, for example, the Watergate cases. It can be safely assumed that Messrs. Haldeman, Ehrlichman, and Mitchell are no longer dangerous (if for no other reason than that they are unlikely ever to be in positions where they could recidivate); nor are they in need of the kind of rehabilitation currently available in prison. But it would be immoral in the extreme for them to be spared imprisonment, since under current sentencing practices imprisonment is the most significant measure of how seriously society regards a crime. For these serious criminals to escape with only a fine would be to minimize their culpability. Were equivalently serious punishments, other than imprisonment, available, it might be fair—and effective—to impose such punishments on the likes of Haldeman et al. But in the absence of such alternative punishments, it would simply be unfair to fine them, since fines— especially at there current levels—are widely regarded as slaps on the wrist or criminal license fees. Yet, at one level, the absurdity of imprisoning these convicted criminals is patent: they simply do not need walls around them. It is only the symbolism of the imprisonment—and the accompanying stigma and deprivation—that justifies imposing this punishment.

The heuristic device employed above is simply intended to demonstrate both the confusion inherent in current sentencing practices—especially as it relates to the sentence of imprisonment—and the impossibility of simple solutions. Despite its criticism, imprisonment is likely to continue as the dominant formal response to conviction for serious crime, not only for dangerous criminals, but also for nondangerous criminals convicted of serious crimes.

An Institutional History of Criminal Sentencing

The literature on the allocation of sentencing responsibility over the last two centuries is surprisingly spotty; authoritative historical accounts are lacking. Nevertheless, it is possible to describe, in general outline, several historical periods characterized by somewhat different sentencing systems.

The Colonial Period

During the colonial period, the primary mechanisms of sentencing were isolation and punishment. Colonial Americans used a variety of nonincarcerative techniques to protect their communities from the threat of crime. One effective method for both preventing and punishing offenses within a particular town was the enforcement of settlement laws: unwanted individuals were simply "warned out" (excluded) by the constable. Specific crimes were punished, according to the colonial criminal codes, with relatively specific penalties. Economic crimes were usually punished by a system of fines,

in addition to orders of restitution. Offenders who simply could not pay were sentenced to forced labor, whipped, placed in the stocks or perhaps branded with a symbol of their offense.

These same corporal penalties were also deemed appropriate for a wide variety of petty offenses. Colonial criminal codes sometimes gave a magistrate a measure of discretion concerning, for example, the duration of an offender's stay in the stocks or the pillory; but, in general, punishments were legislatively prescribed with some precision. Often, that prescription was death.

Incarceration as a punishment or as a "rehabilitative" technique was practically nonexistent. Although some communities had local jails, these institutions did not house convicted offenders serving criminal sentences, but were used to "hold" defendants who were awaiting trial or who had been unable to raise sufficient funds to pay court-imposed fines.

Thus, with few exceptions, criminal sentencing in the colonial period was primarily the responsibility of the legislatures. Statutes dictated relatively fixed sentences: the whip, the stocks, fines, death.

The Pre-Civil War Period

During the period following the Revolution (1790-1820), most states undertook rather complete revisions of their criminal codes, drastically limiting the operation of the death penalty. Similarly, flogging, whipping, branding, and other corporal punishments were abolished in many jurisdictions. Instead of violent physical penalties, the states developed a new—and, in many ways, quite innovative—form of criminal sentence: imprisonment, often with the most idealistic goals for the offender's benefit. When first proposed as a sentencing mechanism, imprisonment was seen as a "reformative" policy merely because it served as a substitute for capital punishment. However, incarceration rather quickly developed its own justifications as an intrinsically "reformative" institution; the penitentiary could, through carefully calibrated systems of discipline, labor, and religious exhortation, "cure" the offender of his criminogenic pathology.[10]

The underpinnings of this optimistic view of the potential for incarcerative reform of the individual offender were first set forth in 1787 at a meeting in the Philadelphia home of Benjamin Franklin. An influential group gathered there to hear Dr. Benjamin Rush deliver a paper concerning the establishment of a modern prison system. Rush urged a prison program which would (1) establish various inmates "classification" programs, for purposes of both inmate housing assignments and various "treatment" plans; (2) devise a self-supporting institutional system based on inmate piecework and agriculture; and (3) impose indeterminate periods of confinement on inmates who would then be released on the basis of evidence of their progress toward "rehabilitation." The Philadelphia Society for Alleviating the Miseries for Public Prisons organized to implement Dr. Rush's idealistic program. In 1790 the society succeeded in prevailing upon the state legislature to authorize the remodeling of Philadelphia's Walnut Street Jail in order to fashion a prison—a "cellhouse"—which could serve as a proving ground for the new theory of individualized reformative incarceration

Over the next few decades—in fact, until the 1870 Declaration of Principles —the practice and theory of criminal sentencing underwent very little substantive revision. The state codes were reworked and capital and corporal punishments gave way to sentences of imprisonment. Legislatures gave courts discretion—within ranges which were rather narrow compared to today's legislatively authorized punishments—to impose sentences which could then be altered only by the executive's pardoning power. Some nineteenth-century statutes set out punishments based on different gradations of offenses which had formerly had only one broad definition.

This period, encompassing almost the entire nineteenth century, can be fairly characterized as one in which the judiciary began to share responsibility with the legislature for criminal sentencing decisions. The legislature set the outside limits within which sentencing discretion could be exercised, but the statutes did not set out specific, detailed criteria to guide judicial sentencing. Once the sentence was imposed by the court upon the individual offender, it was "fixed": it did not include a minimum term and/or a maximum term subject to later decisions by other institutions or persons such as wardens. A sentence of two years meant 730 days (unless, of course, a pardon or some sort of commutation was forthcoming from the executive branch).[11]

In several senses, the sentencing process then in operation was in serious conflict with the developing rhetoric of reformative incarceration. First, despite hortatory calls to vocational and spiritual betterment, an inmate's response in the prison environment mattered very little in determining the duration of his sentence: whether he was a model prisoner or not, he was likely to serve the sentence pronounced by the court.

Second, the length of the sentence was almost invariably a function of how the court—and, in the first instance, the legislature—viewed the seriousness of the crime committed. Courts, as sentencing institutions, rarely concerned themselves with "correctional" goals other than simple punishment for a particular criminal act. If the conviction was for the felony of assault, a New York court, "on a consideration of all the circumstances of the case," could sentence an offender to imprisonment (in solitary confinement at hard labor, or to "simple" incarceration) for any term up to 14 years.[12] The relevant "circumstances," for a court in the nineteenth century, would include such considerations as the ferocity of the attack and the defendant's motive.

The Post-Civil War Period

An "enlightened" view of a sentencing system which would strongly reinforce rehabilitative rather than punitive purposes was given dramatic highlighting at the 1870 National Prison Congress. The delegates to that convention voted for a Declaration of Principles—a call for a variety of penal reforms, among them a radical alteration of the existing sentencing structure. The principles did pay lip service to the punitive rationale for sentencing: "Crime is an intentional violation of duties imposed by law" and "[p]unishment is suffering... in expiation of the wrong done." Nevertheless, and more importantly, crime is:

a moral disease, of which punishment is the remedy. The efficiency of the remedy is a question of social therapeutics, a question of the fitness and the measure of the dose. . . . [P]unishment is directed not to the crime but the criminal. . . .

The supreme aim of prison discipline is the reformation of criminals, not the infliction of vindictive suffering.[13]

With "reformation" as the uncompromised goal of the prison, it followed that release should be effected only upon its achievement. Thus, the Congress declared:

Peremptory sentences ought to be replaced by those of indeterminate duration—sentences limited only by satisfactory proof of reformation should be substituted for those measured by mere lapse of time.[14]

This principle had been most strongly urged by Zebulon Brockway, then the superintendent of the Elmira Reformatory in New York, who had addressed the delegates on "The Ideal of a True Prison System." His ideal was premised on the indeterminate sentence. According to Brockway, the "indeterminate sentence" and the "indeterminate reformatory" were the methods by which the reformation of the criminal and the protection of society could be most effectively achieved. Brockway rejected vengeance (pure punishment) as unjust and deterrence as a failure. He proposed, instead, a system of confinement under which:

all persons in a state, who are convicted of crimes or offenses before a competent court, shall be deemed wards of the state and shall be committed to the custody of the board of guardians, until, in their judgment, they may be returned to society with ordinary safety and in accord with their own highest welfare.[15]

The first explicit indeterminate sentence law for crimes in the United States was enacted at the behest of Zebulon Brockway in the state of Michigan in 1869. It was of extremely limited application, reserved solely for "common prostitutes" and providing for a three-year sentence which could be terminated at any time at the discretion of the inspectors of the Detroit House of Correction.[16] (The maximum punishment for prostitution had been far less than three years.) Eight years later, Brockway secured the enactment of the first indeterminate sentence law of more widespread penal application. His original proposal was for an indeterminate sentence law "without limitation," but "neither public sentiment in general nor the views of the legislators would accept this."[17]

Instead, New York enacted a modified provision which was typical of the statutes enacted in most states in the year following. The New York law limited the term of the sentence to "the maximum term provided by law for the crime for which the prisoner was convicted and sentenced," but left the determination of the exact amount of time to be served to the managers of the reformatory. By 1922, 37 states had similar forms of indeterminate sentencing and seven others had parole systems which were functionally similar to the indeterminate sentence.

As rehabilitation came to be recognized as the prison's primary function, a major reordering of sentencing power was implemented in order to allow the period of incarceration to fit the time required for the particular offender's reformation: hence, the proliferation of parole systems and the indeterminate sentence. Ironically, by the time indeterminate sentencing structures had been established, the belief in man's ability to better his moral faculties was giving way to various schools of physiological and ethnic determinism: the new criminologists suggested that some, if not most, criminal "types" could not overcome their propensities for deviant behavior. So, in a strange inversion, the indeterminate sentence could be used to prolong the incarceration of those offenders felt to be "incurable."

Medical terminology and methodology began to infuse the functioning of the prison system. Ideally, an inmate was carefully "classified" (diagnosed), and treatment plans were prescribed for his individual condition; prisoner's responses to his rehabilitative program was constantly monitored and evaluated; upon recovery from his criminal disease, he was paroled. Of course, some criminal syndromes had no known cures—and those inmates unable to demonstrate that the symptoms and cause of their disorders had somehow disappeared had to remain in prison to serve out their full sentences. The indeterminate sentence was essential to the working of this system. The large amount of discretionary power vested in correctional and parole personnel was necessary in order to give the clinicians (psychiatrists and psychologists, educators, social workers, employment counselors, and others) the needed leeway to tailor their efforts to each individual prisoner.

Current Practices

The indeterminate sentence, which was once viewed as a special form of sentencing, has now emerged as the dominant sentencing structure in the United States. Nor is the indeterminate sentence a unitary concept of precise definition; it is very much a matter of degree. A sentence is more or less indeterminate to the extent that the amount of time actually to be served is decided not by the judge at the time sentence is imposed, but rather by an administrative board while the sentence is being served. Thus, a judicially imposed sentence of one day to life, the actual duration to be determined by the parole board after service of sentence has commenced, is entirely indeterminate; a judicially imposed sentence of life imprisonment with no possibility of parole (or other discretionary reduction) is entirely determinate. Between these terminal points of the continuum lies a wide range of more or less indeterminate sentences. A judicially imposed sentence of not less than five or more than 10 years is partially indeterminate: although its maximum and minimum are fixed at the time of sentencing, the actual time to be served within those limits will be decided subsequently by some administrative authority. Another form of indeterminate sentence is the judicially imposed term of imprisonment for what appears to be a fixed period, say 10 years, but subject to the normal rules of parole, under which an administrative board has discretion to authorize release after a percentage of the "sentence" prescribed by statute has been served. Thus, all sentences subject to parole—the vast majority of prison sentences imposed in the United States today—are indeterminate to some degree.[18]

Models of Criminal Sentencing

It is possible to extract from this history several possible models of prison sentencing. Among the "pure" models are the following.

1. *The legislatively fixed model*— The legislature determines that conviction for a given crime warrants a given term of imprisonment (for example, a first offender convicted of armed robbery must be sentenced to five years imprisonment). There is no judicial or administrative discretion under this model; the legislature has authorized but one sentence. In practice, of course, there would still be discretion at various points in the process: the police and/or prosecutor generally have wide discretion to determine the charge (whether the taking was a robbery or some lesser form of larceny; whether the weapon constituted an "arm"); the executive generally has discretion to commute or pardon. In theory, however, the legislatively fixed sentence model is the least discretionary, in the sense that the sentence is determined in advance of the crime and without knowing who the criminal is.[19]

2. *The judicially fixed sentence model*—The legislature determines the general range of imprisonment for a given crime (for example, a first offender convicted of armed robbery shall be sentenced to no less than one and no more than 10 years imprisonment). The sentencing judge must fix a determinate sentence within that range ("I sentence the defendant to five years imprisonment"). Once this sentence is fixed, it cannot be increased or reduced by any parole board or adult authority; the defendant must serve five years.[20] Under this model, discretion is vested in the sentencing judge (how much depends on the range of imprisonment authorized by the legislature). On the day he is sentenced, however, the defendant knows precisely how long he will serve; there is no discretion vested in the parole board or prison authorities.

3. *The administratively fixed sentence model*—The legislature nominally sets an extremely wide permissible range of imprisonment for a given crime (for example, a first offender armed robber shall be sentenced to a term of one day to life). The sentencing judge must— or may—impose the

legislatively determined sentence ("You are sentenced to one day to life"). The actual duration of the sentence is decided by an administrative agency (for example, after five years of imprisonment, the adult authority decides that the prisoner is "ready" for release). Under this model, vast discretion is vested in the administrative agency and, in practice, in the prison authorities. And the defendant, on the day he is sentenced, does not know—though he probably can make an educated guess based on past practices—how long he will have to serve.

In addition to the "pure" models described above, there are obviously a number of mixed systems. For example, the most common American sentencing system operates as follows: the legislature determines the general range of sentences for a particular crime (a first offender armed robber may be imprisoned from three to 10 years). The judge may select any sentence within that range ("I sentence you to five years"). The parole board may then release him after a specific percentage of his sentence (say one-third) has been served.

An important deviation from these pure models is introduced by the phenomenon of prosecutorial plea bargaining, under which the sentence is determined—or at least critically affected—by negotiations between the prosecutor and the defense attorney. Such negotiations are possible under any of the pure systems, though they may take a different form depending on the model. For example, where the sentence is legislatively fixed, the object of the negotiations will probably be to reduce the charge from a more to a less serious one (thus directly reducing the legislatively determined sentence). Where the sentence is judicially determined,

the object will probably be to reduce the sentence imposed by the judge. Where the sentence is administratively determined, the object will probably be to have the prosecutor put a good word in with the parole board. There can be no practical understanding of any sentencing system without an appreciation of the role that plea bargaining plays in it.

Current Trends and Future Prospects

The era of the indeterminate sentence—of the administrative model of sentencing—is quickly drawing to a close. Reaction is beginning to set in. In the past several years, several influential books were published criticizing the indeterminate sentence. The first, a report prepared for the American Friends Service Committee under the guidance of Professor Caleb Foote of Berkeley, recommended the abolition of indeterminate sentencing and the adoption of a system which proportions the punishment to the act committed (though it advocated the retention of "good time" reductions of sentence with proper safeguards).[21]

Jessica Mitford's more popular work, *Kind and Usual Punishment*, focuses particularly on indeterminate sentencing as it is practiced in California. After describing its humane-sounding qualities, she poses and attempts to answer the following questions:

> Why, then, is [the indeterminate sentence] denounced by the supposed beneficiaries—prisoners and parolees—from coast to coast, its abolition one of the focal demands of the current prison rebellion? And why is it coming under increasing attacks from those criminologists, sociologists, lawyers, legislators who have taken the trouble to look closely at the prison scene and have informed themselves at first hand about the day-to-day realities of prison life?[22]

Mitford finds many reasons for this strident opposition, including "much longer sentences for most prisoners than would normally be imposed by judges,"[23] and total arbitrariness of the bureaucracy that rules every aspect of their existence"[24]—notably the actual duration of their confinement.

The most scholarly and thoughtful of these recent works is Judge Marvin Frankel's Criminal Sentences: Law without Order, which is a general critique of sentencing, especially in the federal courts. Finding that the "movement toward indeterminancy in sentencing is broad and powerful,"[25] Frankel articulates a "minority position" that "indeterminate sentencing, as thus far employed and justified, has produced more cruelty and injustice than the benefits its supporters envisage."[26] Doubting that rehabilitation, an important justification of indeterminancy, is possible in most cases, Judge Frankel opts for a "presumption...in favor of a definite sentence, known and justified on the day of sentencing (and probably much shorter than our sentences tend to run)." There should be:

> a burden of justifying an indeterminate sentence in any particular case—a burden to be satisfied by concrete reasons and a concrete program for the defendant involved. The justification...would consist of identified needs and resources for effective rehabilitation....[27]

In the United States, judicial doubts about the substantive wisdom of particular law enforcement techniques often are reflected initially by the imposition of procedural barriers.

Courts feel more comfortable placing procedural, rather than substantive, limitations on legislatively authorized programs. As Justice Harlan once said: while courts "must give the widest deference to legislative judgments" concerning the substantive criteria for confinement, the judiciary has "been understood to possess particular competence" in assessing the "necessity and wisdom of procedural guarantees." It is not surprising, therefore, that the initial judicial limitations on indeterminate sentencing have taken the form of procedural safeguards. Several important decisions, dealing with a different point in the indeterminate sentence process, have imposed procedural barriers to the easy imposition of indeterminate sentences.[28] Courts have also begun to impose some substantive limitations on the indeterminate sentence.[29]

It is likely that a process of retrenchment is upon us: courts and legislatures will continue to reflect the growing academic and inmate criticism of indeterminate sentencing. What we may well witness over the next several decades is a return to an earlier stage in the inevitable cycle. Legislatures will assume greater responsibility for sentencing decisions. The role of the parole board will probably be significantly curtailed. The sentencing judge and prosecutor may also have limits imposed on their discretion. Then, before long, a reaction may again set in: complaints will be voiced against too much conformity and rigidity; a need for flexibility and discretion will be noted. And the cycle will turn once again.

Notes

[1] See A. M. Dershowitz, "Preventing Preventive Detention," New York Review of Books. (13 March 1969), p. 27.

[2] See A. M. Dershowitz, "Preventive Confine-

ment: A Suggested Framework for Constitutional Analysis," *Texas Law Rev.* 51 (1973), 1277, 1283-88.

³See, Salielles, *The Individualization of Punishment,* p. 186.

⁴The Penal Law is a Categorical Imperative; and woe unto him who creeps through the serpent-windings of Utilitarianism to discover some advantage that may discharge him from the Justice of Punishment...." Immanuel Kant, *Philosophy of Law,* trans. W. Hastie (Clifton, N.J.: Augustus M. Kelley, Pubs., 1887), pp. 195-196.

⁵See, e.g., Cesare Lombroso, *Criminal Man* (unpubl., 1971).

⁶See A. M. Dershowitz, "Indeterminate Sentencing as a Mechanism of Preventive Confinement," in *Law in the U.S.A. in Sociological and Technological Revolution,* ed. John Hazard & Wenceslas Wagner (Brussels, Bel.: unpubl., 1974).

⁷There still is room for questioning the goals sought to be achieved by rehabilitation, even voluntary rehabilitation. See "South Africa Plans Rehabilitation Centers for Blacks Violating Racial Laws," *New York Times* (20 July 1975), p. 4, col. 1.

⁸This formulation deliberately leaves out the entire issue of whether dangerous persons who have not been convicted may be "preventively" confined.

⁹That such a system is not unthinkable is evidenced by the fact that it was proposed by early advocates of indeterminate sentencing: "No man be imprisoned unless it is clear that his freedom is dangerous to others, and that when once imprisoned, no man be free until the danger has ceased." C. Lewis, "The Indeterminate Sentence," *Yale Law J.* 9 (1899), 17.

¹⁰See David J. Rothman, *The Discovery of the Asylum* (Boston: Little, Brown & Co., 1971).

¹¹Some states, such as New York, did however, have "good time" laws which allowed an inmate to earn a set amount of sentence reduction through good behavior in prison.

¹²See *Laws of New York* (1801), ch., 58.

¹³*Transactions of the National Congress on Prisons and Reformatory Discipline,* (Albany, 1871), reprinted by Amer. Correctional Assn., ed. Weed & Parsons (1970).

¹⁴*Ibid.*

¹⁵Zebulon R. Brockway, *Fifty Years of Prison Service* (London: Oxford Univ. Press, 1912), p. 401.

¹⁶E. Lindsey, "Historical Sketch of the Indeterminate Sentence and Parole System," *J. Crim. Law, Criminology & Police Science* 16 (1925), 9.

¹⁷*Ibid.*, p. 21.

¹⁸The concept of indeterminancy is not applicable exclusively to punitive criminal sentences. Orders of involuntary confinement that do not bear punitive labels—such as commitment of the insane, addicts, juvenile delinquents, defective delinquents, and sexual psychopaths—are typically indeterminate; indeed, they tend to be even more indeterminate than criminal sentences. Commitments of the mentally ill, sexual psychopaths, and defective delinquents are wholly indeterminate as a general rule. "Nonpunitive" confinements of juveniles and addicts usually have upper time limits, but give administrative boards discretion to determine the actual duration of the confinement within these limits.

¹⁹Under this model, the legislature does, of course, have enormous discretion to determine which crimes deserve what punishments. And since it is widely known what kinds of persons commit what kinds of crimes, various kinds of prejudice—economic, social, racial, and others—can operate.

²⁰This model does not consider good time provisions or other relatively automatic reductions, nor does it consider commutation or pardon.

²¹A Committee Report prepared for the Amer. Friends' Service Committee, *Struggle for Justice,* (New York: Hill & Wang, 1971).

²²Jessica Mitford, *Kind and Usual Punishment* (New York: Alfred A. Knopf, 1973), p. 81.

²³*Ibid.*, p. 83.

²⁴*Ibid.*, p. 87.

²⁵"A prestigious and influential scholarly product, the Model Penal Code, provides for broadly indeterminate sentences. A number of state legislatures, including several influenced by the Model Penal Code, have opted for indeterminancy in recent revisions of their laws." Marvin E. Frankel, *Criminal Sentences: Law without Order* (New York: Hill & Wang, 1973), p. 88.

²⁶*Ibid.* Judge Frankel acknowledges the impact of prisoners' complaints on resisting the trend toward indeterminancy: "Until the last couple of years, the trend toward indeterminant sentencing has seemed irresistible. Just recently, from the prisons and elsewhere, some voices of dissent have been heard."

²⁷*Ibid.*, p. 98.

²⁸See, e.g., *Specht v. Patterson,* 386 U.S. 605 (1967); *Monks v. New Jersey,* 58 N.J. 233, 277 A2d 193 (1971); *Morrissey v. Brewer,* 408 U.S. 471 (1972).

²⁹See, e.g., *In re Lynch,* 8 Cal. 3rd 410, 503 P.2d 921 (1972); Compare, *People v. Wingo,* 43 U.S.L.W. 2493 [14 Cal.3d 169, 534 P.2d 1001] (1975).

References

Bailey, F. G.
1969. *Stratagemsand spoils.* New York: Schochen Books.

Bittner, E.
1970. *The functions of the police in modern society.* Washington, D.C.: United States government printing office.

Black, D. J.
1968. *Police encounters and social organization.* Unpublished Ph.D. disserta-

tion, Department of Sociology, University of Michigan.

1970. The production of crime rates. *American sociological review* 35 (August): 733-748.

Black, D. J. and Reiss, A. J.
1970. Police control juveniles. *American sociological review* 35 (February): 63-77.

Bordua, D.
1965. Recent trends: deviant behavior and social control. *Annals* 57 (January): 149-163.

Cain, M.
1973. *Society and the policeman's role.* London: Routledge, Kegan Paul.

Chatterton, M.
1973. *A working paper on the use [of] resource changes and practical decision-making in peace-keeping.* Presented at Bristol Seminar on the sociology of the police. Bristol University, England.

Chevigny, P.
1968. *Police power: police abuses in New York.* New York: Pantheon.

Cicourel, A.
1968. *The social organization of juvenile justice.* New York: Wiley.

Clark, A. and Gibles, J. P.
1965. Social control. *Social problems* 12 (Spring): 398-415.

Cohen, S.
1973. *Folk devils and moral panics.* London: Paladin Books.

Edelman, M.
1972. *Politics as symbolic action.* Chicago: Markham.

Erikson, K. T.
1966. *Wayward puritans.* New York: Wiley.

Ferdinand, T., and Lucterhand, E.
1970. Inner city youths: The police and justice. *Social problems* 17 (Spring): 510-527.

Glaser, D.
1970. *Social deviance.* Chicago: Markham.

Goffman, E.
1959. *The presentation of self in everyday life.* New York: Doubleday.

Goldman, N.
1963. *The differential selection of juvenile offenders for court appearance.* National Research and Information Center, National Council on Crime and Delinquency, New York.

Goode, E.
1969. Marijuana and the politics of reality. *Journal of health and social behavior* 10 (June) 83-93.

Hughes, E. C.
1963. Good people and dirty work. *The other side,* edited H. S. Becker. Glencoe: The Free Press.

Knapp, W., et. al.
1972. The knapp commission report on police corruption [in New York City]. New York: George Braziller.

Long, N.
1958. The local community as an ecology of games. *American journal of sociology* 54 (November) 251-261.

Manning, P. K.
1971. The police: mandate, strategies, and tactics. *Crime and justice in American society,* edited by J. D. Douglas. Indianapolis: Bobbs-Merrill.

1974. *Organizations as situationally justified action* presented at the VIII World Congress of Sociology, Toronto, Canada.

McEachern, A., and Bauer, A.
1967. Factors relating to disposition in juvenile-police contacts. *Juvenile gangs in context,* edited by Klein and Neyerhoff. Englewood Cliffs: Prentice Hall.

Niederhoffer, A.
1967. *Behind the shield.* New York: Doubleday.

Parsons, T.
1951. *The social system.* Glencoe: The Free Press.

Piliavin, I. and Briar, S.
1964. Police encounters with juveniles. *American journal of sociology* LXX (September): 206-214.

Pitts-Rivers, J.
1967. Contextual analysis and the laws of the model. *Archives of european sociology* VII: 15-34.

Rappaport, R. A.
1971. Ritual, sanctity and cybernetics. *American anthropologist* 73 (February): 59-76.

Reiss, A. J. Jr.
1971. *The police and the public.* New Haven: Yale University Press.

Selznick, P.
1966. *TVA and the grassroots.* New York: Harper Torch Books.

Silver, A.
1967. The demand for order in civil society. *The police,* edited by David Bordua. New York: Wiley.

Skolnick, J.
1966. *Justice without trial.* New York: Wiley.

Stark, R.
1972. *Police riots.* Belmont, California: Wadsworth.

Terry, R.
   1967. The screening of juvenile offenders. *Journal of criminal law, criminology and police science,* **58**: 173-181.

Westley, W.
   1953. Violence and the police. *American journal of sociology* **59** (July): 34-41.

Wilson, J. Q.
   1967. A reader's guide to the presidents' crime commission reports. *Public interest* (Fall).

   1968. *Varieties of police behavior.* Cambridge: Harvard University Press.

Wilson, O. W., and McLaren, R.
   1972. *Police administration.* New York: McGraw Hill.

Young, J.
   1971. The role of the police as amplifiers of deviance, negotiators of reality, and translators of fantasy. *Images of deviance,* edited by S. Cohen. Harmondsworth: Penguin.

9. *Our sentencing laws, according to Dershowitz, reflect either social concern with the practicality of social justice or the philosophic obligations of individual justice. The two concepts have been approached as being mutually exclusive: hence the difficulties of judgment.*

The problem of seeing "that justice is not only done but [that it] appears to be done"* is further complicated by the present educational and professional preparation of individuals for the judicial seat. Frankel, in his criticism of law school curricula, states that very little emphasis is placed on sentencing. This is accountable for the situation Dershowitz describes (Article #8) in the following quote: "Courts feel more comfortable placing procedural, rather than substantive limitations on legislatively authorized programs." That is, the subtleties inherent in deciding the fate of another individual provide unsteady ground for judges who are, according to Frankel, uncomfortably aware that they are "only human." Strict procedural considerations, on the other hand, supply adequate guidelines for those who are unwilling to jeopardize their sense of authoritative superiority.

Frankel also ascribes the rather impotent state of our courts to the lack of "professional criteria [that do not] include meaningful inquiries as to whether the prospective judge is fit to wield the awesome sentencing power." The complicated nature of sentencing trends alone (as Dershowitz explains in his historical analysis) is enough to discourage the most astute of judges. The lack, then, of "meaningful inquiries" in deciding who can and who cannot judge severely exacerbates courtroom attempts to even appear just in sentencing decisions.

The author of "Individualized Judges" tells the reader that he is compelled to write on "the large and unregulated character of the sentencing power, the resulting arbitrariness permitted in its exercise, [and] the frightening chanciness of judicial tempers and reactions." The state of our sentencing laws, his first concern, is fully examined by Dershowitz in Article 8 of this section. Frankel concentrates most of his discussion on the "whys" of courtroom inequities. The judicial personality that Frankel touches upon lightly but nonetheless disconcertingly, is elaborated upon in Article 10, "The Psychology of Judges."

*See also the introductory essay to Article 11.

INDIVIDUALIZED JUDGES

MARVIN FRANKEL

The absurdities of our sentencing laws would remain aesthetically repulsive, but might be otherwise tolerable, if our judges were uniformly brilliant, sensitive, and humane. Though I yield only to numerous judges in my admiration for those on the bench, I must acknowledge that we do not, in fact, approach any such state of affairs. Judges, I think, tend to be like people, perhaps even some cuts above the mine run but, unfortunately, less than gods or angels. And how, after all, could we dream it might be otherwise? Consider whence we acquire our judges, how we select them, how they are trained before and after they don robes.

To start near the beginning, most of our judges have been trained as lawyers. (There is a disappearing breed of petty magistrates for whom this is not necessarily true, and the picture is more bleak with respect to them.) Substantially nothing in the law curriculum is relevant to problems of sentencing. Indeed, until the last decade or so, the entire field of criminal law, being neither lucrative not prestigious, occupied only a small and disfavored corner of our law schools' attention. While that state of neglect has undergone extensive repairs, these have scarcely grazed the area of interest here. Law students learn something about the rules of the criminal law, about the trial of cases, and, increasingly, about the rights of defendants before and during trial. They receive almost no instruction pertinent to sentencing. They may hear some fleeting references to the purposes of criminal penalties—some generalities about retribution, deterrence, etc. But so far as any intentional consequences of their legal education are concerned, they are taught by people and exposed to curricula barren of even food for thought about sentencing.[1]

From among the total supply of law graduates who have not studied sentencing, there emerges in twenty or thirty years the narrower group from which we select the bulk of our judges. The most notable thing about this group for present purposes is that its members have mostly remained unencumbered by any exposure to, or learning about, the problems of sentencing. Characterized by their dominant attributes, our judges are men (mostly) of no longer tender years who have not associated much with criminal defendants, who have not seemed shrilly unorthodox, who have not lived recently in poverty, who have been modestly or more successful in their profession. They are likely to have had more than an average lawyer's amount of experience in the courtroom, though it is a little remarkable how large a percentage of those who go on the bench lack this credential.[2] They are unlikely to have defended more than a couple of criminal cases, if that many. They are more likely to have done a stint as prosecutors, usually as a brief chapter in the years shortly after law school. However much or little they have been exposed to the criminal trial process, most people ascending (as we say) the bench have paid only the most fleeting and superficial attention to matters affecting the sentences of convicted defendants. In this respect, the pattern set in the law school is carried forward and re-enforced. The professional show ends with the verdict or the plea. The histrionics later on at the sentencing proceeding may be moving or embarrassing, even effective on occasion, but are no part of the skills the average lawyer prizes and polishes as special tools of his trade.

Whatever few things may be said for them, our procedures for selecting judges do not improve the prospects of sensitive, knowledgeable sentencing. It may happen sometimes, but I do not recall ever hearing anything relevant to that subject in discussions of the qualifications of prospective judges. I put to one side for this purpose the disgraceful process, widely used, of political nominations, where the candidates are too often selected without concern for any of the qualities supposedly wanted in suitable judges. Even where relevant questions are asked, the professional criteria, reflecting the training and the profession at work, simply do not include meaningful inquiries as to whether the prospective judge is fit to wield the awesome sentencing power. Apart from elementary, and usually superficial, glances at vague qualities of "temperament," we would not know really where to look or what to ask on a subject destined to loom so large among the prospective judge's impacts upon his fellow citizens.

The judges fetched up in the process are a mixed bag, without many surprises. Some grow to be concerned and spend substantial time brooding about their sentencing responsibilities. Most, I think, are not so preoccupied. Judges are commonly heard to say that sentencing is the grimmest and most solemnly absorbing of their tasks. This is not exactly hypocrisy. It is, however, among the less meaningful things judges report about their work. Measured by the time devoted to it, by the amount of deliberation and study before each decision, and by the attention to the subject as a field of intellectual concern in general, the judges' effective expenditures of themselves in worries over sentencing do not reflect a profound sense of mission. Judges don't talk much, to each other or to anyone, about the issues and difficulties in sentencing. They don't read or write about such things. Because strictly "legal" problems are rare in this area, and appeals are normally not allowed to attack the sentence, the reading pile rarely contains anything pertinent. The judge is likely to read thick briefs, hear oral argument, and then take days or weeks to decide who breached a contract for delivery of onions. The same judge will read a presentence report, perhaps talk to a probation officer, hear a few minutes of pleas for mercy—invest, in sum, less than an hour in all—before imposing a sentence of ten years in prison.

Some judges, confronting the enormities of what they do and how they do it, are visited with occasional onsets of horror or, at least, self-doubt. Learned Hand—to some, the greatest of our judges; to all, among a small handful of the greatest—reflecting such sentiments. Never accounted soft toward criminals among any who knew his work, he said of his role in sentencing: "Here I am an old man in a long nightgown making muffled noises at people who may be no worse than I am." A distinguished committee of federal judges, with Hand among its members, acknowledged "the incompetency of certain types of judges to impose sentence." It spoke of judges "not temperamentally equipped" to learn this task acceptably, of judges who compensate for their own inadequacies by "the practice of imposing severe sentences," of judges "who crusade against certain crimes which they feel disposed to stamp out by drastic sentences."[3] Other judges have expressed similar misgivings—about their own and (perhaps more strongly) about their colleagues' handling of powers so huge and so undefined over the lives of their fellow men.

Self-criticism, uncertainty, and a resultant disposition toward restraint are useful qualities in judges—for sentencing and for other aspects of the job. They are not, however, in oversupply. The kinds of people who make their way onto the bench are not by and large given to humility. If there are seeds of meekness to begin with, the trial bench is not the most fertile place for their cultivation. The trial judge may be reversed with regularity; he may be the butt of lawyers' jokes and an object lesson in the law schools; but the incidents of his daily life—the rituals of deference, the high bench, the visible evidences of power asserted directly and face-to-face—are not designed to shrink his self-image. It should be said in all fairness that the Hamlets of this world are not suited to the business of presiding over trial courts. Scores of things must be decided every day. It is often

> ## "the Hamlets of this world are not suited to the business of presiding over trial courts."

more important, as Brandeis taught, that the decisions be made than that they be correct. Both the volume and the nature of the enterprise—the regulation of the flow of evidence, the predictable eruption of emergencies, the endless stream of cloudly questions demanding swift answers—generate pressures for decisive action. And so the trial judge, who starts his career well along the course of a life in which self-effacement has not been the key thing, is encouraged to follow his assertive ways.

Conditioned in the direction of authoritarianism by his daily life in court, long habituated as a lawyer to the stance of the aggressive contestant, and exercising sentencing powers frequently without practical limits, the trial judge is not discouraged from venting any tendencies toward righteous arrogance. The books and the reliable folklore are

> ## "the trial judge is not discouraged from venting any tendencies toward righteous arrogance."

filled with the resulting horror stories—of fierce sentences and orgies of denunciatory attacks upon defendants. One need not be a revolutionist or an enemy of the judiciary to predict that untrained, untested, unsupervised men armed with great power will perpetuate abuses. The horrible cases may result from moral or intellectual or physical deficiencies—or from all together. But we can be sure there will be some substantial number of such cases.

Everyone connected with this grim business has his own favorite atrocity stories. James V. Bennett, the enlightened former Director of the Federal Bureau of Prisons, wrote this often-quoted passage, which appears in a 1964 Senate Document:

> That some judges are arbitrary and even sadistic in their sentencing practices is notoriously a matter of record. By reason of senility or a virtually pathological emotional complex some judges summarily impose the maximum on defendants convicted of certain types of crimes or all types of crimes. One judge's disposition along this line was a major factor in bringing about a sitdown strike at Connecticut's Wethersfield Prison in 1956. There is one judge who, as a matter of routine, always gives the maximum sentence and who of course is avoided by every defense lawyer. If they have the misfortune of having their case arise before him they lay the ground for appeals since experience has indicated the appeals court is sympathetic and will, if possible, overturn the sentencing court. I know of one judge who continued to sit on the bench and sentence defendants to prison while he was undergoing shock treatments for a mental illness.[4]

Foregoing the temptation to parade more lurid instances, I think a couple of mild, substantially colorless cases within my own ken give some sense of the unchained sentencing power in operation. One story concerns a casual anecdote over cocktails in a rare conversation among judges touching the subject of sentencing. Judge X, to designate him in a lawyerlike way, told of a defendant for whom the judge, after reading the presentence report, had decided tentatively upon a sentence of four years' imprisonment. At the sentencing hearing in the courtroom, after hearing counsel, Judge X invited the defendant to exercise his right to address the court in his own behalf. The defendant took a sheaf of papers from his pocket and proceeded to read from them, excoriating the judge, the "kangaroo court" in which he'd been tried, and the legal establishment in general. Completing the story, Judge X said, "I listened without interrupting. Finally, when he said he was through, I simply gave the son of a bitch five years instead of the four." None of the three judges listening to that (including me) tendered a whisper of dissent, let alone a scream of outrage. But think about it. Not the relatively harmless, if revealing, reference to the defendant as a son of a bitch. But a year in prison for speaking disrespectfully to a judge.[5] Was that, perhaps, based upon a rapid, subtle judgment that a defendant behaving this way in the courtroom showed insufficient evidence of remorse and prospects of reform? I confidently think not. Should defendants be warned that exercise of their "right" to address the court may be this costly? They are not.[6] Would we tolerate an act of Congress penalizing such an outburst by a year in prison? The question, however rhetorical, misses one truly exquisite note of agony: that the wretch sentenced by Judge X never knew, because he was never told, how the fifth year of his term came to be added.

That short story epitomizes much that prompts me to be writing this: the large and unregulated character of the sentencing power, the resulting arbitrariness permitted in its exercise, the frightening chanciness of judicial tempers and reactions. Whatever our platonic vision of the judge may be, this subject, like others, must be considered in the setting of a real world of real, mixed, fallible judicial types.

Let me turn here to my second, somewhat more appalling, anecdote. I happened a few years ago to preside at

> *". . . this subject, like others may be considered in the setting of a real world of real, mixed, fallible judicial types."*

a widely publicized trial of a government official charged with corrupt behavior and perjury, convicted finally on a perjury count. While the conviction was for perjury only, the aura of corruption tended to overhand the case. In the weeks between the verdict and the sentence, as sometimes happens, I received some unsolicited mail, often vindictive in tone, not infrequently anonymous. One letter was from a more august source. A state trial judge, from Florida, wrote as follows:

Dear Judge Frankel:
I have read with interest the proceedings in the case involving above Defendant and his influence peddling, perjury, etc....
One of the more serious problems

*confronting Judges in the State
Courts, such as the one in which I
preside, is the leniency extended by
the Federal Judiciary and the pam-
pering of prisoners and parolees by
the Federal Penal and Parole
Systems. It is difficult for me to
justify giving an individual 10, 15, 20
years or life for armed robberies
involving a few dollars when persons
in the Federal Judicial System are
usually given much small sentences
and are paroled after having served a
few months or years of their sentences, and then are proceeded to be
loosely supervised by an overly
compassionate and headturning
parole system.*

*Accordingly, as an individual, as a
Judge in the State Court, as a father
of a young man serving upon the
High Seas of the country as an
enlisted man, and as the step-father
of a drafted Army Private on Asiatic
soil, and as an individual who has
served honorably for five years in the
service of the United States Navy in
wartime, let me strongly urge upon
you that you impose the maximum
sentence as provided by law upon
the above Defendant, and upon any
other individuals who would tend to
destroy and demoralize our nation's
government from within.*

The author of that letter was deeply
in earnest. What he wrote was not
intended as a caricature. I am sure he
did not mean to document the
enormities we invite when we em-
power untested and unqualified officials to spew wholesale sentences of
"10, 15, 20 years or life for armed
robberies involving a few dollars...."
He was not applying for the analyst's
couch when he tendered up his
generations of patriotism, his cruelty,
and his confident ownership of ultimate truths. He was not—I assume,
regretfully, he still is not—slowed for
a second by any shibboleth about
"individualized treatment" when he
offered advice on sentencing to a
fellow judge based upon newspaper
intelligence, without even seeing the
defendant or reading a presentence
report.

What that Florida colleague did was
merely to dramatize the macabre point
that sweeping penalty statutes allow
sentences to be "individualized" not
so much in terms of defendants but
mainly in terms of the wide spectrums
of character, bias, neurosis, and daily
vagary encountered among occupants
of the trial bench. It is no wonder that
wherever supposed professionals in
the field—criminologists, penolo-
gists, probation officers, and, yes,
lawyers and judges—discuss sentencing, the talk inevitably dwells upon
the problem of "disparity." Some
writers have quibbled about the defini-
tiveness of the evidence showing
disparity. It is among the least
substantial of quibbles. The evidence
is conclusive that judges of widely
varying attitudes on sentencing,
administering statutes that confer
huge measures of discretion, mete out
widely divergent sentences where the
divergences are explainable only by
the variations among the judges, not
by material differences in the defendants or their crimes. Even in our age
of science and skepticism, the conclusion would seem to be among
those still acceptable as self-evident.
What would require proof of a weighty
kind, and something astonishing in
the way of theoretical explanation,
would be the suggestion that assorted
judges, subject to little more than
their own unfettered wills, could be
expected to impose consistent
sentences. In any event, if proof
were needed that sentences vary
simply because judges vary, there is
plenty of it. The evidence grows every
time judges gather to discuss specific
cases and compare notes on the
sentences they would impose upon
given defendants. The disparities, if
they are no longer astonishing, remain

horrible.

The broad experience of former Prison Director Bennett merits another quotation here from the 1964 Senate Document mentioned earlier:

> Take, for instance, the cases of two men we received last spring. The first man had been convicted of cashing a check for $58.40. He was out of work at the time of his offense, and when his wife became ill and he needed money for rent, food, and doctor bills, he became the victim of temptation. He had no prior criminal record. The other man cashed a check for $35.20. He was also out of work and his wife had left him for another man. His prior record consisted of a drunk charge and a nonsupport charge. Our examination of these two cases indicated no significant differences for sentencing purposes. But they appeared before different judges and the first man received 15 years in prison and the second man 30 days.
>
> These are not cases picked out of thin air. In January the President of the United States commuted to time served the sentence of a first offender, a former Army lieutenant, and a veteran of over 500 days in combat, who had been given 18 years for forging six small checks.
>
> In one of our institutions a middle-aged credit union treasurer is serving 117 days for embezzling $24,000 in order to cover his gambling debts. On the other hand, another middle-aged embezzler with a fine past record and a fine family is serving 20 years, with 5 years probation to follow. At the same institution is a war veteran, a 39-year-old attorney who has never been in trouble before, serving 11 years for illegally importing parrots into this country. Another who is destined for the same institution is a middle-aged tax accountant who on tax fraud charges received 31 years and 31 days in consecutive sentences. In stark contrast, at the same institution last year an unstable young man served out his 98-day sentence for armed bank robbery.[7]

Protesting more than enough, let me say again that the tragic state of disorder in our sentencing practices is not attributable to any unique endowments of sadism or bestiality among judges as a species. Without claiming absolute detachment, I am prepared to hypothesize that judges in general, if only because of occupational conditioning, may be somewhat calmer, more dispassionate, and more humane than the average of people across the board. But nobody has the experience of being sentenced by "judges in general." The particular defendant on some existential day confronts a specific judge. The occupant of the bench on that day may be punitive, patriotic, self-righteous, guilt-ridden, and more than customarily dyspeptic. The vice in our system is that all such qualities have free rein as well as potentially fatal impact upon the defendant's finite life.

Such individual, personal powers are not evil only, or mainly, because evil people may come to hold positions of authority. The more pervasive wrong is that a regime of substantially limitless discretion is by definition arbitrary, capricious, and antithetical to the rule of law. Some judges I know believe (and act on the belief) that all draft resisters should receive the maximum sentence, five years; this iron view rests variously upon calculations concerning time off for good behavior, how long those in uniform serve, how contemptible it is to refuse military service, etc. Other judges I know have thought, at least lately, that persons opposing service on grounds of moral or other principle, even if technically guilty of a felony, should be subjected to token terms in prison, or none at all. It is not directly pertinent here whether either category of judge is right, or whether both have failed to exercise, case by case, the discretion with which the law entrusts them. The simple point at the moment is the contrast between such individual, personal, conflicting criteria and the ideal of the rule of law.

Beyond the random spreads of judicial attitudes, there is broad latitude in our sentencing laws for kinds of class bias that are commonly known, never explicitly acknowledged, and at war with the superficial neutrality of the statute as literally written. Judges are on the whole more likely to have known personally tax evaders, or people just like tax evaders, than car thieves or dope pushers. Dichotomies of a similar kind are obvious beyond the need to multiply examples. Can such items of personal experience fail to have effect upon sentencing? I do not stop at simpleminded observations about the substantial numbers of judges who simply do not impose prison sentences for tax evasion though the federal law, for example, provides a maximum of five years per count (and tax-evasion prosecutions frequently involve several tax years, with each a separate count). There are more things at stake than judicial "bias" when tax evaders average relatively rare and brief prison terms, while more frequent and much longer average terms (under a statute carrying the same five-year maximum) are imposed for interstate transport of stolen motor vehicles.[8] Whatever other factors may be operating, however, it is not possible to avoid the impression that the judges' private senses of good and evil are playing significant parts no matter what the law on the books may define as the relative gravity of the several crimes. And, although it anticipates a later subject, this is certainly the focus of the familiar jailhouse complaint that "the more you steal, the less of a sentence you get." I believe the complaint has a basis in the fundamental realities and in the way justice is seen to be dispensed. The latter aspect is important in itself; among our sounder aphorisms is the one teaching that justice must not only be done, but must appear to be done. Both objectives are missed by a system leaving to individual preferences and value judgments the kind of discretion our judges have over sentencing.

I have touched upon individual traits of temperament and variations of an ideological, political, or social character. The sentencing power is so far unregulated that even matters of a relatively technical, seemingly "legal" nature are left for the individual judge, and thus for whimsical handling, at least in the sense that no two judges need be the same. Should a defendant be deemed to deserve some leniency if he has pled guilty rather than going to trial? Many judges say yes; many, perhaps a minority, say no; all do as they please. Should a prior criminal record enhance punishment? Most judges seem to think so. Some take the view that having "paid the price" for prior offenses, the defendant should not pay again now. Again, dealer's choice. Many judges believe it a mitigating factor if defendant yields to the pressure, moral or other, to pay back what he has taken. Others condemn this view as an illicit use of criminal sanctions for private redress. Once more, no rule of law enforces either of these contradictory judgments. There other illustrations—relating, for example, to family conditions, defendant's behavior at trial, the consideration, if any, for turning state's evidence—all subject to the varying and unregulated views of judges. The point is, I hope, sufficiently made that our sentencing judgments splay wildly as results of unpredictable and numerous variables embodied in the numerous and variegated inhabitants of our trial benches.

Among the articles of wisdom for which we honor those who wrote the American Constitution was the keen concern to test all powers by the possibility of having wicked or other- wise unsound men in office. In this realistic light, it was deemed vital to confine power as much as possible and to hedge it about with checking and balancing powers. Like every- thing, such precautions can be over- done. But we have lost sight of them almost entirely, and without justifica- tion, in our sweeping grants of sentencing authority.

Notes

[1]Everything in law, as in life, has exceptions. So I should acknowledge that there are here and there in the law schools some meaningful offerings on the subject. Prof. Leonard Orland of the Univ. of Conn. Law School has lately been giving a well-stocked course on post-conviction matters, including significant and provocative ideas about sentencing. My thoughtful and energetic colleague on the Federal District Court for the So. Dist. of N.Y., Judge Harold R. Tyler, Jr., has been finding time in recent years to offer enlightenment on similar subjects at the N.Y. Univ. School of Law. I am certain there are other things of the sort in progress elsewhere. The general point I have made remains basically accurate even today and was sound without noticeable qualification when people now judging went to law school.

[2]I am not myself in a position for exuberant stone-throwing. Before, I became a trial judge in 1965, I had spent many years working mainly as an appellate lawyer. I had tried some cases and done a fair amount of trial lawyer's work, but had managed somehow never to face a jury. I had argued criminal appeals, but had never been on either side of a criminal trial. In defense of myself and the bar-association committees that found me acceptable, if not the answer to their prayers, I think it fair to add that the mechanics and economics of big-city law practice lead the members of large, respectable law firms to settle most of their clients' disputes short of actual trial.

[3]Judicial Conference of Senior Circuit Judges, *Report of the Committee on Punishment for Crime* (1942), pp. 26, 27.

[4]"The Sentence—Its Relation to Crime and Rehabilitation," in *Of Prisons and Justice*. S. Doc. No. 70, 88th Cong., 2d sess., (1964), p. 311.

[5]Only the prissiness of a lawyer's training would require a footnote here to acknowledge that I have neglected the calculation of probable time off for good behavior.

[6]Dr. Willard Gaylin, in his work *In the Service of their Country—War Resisters in Prison* (New York: Viking Press, 1970), p. 283, reports an episode identical with mine about Judge X. There is other evidence—including, I fear, some results of my own introspection—that the defendant's rare outburst may carry a monstrous price.

[7]"Countdown for Judicial Sentencing" in *Of Prisons and Justice, supra* note 4.

[8]It may serve only to confirm a priori hunches, but consider these illustrative figures for federal sentences in the fiscal year 1969. Of 502 defendants convicted for income tax fraud, 95, or 19 percent, received prison terms, the average term being 3 months. Of 3,791 defendants sentenced for auto theft, 2,373, or 63 percent, went to prison, the average term being 7.6 months. From the Administrative Office of the U.S. Courts' publication, *Federal Offenders in the United States District Courts,* 1969, pp. 146-7 (1971).

10. *All criminal justice agencies suffer from the public's tendency to believe that "the law [is] a closed system of great orderliness that manifests a grand design which rules the legal relations of men." Therefore, when criminal justice personnel err, the public often overreacts; human fallibility displayed by agents of social control causes social insecurity. Hence, FBI Director Clarence Kelly's use of federal funds for window valances—an innocent faux pas in view of the Watergate days—leads to sanctimonious moralizings of "What's this world coming to?"*

The judge holds an exalted position in our society. For years, as indicated by the studies cited in this excerpt, researchers have been concerned with "the formal ethics and actual practice" of judges. The authors of the next article begin their discussion by describing the ideal judge, his duties, and the extent of his influence on other members of the courtroom. Their article gains impetus, once given this idealistic description of the judicial role, as it reveals the impossibilities of any judge being perfect— the impossibility, in other words, of complete judicial objectivity. As the authors anticlimatically state, in their denouncement of the "ideal judge," in a real world, "the dissonance between the individual's life style and the demand of his role may lead to problems."

THE PSYCHOLOGY OF JUDGES

CHARLES WINICK, ISRAEL GERVER, and ABRAHAM BLUMBERG

De Tocqueville wrote over a century ago that in America most major, as well as minor, problems ultimately find their way into the courts (De Tocqueville, 1945). For example, in one year 1,330,000 people used the courts in the states of New York and California alone (Blaustein and Porter, 1954). Of the 7,903 judges officially reported in the courts of America, 621 are on the federal bench, 5,041 are state or county judges, and 2,241 sit in city courts (Bureau, 1958). Many other thousands of judges serve in police courts or as justices of the peace, although many of them may have other occupations. Perhaps as many as 5 percent of the country's approximately 250,000 lawyers are thus serving as judges at any one time.

The judge represents one of the few occupations which enjoys extremely high status in practically all modern cultures. The exceptionally high status of judges and their removal from ordinary interpersonal contact is underscored by their robes of office, the judges' sitting above the general room level, and the rather absolute power of judges in their courtrooms. Great respect is generally shown for the office, which is usually designated by very honorific titles. Judges indicate awareness of the reification and depersonalization of their offices by referring to themselves as "the Court" or "the Bench." Many if not most lawyers see judgeship as a proper climax to a career in the law.

The image of the judiciary is thus, at least since Old Testament days, of a group of aloof holders of great power. In some ways they are analogous to revered theologians who interpret Scripture, and they have been instrumental in developing the law into a kind of secular theology. Just as the meaning of Scripture is continually being modified by commentators, the meaning of the law is continually being modified by other judges.

The enormous prestige of the judge in America is exemplified in two situations involving judges which have resulted in much popular and other reaction. The discussion over the mysterious disappearance in 1930 of New York's Justice Crater continues to this day because it is inconceivable that a judge would disappear voluntarily. When Federal Judge Manton—an exponent of Natural Law—was found guilty in 1939 of accepting bribes, the expectations of his high office were stridently violated, and the case occasioned much comment. A federal judge, in contrast to more ordinary mortals, was assumed to be immune from such temptation.

The great importance of the work of judges makes it curious that there is relatively little agreement on the qualities of a good judge or on how judges reach their decisions. This lack of agreement, however, helps to explain why the judiciary is the only profession in our society for which there is no specific training or preparation. Inasmuch as the great

> **"the judiciary is the only profession in our society for which there is no specific training or preparation."**

majority of our judges are elected and not appointed, it is the voters of America who are regularly called upon to evaluate the background of candidates for the bench.

The Judge's Job

Although there is not a complete agreement on the exact qualities of a good judge, Hobbes's discussion has been the basis for most later commentators: "The things that make a good judge...are, first, a right understanding of that principal law of nature called equity, which depends...on the goodness of a man's own natural reason, and meditation. . . . Secondly, contempt of unnecessary riches and preferments. Thirdly, to be able in judgment to divest himself of all fear, anger, hatred, love and compassion. Fourthly and lastly, patience to hear, diligent attention in hearing, and memory to retain, digest and apply what he has heard" (Hobbes, 1950).

These qualities are relevant to the work of the judge. The judge is the umpire in the courtroom warfare known as the trial. The trial judge has a role in jury selection and in the admission of evidence; by his rulings on specific applications of law, he is contributing toward the record of the trial that will be necessary in any appeal which may be taken. The judge's subpoena powers enable him to compel the production of records and the appearance and testimony of witnesses. The judge maintains order and discipline and exerts extraordinary control over the conduct of attorneys and other participants in a trial. The judge's power to set aside verdicts, to direct verdicts, to rule on the various motions of counsel, and to effect settlements enables him to dominate the course of litigation.

The judge has a major role in connection with the historic doctrine of judicial review, by which the judge can declare legislative acts unconstitutional (Marbury, 1803). The judge's sentencing power in criminal cases enables him to reinforce the values of society and the distinction between the transgressor and the society which exercises the sentencing power. Ross has stressed that "punishment must not appear as natural brute violence, but as the act of God or of Justice. It must firmly ally itself with the religious and moral ideas of the time, and avoid the appearance of being a blow dealt by a victor to his prostrate foe" (Ross, 1926).

In spite of the enormous importance

of the judge's sentencing power in criminal cases, the bulk of the work of the courts is devoted to civil cases and to the resolution of disputes affecting property. In the prestige hierarchy of judges and lawyers, those engaged in the criminal courts are generally on lower levels of prestige, however important their work is. The civil courts oversee the orderly transfer of wealth in our society by their appointment of receivers, executors, administrators, trustees, guardians, and other caretakers of property.

The Making of Judicial Decisions

One of the central activities of the judge is making decisions. The decision has both a public or manifest and a private or latent aspect. The public aspect consists of what the judge communicates publicly, either orally in the courtroom or in a written opinion. An opinion is a statement by a judge in which he explains why he decided as he did. He states the facts as he sees them and the legal rules he applied. Any such public communication of a decision is likely to be made by the judge in accordance with the well-established principle of social psychology that a communicator's message is modified by his perception of his audience (Pool and Shulman, 1959).[1]

Different judges may be talking to different audiences in their decisions and opinions. Some judges seem to be talking to the general public in comments associated with decisions in the sentencing of criminal offenders. These comments may be reflections of the judge's belief in the power of his observations to deter future criminals, a desire to maintain a particular reputation, a wish to cater to public pressures, or a desire to keep his name before the voters for purposes of re-election or election to other office. Those judges who seem to be communicating with their col-

leagues may be demonstrating, for several reasons, their awareness of the human condition, or their flair for fine reasoning, apt citations, or legal scholarship. These reasons may include the edification of other lawyers in the courtroom or they may include unseen audiences or "hidden perceivers"—posterity, other judges, other colleagues who may be instrumental in helping the judge in his career, and so on. Or the judge may be giving his opinion in order to avert possible higher judicial reversals or to obtain agreement and support for his opinion at peer levels and from superiors. The specific audience to which the judge is addressing himself is seldom explicitly stated in his decision and can only be inferred on the basis of the context and circumstances of the decision.

Some Contextual Pressures on Judicial Decisions

The specific context and level of jurisdiction of a court may be related to the kind of decision which its judges typically make. The higher the level of a court, the more scrupulous is the care likely to be shown to procedural matters and the greater the concern for all legal rights and protocol. The area of responsibility of a court may be relevant to how its judges perceive their cases. A lower court, such as a magistrate's court in a large city, can, and almost invariably does, pass a case along to another court if there is any indication that the case is problematical, thus postponing its role in the entire decision-making process. A traffic court or a justice of the peace in a smaller community may dispense rough and ready justice which often violates the rights of defendants, but this may seldom be discovered because such cases are only rarely appealed to a higher court. Such a judge is likely to be relatively freewheeling in his decisions.

In addition to this dimension of the level of the court at which the judge presides, there is the important dimension of whether a court has original or appellate jurisdiction. The judge who sits in the court of original jurisdiction, in his role as trial judge, arbiter, sentencer, or awarder, is likely to become involved in the legal, interpersonal, and emotional dynamics of the small group in the courtroom of which the judge is the hub. Even though they are together for a short time, the members of the courtroom group interrelate with each other. The judge in the court of original jurisdiction not only is reacting to witnesses and lawyers, but may also be aware of the shadow of an appellate court passing on any actions or decisions of his which are dubious. He must thus maintain professional impassivity in the courtroom and make his decision with the possibility that the "hidden perceivers" may engage in an appellate review and possibly rebuke him, either because of his application of a specific rule of law to specific facts or because of the facts he has selected as important in a given case or because he has behaved arbitrarily and unreasonably.

The appellate judge is more removed from the original dispute or offense and is therefore relatively unconcerned with the actual interpersonal dynamics in the case. He studies not only the case record on appeal but also what the judge did with the case and whether the original judge behaved with propriety and in accordance with the law. The great majority of cases, however, are not appealed beyond the trial judge's decision; hence the trial judge is a very important figure. In spite of this, the great judges of American tradition are almost always found in appellate courts rather than in courts of original jurisdiction.

Another component of the context within which judicial decisions are made is the pressure upon the judge to reduce a sentence, in response to a request by the prosecuting attorney that he do so in return for a defendant's pleading guilty to a lesser charge. The prosecuting attorney can enter upon discussions with a defendant to plead guilty to a lesser charge only if he has support from the judge. The judge is usually satisfied to do so so long as he regards the sentence for the lesser offense to be adequate punishment (Ohlin and Remington, 1958). The prosecutor initiates such a request in order to avoid overcrowding of trial calendars and long delays. The defendant is usually told that no promises about a lesser sentence can be made to him in response to his plea of guilty, but he is informally advised that it is likely that he will get special consideration.

Another variable related to the social structure of the court is the role of the judge's law clerk or legal secretary. He is usually a lawyer, and either may have political connections or may have graduated from a law school with distinction. Some members of the Supreme Court have been attacked for giving too much responsibility to their law clerks, who are usually recent honor graduates from the national law schools. Whether or not these attacks are justified, they have served to focus attention on the exact role of the law clerk, which may range from legal errand boy and citation searcher through being a sounding board for the judge and actually participating in making decisions in important cases. There is reason to believe that these anonymous law clerks may be important contributors to some decisions. One former law secretary to Justice Holmes has discussed the clerks' influence on the Supreme Court (Konefsky, 1956).

Political pressures may also be among the larger social factors contributing to the context of the judge's decision. There may be some pressures, visible or invisible, on the judge for reasons of partisan politics or business. Even though there may b no pressures on specific cases, t judge may not wish to offend th who have contributed to his past, may control his future when he comes up for reappointment or renomination. Only federal judges and some trial and higher appellate state justices are appointed for life and are thus presumably above political pressures; yet even they may be interested in promotion. Inasmuch as most judgeships are often likely to be political rewards, there is likely to be an assumption of repayment by the judge for the reward, although such assumptions are apt to be tacit on both sides. Appropriate repayment may be in the form of judicial sympathy for the interests of the sponsors or former associates of the judge when litigation involving such interests comes before him. Probate court judges in ten states are permitted to practice law, and it is easy to see how the pressures of the private practice of such judges might affect their judicial functioning.

In order to help judges cope with this kind of difficult contextual situation, the legal profession, through the American Bar Association, has promulgated its own Canons of Judicial Ethics (Cheatham, 1955). These moral guidelines to judicial conduct are based on sources like the Magna Charta (XLV), the Bible (Deuteronomy 16), and Francis Bacon's essay on judicature. The canons range from precepts on the virtues of promptness to the evils of ex parte communication (communication from one litigant without an equal opportunity being afforded the other). The twenty-eighth canon almost spells out the necessity for a judge to avoid political party

120 / THE DYSFUNCTI

Some Personal
Judge's Career

A number
tics of judg
enter into
make de
as well
him
crim
ex

resr
pa
a

press.
tive.

There is som
extent to which judg
the Canons of Judicial Eth
relationship between the forma
and actual practice is a fascinatn.
one for the psychologist to observe.

"the relationship between the formal ethic and actual practice is a fascinating one for the psychologist to observe."

First-person and other accounts by judges generally make it clear that the relationship is also one which is of concern to judges (Botein, 1952; Ulman, 1933; Lummus, 1937). It is difficult to tell whether judges' conduct is ever evaluated dispassionately by others in terms of how judges face these conflict situations. The fact that in the last thirty years *not one* judge has been removed from office by impeachment, which is the appropriate procedure for removal from judicial office, suggests that either judges' handling of these conflicts is impeccable, or there is a feeling that judges' behavior is above reproach and their handling of conflicts of interest is best left unscrutinized.

Variables in the

of personal characteris-
es may be presumed to
the process whereby they
isions. The age of the judge
as the age of the litigant before
nay be relevant. Observers in
nal courts have noted, for
mple, that younger offenders are
kely to get more lenient treatment
from some judges than are older
offenders.

A career on the bench has its own life cycle, and a judge who has just assumed his robe of office may perceive his duties and responsibilities quite differently from the way an older judge perceives his. In contrast to an older judge, the younger man may be very eager to make his mark. It has been noted that many judges tend to become more cautious with age. Other judges tend to become more confident and less susceptible to pressures as they grow older. The older judges, as do ordinary citizens, may become more conservative and tradition-oriented and less experimental. With the experience of years on the bench, some judges tend to be more reserved than they originally were in giving the specific rationale behind a decision. Aging is doubtless a factor in aberrant behavior of judges, and is particularly important because judges are generally named to the bench fairly late in life. There is sometimes a conflict between the relative youth of judges' law clerks and the relative age of the judges themselves.

Ethnic, nationality, religious, and race factors may help or hinder a judge in being appointed or elected or promoted. In American political life, judgeships are often regarded as offices which should be allocated on the basis of these factors. Certain judgeships often seem to be especial-

ly available for persons of specific backgrounds that seem to be under-represented on the bench, especially at election time. Political leaders often make a tacit assumption that the bench's ethnic composition, writ large, should be the same as the electorate's. These background factors may also be very relevant to the judge's judicial behavior. It is likely, for example, that a judge from a minority group might be very harsh on litigants of the dominant ethnic group, perhaps as one means of demonstrating some of his feelings about the dominant group. Another judge from such a group might be "soft" on litigants of the dominant ethnic group as one way of expressing his identification with the regnant group. But to avoid any imputation of favoritism a judge from the minority group might be especially harsh with a litigant from the same group.

Still another judge from the same minority group might be an exceptionally hard worker in order to demonstrate that he made his way to the bench on the basis of merit alone. In all these cases, the specific background of the judge would be directly related to his judicial behavior.

The number of women judges is increasing, especially in courts concerned with family matters and children. There is some reason to believe that a woman who becomes a judge is likely to be a relatively superior person, because of the general prejudice against women lawyers and judges. Some women judges may overreact to this stereotype and be exceptionally rigorous in their decisions, as if to demonstrate that cliches about women's emotionalism are false.

The marital status of the judge may enter into his decisions, especially in matters involving paternity actions, family difficulties, separation or divorce, neglected children, or juvenile delinquency. The divorced judge's attitude toward a divorce action may be quite different from that of a bachelor judge. In one jurisdiction, lawyers representing the husband in marital action are delighted when a particular judge is assigned to the case because the judge's difficulties with his own wife— which are known to the lawyers—often make him especially sympathetic to the husband's side of the story. Whether the judge has any children himself may enter into his decisions involving children, ranging from oversentimentality to avoidance (the judge might say that his "hands are tied by the law"), to extreme vigor in punishing either parents or children for violations of the law.

The socioeconomic status from which the judge came may be relevant to his decisions, depending on the extent to which he has internalized the biases of his particular group. Thus a judge whose father was a successful attorney or a member of any other elite occupation is often likely to have adopted the conservative point of view of his father's occupational group. A judge whose father was a small retail storekeeper, or had some other equally marginal status, may have resented his background and have sought the elite status of a judge and so be ultraconservative. One judge who is the son of a conservative father may be relatively radical, whereas a judge who is the son of a radical may be relatively conservative on the bench, although both men are reacting to their fathers' backgrounds. This kind of inconsistency between social class background and judicial attainment may have resulted in some unusual decisions and opinions.

The law school which the judge attended may have a considerable effect on his decisions. It is curious that the typical judge is more likely not to have attended law school than

is the typical lawyer, and of those judges who did go to law school, there are proportionately more among graduates of unapproved law schools than among graduates of approved law schools (Blaustein and Porter, 1954). The bench clearly is not getting the lawyers with the best training, although this situation may be changing for the better.

The kind of legal practice in which the judge engaged before his appointment undoubtedly has some relationship to the type of decisions he gives. A judge who has been a corporation lawyer is likely to see things differently from the way a judge who has been a criminal lawyer sees them. Individual differences are important because a judge who was a criminal lawyer, as in one case, may become an extremely harsh and tough-minded judge when dealing with the kind of criminals he used to defend, whether because he is reacting against his past or because he believes in severe punishment or because of other reasons. Another judge who was a criminal lawyer may be relatively lenient toward his former clients because he does not believe in severe sentences, as one means of identification with his past, or because of other reasons.

A judge who as a lawyer represented insurance companies in negligence actions, and a judge who used to represent people suing insurance companies are likely to approach a negligence case with different kinds of prebench points of view, which may or may not enter [into] their work as judges. If the financial status of a litigant or lawyer is unusual, whether the judge is relatively wealthy or just struggling along on his salary may enter into his attitudes toward such litigants or their lawyers.

Previous political activity is also often a factor in the context within which the judge will make his decision. A number of similar dimensions of the judge's career lines can be distinguished. They seem to suggest a typology of at least three different kinds of judges. The existence of such types has possible importance because it is likely that each of the different kinds of judges perceives the bench differently and has different motivations for it, and thus may behave differently as a judge.

What can be called the Lower Level of judicial career development is the course followed by perhaps the great majority of lawyers who become judges. Such a person has usually attended a low-level law school and has joined a political club as well as a variety of fraternal, benevolent, and religious organizations. This kind of lawyer will generally take all kinds of cases, perhaps even including some at the suggestion of political leaders. After years of faithful service to his party, such a lawyer will be given a vacancy on the bench. This kind of "ideal type" pattern is likely to be found in many courts of first instance and appearance, such as justices of the peace, traffic courts, and magistrates.

A Middle Level career pattern—would typically include graduation from a law school which is accredited but above the level of the "factory" and below the level of the national law schools. Such a lawyer is likely to have a moderately successful and discriminating practice, more dignified than "ambulance chasing," but he is not with a first-rate law firm. He is likely to exhibit political leadership substantially above the routine service of the Lower Level judge, and to get a Higher Level judgeship.

The Upper Level judge is likely to have come from an elite family, to have been graduated from a national law school, and to have been a member of a well-regarded law firm (Miller, 1951; Mills, 1951). He is also likely to have held relatively important political office and to have demonstrated exceptional ability before getting a relatively High-Level judgeship.

There are, of course, many judges who do not fit into these "ideal types." No typology can adequately capture the range of judicial career patterns. Some lawyers may get to the bench because they are special friends of an unusually well-placed politician. Some lawyers may be wealthy enough to be able to give a large sum to their political party and, all other factors being equal, such a lawyer is more likely to get to the bench than an equally qualified lawyer who has not given any money to the party in power. Two scholars recently reported that it was "rumored" that the "going rate" for judgeships in New York City was the equivalent of two years' salary for the office (Sayre and Kaufman, 1960). Some lawyers may be singled out for the judiciary merely because of their brilliance and knowledge. Some law school professors who have not practiced may be tapped for the bench, but this is relatively infrequent.

There is some reason to speculate on the way in which the judge's career pattern is related to the kind of decision he makes. Of special interest are atypical cases, where a lawyer with one kind of background gets a judgeship that is not one it would be logical to expect him to get. Deviant behavior on the part of judges, like intemperate language or actual crime, as in the case of a recently convicted former Westchester County Surrogate, seems to occur mainly in judges whose position on the bench does not flow naturally from their previous careers. As we would expect from studies into the causes of other forms of deviant behavior, the dissonance between the individual's life style and the demand of his role, may lead to problems (Zajonc, 1952).

Differing Views on the Basis for Judicial Decisions

Some four thousand years ago, when the Code of Hammurabi was promulgated, it was believed that judges' decisions and the law came directly from the gods. By the time of Holme's pioneering studies in the late nineteenth century, it was becoming clear that law was the result of human experience. Up to the early twentieth century, writers on jurisprudence had generally held that judges were able to keep their personalities out of their decisions. Soon after the turn of the century, some students of the courts who were less "tough-minded" than the legal realist school (which held that the law was the decision of judges in particular cases—in contrast to the traditionalist view that the law consists of general rules) were developing the thesis that law is a form of social control. Some of the great exponents of what has been called sociological jurisprudence noted that even distinguished Supreme Court judges like Marshall and Taney differed in their interpretation of the Constitution, and that such differences are partially attributable to the different social, economic, and political backgrounds of the judges (Pound, 1923). These scholars were not suggesting that judges were making decisions on the basis of their economic backgrounds. They were suggesting that the judge's professional education and experience were influential in his decision.

The anthropological approach to judges' decisions has been followed by some writers. Llewellyn has pointed out that there is a procedure for getting rid of precedents which are troublesome and another procedure for using precedents that seem helpful. The same doctrine may be used for a specific purpose as well as for its exact opposite (Llewellyn, 1951). He has suggested that the main function of the courts is not to resolve disputes but to establish "working rules" for society (Llewellyn, 1925). He has urged the study of what judges and courts actually do, and Dean Roscoe Pound has added his great prestige to encouraging the application of the social sciences to the study of what the courts are doing (1938).

Other writers have said that it was less important to study the courts than to study the judges, in terms of what can be called the latent or private aspects of their decisions. As long ago as the sixteenth century, Montaigne commented that the judge's mood and humor varied from day to day and were often reflected in his decisions. Legal scholars have occasionally mocked the importance of such nonrational aspects in a decision and referred to them as "gastronomical jurisprudence," or an explanation of a judge's decision in terms of factors like gastronomical ailments. Such factors doubtless do enter into many judges' decisions, but they are hardly likely to be explicitly stated in the formal decision.

Candid statements about the way in which the judge's personality enters into his decisions have been made by some of America's leading judges. One of the great American judges, who was an outstanding figure in the development of law in New York State, Chancellor James Kent, said well over a century ago, in explaining how he reached a decision: "I might once in a while be embarrassed by a technical rule, but I almost always found principles suited to my view of the case..." (Frank, 1930). Even the famous legal philosopher, Justice Oliver Wendel Holmes, who is perhaps the classical exponent of the modern approach to law, has said that " a decision is the unconscious result of instinctive prejudices and inarticulate connections," and "even the prejudices which judges share with their fellow men have a good deal more to do than the syllogism in determining the rules by which men should be governed" (Holmes, 1881). Justice Cardozo stated that forces which judges "do not recognize and cannot name have been tugging at them... and the result is an outlook on life..." (Cardozo, 1921).

One federal judge, after years of service, concluded that he reached his decisions by hunch or feeling: "I... give my imagination play, and brooding...wait for the feeling, the hunch—that intuitive flash of understanding...." (Hutcheson, 1929). Writing a few years later, a distinguished judge said that a judge reaches his decision "by a 'hunch' as to what is fair and just or wise or expedient...the personality of the judge and the judicial hunch are not and cannot be described in terms of legal rules and principles" (Frank, 1932). Frank has pointed out that the "sentence" which the judge pronounces comes from the Latin verb *sentire,* which means "to feel," and that the judge experiences his decision on an emotional level. In a decision, he wrote that "much harm is done by the myth that merely by putting on a black robe, and taking the oath of office as a judge, a man ceases to be human...If the judge did not form judgments of the actors in those courthouse dramas called trials, he could never render decisions" (Frank, 1946).

The English jurist Lord Macmillan also underscored that "the judge's mind remains a human instrument working as do other minds" (Macmillan, 1937).

A Supreme Court justice frankly stated: "I know that in this great mass of opinions by men of different temperaments and qualifications and viewpoints, writing at different times and under varying local influences, some printed judicial word may be found to support almost any plausible proposition" (Jackson, 1944). This suggests that the judge first reaches his decision and then may look for a precedent to document his "decision," in contrast to the usual view that the precedent search precedes the decision. Just how much of an opportunity a judge has to find the "judicial word" with which he is comfortable can be seen in Justice Stone's estimate that a good law library, as of 1923, would have about 18,500 volumes of reports and 5,500 volumes of statutes, with 350 new volumes of reports and 250 new volumes of statutes each year (Stone, 1924). He estimated that a good law library around A.D. 2023 would have 1,850,000 volumes of reports and 550,000 volumes of statutes. Judges have pointed out that the judge is a human being and does not "clink out" decisions as a computer does (Tate, 1958), but is practicing an art (Yankwich, 1957).

A number of judges have thus stated quite frankly that instead of following a formal logical scheme, they reach their decisions by a kind of intuitive Gestalt impression of the case and its issues. If there are many judges who do reach their decisions in this way, it is important to know this as well as to know how many judges do so. Its implications for juridical science are central: it is like the difference between explaining a particular learning phenomenon in Gestalt principles in contrast to the traditional theory that judges reach their decisions by a logical process akin to learning theory. Among the possible implications for the student of the bench is that the precedents and legal reasoning cited by the judge may not actually be the private rationale for some decisions.

One authority who conducted psychological studies of judicial decisions said flatly that every judicial opinion "amounts to a confession" by the judge (Schroeder, 1918). He presented a hypothetical case in which the judge's decision was a direct reflection of "fearful phantasies from his own past," instead of a wise adjudication. A pioneering student of personal factors in judges' decisions examined the way in which different New York magistrates, in 1916, were handling the same offense (Haines, 1923). He found that the proportion of cases dismissed ranged from 6.7 percent for one magistrate to 73.7 percent for another. One magistrate discharged 18 percent of his disorderly conduct cases and another discharged 54 percent. Haines reasoned that personality factors in each judge were probably responsible for the huge spread between the sentencing behavior of one judge and another. The fate of a litigant who appeared in this court was thus clearly a function of the judge before whom he was fortunate or unfortunate enough to appear. Another empirical investigation of court behavior found "criminal courts in Chicago today... twisting the law and inventing fictions to attain results they regard as just" (Hall, 1935). Other studies have suggested the possibility that some judges have favorite numbers which they use in establishing sentences (Burtt, 1931; Gaudet et al., 1934).

Legal scholars have discussed the personal and even idiosyncratic components in the work of the bench. Dean Roscoe Pound has praised Bergsonian intuition in a judge as a desirable quality (Pound, 1925). One noted student of the logic of law admitted that "unmistakable directions, irrestible implications, are few" for the judge (Radin, 1925). One member of what can be called the realistic school of judicial interpretation said that the behavior of judges exhibits a "predictable uniformity" because human values of judges suggested the kinds of decisions they

would render (Cohen, 1935).

A related viewpoint is that many judicial decisions are essentially fictions because "many of the most beautifully intricate and subtle of legal theories are merely a form of legal rationalization or fiction....Theories are now recognized as often a means of justifying decisions rather than as reasons for making them" (Bohlen, 1935). Another scholar presented the view that judges engage in a kind of mental gymnastics or "jurisprudential fictions," which they use in order to justify and rationalize their decisions (Fuller, 1931), and he established a typology of legal fictions. One scholar has frankly stated that judges seldom give the "real motives and reasons" behind their decisions (Rohrlich, 1931), although he believes it is best that the public not know of these "real" motivating factors.

Even though experienced jurists and scholars have repeatedly emphasized the personal factors which are related to the judge's decision, the more formal point of view toward judicial decisions has also been a continuing tradition (Radin, 1925; Dewey, 1924). Some legal scholars have suggested the possibility that law can some day be made almost as precise as geometry (Cairns, 1941). Justice Frankfurter has repeatedly urged that the message of the statutes is clear and that judges should do as the statutes suggest (Frankfurter, 1947). He has urged that a judge "move within the framework of relevant legal rules and the covenanted modes of thought for ascertaining them.... This is achieved through training, professional habits, self-discipline and that fortunate alchemy by which men are loyal to the obligation with which they are entrusted...." (Frankfurter, 1952).

Justice Frankfurter has urged that, in the absence of obvious constitutional defects, courts be loath to overturn legislative judgments as embodied in statutes. He has also indicated in the strongest terms that judges desist from substituting their proclivities, tastes, and notions of justice or goodness for that of the people as they have expressed themselves through their legislatures.

Another point of view on the judge's function sees the decision as an instrument of social control in the hands of a completely rational judge (Michael and Adler, 1933). Justice Douglas is representative of what can be called a social control or libertarian view on the current Supreme Court, and has clearly stated his belief that the judge is not an impersonal arbiter (Douglas, 1959; Schwartz, 1957). The widely discussed differences between the "liberal" and "conservative" (Larson, 1955) members of the Supreme Court have made it clear that even on this highest level, judges may perceive their function differently, and that a study of the personal and social backgrounds of the men on the Court would be as realistic an approach to their decisions as the more usual legal approach (Carr, 1942; Lerner, 1957).

The Psychology of the Judge

The frequent references by legal scholars to the "personality" of the judge are almost never carried into an extended discussion of the subject. If we define "personality" as everything about a person which has relevance to his relations with other people, then it is obvious that many different dimensions of the personal and social background of the judge are relevant. His possible interest in dominance, his needs, his self concept, his ways of achieving security, and his use of unconscious defense mechanisms like projection, rationalization, sublimation, repression, and suppression may all be important.

The behavior of the judge represents a kind of natural convergence between the area of "decision theory" and the area of "role theory" in social psychology. The judge is a person who must make a decision, but under circumstances in which his role as a judge is a reflection of his other and previous roles and of his several group memberships. Any kind of multiple group identification creates problems for the individual (Hartley, 1951). Different judges may have different reference groups (groups with which they identify and which provide standards for decisions). These groups may include the great leaders of the judiciary like Holmes, their colleagues on higher courts, the common man seeking justice, the impersonal majesty of justice, the established power structure of society, an ideal of social amelioration, the lawyers who appear before them, and many others. Conflict between the judge's reference groups may be reflected in his decisions.

The power over other persons which judges wield has been a source of concern to many students of the bench. Some may glory in the power, some may dislike it, and others may be ambivalent about it. It is possible that the power and dominance of the judge's role attracts persons who have an authoritarian inclination. Psychological research has extensively documented that the authoritarian persons are likely to see things in an either-or fashion, rather than in the balanced and democratic manner which is traditionally associated with the judicial temperament (Adorno, 1950). The process of socialization in office may temper the power strivings of judges.

There are courtroom observers who have suggested that perhaps overenthusiastic generalization that some judges are basically insecure people who seek security in the ritualized power embodied in the judicial robe.

Other observers have called attention to the latent psychological functions which may be served for some judges by sentencing.

Since our courts are based on the adversary system, in which points of difference and conflict are explicitly the foci of courtroom discussion, it is possible that there is some self-selection of lawyers who seek the bench because of their interest in this kind of expression of disagreement. Many years ago, in his famous novel *Bleak House,* Charles Dickens expressed the view that there is a specific kind of judge who enjoys the battle of the courts. If Dickens's vision were found to apply to any considerable proportion of the American judiciary, this would certainly be relevant to the study of the psychology of the judge.

The courtroom may provide an outlet for the kind of exhibitionism which has traditionally characterized actors and other near exhibitionists. The judge has a captive audience, in contrast to the actor whose audience may walk out on him at any time, or not even buy a ticket to the theatre. No matter how egocentric the judge's behavior becomes, the lawyers for either side are hardly likely to complain about it. As is true of most professionals, but perhaps especially because his name is affixed to his opinions, the ego of the judge is likely to be deeply involved in his work.

Judges' perception may be very important because their alertness in a trial is of critical importance to both sides. The psychology of perception is as applicable to a judge as to any other person (Bruner and Tagiuri, 1954). One outstanding example of idiosyncratic perception of judges occurred not long ago when a federal trial judge revealed, after years on the bench, that he always assumed that any witness who rubbed his hands while testifying was a liar (Frank, 1949). It is only possible to speculate on the number of unfair decisions which such a judge gave.

The well-established difficulties of memory and cognition which plague witnesses are likely to be multiplied in the case of a judge, who is a witness of the witnesses, and thus perceives at two removes from the reality of the circumstances which gave rise to a trial. One noted student of the law has reported that his task as a young lawyer was to drop books on the floor when a judge began getting drowsy (Gross, 1947).

Predicting Decisions

Professor Oliphant of Columbia Law School was not the first who believed that judicial decisions could be predicted by studying the stimuli, or facts, which were presented to the judge. Oliphant first presented his views in 1928. A well-known mathematician, at about the same time, was exploring the possibility of establishing a science of prediction of judges' decisions (Keyser, 1929). More recently a lawyer and a political scientist have suggested the feasibility of a science of judicial prediction, even though they recognize the role of personality factors of judges and others connected with the trial (Lasswell and McDougal, 1943). One scholar has called for appropriate statistical and probability techniques to summarize how individual judges behave in different kinds of cases (Loevinger, 1949).

One study identified several areas of judicial action to which quantitative methods have been applied with meaningful results (Schubert, 1958). Another study has attempted to quantify any rule of law that makes a decision dependent on combinations of specified controlling circumstances (Kort, 1960). These promising starts have made the possibility of a science of prediction of judicial decision much more realizable.

Suggested Changes

Many recommendations have been made for improving the quality of the work of judges. Such recommendations are usually made very cautiously because of the established tradition of being very reluctant to criticize the judiciary, even inferentially. One such recommendation is that trial judges make written findings of fact (Note, 1948). This might help in the review of a case, define the scope of the decision, increase public confidence in the courts, and reassure the litigants that their case had been carefully considered by the judge. Findings of fact will, it has been suggested, act as a partial check on the judge's subjectivity.

A number of students of the courts, including the Survey of the Legal Profession of the American Bar Association, have recommended that courts use more of the method of relatively informal conferences of all the parties in chambers with the judge (Blaustein and Porter, 1954). It is interesting that judges have often met the recommendation that they seek consonances rather than arbitrate among dissonances with less than marked enthusiasm, a fact which suggests that there are judges who enjoy the combat of the courtroom.

Another suggestion made by an imaginative lawyer and judge urged that prospective judges undergo some kind of psychoanalytic treatment (Frank, 1949), as one way of recognizing the great power of the judge's "personal equation." Such self-exploration, he felt, should be of great help in reducing judicial bias and prejudice. Ideally, such treatment would be repeated throughout the judge's career on the bench. The same student has questioned the whole system of precedent-following by judges, saying that it has roots in emotional immaturity and a need for certainty. Good judges "will not talk of 'rules' and 'principles' as finalities while unconsciously using them as soporifics to allay the pains of uncertainty" (Frank, 1930).

Federal Judge Julian Mack refused to wear a robe when presiding at a trial, and often conducted trials in his chambers, sitting on the same level with the witnesses and lawyers. Others have recommended that judges not wear robes, pointing out that Thomas Jefferson was opposed to any distinctive costume for federal judges. Robes have priestly connotations which many observers believe to be irrelevant to modern life, and which may help lead to stilted and awkward testimony. Other students of the courts have suggested that, as part of becoming more informal, courts abandon the complicated language which they currently use in decisions and speak more plainly, so that they can be both understood and criticized more directly. As long ago as 1898, Justice Brewer suggested the possible value of being critical of the Supreme Court, noting that "the life and character of its Justices should be the objects of constant watchfulness by all." The robe is a symbol of the judge's sealing himself off from criticism.

One suggestion for improving judicial decisions which has been made by a number of legal students is to incorporate more behavioral science into court findings, and possibly train judges in the nature of behavioral science. Critics have observed that classical sources, like Wigmore on Evidence (Wigmore, 1940), do not appear to take any cognizance of what modern behavior science says on subjects like perception and consciousness. Judges daily deal with subjects on which the behavioral sciences have collected much data, and they almost never refer to such data. The 1954 Supreme Court desegregation decision was a major decision that did draw on such materials (Brown, 1954). In another series of decisions the Court has stated that a jury must be representative of the community from which it is drawn if it is to be impartial, thus recognizing dimensions similar to those used in selecting a sample by survey technicians (Robinson, 1950). Such use of behavioral science is rare.

Despite some of the statements made about the wisdom of integrating social science findings with legal materials in the desegregation decision, such materials were used in the courts over a half century ago. In an epoch-making brief (Muller, 1908), Brandeis successfully urged that economic and social data were as relevant in a case involving the constitutionality of a law limiting the working hours of women as the legal principles. Ever since, the Brandeis Brief has been the designation for a brief which includes nonlegal material of probative value to the propositions being urged upon a court. Since such procedures are established, their relative nonuse by judges leads to speculations on the reasons for their nonuse.

One such reason is that judges may be afraid of being considered "unlawyerlike" and possibly overruled. Another reason is the nature of law school training and the history and development of legal institutions including the common law. The writings of legal philosophers and judges, beginning with Henry De Bracton in the thirteenth century, express an overt or covert yearning for predictability and certainty. As Redmount points out, the law often appears to be a closed system of great orderliness that manifests a grand design which rules the legal relations of men. Judges trained in such a system and accustomed to the doctrine of *state decisis,* or the following of precedent, may understandably be reluctant to use social science materials which are seldom as precise and definitive as statements in the law. The long struggle between lawyers and psychiatrists is a good example of the "legal ethnocentrism" which has characterized judges' attitudes toward the materials of behavioral science.

Suggestions for improving the functioning of the courts have included modification of the procedures whereby judges are selected. All federal judges are appointed for life, but judges are elected in about three fourths of the states, for terms ranging from 2 years in Vermont to 21 in Pennsylvania (Institute, 1956). It has been alleged that the electorate is not competent to appraise the qualifications of a given candidate for judicial office, and the appointive system has been attacked because of the element of political patronage. The American Bar Association has favored a plan (the Missouri Plan) whereby a state governor would select a candidate from a panel of names submitted by a nonpartisian judicial nominating commission, and the candidate would then be confirmed by the electorate at the next general election. The California Plan calls for appointment by the governor and confirmation by the majority of an ex officio commission as well as subsequent confirmation by the electorate. Another plan would have local bar associations nominate candidates who would be recommended to the political parties.

The more actively the work of the courts is discussed, the more likely is it that we shall begin to bring theory and practice together in the optimum selection and functioning of judges. It is to be hoped the introduction of the concepts of psychology and other social sciences into the discussion of the work of the bench will lead to ever-improving methods for the administration of justice in the courts—a goal which all believers in the democratic process can only endorse.

It is necessary to realize that progress in improving court procedures is likely to be relatively slow. Almost twenty years after the American Bar Association, in the late 1930's, had adopted minimum practical standards of judicial administration, complete conformity to these standards had not been achieved in even a single state, with the possible exception of Alaska. The enormous importance of the judiciary in the lives of men makes it urgent that continuing effort, from all relevant disciplines be continued with the patient cooperation of all who are interested in improving the work of the courts. The judge, after all, is a key link between the individual and the agencies of social control.

Notes

[1] The judge's opinion generally has two parts—the "holding" and the "dictum." The "holding" consists of judicial observations necessary to the decision of the case. The "dictum" consists of comments not necessary to the actual decision. The opinion is an intellectual rationale which is buttressed by a hierarchy of legal precedents, usage, and case law synthesis, which lead up to the "holding" or *ratio decidendi.*

References

Adorno, T. W., *et. al.*
1950. *The authoritarian personality.* New York: Harper

Blaustein, A.P. and Porter, C.O.
1954. *The American lawyer.* Chicago: University of Chicago Press.

Bohlen, F. H.
1935. The reality of what the courts are doing. *Legal essays in tribute to Orrin K. McMurray,* edited by Max Radin Berkeley: University of California Press.

Botein, B.
1954. *Trial judge.* New York: Simon and Schuster. Brown v. Board of Education, 347 U.S. 483, 1954; 349 U.S. 294, 1955.

Bruner, J. and Taguiri, R.
1954. The perception of people. *Handbook of Psychology* Cambridge: Addison Wesley.

Bureau of the Consensus
1958. Statistical abstract of the United States. Washington, D.C.: U.S. Government Printing Office.

Burtt, H. E.
1931. *Legal psychology.* Englewood Cliffs: Prentice Hall.

Cairns, H.
1941. *The theory of legal science.* Chapel Hill: University of North Carolina Press.

Cardozo, B. N.
1921. *The nature of the judicial process.* New Haven: Yale University Press.

Carr. R. R.
1942. *The Supreme Court and judicial review.* New York: Holt, Rinehart and Winston.

Cheatham, E. E.
1955. *Cases and materials on the legal profession.* Brooklyn: Foundation Press.

Cohen, F. S.
1935. Transcendental nonsense and the functional approach. *Columbia Law Review,* 35, 809-849.

de Tocqueville, A.
1945. *Democracy in America.* New York: Knopf.

Dewey, J.
1924. Logical method and law. *Cornell Law Quarterly,* **10,** 17-27.

Douglas, W. O.
1959. On the misconception of the judicial function and the responsibility of the bar. *Columbia Law Review,* **59,** 227-233.

Frank, J.
1930. *Law and the modern mind.* New York: Brentano, 104, 166.

1932. What courts do in fact. *Illinois Law Review,* **26,** 762-776.

1946. In re J. P. Linehan and Company, 138 F (2d), 651-654.

1949. *Courts on trial.* Princeton, N.J.: Princeton University Press, 250, 270, 335.

Frankfurter, Felix
1947. Some reflections on the readings of statutes. *Columbia Law Review,* 520-546.

1952. In Public Utilities Commission v. Pollack, 343 U.S. 451; 725 Ct. 813.

Fuller, L. L.
1931. Legal fictions. *Illinois Law Review,* **25, 513-546.**

Gaudet, G. F., Herrich, G. F., & St. John, G. W.
1934. Individual differences in penitentiary sentences given by different judges. Journal of Applied Psychology, **18**, 675-686.

Gross, H.
1947. A psychological theory of law. *Interpretations of modern legal philosophies*, edited by Paul Sayre. New York: Oxford University Press, 766-775.

Hains, C. G.
1923. General observations on the effects of personal, political, and economic influences in the decision of cases. *Illinois Law Review*, **17**, 96-116.

Hall, J.
1935. *Theft, law, and society*. Boston: Little, Brown, 264.

Hartley, E. L.
1951. Multiple group membership. *Social psychology at the crossroads*. New York: Harper, 371-387.

Hobbes, T.
1950. Leviathan. New York: Dutton, 242.

Holmes, O. W., Jr.
1881. *The common law*. Boston: Little, Brown, 35.

Hutcheson, J. C.
1929. The judgment intuitive: The function of the "hunch" in judicial decisions. *Cornell Law Quarterly*, **14**, 274-278.

Inheles, A., and Rossi, P. H.
1956. National comparisons of occupational prestige. *American Journal of Sociology*, **61**, 329-339.

Institute of Judicial Administration
1956. *Selection, tenure and removal of judges in 48 states, Alaska, Hawaii, Puerto Rico*. New York: Institute of Judicial Administration.

Jackson, R.
1944. Decline of state decisis is due to volume of opinion. *Journal of American Judicature Society*, **28**, 6-8.

Keyser, C. J.
1929. On the study of legal science. *Yale Law Journal*, **38**, 413-422.

Konefsky, S. J.
1956. *The legacy of Holmes and Brandeis*. New York: Macmillan, 94.

Kort, F.
1960. The quantitative content analysis of judicial opinions. **PROD, 3,** 11-14.

Larson, A.
1955. The lawyer as conservative. *Cornell Law Quarterly*, 40, 183-194.

Lasswell, H.D., and McDougal, M.S.
1943. Legal education and public policy: Professional training in the public interest. *Yale Law Journal*, **52**, 203-295.

Leiner, M.
1957. *American as a civilization*. New York: Simon and Shuster, 446.

Llewellyn, K.
1925. The effect of legal institutions upon economics. *American Economic Review*, 15, 665-671.

1951. *The bramble bush*. New York: Oceana Publications.

Loevinger, L.
1949. Jurimetrics. *Minnesota Law Review*. **33**, 455-494.

Lummus, H. T.
1937. *The trial judge*. Chicago: Foundation Press.

Macmillan, H. P.
1937. *Law and other things*. Cambridge, England: Cambridge University Press.

Marbury v. Madison
1803. 1 Cranch 137; 2 Lawyer's Ed. 60.

Micheal, J. and Adler, M. J.
1933. *Crime, law, and social science*. New York: Harcourt, Brace.

Miller, W.
1951. American lawyers in business and in politics. *Yale Law Journal*, **60, 66-76.**

Mills, C. W.
1951. *White collar*. New York: Oxford University Press, 121-128.

Muller v. Oregon
1908. 208 U.S. 412.

Ohlin, L. E. and Remington, F. J.
1958. Sentencing structure. *Law and Contemporary Problems*, **23**, 495-507.

Pool, I. and Shulman, I.
1959. Newsmen's fantasies, audiences and newswriting. *Public Opinion Quarterly*, **23**, 145-158.

Pound, R.
1923. A theory of judicial decision for today. *Harvard Law Review*, **36**, 940-959.

1925. *An introduction to the philosophy of law*. New Haven: Yale University Press, 101-130.

1938. Fifty years of jurisprudence. *Harvard Law Review*, **51**, 777-812.

Radin, M.
1925. The theory of judicial decisions. *Journal of the American Bar Association*, **11**, 357-362.

Robinson, W. S.
1950. Bias, probability, and trial by jury. *American Sociological Review*, **15**, 73-78.

Ross, E.
1926. *Social control*. New York: Macmillan, 112.

Sayre, W. S. and Kaufman, H.
1960. *Governing New York City*. New York: Russell Sage Foundation.

Schroeder, T.
1918. The psychologic study of judicial opinions. *California Law Review*, **6**, 89-113.

Schubert, G. A.
1958. The study of judicial decision-making as an aspect of political behavior. *American Political Science Review,* **52,** 1007-1025.

Schwartz, B.
1951. *The Supreme Court.* New York: Ronald. 363.

Stone, H. F.
1924. Some aspects of the problem of law simplification. *Lectures on Legal Topics,* New York: Macmillan, 209.

Tate, A.
1958. The judge as a person. *Louisiana Law Review,* **19,** 438-447.

Ulman, J. N.
1933. A judge takes a stand. New York: Knopf.

Wigmore, J. H.
1940. *Wigmore on evidence.* Boston: Little, Brown.

Yankwich, L. R.
1957. The art of being a judge. *University of Pennsylvania Law Review.* **105,** 374-389.

Zajonc, R. B.
1952. Aggressive attitudes of the "stranger" as a function of conformity pressures. *Human Relations,* **5,** 205-216.

11. *In his mock epic, The Faery Queen,* Spenser reveals his hero knights as masters in the art of appearances. Throughout the tales, the heroes as well as the villians "seem" rather than are virtuous, brave, chaste, and so on. The reason being that "nothing is sure that grows on earthly ground"—that true honesty, temperance, and justice are imposs- ible human objectives because con- cepts of morality are mutable, not absolute.*

In courtroom activities, the appear- ance of justice, of "seeming" just, has taken precedence over being just. In criminal trials, many lawyers have cultivated the art of seeming to pursue the truth. Equipped with emotional rhetoric and other more subtle tactics, the criminal lawyer strives to crush his opponent and convince the jury that he alone is the bearer of truth.

Why is this adversary system perpetuated especially if, as Wood indicated in Article 12, it is contrary to the positive values of professional camaraderie. According to Dressler, to work together in the solemn search for truth rather than engage in courtroom gladitorial rites would end the ro- mance of the dynamic criminal lawyer who shines above his mediocre comrades. It would also end the emphasis on individual reputation and create the need for a new strain of lawyers—lawyers who actually realize that "the liberty and perhaps the life of a defendant is at stake in every criminal trial."

According to Dressler, the adversary system is sustained simply because it is an interesting game—a game that challenges the wit and deftness of the participants and yet is dictated by often clean-cut, obvious strategies. Conversely, a conscientious search for truth demands an understanding of law "as an institution of society, as a philosophy, a science, and a craft." It

is understandable that "the un- leavened mass of lawyers who are abundantly satisfied with things as they are" would be hesitant to embark on such an industrious restructuring of their professional perspective when they can depend on the benefits of "seeming" rather than being true defenders of the truth.

*Edmund Spenser, Selections from the Poeti- cal Works of Edmund Spenser (Boston: Hough- ton Mifflin, 1970).

TRIAL BY COMBAT

DAVID DRESSLER

The average criminal trial, said the late Judge Jerome Frank, is a "subli- mated brawl." A decade ago, few of Judge Frank's colleagues bothered to defend their profession when he made the charge in his crusading book, *Courts on Trial;* today many progres- sive lawyers and judges are battling for the very reforms he championed, and in some Federal and state courts the ancient rituals are changing. But even now in the United States, despite our prevailing respect for the scientific search for truth, trial techniques are as unscientific as an appendectomy performed with a tomahawk. With the sensational Finch murder trial in court for the *third* time in California, the law is still "a ass, a idiot," as Mr. Bumble put it—if not worse.

Unfortunately for advocates of reform, most lawyers are proud of this instance of cultural lag. Our so-called adversary theory against which judge Frank inveighed sets the rules of trial procedure. It stems from medieval trial by combat and is basic both to English common law and to American legal codes. In the old days accuser and accused met on the field of battle and had at each other with sword or lance. If the accused fell, he was guilty. If the accuser died, that proved he didn't have a just cause to begin with. Thus was "truth" revealed.

Today, instead of fighting with lethal weapons, we use legal arguments. Where combatants formerly met face to face, they now have surrogates—attorneys—who fight for them. The judge acts as referee, theoretically protecting the contenders against foul blows. The jury decides which "side" fought the better fight. But fight it is and the object is to win, not necessarily to reveal the truth.

The heart of the adversary system —and the source of many of the evils which the reforms now in progress aim to eliminate—is "surprise," a technique which some lawyers call "trial from ambush." The intent of surprise is to time a sudden blow so as to throw the opposition off balance and overwhelm it before it can recover.

An example of a successful surprise is the following: A Chicago attorney, Luis Kutner, was in Federal Court defending William Henderson, who had been charged with piracy on the high seas. Henderson had boarded a sight-seeing motor launch operating on Lake Michigan and, when it left its moorings, pulled a pistol and robbed the passengers. At trial, thirty erstwhile passengers positively identified the defendant as their assailant. Kutner cross-examined diffidently, as if his cause were hopeless. He presented no evidence on his own, and listened respectfully as United States Attorney Al Bosworth summed up and rested his case, by which time Henderson's guilt was plain as a wart.

Then Kutner addressed Judge James H. Wilkerson: "Your Honor, the defense moves for a directed verdict of acquittal, on grounds this court lacks competent jurisdiction." Under Federal law, counsel pointed out, the port of registry of a vessel determines jurisdiction. "The boat in question is registered out of Milwaukee. Chicago is therefore not the venue of the crime."

The judge ordered acquittal.

Now, as he told me in an interview, Kutner knew all along that the case belonged in a Milwaukee court. He could have moved for change of venue before the trial opened in Chicago. Instead, he let it run its course. He allowed the prosecution to rest its case, confident it had won. Then he sprang his trap. In the eyes of the law, Kutner's conduct was entirely ethical. Under the adversary theory he was an advocate, which is to say he was obliged to be strictly partisan. As a partisan, he was entitled to use surprise.

Tongue in cheek, attorneys insist that the adversary system guarantees revelation of all facts bearing on an issue, and so it furthers the scientific method in trial practice. A lawyer buried beneath a mountain of books in the Los Angeles County Law Library told me, "I am here seeking the matter that will win a certain action. My opponent is here, too, with the same purpose. I search with fervor and frenzy. Nothing favorable to my position will escape me. The same is true of my opponent, dammit! He and I will search and together we will bring in facts so plain that even a jury of potato peelers and peanut vendors will understand them."

Maybe. But when I headed the New York State Division of Parole, I had been in and out of courts for seventeen years and most of the time I felt those potato peelers and peanut vendors were licked. They would not get at the truth because it lay hidden behind a curtain of flimflam and obfuscation. Each attorney was out to help his side and his side only, at almost any cost. Each wanted the jury to believe that he and he alone was the bearer of the Holy Grail, while his opponent was a knave out to suppress the truth. Each witness swore he was telling nothing but the truth, even when his story was directly contrary to what a witness for the other side swore was true. No witness was permitted to tell all he knew, although under oath to tell "the whole truth." No witness could tell what he did tell in his own way. The attorney on his side suggested by his questions what the witness should say. In cross-examination the opposing lawyer tried to trap him into saying something else. Each counselor hoped to cajole the jury into disregarding everything the other lawyer or witnesses said. The net outcome, all too often, probably was that the talesmen agreed with the wag who said that cases are decided only "according to the preponderance of the perjury." They voted for the side that seemed to tell fewer lies.

Juries might get at the truth if counsel researched cases scientifically. When two research men investigate causes of cancer they make a hypothesis and check it with an open mind. They may pursue different courses but they clear their findings with each other.

Not so in criminal trial practice. According to the late eminent attorney, Charles P. Curtis, the counsel who sets out to build evidence "will waste a lot of time if he goes with an open mind." Unlike a scientist, he will not sit down with his opposite number and say, "Here is what I found. What did you find? We are both after the same thing—truth. What can we agree on, in the interest of justice?" Instead, he squirrels away his evidence, citations, and arguments—his putative "facts"—hoping his opponent will be overwhelmed by them in the courtroom.

An attorney told a Bar Association audience: "Of course surprise elements should be hoarded. Your opponent should not be educated as to matters concerning which you believe he is still in the dark. Obviously, the traps should not be uncovered. Indeed, you may cast a few more leaves over them so that your adversary will step more boldly on the low ground believing it is solid."

The leaves over the low ground are yellowed pages of musty law books containing ancient trial decisions, which serve as precedents. Precedents are hallowed. What was good enough for great-great-grandpappy is all the better today because it is aged-in-the-book. The contemporary counselor who has a talent for digging these vintage morsels becomes a scholar in the law, highly respected and extravagantly paid. More important, he gains an advantage. The older a precedent, the less likely it is his adversary will find it, too. In court, before an amused jury, the opposing lawyer is trapped and the victory may go to the legal scholar.

What makes such tactics more deplorable is that the precedents often fail to go to the heart of a matter. They award a decision, not on the essence of a case—that is, whether the defendant is guilty or not—but more frequently on mere technicality. If, as happened in one Florida case, the judge simply has to leave the bench to answer the call of nature while counsel is summing up for the jury, the opposing lawyer will make no demur. He has an early precedent up his sleeve that holds if a judge has to go, the trial should be recessed, even though all the evidence is in and only summation is in progress. Then, if the verdict is against his side, the lawyer will jostle the precedent loose and demand a new trial.

There are literally hundreds of thousands of technicalities that have won cases in the past. Many of them are contradictory. The lawyer who can't find the special one that fits his case had better turn in his diploma.

In one case, the advocate found just what he needed to defend his client, a North Carolinian who had fired across the state line and killed a man in Tennessee. When North Carolina attempted to charge him, the attorney cried foul. The act, he pointed out, was completed in Tennessee, and the law requires a man be tried where the act was completed. North Carolina had to agree. Tennessee then tried to extradite the killer as a fugitive from justice. Impossible, counsel fumed. Since his client had never been in Tennessee how could he be a fugitive from that state? Tennessee gave up. Thus, remarks Roscoe Pound, dean of legal philosophers, "The state which had him could not try him, while the state which could try him did not have him and could not get him."

If, by amazing mischance, a counselor finds no precedent, *circa* 1800, to prove his case, he might try another form of surprise, the hit-run tactic. He may fire an improper question at a witness, knowing it must be withdrawn. It will be expunged from the record but not from the recollection of the jurors.

When the Teamsters' president James R. Hoffa was tried for bribery in 1957, his attorney, Edward Bennett Williams, was content to have eight Negroes on the jury. I was an observer in the court and saw John Cye Cheasty, a prosecution witness, come up for cross-examination. Out of a clear sky, Williams asked him if he had not once been engaged by a bus line to investigate the National Association for the Advancement of Colored People during a Florida labor dispute.

The horrified prosecutor jumped to his feet, protesting that the question was altogether immaterial to the matter at issue. The judge sustained the objection and ordered the jury to disregard the question—one of many neat legal fictions is that jurors can forget what they have heard. Actually, the damage was done. It seems reasonable to assume that at least eight veniremen considered Cheasty's testimony as the biased mouthings of an enemy of labor and minorities.

Soon after, another dramatic surprise staggered the prosecution. Ex-champion Joe Louis sauntered into the courtroom, put an arm around Hoffa, and explained to newsmen, "I just came over to say hello to my friend Jimmy." Acquittal for the friend of the oppressed followed.

While in the Hoffa case surprise benefited the defense in court, the prosecution usually has a distinct advantage in preparing certain surprises before trial. For example, the findings of the police laboratory are available to it, rarely to the defense.

In one Los Angeles case, a defendant charged with murder convinced his attorney he was absolutely innocent. Although some attorneys consider it their duty to defend guilty clients, and the canons of the bar hold that this is the one way to assure that mitigating circumstances will be put before a jury, this particular attorney prefers not to handle such cases. He feels he cannot win unless he goes into court convinced in his own mind he is defending an innocent man. At trial, the state produced a police witness who testified he photographed the latent print of the palm of a hand, found on the window sill over which the slayer climbed to gain entrance. The print was the defendant's. Had defense been apprised of this before trial, it might have prepared a better argument in favor even of a guilty client. Taken by surprise, it surrendered the decision to the prosecution. Almost certainly a guilty man was convicted in this instance, but it is our theory that even a guilty man is entitled to the best possible defense.

A case which is still moot as this is written offers another illustration, this time in a situation where we do not know whether the defendant was guilty or innocent. In the first trial early last year of Dr. R. Bernard Finch and Carole Tregoff Pappa for the murder of the physician's wife, the district attorney let Dr. Finch, called by the defense, testify to details of the fatal struggle. He alleged his wife came at him with a gun, he seized it in self-defense and it was accidentally discharged, killing Mrs. Finch. Thereupon the prosecutor on the seventy-first day of the trial brought in tape recordings of an interview between the physician and police shortly after his arrest. On the tape, Dr. Finch gave testimony directly contrary to what he had just given on the stand. Neither the accused nor his counsel knew the interview was recorded. The prosecutor had hoarded the tapes for just such a purpose. It would seem that if a trial is intended to discover truth, both sides should have known of the existence of the tapes. Each side would insist that the truth ought to be brought into court. How could it hurt, then, to reveal it before the trial?

Nevertheless, when I asked a Los Angeles police official whether police findings should not be shared with the defense, he replied, "Do the Dodgers give the Giants their signals?" No, but human beings are not baseballs, trials are not baseball games, and the stakes are not pennants. The liberty and perhaps the life of a defendant is at stake in every criminal trial. Police science should be employed in the interest of truth and justice, not to win a battle for one side.

Because adversary methods sanction a battle of wits rather than a search for truth, a few leaders in the law have become restive. They know that we have at hand methods of finding evidence scientifically, that trials can be made more truthful and

> "*Police science should be employed in the interest of truth and justice, not to win a battle for one side.*"

just than they usually are at present. Largely as a result of their efforts, the American Bar Association has at long last instituted reforms in the adversary method, though much more remains to be done. The first attack was on surprise. To minimize the unfairness and inefficiency of this technique, the American Bar Association produced what it calls "discovery."

Judge Frank likened surprise to a cat-and-mouse game. He thought the mouse should at least have "a peek at the cat's claws." That peek is now provided by discovery. This is, in essence, legal machinery by which one side is required to inform the other, in advance of trial or sufficiently in advance during trial, that certain evidence will be introduced. Forewarned, the other side has time to prepare its case.

As far back as 1848, England provided a first step in discovery. By changes in procedure, the prosecution was obliged to place before a magistrate all the evidence it planned to produce at trial. The defense was to be present and thus would have the information and could prepare adequately. The U.S. waited almost a century to follow suit. But in 1946, Federal Courts began operating under revised Rules of Criminal Procedure, developed under the sponsorship of the American Bar Association. For the first time, some discovery was officially sanctioned in criminal cases before Federal tribunals. Under the new Rules, defense may move, and the court order, that the Government shall show to the defendant's counsel specific documents and tangible objects material to preparation of the case for the accused.

Suppose John Smith is charged with kidnaping a child in violation of Federal statutes. The father is to be the principal Government witness. He has given the United States Attorney a sworn statement that the kidnapper sent him a ransom note. The note itself is in the prosecutor's possession. Defense counsel goes before a Federal judge, in the presence of the U.S. Attorney, and asks to see the statement. He also wants a photostat of the ransom note, so the handwriting may be compared with his client's.

The requested data would be essential to a reasonable defense in this instance, and would probably be furnished. This would not always be the case. It is not the purpose of discovery to facilitate "fishing expeditions" that will give away the Government's case in each and every respect. The buckshot approach to discovery will not be permitted. Counsel must satisfy the judge that the requested information is material to building a defense and that denial would place the defendant in an untenable position at trial. Only then will discovery be ordered.

Because it is and undoubtedly should remain discretionary with the court, discovery was rarely granted in the first decade under the revised Rules. Beginning about the late 1950s Federal Courts became more liberal, but even now discovery is the exception rather than the rule.

But the trend has begun. The American Law Institute has stimulated the states to follow the Federal example. California, Delaware, Florida, Maryland, Michigan, New Jersey, and Ohio have enacted statutes authorizing some degree of discovery, and in the past several years the effects are being felt in state courts. In the majority of jurisdictions the prosecution must provide the defense with a list of its witnesses. In some states the substance of the expected testimony must also be revealed before trial.

Most discovery is in the interest of the defense, since it is the prosecution that brings the charge and believes it has evidence to sustain it. But some disclosure favors the prosecution. In several states the defense is required to notify the prosecutor when it plans to plead not guilty by virtue of insanity. Michigan, Arizona, Ohio, Kansas, Wisconsin, require that the prosecution be notified if the defense claims an alibi.

The disclosure of alibi was required by law even before 1946 in at least one state—Ohio. Its value is illustrated by the case of "Roaring Bill" Potter, a politician murdered in Cleveland. Racketeer Hymie Martin was arrested in Pittsburgh for the offense, and extradited. He would have escaped conviction but for the Ohio law which specified that the defendant must give three days' notice of a proposed alibi. County Prosecutor Ray T. Miller, was so notified and, checking, learned that at the extradition hearing in Pittsburgh, Martin's attorney brought witnesses who swore the accused was in that city when Potter was murdered. The testimony apparently failed to convince.

At the trial in Cleveland, the same attorney presented different witnesses who testified Martin was in Akron the day of the murder. All the County Prosecutor had to do was place in evidence the testimony given at the extradition hearing. Since the defendant could not have been in Pittsburgh and Akron simultaneously, the conflict was obvious. The credibility of the alibi was destroyed and Martin was convicted.

Does discovery make it harder to convict the guilty? Not so, says Maryland's Supreme Court. "We are not impressed by the fear.... It apparently has not had that effect."

Professor Abraham S. Goldstein, of Yale Law School, in an article prepared for *The Yale Law Journal,* suggests a safeguard if it be feared that discovery will tip the balance to the side of the defense. In return for discovery the accused could be required to waive immunity from self-incrimination. He could be required to take the stand. That would give the prosecution an opportunity for its own discovery, direct from the man who, by the prosecution's presumption, knows most about the crime. Professor Goldstein holds the law could be so written as not to conflict with the Constitutional guarantee that a defendant may not be forced to testify against himself.

The trend toward discovery is impressive but as yet limited. It continues to meet with resistance by a majority of attorneys. Professor W. T. Morgan, of Harvard Law School, has explained why: "Some of the finest legal minds today are anxious for revolutionary changes in procedure, but they are as voices crying in the wilderness compared to the great unleavened mass of lawyers who are abundantly satisfied with things as they are. With even a slight modification of procedure in civil and criminal cases the United States could dispense with half her lawyers. The average citizen, therefore, need not expect the legal profession to commit hari-kari."

It will take an entirely new generation of lawyers, trained in a loftier philosophy, to bring a more effective justice into our courts. Most attorneys today come from law schools that imbue them with the theory of winning decisions at almost any cost. They have been taught to use not only surprise but every other questionable advantage which a complacent judge, himself a product of such schools, will allow.

Logic argues that a witness belongs to neither side. He should mount the stand to tell what he knows, whatever the outcome. But budding lawyers study textbooks that teach them to consider witnesses either "friendly" or "hostile." According to such texts, the hostile witness is an outsider and, as Charles P. Curtis says in *The Ethics of Advocacy,* "A lawyer is required to treat outsiders as if they were barbarians and enemies."

Is the hostile witness honest but egotistic? One test advises the cross-examiner he might "deftly tempt the witness to indulge in his propensity for exaggeration, so as to make him 'hang himself.' " A truthful but irascible fellow? "Make him lose his temper and seem spiteful." One recent text by Lewis W. Lake has a section titled "How to Humiliate and Subdue a Recalcitrant Witness." Not a dishonest witness, mind you, but merely one who is recalcitrant, meaning he won't go along with the cross-examiner. The neophyte is instructed:

When you have forced the witness into giving you a direct answer to your question you really have him under control; he is off-balance, and usually rather scared. This advantage should be followed up with a few simple questions such as, "You did not want to answer that question, did you?" If the witness says that he wanted to answer it, ask him in a resounding voice, "Well, why did you not answer it when I first asked you?" Whatever his answer is you then ask him, "Did you think that you were smart enough to evade answering the question?" Again, whatever the answer is you ask him, "Well, I would like for the jurors to know what you have behind all this dodging and ducking you have done." ...This battering and legal-style "kicking the witness around" not only humiliates but subdues him.

We have barely emerged from the era of the self-made lawyer, who needed only a mail-order law book and a fireplace in front of which to study. That was good enough in Abe Lincoln's day, but we can do better today. This is an age of specialization, but one in which we believe the specifics of professional practice should be superimposed on a foundation of general education. Yet over half of today's attorneys are trained in the law without learning to understand the society for which law is created. They

> *"over one half of today's attorneys are trained in the law without learning to understand the society for which law is created."*

do not have college degrees. The majority attended schools of a type which a Columbia University dean called "vocational bargain basements." An investigator for the American Bar Association reported in 1954 that of nine law schools he inspected, six "showed no impact of the modern world whatsoever."

But a measure of improvement is on the way. The great universities now require a liberal art base for the law degree. They teach law as an institution of society, as a philosophy, a science and a craft. When enough of their students have been graduated, law will be practiced with a sense of responsibility for the ethics of modern life. At any rate, there is a chance that lawyers will accept the obligation to make law serve society.

A Daumier print shows a lawyer arguing in court. Nearby sit a woman and child. The caption reads: "He defends the widow and orphan unless he is attacking the orphan and the widow." That's trial by combat under adversary rules. We require much better in our time.

12. *U.S. Attorney General Edward Levi stated in a recent address that "the assumption that government by its nature will inevitably be an instrument of good, or that its judgments will always be wise, is not the necessary product of experience." In the preceding articles in this section, it has been shown that the courtroom is a living institution—its judgments are not always wise, its judges not always judicious.*

The predominant theme in the next article is that lawyers experience anxieties caused by the discrepancies that exist between the realities of their tasks and the dictates of true professionalism. Wood's contention that "informal social structures emerge from strains in the operation of the formal system" is obvious. Yet the fact that these informal patterns affect the administration of justice is serious. Wood states, "the informal patterns are actually an attack on justice."

Wood's discussion is similar to the arguments found in Part I on police and their reactions to the ideal police role. In a search for professional security, lawyers form cliques— "informal groups that often support...unprofessional practices and miscarriage of justice as well as... encouraging the normal courtesies that may be expected among friends." If a lawyer finds this repugnant, it remains an unfortunate fact that "a career in law is particularly difficult for the solo practitioner." Another situation beginning lawyers find difficulty adjusting to is the adversary system— what Wood calls "combat justice." This is a formal condition of court that calls for a battle for truth—a battle that concludes in the friendly acquiescence of the "loser" once justice is achieved. The problem in accepting this is that the loss of a case is detrimental to the reputation of a

lawyer regardless of the situation. Also, the very idea of battle "runs contrary to both professional norms of courtesy to one's colleagues and the community value of friendliness."

These are two examples of the strains criminal lawyers experience as they try to both achieve justice and to maintain a professional reputation. The lawyer, similar to the policeman who must protect society and be suspicious of it, has three major objectives which must be regarded as contradictory; he must protect his client, maintain his professional integrity, and defend the law. No small occupational hazard is the ulcerative situation that exists if he does not satisfy these goals equally or at least seem to: he can be denounced as incompetent by his client by attempting to reveal the truth regardless of what it reveals; unprofessional by his colleagues if he refuses to join cliques and is overly honest in his disregard of political and business interests; or undemocratic by the public when "his interest in the protection of accused persons takes precedence over the public's interest in the conviction of guilty persons."

INFORMAL RELATIONS IN THE PRACTICE OF CRIMINAL LAW

ARTHUR L. WOOD

In this study of the informal relations in the practice of criminal law,[1] the frame of reference is a constructed typology of the social structure of a profession as it is generally described in the literature. This includes institutionalization of a program of specific training and requirements of admission to guarantee minimum competence and a code of ethics covering relations with clients and the community.[2]

The formal structure of a group refers to its system of official rules or laws, explicitly stated, widely known, and presumed to be generally enforced by its regular officers; or, from a behavioral standpoint, it is that conduct which tends to conform with these rules. For the legal profession the formal structure is described in statutory law, court precedents, and bar association codes.

The informal structure of a group consists of the patterns that arise out of spontaneous interaction of persons or the customary relationships recognized by members of the group but not explicitly sanctioned by regular officials. For the practice of law these are the extra-legal patterns of behavior and conduct not specifically recognized in codes of ethics, which are found in the relationships between practitioners and public officials, their clients, and other lawyers.[3] The informal practices are not necessarily unethical, although they supplement or may deviate from formal norms.

In order to analyze the conditions under which the informal patterns arise and to test the hypothesis that informal social structures emerge from the strains in the operation of the formal system, the informal patterns themselves will be described.

For purposes of research a criminal lawyer was defined as an attorney who devotes 10 per cent or more of his practice to criminal law. During the summer of 1951 lawyers were interviewed in five different areas of the United States: three large metropolitan cities (one in the Deep South and two on the eastern seaboard) and two smaller cities (in New England and the Middle West). From two of the larger cities a sample of over 40 per cent was randomly selected, and virtually all criminal lawyers were included in the

three other cities—making a total sample of 101 attorneys in criminal law. From the same cities random samples of civil lawyers (defined as all other practicing lawyers) were interviewed for purposes of comparison—a total of 104.[4]

Community and Political Activities

Lawyers are generally expected to be active in community and political organizations.[5] These activities are clearly an aspect of the informal relationships and are related to professional practices and careers in law. Such participation, as many are frank to say, brings about contacts for obtaining clients and sometimes for rendering them service. For example: "I find veterans' affairs a most satisfying activity for two reasons: I sympathize with the problems of the veterans and also because veterans' organizations have been very good to me—they have really been the backbone of my clientele." Said another respondent: "Most juries know of my activities, and, though I think this is wrong, they have, I think, decided many cases in my favor because of this." There are also those dedicated to community and political causes and, at the other extreme, those irritated by pressure to serve which is exacted in organizations wishing to use their names or to obtain free legal counsel.

Although both criminal and civil lawyers participate in a wide variety of community and political organizations, there are characteristic differences between them.[6] The former group of attorneys tend to dissociate themselves from the business community. Thus criminal lawyers are less frequently officers of these community organizations, and they more often express a dislike for civic and recreational clubs and religious lay groups (Table 1, Nos. 1 and 2), the majority of which are dominated by persons in the business world. They less often choose bankers and corporation lawyers for friends (Nos. 3 and 4); and they less frequently include businessmen among their intimate friends (No. 5).

At the same time, criminal lawyers more frequently participate in charitable organizations[7] (No. 6), and they express a liking for this activity (No. 7); their friends are more often among professional persons (mostly lawyers of lower status) and those from occupations with lower status rathe than businessmen (No. 5). They would choose social workers for intimate friends more often (No. 8); and they are much more active in political party work than their colleagues in civil law (No. 9). From different cities, two comments by criminal lawyers illustrate a common attitude toward politics: "Most lawyers are, and have to be, active in politics. The law and politics are tied up with one another. It is important to have contacts—allows you to avoid loss of time in your law practice; you also get advice." "I like to have my fingers in the pie. Frankly, politics has meant good business for me."

These differences are compatible with the following propositions:

1. Compared with other attorneys, criminal lawyers have lower status among members of the bar as well as in the community at large. This judgment is often made by respondents from both fields of practice. Moreover, it is suggested by the relative infrequency with which they have held positions of leadership in community activities, even though combined rates for all activities (including lay religious, civic and recreational, cultural, professional, and charitable organizations) show the two groups to participate to the same extent.

2. Participation in various civic and recreational clubs is not so useful for criminal lawyers in obtaining clients as for attorneys who practice business law or in other ways serve the middle and upper classes. On the other hand, the criminal lawyers' political connections may aid them in obtaining and servicing clients and in election and appointment to government positions. Their relatively low status in the community and as members of the bar, however, may explain why they have not held government positions more often than have other attorneys.[8]

3. Criminal lawyers more often are motivated by humanitarianism or sometimes even by identification with underprivileged persons. Their concern for the legal rights of indigents and those accused of crime is generally evidenced by their activity in charitable groups and preference for this activity; their more frequent voting for Democratic or more "liberal" candidates (No. 10); their choice of social workers as intimate friends; and perhaps their sense of moral indignation toward persons with whom they disagree (No. 11). These attitudes are compatible with a law practice which counsels persons accused of crime.

Relations with Government Officials

Unique to the practice of criminal law is the attorney's extraordinary dependence on government agencies. Virtually every service for the client rests on a decision by some official: seeing the client in jail, obtaining information on the case against client, setting bail, bargaining for an informal settlement,[9] scheduling the time and place of trial, and requesting a "reasonable" sentence. On the other hand, in civil law legal counseling is designed to prevent litigation (almost nonexistent in criminal practice); argumentation and settlement are largely restricted to negotiations with private attorneys; and relations with government officials may be limited to the filing of legal papers.

Although the institutional system places the defense attorney and government officials in opposition (and perhaps because of this fact), relationships of a friendly character are compatible with the interests of both parties. Because antagonism between participants leads to unpredictability of the outcome and to professional insecurity, informal agreement may be mutually desired —police officials wish to evade cross-examination by defense, the prosecution wants to avoid the work and risk of a trial, and the defense desires a reasonable disposition. These interests consequently become the basis for compromise.

Criminal lawyers were asked: "How friendly must a lawyer be with the district attorney for a successful practice of criminal law?" A similar inquiry was made about relations with police. Including those who qualified their answers, 57 per cent believe that personal connections with the district attorney are helpful, while 80 per cent believe it of the police. Among respondents who were asked about their own practice, half admit friendly contacts with police and district attorney.

A minority of criminal lawyers, particularly the highly specialized, remain aloof from personal involvement with these officials. They may have contempt for officials; they rarely settle a case out of court; and they are inclined to follow the *"combat theory of justice."*[10] The patterns of informal justice are more typical of those just beginning practice and those who have never successfully specialized in any field of law.

Systems of Informal Relations

In the five cities studied, regular or permanent informal relationships with public officials do not exist in all jurisdictions. Their development is unrelated to the size of the city's population but appears to depend on local traditions, politics, and the professional outlook of individual officials. In one of the large cities, for instance, the judges and prosecutors are so professionally oriented that virtually no "personal" relationships exist. Nevertheless, in the same community criminal lawyers are likely to maintain regular connections with the police department, and, in fact, several members of the force act as "runners" to channel clients to certain criminal lawyers. In another the police are widely distrusted, and only an occasional attorney maintains intimate associations with them. In the third large city, however, many attorneys in criminal law are members of an informal group to which prosecutors and clerks of court belong. In this case, as well as where the police refer clients to lawyers, it seems proper to speak of established patterns in which connections are no longer matters of individual bargaining but rather *systems* organized for mutual exchange of benefits.

Cliques of Lawyers

Informal relations among members of the bar, however, appear to be present everywhere in the form of cliques. Membership in cliques, in general, parallels political, ethnic, and religious affiliations as well as fields of specialization. For example, an informal grouping of attorneys in corporation law and allied fields is usually identified with the political and ethnic elite, just as those who have a criminal, negligence, and domestic relations practice maintain informal relations with persons of lower status. Cliques in many ways further a successful practice—for referral of clients, legal and other advice, and contacts outside the bar for obtaining or servicing clients such as banks, real estate and insurance agents, and bondsmen.

In one of the smaller cities a more intensive study of informants who were themselves members of these informal groups revealed five well-developed cliques with three or more members each, in addition to several groups with two members. Over half of all members of the local bar belong to such a group. One commonly joins a clique by accepting or performing a favor with the expectation that it will be reciprocated.

If he is not in one of these informal groups, a career in law is particularly difficult for the solo practitioner. Moreover, cliques may furnish support for unprofessional practices and miscarriage of justice as well as for encouraging the normal courtesies that may be expected among friends. Generally, they discriminate against men they do not want in a particular field of practice. As a clique grows in the service of its members, it ceases to function solely on the basis of friendship: its membership may cross political, ethnic, and religious lines,

the better to serve a variety of interests and a diversity of clients.

The Political Machine

The maximum development of an informal system of relationships occurs in an area controlled by a political machine. In one large city the recent defeat of a machine many years intrenched in power provided a natural experiment on its effect on the practice of criminal law. Several successful criminal lawyers who had once been connected with the political machine reported to us that, mainly through the prosecutor's office, they and their clients were given favored consideration. Accused racketeers and professional criminals normally went to these lawyers, while ordinary criminals were also received by referral through local political clubs.

The significance of the political machine is revealed by the following facts: (1) This was the only city in which the average income of criminal lawyers was greater and where criminal lawyers more often had sources of income outside the practice of law than did their colleagues in civil law.

TABLE 1
COMPARISONS OF CRIMINAL AND CIVIL LAWYERS*

CHARACTERISTIC	CRIMINAL LAWYERS	CIVIL LAWYERS
1. *Officers of community organizations during career:*		
Never	42	27
One or more positions held	59	77
Total respondents	101	104
$x^2 = 4.92$		

*All comparisons show differences at the 5 per cent level of statistical significance. "Correction for continuity" used for x^2 in 2 x 2 tables.

TABLE 1 (*Continued*)

Characteristic	Criminal Lawyers	Civil Lawyers
2. *Activities found least satisfying:*		
Civic and recreational, and religious	16	6
Charitable, professional, and political	11	18
"None of them," "All of them," "Don't know," etc.	34	40
Total respondents	61	64
$x^2 = 6.65$		
3. *Choice of bankers for intimate friends:*†		
Among first two choices	4	17
Not chosen	58	54
Among last two choices	14	7
Total respondents	76	78
$x^2 = 10.50$		
4. *Choice of corporation lawyers for intimate friends:*†		
Among first two choices	14	37
Not chosen	56	39
Among last two choices	6	2
Total respondents	76	78
$x^2 = 15.39$		
5. *Status of three best friends:*		
All professional persons	23	14
Business and professional persons..................	55	77
One or more lower-status persons....................	18	8
Total respondents	96	99
$x^2 = 9.66$		
6. *Participation in charitable organizations:*		
Low participation	67	83
High participation	34	21
Total respondents	101	104
$x^2 = 4.08$		
7. *Activities found most satisfying:*		
Civic and recreational, and religious	23	28
Charitable, professional, and political	27	15
"None of them," 'All of them," "Don't know," etc.	17	27
Total respondents	67	70
$x^2 = 6.13$		

†Respondents ranked the following occupations: accountant, banker, corporation lawyer, criminal lawyer, family doctor, high-school teacher, independent small store owner, lawyer-general practitioner, minister, optometrist, owner of factory employing about 100 persons, social worker, and surgeon.

TABLE 1 (*Continued*)

CHARACTERISTIC	CRIMINAL LAWYERS	CIVIL LAWYERS
8. *Choice of social workers for intimate friends:*†		
Among first two choices	9	1
Not chosen	49	47
Among last two choices	18	30
Total respondents	76	78
$x^2 = 9.42$		
9. *Participation in political party activity:*		
Never	28	43
Currently active	54	38
Formerly active	18	23
Total respondents	100	104
$x^2 = 6.49$		
10. *Candidates favored in 1948 presidential election:*		
Republican, Dixiecrat	35	56
Democratic, Progressive, Socialist, Farmer-Labor	62	45
Total respondents	97	101
$x^2 = 6.71$		
11. *Reasons for last choice of occupations for intimate friends:*		
Moderate dislike (boring, unpleasant, uninteresting)	18	34
Extreme dislike (unintelligent, narrow-minded, hypocritical, "intimate friendship inconceivable")	23	15
Other reasons	7	4
Total respondents‡	48	53
$x^2 = 7.20$		

†Respondents ranked the following occupations: accountant, banker, corporation lawyer, criminal lawyer, family doctor, high-school teacher, independent small store owner, lawyer-general practitioner, minister, optometrist, owner of factory employing about 100 persons, social worker, and surgeon.

‡Question not asked in two cities.

(2) The most successful criminal lawyers during the days of the machine have been replaced under the new regime by others who are now the most successful, and some of their predecessors are in the process of establishing themselves in other fields of law. Some of the extremes of misgovernment are currently, at least, in abeyance under the "reform"-party rule. Nevertheless, the strong local tradition of political partisanship among criminal lawyers has meant that the machine lawyers are out of favor with the prosecutor's office and others are in.

Institutional Strains and Informal Relations

The informal relationships in the practice of criminal law have their effect whenever the formal system and the conditions of practice put a strain on professional norms of conduct. Three situations of strain resulting in informal evasions of the formal system are the starting of a practice and obtaining clients, the adversary system of justice, and the rendering of service.

Starting a Practice and Obtaining Clients

In theory at least, a private professional practice is achieved by a display of technical competence, by ethical conduct, and by hard work. Since publicity by advertising is ruled out, the establishment of a practice is difficult, no matter what the professional abilities of the practitioner. More fortunate beginners may enter a firm, take over another's practice, or receive benefits from other contacts. Perhaps a majority of those entering the bar, however, come from positions of lower status or, for one reason or another, have no connections with those who could help them. Consequently, we find a large proportion of inexperienced lawyers as well as the less successful of the older attorneys among those willing to accept criminal cases. They take minor cases from the police, prosecutor's office, or on assignment from the court, even though the fees, if any, are small. These are their clients, and only through them can reputations be established; moreover, there is always the possibility of an important case. Cases mean newspaper and other publicity.

It is obvious that the extensive informal connections with administrative officials and others from whom referrals can be obtained are desired, just because of the difficulties described here. Formal institutional norms do not shed light on this problem for the individual practitioner, and law-school training does not prepare the candidate to meet the situation. The systems of mutual obligation tend to fill the vacuum.

The Adversary System of Justice

In formal outline the adversary system of criminal justice is litigious and inflexible. Providing for public battle in which one side must win, it naturally arouses anxiety among the participants. For either side there is always a risk in taking a case to trial. Also, the public battle runs contrary to both professional norms of courtesy to one's colleague and the community value of friendliness. This system of litigation could exist only under conditions of the institutionalized trial, which formalizes the conflict under the close supervision of a judge. The antagonism in the formal combat is brought to an end by the customary friendly greeting between opposing attorneys when the trial is completed.

Strains from the adversary system arise out of both professional and personal interests. The obligations of

> "Strains from the adversary system arise out of both professional and personal interests."

his office require the prosecutor to take action against all those for whom he has reasonable evidence of guilt, but limited staff, money, and time, doubts as to jury finding, and public opinion often make avoidance of trial a desirable alternative. Analogous considerations exist for the defendant lawyer.

Since the outcome of a trial is uncertain and because it is a public event, this type of litigation is often to be avoided in the interests of a successful career. In the formal patterns, loss of a case in court need not reflect on the attorney's skill—cases are won or lost on the basis of their merits—but every lawyer knows that successful careers are not based on failures in court. Some lawyers admit their willingness to avoid public trial; some have a personal distaste for trial work. In spite of the fact that criminal lawyers do much more trial work than their colleagues in civil law, over half of the former practically never take a case to trial court. The stereotype of the criminal *trial* lawyer applies to less than a fourth who practice in this field. The personal as well as the professional strain from litigation in court leads to informal evasions and extra-legal settlements.

Rendering Service

Finally, strains are felt by the defendant lawyer in the rendering of service. The majority of clients are guilty of some crime. With little basis for their defense, the most an attorney can do is something less than a trial. Contact with police can make possible negotiations over the evidence. More frequently, the prosecutor can arrange a compromise solution for the client: with a plea of guilty, the attorney may get charges for a lesser offense, recommendation for leniency in sentence, or a reduction in bail bond. This bargaining exists in every jurisdiction, but the extent to which it is influenced by informal relationships varies in accordance with local conditions. In "bargain justice,"[11] the attorney substitutes for technical service his skill in dealing with public officials and thereby facilitates his service to clients.

To recapitualate, the informal patterns tend to relieve strains in the practice of criminal law: they provide a form of "security" for the attorney in facilitating the search for clients, mitigating the rigors of the adversary system of justice, and rendering service to clients. In effect, they are a substitute for the areas of influence which law firms and their connections with the business world maintain in other areas of practice.

An analysis of these patterns shows them to be both functional and dysfunctional for formal justice. In the former case the bargain system of justice helps to clear the court calendar of work which would otherwise overtax the facilities for formal legal procedures. Moreover, the cliques of criminal lawyers strongly support the procedural rights of accused persons. Though this support is in part derived from the career interests of these attorneys, the cliques also help to maintain the formal basis for a democratic system of justice.

On the other hand, there are dysfunctional aspects of the informal relationships for a constructed typology of abstract justice. The informal system may deprofessionalize the practice of criminal law. This is seen in the tendency for personal contacts to be substituted for legal deftness in the service of clients; in ramified arrangements which sometimes ward off rigorous action by local grievance committees.[12] The informal patterns are often actually an attack on justice: when, for example, interest in protection of accused persons takes precedence over the public's interest in the conviction of guilty persons. Affective neutrality and functional specificity, two characteristics of the professional role, tend to be compromised by the system of informal relations.

The data at hand show that a majority of practitioners in criminal law maintain informal connections. This generalization holds regardless of the size of the city, the religious affiliations of the lawyers, the degree of specialization in criminal law, the extent of college education, or income.[13] The quality of the informal relations, however, varies consider- ably between jurisdictions, largely as an effect of the policies of the prosecutor's office and the degree of political influence in the administration of justice.

Notes

[1]This report, read at the annual meeting of the Amer. Sociological Society in 1955, is part of a larger study of the criminal lawyer sponsored by the Survey of the Legal Profession of the American Bar Association. Research assistants of the project were David Caplovitz, Harold R. Katner, Sol Levine, Donald J. Newman, & H. Carl Whitman. The author is indebted to them for their efforts and helpful suggestions.

[2]Talcott Parsons characterizes the prerequisites for the professional role to include functional specificity, a universalistic orientation or equal service to all, and affective neutrality in regard to the particular case. Cf. his "The Professions and Social Structure" in Essays in Sociological Theory: Pure and Applied (Glencoe, Ill.: Free Press, 1949).

[3]Sociology needs an operational definition of "informal." In the lawyer interviews and this article the terms "personal" and "friendly" refer to types of informal relations in contrast with relations that are ideal typical institutionalized professional or formal. Empirical evidence is found in types of treatment: relationships and agreements relying on the spoken word and degrees of courtesy and discriminations relative to the unofficial position of an attorney in a clique versus agreements using legal forms and requiring signatures.

[4]Prior to being interviewed, each lawyer received a letter describing the purpose of the study and its sponsorship by the Survey of the Legal Profession of the ABA and one from an officer of the local bar or judge of the county court. Each lawyer of both samples was interviewed by using a pretested schedule of questions. Each of the five research assistants was largely responsible for interviewing in one of the five cities. A copy of the questionnaire is available upon request from the author. Approximately 5% of the original samples of lawyers were not interviewed.

[5]Cf. Walter I. Wardwell and Arthur L. Wood, "The Extra-professional Role of the Lawyer," Amer. J. Sociology, 61 (Jan. 1956), 304-7.

[6]Table 1, infra, gives frequencies and values of chi square for all these differences.

[7]As indexes of participation in religious, professional, civic and recreational, cultural, and charitable organizations we gave one point for membership and two points for attending meetings two or more times a year.

[8]About 40% of each group have held or currently hold such positions.

[9]"Informal" and "compromise" settlements are agreements by which the prosecutor accepts from defense counsel a plea of guilty to a lesser crime than that originally charged in return for a promise of some form of leniency, thus avoiding formal court trial.

[10]"Combat justice" is a non-technical legal expression referring to settlement of disputes by trial court, where compromise solutions are minimized and the case becomes a formal contest between opposing lawyers.

[11]Roscoe Pound referred to the informal settlements as "convictions" obtained on "bargain days" in Criminal Justice in America (New York: Henry Holt & Co., 1930), p. 184; hence the results of this procedure are currently called "bargain justice." Although Pound spoke disparagingly of the procedure, many legal authorities now believe it to be necessary, judging it on the basis of how the privilege is used by the prosecutor's office. "Bargain justice" as used here is merely descriptive, referring to compromise settlements.

[12]These subjects are dealt with at some length in the author's report to the Survey of the Legal Profession (unpubl.).

[13]In the statistical analysis, criminal lawyers were divided into subcategories by religion, specialization, income, and education. These breakdowns made practically no differences in the comparisons reported between criminal and civil lawyers.

13. *Justice is defined in Webster as "the maintenance or administration of what is just especially by the impartial adjustment of conflicting claims or the assignment of merited rewards or punishments." As the readings in this collection suggest, it would be naive to assume that courtroom officials can adhere to the standards the above definition requires in "doing justice." The difficulty in achieving impartial judgment is that the courtroom drama is determined, ostensibly by law, actually by human caprice. Dressler's metaphor, "trial techniques are as unscientific as an appendectomy performed with a tomahawk," and Frankel's statement that "daily vagary" is not an unusual characteristic of trial courts are common criticisms found throughout criminal justice literature. The following quotation indicates why social scientists and criminal justice researchers are also concerned with the equality of justice as administered in trials by jury:*

> *...the jury is the worst possible enemy of the ideal of the 'supremacy of law.' For jury-made law is par excellence, capricious and arbitrary, yielding to the maximum in way of lack of uniformity, and of unknowability.*

> *Jerome Frank*

Robert Carp's findings in the following study of the grand jury indicate why Frank and other critics of the jury are suspicious of the decisions made by a trial jury—why jury decisions cannot be depended on to reflect an adequate understanding of "merited rewards and punishments." Although its ideal task is to check prosecutorial zeal to bring indictments against persons suspected of criminal behavior, the grand jury is often biased in favor of the prosecutor. In addition, because case loads are heavy and decision-making wearisome, especially when dissents encumber the process, grand jurors cannot deliberate over long nor can they debate an issue to the extent that everything crucial to the case is weighed and considered with excruciating exactness. To add to this inability to decide a case in a truly responsible manner, jurors bring with them specific values which cannot be temporarily discarded in "the line of duty."

The grand jury, then, according to Carp, is beset by "psychological, institutional, and sociological variables" that cloud an impartial understanding of the cases it must decide. This author concludes his discussion with three specific suggestions for future research that might possibly bring justice into sharper focus within the courtroom: (1) jurors must be understood as value-laden individuals who can be manipulated in the cause of prosecutorial victory rather than truth; (2) organizational impediments such as the amount of cases a grand jury must decide over a short period of time and prosecutorial influence should be studied and rectified; and (3) the degree of impartiality that can feasibly be attained in a courtroom of men and then of laws must be ascertained.

THE BEHAVIOR OF GRAND JURIES: ACQUIESCENCE OR JUSTICE?

ROBERT A. CARP

For several decades students of the judicial process have had measured success in parting the veil of secrecy which surrounds the deliberations and internal dynamics of American *trial* juries. The classic study of Kalven and Zeisel of jury behavior in Chicago[1] and other related projects[2] have provided keen insights into the types of psychological, institutional, and sociological variables which influence the "output" of trial jury deliberations. In addition, psychologists and sociologists have generated numerous theories about the behavior patterns of small groups,[3] and many of these theories have served as the basis of highly sophisticated studies of the interpersonal relations and voting behavior of small groups of judicial decision-makers.[4] Many of these latter studies have obvious application to the study of trial juries as small groups.

While the literature on petit jury behavior has increased, both in quantity and in theoretical and methodological sophistication, such research has not been extended to the subject of grand juries. Even though the grand jury is a vital aspect of the federal judicial process and is part of the due process guarantee in half of the state constitutions, it has received scant and generally unsophisticated treatment by judicial scholars. Grand jury literature tends to fall into three general categories: (1) studies of the history and evolution of the grand jury,[5] (2) analyses of the legal powers and prerogatives of grand juries vis-a-vis the rights and immunities of the accused;[6] and (3) critiques of the grand jury system and/or proposals for reform.[7] Although there are a few studies which purport to analyze the process of recruitment to grand juries and to speculate on the possible effects on grand jury "output" of one form of recruitment over another, these studies are neither based on quantitative data nor performed with much methodological rigor.[8]

This study is intended to help remedy the paucity of empirical data on the recruitment and internal dynamics of grand juries by reporting the results of a case study of grand jury operations in Harris County (Houston), Texas. The study may be distinguished from the existing grand jury literature, first, because the author had access to data which has not heretofore been available to judicial scholars, and, second, because the data permitted the researcher to respond concretely to questions which until this time were only subjects of speculation among students of the judicial process. The study is concerned with two major substantive questions. (1) What are the distinguishing characteristics of grand jury behavior? It is suggested that the basic behavioral traits include an excessively rapid processing of cases with little deliberation, a high level of internal agreement on the resolution of cases, and an overwhelming acquiescence in the district attorney's recommendations. (2) How are the basic behavioral characteristics of the grand jury to be accounted for? It is then argued that grand jury behavior is explained by the type of people who become grand jurors, by the grand jurors' inadequate training and preparation for their duties, by the pressures of a very heavy caseload, and by a variety of institutional and legal factors which ensure the prosecutor's domination of the grand jury.[9] Finally, some suggestions for future research on the subject of grand juries are offered.

Methodology

Data for this study derive from three principal sources. First, as a participant-observer on the 177th District Court Grand Jury (which met in Houston, Texas, between November, 1971, and February, 1972), the author had the opportunity to perform a case-by-case content analysis of the 918 cases considered by that grand jury. This analysis includes a complete record of all votes taken, the amount of time spent deliberating on the various cases, and extensive notes on the discussions among the grand jurors and between members of the grand jury and the district attorneys. Because of the oath of grand jury secrecy to which the author is bound, the information here provided must deal with the cases in the aggregate—not individually—and great care has been taken not to divulge specific information about sensitive or confidential subject matter.

Second, in-depth interviews were conducted with former members of Harris County grand juries. The interviewees were not selected at random but rather with an eye toward including as many *recent* grand jury members and jury foremen as possible. Twenty-three such persons in all were contacted (including six jury foremen) and all of them agreed to be interviewed. The primary purpose of these interviews was to compare the grand jury experiences of this author with those of others who have similarly served so as to determine how typical was the performance of the 177th Grand Jury from which the hard data were drawn. No attempt was made to quantify the results of the in-depth interviews, and therefore the information they provide is anecdotal although frequently interesting and insightful.

Third, the study contains data from a questionnaire mailed to all persons who served on Harris County grand juries between 1969 and 1972. Of the 271 questionnaires mailed to the grand jurors, 156 (58 percent) were returned and included in the analysis. The questionnaire solicited information about the socioeconomic characteristics of the grand jurors and about the nature of their grand jury delibera-

tions and experiences. The results are used throughout the study to supplement the other sources of research data and to provide a comparison and contrast between the data of the 177th Grand Jury and the other grand juries which immediately preceded and followed it.

Behavioral Characteristics of the Grand Jury

In principle the grand jury is supposed to carefully determine whether the evidence presented to it by the prosecutor is sufficient to warrant the time and expense of placing a person on trial for a felony offense. Ideally the grand jury serves as a check against an over-zealous district attorney to protect the citizen against unwarranted harassment and prosecution by the state. How well such a function is performed in practice may be ascertained by examining the real, observable defining characteristics of grand jury behavior. First, it will be shown that the grand jury spends an extremely small amount of time deliberating on the vast majority of its cases. Second, the data will indicate a surprisingly low level of internal conflict in the grand jury decision making process. Finally, the grand jury's overwhelming approval of (or acquiescence in) the district attorney's recommendations will be demonstrated.

Time allotted to each case: The failure to deliberate adequately

To determine whether or not the grand jury sufficiently deliberates its cases it seems logical to begin by asking this question: how much *time* does the average grand jury spend with each case to determine whether there is enough evidence to place a man on trial for a felony offense?

Although there is considerable variation in the amount of time spent deliberating on the various categories of cases, the evidence reveals that the typical grand jury spends only five minutes per case. (In 1971, twelve Harris County grand juries spent an estimated 1,344 hours deliberating on 15,930 cases).[10] This average time of five minutes includes the assistant district attorney's summary of the case and his recommendation as to how the case should be decided (about one minute per case), the hearing of testimony by whatever witnesses are called, and the actual secret deliberations by the grand jury on each case individually. By any man's standards, "justice" is indeed swift!

Does the grand jury become more efficient as its term progresses, that is, is it able to deal with a larger number of cases per hour toward the end of its term than at the beginning? Eighty-four percent of the questionnaire respondents indicated that this was their impression. Table 1 (panel a) suggests that such was also the case with the 177th Grand Jury despite a slight initial increase in the amount of time spent per case.

This grand jury spent an average of 7.4 minutes per case during its first

TABLE 1

BEHAVIORAL CHARACTERISTICS OF THE 177TH GRAND JURY
(Number of Cases in Parentheses)

	Time Periods[1]							
	Nov. 3-10	Nov. 15-22	Nov.29—Dec.6	Dec. 8-29	Jan. 3-10	Jan. 12-19	Jan. 24-31	Overall Average
Average number of minutes per case spent deliberating on cases by the 177th Grand Jury	7.3	7.5	8.0	7.6	6.5	6.0	5.6	7.0
Percentage of cases discussed by the 177th Grand Jury	24	26	33	25	5	20[2]	6	20
Percentage of divided votes for the 177th Grand Jury	9	3	6	3	2	6[2]	1	5
Percentage of cases on which the 177th Grand Jury did not follow the district attorney's recommendations	11	10	11	5	4	5	2	7
Total (N)...............	(148)	(112)	(135)	(146)	(111)	(154)	(112)	(131)

[1]Each of these time periods includes three working sessions except the period December 8 through the 29th, which includes five working sessions. The three month session is divided into seven time periods each of which includes an average of 131 cases.

[2]Time period six tends to deviate from the overall tendency. This was primarily because one grand juror suddenly insisted on discussing all of the usually routine driving-while-intoxicated cases. This was the result of an unpleasant personal encounter he had had with law enforcement officials relating to a drunken driving charge during the New Year's holiday.

six working sessions while spending but 5.9 minutes per case during the final six working days.

> ## "In 1971, twelve Harris County grand juries spent an estimated 1,344 hours deliberating on 15,930 cases."

Another question about the deliberation process is how many (and what types of cases) are actually discussed by the grand jury and how many are simply voted on without any discussion at all after the district attorney's one minute summary of the facts of the case. For the 177th Grand Jury a full 80 percent of the cases were voted on with no discussion whatsoever.[11] This percentage is probably even greater for most other Harris County grand juries since the 177th Grand Jury spent a mean time of seven minutes per case, whereas the average figure for the other grand juries between 1969 and 1971 was five minutes.

Table 1 (panel 6) also suggests that after a slight initial increase the percentage of cases discussed by the grand jury tends to decrease as the term progresses.[12] For instance, during its first nine sessions (November 3rd through December 6th) the 177th Grand Jury chose to discuss 27 percent of its cases, whereas it decided to discuss only 12 percent during its final nine meetings (January 3rd through the 31st). Why this is so is explained in part in this statement by a former grand jury foreman:

> As time went on fewer and fewer of the cases were actually discussed.

Toward the end of the term someone would say he wanted to discuss a particular case, and then when someone else would pop up and say "What's the point of discussing this case? We had a case just like it a couple weeks ago. You know where I stand on cases like this, and I know where you stand. Why discuss this all over again? Let's just vote on it and get on to the next case." And more often than not, nothing more would be said. We would just vote without discussing the case.

The phenomenon of discussing fewer and fewer cases as the term progresses probably explains the increasingly grand jury "efficiency" as outlined in panel a of Table 1.

The evidence also suggests that grand juries do discriminate in the amount of time allotted to specific categories of cases, that is, while a grand jury might spend several hours investigating and discussing a prominent murder or rape case, it might spend less than a minute dealing with the average robbery or drunken driving case. When asked on the questionnaire about which types of cases his grand jury spent the most time deliberating, the frequency distribution of responses was in the following rank order: (1) drug cases, 29 percent; (2) crimes of passion, e.g., murder, rape, 27 percent; (3) burglary, 9 percent; (4) forgery and embezzlement, 9 percent; (5) theft, 8 percent; (6) victimless sex crimes, e.g. sodomy, 8 percent; (7) robbery, 5 percent; and (8) driving while intoxicated, 5 percent.

The 177th Grand Jury likewise gave differential treatment to certain types of cases at the expense of others. This panel chose to discuss two-thirds of its victimless sex crimes cases while deciding to talk about only 5 percent of the driving while intoxicated cases. Crimes of passion and drug cases were discussed about a third of the time while 28 percent of the theft cases and 19 percent of the burglary cases were talked about. This was followed by robbery cases and the cases involving forgery and embezzlement which were discussed respectively 9 and 6 percent of the time.

The high level of unanimity in Grand Jury decision making

The most striking feature of grand jury voting patterns is the exceptionally high degree of unanimity. This is confirmed by interviews with former grand jury members and by examining the voting record of the 177th Grand Jury: of the 918 cases decided by that Grand Jury, a non-unanimous vote occurred in a mere 42 cases (5 percent). The evidence further indicates that as the grand jury term progresses, there is a tendency toward increased unanimity in its voting patterns. This is in accord with one of Bales' conclusions about small group decision-making behavior: as the small group continues to deliberate on a matter (or on a series of questions), there is an increased tendency toward group solidarity.[13]

The results in panel c of Table 1 show that during its first nine working days the 177th Grand Jury cast less than unanimous votes in 6 percent of its cases, whereas during its last nine sessions there was a divided vote in only 3 percent of its decisions. This excerpt from a journal kept by one former grand jury member is insightful:

In general there is a fairly unified spirit among us, and I think we all feel that pressure to "dissent only when absolutely necessary," as Chief Justice Taft used to urge. I myself today felt inclined to bring a T.B. (true bill) in a case this afternoon, but I could see no one else agreed with my position, and so

when the vote was taken I held my peace.

Victimless sex crimes was the only category of cases which served to create disharmony on the 177th Grand Jury; a divided vote resulted in one-third of all such offenses. Disagreement on the other types of cases did not exceed the 6 percent level.[14] As for the former grand jurors who were asked in the questionnaire to cite cases on which their respective panels had the largest amount of internal dissension, drug cases led the way with 40 percent, followed by crimes of passion at 25 percent. No other category of cases was cited more than 9 percent of the time.[15]

Thus the evidence suggests that grand jurors most frequently divide on drug cases, crimes of passion, and victimless sex crimes while being significantly more unified on the other categories of cases. Such findings are not too surprising when one considers that cases in the three aforementioned categories are not only likely to be the most serious and complex, but they are also cases about which society in general seems to be most divided as to whether such offenses are really crimes at all or merely the actions of social dissidents and psychopaths.

The Grand Jury's acquiesence to the demands of the prosecutor

A third defining characteristic of grand jury behavior is the almost total approval of the district attorney's recommendations. Although the interview data suggest that grand jurors are often critical of the prosecutor for inadequate and careless preparation of cases, for insensitivity to the inequities of our legal system, and for presenting the grand juries with inordinately heavy caseloads, the evidence also reveals that most grand juries tend (or are forced by circumstances) to rely heavily on the skill and integrity of the district attorney in deciding whether or not to bring an indictment. When asked on the questionnaire about the *usual* practice of the grand jury in bringing an indictment, 47 percent of all grand jurors indicated that their grand juries indicted (or refused to indict) solely on the basis of what the district attorney said the file of the accused contained. Another 21 percent noted that their grand jury usually did examine the file of the accused while about a third claimed that their grand jury usually required proof "sufficient to convict, including the calling of witnesses."[16]

What is perhaps most significant, then, is that nearly half of all grand juries (and the author believes this to be a highly conservative figure) usually take action on cases solely on the basis of what the district attorney says the defendant's file contains without the grand jury even bothering to examine the file or to require full demonstration by the district attorney.

On which categories of cases is the grand jury most likely to refuse to follow the recommendations of the district attorneys?[17] The response to this query by the questionnaire recipients generated the following frequency distribution: (1) drug cases, 44 percent; (2) crimes of passion, 18 percent; (3) victimless sex crimes, 11 percent; (4) driving while intoxicated, 9 percent; (5) forgery and embezzlement, 6 percent; (6) theft, 5 percent; (7) burglary, 3 percent; and (8) robbery, 3 percent. Thus the crimes which were likely to cause the greatest amount of dissension among the grand jurors are the very felonies which were likely to result in the most disagreements between grand juries and the district attorneys; viz., drug

cases, crimes of passion, and victimless sex crimes.

The above results parallel exactly the data emanating from the 177th Grand Jury. That Grand Jury, which refused to follow the district attorney's recommendations only 6 percent of the time, disagreed with the district attorneys in 28 percent of the drug cases, 27 percent of the victimless sex crimes cases, and 17 percent of the crimes of passion.[18]

Panel d of Table 1 suggests that the longer the grand jury is in session the more its decisions are likely to be in accord with the district attorney's recommendations. More careful analysis reveals, however, that this is not necessarily the case. For the 177th Grand Jury the evidence indicates that the district attorneys were less and less likely to present to the Grand Jury cases with which they believed the Jury would go against their recommendations. For example, of the first 137 cases presented to the Grand Jury, 25 (18 percent) were drug cases, whereas only 3 (2 percent) of the following 123 cases dealt with drug crimes. Apparently the district attorneys had determined after a few weeks that they would be more successful taking their drug cases to one of the other two grand juries sitting at the same time. In fact this was conceded by one of the district attorneys during one of the working sessions when a grand juror asked, "Why aren't you giving us any more drug cases?" The candid reply was, "Well, you folks are requiring so much (proof) of us with those cases, that we've had to take them to the other grand juries or we're going to get way behind." Therefore, a phenomenon which may well occur in Harris County is for the district attorneys to "size up" the grand juries during their first several working sessions and then to present cases to the grand jury which is most likely to act in accordance with the district attorneys' wishes. To what extent this occurs is unknown, but that it does occur to some degree is beyond doubt.

Partial Explanation of Grand Jury Behavioral Characteristics

The evidence presented to this point suggests the following portrait of grand jury behavior. Burdened with an inordinately heavy caseload, the grand jury rapidly processes almost all of its myriad of cases, according full and adequate deliberation to only a select few which arbitrarily manage to pique the interest of the jury panel. The expedition of the huge caseload is facilitated by a very low level of internal conflict as evidenced by a record of unanimous voting on approximately 95 percent of the cases. Such internal harmony extends to the relations between the grand jury and the district attorney's staff, the former following the latter's recommendations without so much as a question about 94 percent of the time.

If such are the behavioral characteristics of the grand jury, the next logical question is: how are such behavioral patterns to be accounted for? Why doesn't the grand jury deliberate with greater thoroughness on its cases? Why is there so little internal dissension on the resolution of the many issues confronting the grand jury? And why is the public prosecutor able to so effectively dominate grand jury behavior? Partial answers to these questions have already been suggested in the preceding material, but it is the purpose of this segment of the article to provide a more systematic explanation for grand jury behavior.

The type of people who become grand jurors

One possible explanatory factor accounting for some of the behavior patterns lies in the selection and composition of the individual members of the jury panel. This is based on the reasonable assumption that a grand jury composed of a truly random cross-section of the community might well exhibit different behavior from a jury composed largely of upper-middle class whites, or of radical members of the black community, or of a combination of poor whites and Mexican Americans. Therefore, we must explore the grand jury selection process and provide a profile of its members.

The process of selecting grand jurors in Texas is as intricate as it is arbitrary. Unlike many of its sister states which non-discriminately select the names of grand jurors from a lottery wheel containing the names of hundreds of potential jurors, Texas grants jury commissioners almost unlimited discretion to compile a small list of names from which the grand jury is impaneled. Very little is known about these jury commissioners and about the criteria by which these officers of the court select prospective grand jurors. However, preliminary evidence suggests, first, that a significant disproportion of the commissioners are upper-middle class Anglo-Saxon white males; and, second, that the commissioners tend to select as grand jurors their friends and neighbors who have similar socioeconomic characteristics.[19] Historically most jurists have argued, and the courts have officially determined, that grand juries, like trial juries, should be representative of the population of the community as a whole. Although there is still considerable uncertainty about how this goal is to be achieved, the U.S. Court of Appeals for the Fifth Circuit has determined that the Constitution requires that members of Texas grand juries represent "a fair cross section ...[of the] ... community's human resources...."[20] In light of this judicial determination it is fair then to ask the question: how representative are Texas grand juries of the county populations from which they are selected? This is largely an empirical question, and for a partial answer we may compare the results of the mailed questionnaire sent to former grand jurors in Harris County with the 1970 census figures for this same county.

Table 2 shows that the typical Harris County grand juror is an Anglo-Saxon male college graduate about 51 years of age who is quite likely to earn about $25,000 per year while working either as a business executive or as a professional man. How does this profile compare with what the 1970 census data indicates about the "typical" citizen of the county? A brief summary of these data reveals the following about the residents of Harris County: 49 percent are male and 51 percent are female; the median adult age is 39; 69 percent are Anglo-Saxon, 20 percent are black, and 11 percent are Mexican American; the median education is 12 years (a high school degree); and the median family income is $10,348.[21] These figures clearly demonstrate that even by rudimentary standards Harris County grand juries do not meet the judicial criterion of a "fair cross section... [of the] ...community's human resources." Grossly under-represented are women, young people, Negroes, Mexican Americans, the poor, and those with less extensive educational backgrounds.[22]

The evidence suggests that the highly non-representative composition of the grand jury manifests itself in several of the jury's behavior patterns. First, it is probably responsible to a large degree for the low level of internal conflict among the grand jurors. Jury members with highly similar backgrounds of education, income, employment, sex, age, and race are more likely to think alike and disagree less than a panel composed of individuals with highly dissimilar—or even randomly distributed—background characteristics.

Second, the upper middle class white bias of the grand jury is undoubtedly reflected in the selection of that small 5 percent of the cases which the jury does choose to deliberate on at length. The evidence reveals that the vast majority of those cases in the 5 percent category are those which include the bizarre, unusual, or "important" cases which are covered by the news media and which frequently involve the names of well-known local personages, businesses, organizations, etc. The murder of a prominent socialite, corruption in the local fire department, alleged immoral conduct by professors at a local state university have all been subjects of extensive and exhaustive grand jury investigations in the county under study. Cases such as these are regarded as significant by upper-middle class grand juries because the subject matter has a special appeal to the moral, ethical, or even salacious instincts of the middle class mentality. On the other hand, the robbery of a liquor store, the stabbing death of a derelict in a ghetto bar, or the forgery of a credit card tend to be regarded as routine, boring, and worthy of little interest by most grand jurors. As one grand juror said in this candid jest, "We kind of looked forward to the rape and sodomy cases

TABLE 2

SOCIOECONOMIC CHARACTERISTICS OF HARRIS COUNTY GRAND JURORS
COMPARED WITH 1970 COUNTY CENSUS FIGURES FOR ADULT POPULATION,
IN PERCENTAGES
(N = 156 for the Questionnaire Sample)

Characteristic	Grand Jury	County
Sex		
Male..........................	78	49
Female........................	22	51
Age		
21-35 years.....................	10	23
36-50 years.....................	43	18
51-65 years.....................	37	8
Over 65........................	10	5
Median juror age, 51—Median adult age, 39		
Income		
Under $5,000...................	1	16
$ 5,000-$10,000................	3	31
$10,000-$15,000................	25	29
$15,000-$20,000................	16	9
Over $20,000	55	15
Median juror income, $25,000—Median family income in County, $10,348		
Race		
Anglo..........................	82	69
Negro..........................	15	20
Mexican American	3	11
Education		
Less than high school	0	24
Some high school...............	3	23
High school degree	8	25
Some college...................	34	13
College degree	32	15
Graduate degree	23	15
Median juror education, 16 years—Median County residents education, 12 years		
Employment		
Business executive..............	35	
Proprietor......................	7	
Professional	20	Comparable data
Employed worker	13	not available
Retired	13	
Housewife......................	11	
Other	1	

and stuff like that because they broke the routine. I mean if you've heard one bad check case, you've heard them all. But the unusual cases were a little more interesting, and we kind of took our time with them." The result of all this may be that the more bizarre, infamous, or salacious the case, the greater the likelihood that it will be among the small percentage of cases on which the grand jury gives careful and exhaustive investigation. And, conversely, the more routine and uninteresting the case, the greater the likelihood that it will be passed over with scant attention, the grand jury being willing to follow the often-heard advice of the district attorney: "If we make a mistake here, they'll catch it when the cases come to trial." Since 46 percent of all grand jury indictments end in either dismissals or acquittals, one may well assume that many mistakes are indeed passed over by bored, unresponsive, and over-worked grand juries.[23]

Finally, the data reveal that some of the complex social problems which divide society as a whole, such as marijuana and hard drug laws, the possible pathology of the murderer and the rapist, the permissibility of "abnormal" sexual relations between consenting adults, all manifest themselves in the give-and-take of grand jury deliberations. This is evidenced by the comparatively high level of disagreement on the resolution of cases dealing with these subjects, not only among individual members of the grand jury but also between the grand jury and the district attorney's staff. Moreover, the inordinant amount of time the grand jury spends deliberating on these cases and the level of dissension which these discussions evoke are also a probable reflection of the upper-middle class composition of the grand jury. It is now common

knowledge among social scientists that concern with reform of the narcotic laws, revision of the criminal code pertaining to sexual mores, etc., are almost exclusively middle and upper middle class phenomena.

The Grand Jury's inadequate training and preparation for their duties

A second reason to account for some of the grand jury's behavior patterns is found in the process by which newly-selected jurors are trained and socialized. In Harris County all new grand jurors are provided with a training program of sorts which entails three different aspects: a *voluntary* one-day training seminar conducted primarily by police and sheriff's department officials; two booklets pertaining to grand jury procedures and instructions, one composed of the district attorney and the other prepared by the Harris County Grand Jury Association; and, finally, an in-depth, give-and-take discussion between the grand jury and an experienced member of the district attorney's staff. Let us examine each aspect of the program separately.

First, the series of lectures by law enforcement officials seems to be of limited utility for the novice grand juror. Not only do these lectures come several days *after* the formal work of the grand jury has begun, but most grand jurors tend to agree with an evaluation which was included in a recent grand jury report: "The day-long training session was interesting, but for the most part the lectures were irrelevant to the primary functions of a Grand Jury, and many of us noted rather unsubtle political overtones in the formal presentations."[24] Interviews with more than a score of former grand jurors and a content analysis of grand jury reports reveal that the primary function of the law enforcement lectures is to explain and to "plug" the work of the respective departments rather than to provide the grand juror with substantive insights into what his grand jury duties entail.

The pamphlets prepared separately by the county Grand Jury Association and by the district attorney are well-written and provide a good summary of the formal duties and functions of the grand jury. However, since these booklets are not provided until the first day of jury service, the earliest they could be read is after the grand jury has put in one full day of work, which usually means hearing at least 50 cases. More important, however, is the fact that interviews with former grand jurors indicate that very few jurors bother to read and study these booklets. This comment by one former grand juror is typical:

> Yes, I took the books home with me that first night and I glanced through them, but I can't say I really read them. I figured that we'd meet our problems as we came to them, and that's about what happened. If we had a question during our deliberations, one of us would usually say, "Let's see if the booklet says anything about this." That's how we used the books when I was on the jury. I don't think any of us actually read them as such.

The give-and-take discussion between the grand jury and an assistant district attorney is usually scheduled for the first working session, and it is the final aspect of the grand juror's formal on-the-job training. When such a discussion does indeed occur, it appears to be of some utility in acquainting grand jurors with their new duties. However, this comment by a recent member of a grand jury was far from atypical:

> Yes, we were supposed to meet with one of the D.A.'s at the end of the first day, and he was supposed to explain to us what the hell was going on. But can you believe this? They [the assistant district attorneys] presented us with so many cases on our first day, it got to be five o'clock and we didn't have time for anyone to explain to us what we were supposed to be doing. We heard dozens of cases the first day, and when I got home that night I was just sick. I told my wife, "I sure would hate to be one of those guys who had his case brought before us today."

How long does it take, then, for the average grand juror to understand substantially what the duties, powers, and functions of a grand jury are? The results of the questionnaire survey reveal that the typical grand juror does not claim to fully understand his basic purpose and function until well into the third full working session of the grand jury.[25]

Using the average daily workload of 1971 as a base (58 cases per working session), this means that the grand jury hears a minimum of 116 cases before its members even claim to understand their primary duties and functions. Since the average grand jury in 1971 considered 1,328 cases,[26] the data suggests that most grand jurors stumble through the first 8 percent of their cases without fully knowing what is incumbent upon them.

The inadequate training and socialization of the grand jury is clearly one factor accounting for many of its behavioral characteristics. Since grand jurors do not learn systematically from an independent source the full measure of their duties, functions, and prerogatives, there exists the strong potential that they will become "rubber stamps" of the district attorney's staff. This is not to suggest that all grand juries become mere tools of the district attorney, but the potential for this result is by no means minimal. Jurors who do not fully understand their functions, who do not comprehend the meaning of "probable cause," and who do not know how to conduct careful, complete investigations of each case are prime candidates to be "led by the nose" by artful and experienced public prosecutors. Moreover, the evidence indicates that

> "Jurors ... are prime candidates to be 'led by the nose' by artful and experienced public prosecutors."

the district attorneys do indeed take advantage of ignorant grand juries to accomplish their desired ends. This is primarily so because the prosecutors frequently keep significant pieces of information from grand jury purview and because they occasionally deliberately route cases to the grand jury which is expected to act most favorably in accordance with their wishes.

The pressure to decide cases quickly

A third explanatory variable for grand jury behavior is found in the enormous size of the caseload with which both the prosecutor and the grand jury are forced to deal. Just as the heavy caseload at the trial court level produces pressures sustaining the plea-bargaining system, so, too, the huge workload of the grand jury has generated pressures to find alternatives to comprehensive review of each case. As indicated previously, the average grand jury, meeting but two days per week, is presented with approximately 1,328 cases during the three-month term. Since Texas law guarantees to all persons charged with a felony the right to a grand jury indictment, the district attorney is required to process all of these cases through the machinery of the grand jury. Given the small number of grand juries and the limited number of days they can work, there is little wonder that cases are processed with such careless speed. If each case were to receive adequate deliberation, the grand jury would fall hopelessly behind in its workload: if Harris County grand juries were to spend so much as an average of 20 minutes per case, their output of cases would drop by 75 percent! Thus, the sheer size of the caseload precludes careful, serious discussion of the cases.

Besides forcing the grand jury to work much too rapidly, the heavy workload is also partially responsible for the grand jury's excessive reliance on the expertise and good faith of the district attorney. To question the prosecutor's judgment, to make him "do his homework," are luxuries which efficiency-conscious grand juries cannot afford. The district attorney is hardly ignorant of this fact since he frequently admonishes the grand jury that requiring too much evidence of the prosecutor causes the grand jury "to fall behind the other grand juries" or that "grand jury delays result in innocent persons languishing in jail because they can't get their cases heard."

Factors resulting in the district attorney's domination of the Grand Jury

In spite of the considerable legal powers and independence of the grand jury and despite the wishes of most grand jurors to the contrary, it is clear that the district attorney dominates the behavior of the grand jury. Why this is so has already been discussed and implied throughout the article, but it seems useful at this point to put all of the major reasons into summary perspective.

First, it is the prosecutor who has the primary role in training and indoctrinating the grand jurors. It is his office which writes the grand jury handbook, which plans the training seminars, and which instructs the jurors about their primary powers and responsibilities. Given the considerable ignorance of most grand jurors about their proper role and duties, the district attorney has the first and only real opportunity to write on this blank slate that the primary function of the grand jury is to expedite the work of the prosecutor's office with a minimum of time and obstruction.

Another factor resulting in the prosecutor's dominance is his continuing control over the sources of information throughout the three-month term. Perceived as an expert, as a professional, the district attorney is constantly looked to for guidance and information as to the proper disposition of cases and as to the legitimate functions of the grand jury. The prosecutor is fully aware of the grand jury's reliance on him in this regard and his subsequent behavior fully verifies the maxim that knowledge is power. The phenomenon is further heightened by the extremely heavy workload which forces the grand jury to trust the competence and judgment of the district attorney since the alternative is to throw sand in the gears of the judicial machinery and risk bringing it to a virtual halt.

Besides his control over the socialization of the grand jury, the prosecutor possesses some additional powers and prerogatives which ensure his dominant role. The district attorney's ability to control the agenda, that is, the sequence in which cases are presented, is worthy of mention. This power enables the prosecutor, if he is so inclined, to do such things as: (1) initially present the grand jury with a wide variety of cases to determine which ones the jury processes without question and on which cases the grand jury challenges the district attorney, thus enabling the prosecutor to channel subsequent cases to those grand juries which give him the least trouble; and/or (2) increase the size of the agenda for a grand jury which is causing him difficulty, thereby pressuring that grand jury into spending less time with its cases in order to complete the daily agenda. In addition, the district attorney has the right to take a case that has already been voted on by a grand jury to a second such jury for its consideration. This is done whenever the prosecutor is unsatisfied with the vote of the first grand jury, and it enables him to keep trying until his will ultimately prevails in the vote of a more compliant grand jury.

Conclusion

In sum, grand jury behavior is characterized by a rapid processing of cases with little deliberation (except for a small handful of cases of special interest to upper middle class citizens), by low internal conflict in reaching decisions, and by overwhelming approval of the district attorney's recommendations. Such behavior patterns are largely accounted for by the kind of people who become grand jurors, by the inadequacy of the grand jury training process, by the heavy caseload which requires speedy processing of cases for adequate system maintenance, and by a variety of institutional and legal factors which give the district attorney's office a monopoly on the sources of vital information and which insure his capacity to manipulate grand jury activities.

This study cannot end without making some general and specific suggestions for future research on grand juries. First, much more needs to be learned about the selection of grand jurors. We need specific answers to questions such as these: who are the jury commissioners and on what basis are they selected? What standards does the judge use in designating grand jury foremen?

Second, studies must acquire more knowledge about the grand jurors themselves. What are their values and what are their attitudes toward the police, the judicial system, and those arrested for a variety of crimes? The additional use of questionnaires and in-depth interviews with a large cross-section of grand jurors is necessary before we can draw an accurate profile of the typical grand juror.

More evidence is also needed about the internal dynamics of grand jury deliberations. Which types of grand jurors are likely to have more influence in the deliberations than others? Some evidence in this study suggests that the profession or race of the individual grand juror may cause other members of the jury to defer to him in cases which hinge on matters tangent to the grand juror's specific background. For example, on the 177th Grand Jury the lone black member was usually listened to with great attention in cases where an obviously black defendant was charging police harassment, and the only lawyer on the jury was given considerable deference in cases which hinged on highly technical legal questions. Do grand juries develop a form of *stare decisis* as their terms progress (as was clearly the case with the 177th Grand Jury)? That is, are grand jurors, well into their term, likely to say about a case, "We had a case like this last month and we did such and such with it. We must then do the same with this case so we'll be consistent with ourselves." Also, is the grand jury foreman more likely to be on the winning side of divided votes than other grand jurors?

Finally, we need more data on the influence and role of the assistant district attorneys vis-a-vis the grand jury. Are some district attorneys more successful than others in obtaining the desired results from the grand jury? What tactics and strategies do district attorneys employ in preparing and presenting cases to grand juries? To what extent do district attorneys divert specific cases (or types of cases) from a grand jury to which the case(s) would routinely go to a grand jury which is more likely to resolve the case(s) in accordance with the district attorneys' wishes?

If answers to the above questions are found, we will be well on our way to understanding an institution and a process which at this time remains largely unexplored by students of the judicial process.

Notes

[1]Harry Kalven, Jr. & Hans Zeisel, *The American Jury* (Boston: Little, Brown & Co., 1966).
[2]*Ibid.*, see bibliographic references on pp. 541-545.
[3]Robert F. Bales, *Interaction Process Analysis: A Method for the Study of Small Groups* (Cambridge, Mass.: Addison-Wesley Press, 1950); "The Equilibrium Problem in Small Groups," ch. 4 in Talcott Parsons, Robert F. Bales, & Edward A. Shils, eds., *Working Papers in the Theory of Action* (Glencoe, Ill.: Free Press, 1953); R.F. Bales, "Task Status and Likeability as a Function of Talking and Listening in Decision-Making Groups," in Leonard D. White, ed., *The State of the Social Sciences* (Chicago: Univ. of Chicago Press, 1956), pp. 148-161; R.F. Bales, "Task Roles and

Social Roles in Problem-Solving Groups," in Eleanor E. Maccoby, Theodore M. Newcomb, & Eugene L. Harley, *Readings in Social Psychology* (New York: Holt, 1958), pp. 437-447; R.F. Bales, *Personality and Interpersonal Behavior* (New York: Holt, Rinehart & Winston, 1970). Also, P.E. Slater, "Role Differentiation in Small Groups," *Amer. Sociological Rev.*, 20 (June 1955), 300.

Also, Leonard Berkowitz, "Some Effects of Leadership Sharing in Small, Decision-Making Conference Groups" (unpubl. Ph.D. diss., Dept. of Psych., Univ. of Mich., 1951); L. Berkowitz, "Sharing Leadership in Small, Decision-Making Groups," *J. Abnormal & Social Psych.*, 48 (Apr. 1953), 231.

[4]See, e.g., Thomas P. Jahnige & Sheldon Goldman, eds., *The Federal Judicial System* (New York: Holt, 1968), part 3, sec. C. Also, see Glendon Schubert, ed., *Judicial Behavior: A Reader in Theory and Research* (Chicago: Rand McNally, 1964), chs. 3, 4, 5.

[5]See, e.g., Richard D. Younger, *The People's Panel: The Grand Jury in the United States, 1634-1941* (Providence, R.I.: Brown Univ. Press, 1963); J. Van Voorhis, "Note on the History in New York State of the Powers of Grand Juries," *Albany Law Rev.* 26 (Jan. 1962) 1; George J. Edwards, Jr., *The Grand Jury* (Philadelphia: George T. Bisel Co., 1906).

[6]See, e.g., S.A. MacCorkle, *The Texas Grand Jury* (Austin, Tex.: Institute of Public Affairs, Univ. of Texas, 1966); S. A. MacCorkle, "Grand jury—evidence obtained from testimony of prospective defendant cannot be used as basis of indictment," *Fordham Law Rev.* 30 (Dec. 1961), 365; S.A. MacCorkle, "Rule of evidence as a factor in probable cause in grand jury proceedings and preliminary examinations," *Washington Univ. Law Quart.* (Feb. 1963), p. 102; and S.A. MacCorkle, "Criminal procedure —Pretrial disclosures—defendant indicted for suborning witness to testify falsely before grand jury may inspect transcript of witness' testimony before grand jury," *Univ. of Pittsburgh Law Rev.* 23 (June 1962), 1024.

[7]See, e.g., W. Coates, "Grand Jury, the Prosecutor's Puppet. Wasteful Nonsense of Criminal Jurisprudence," *Pennsylvania Bar Assn. Quart.* 33 (Mar. 1962), 311; W. Coates, "California Grand Jury—Two Current Problems. Grand Jury: Some Problems and Proposals," *Chicago Bar Record*, 43 (Oct. 1961), 9; A. H. Sherry, "Grand Jury Minutes: the Unreasonable Rule of Secrecy," *Virginia Law Rev.* 48 (May, 1962), 668.

[8]See, e.g., W. Burnett, Jr., "The Texas Grand Jury Selection System—Discretion to Discriminate," *Southwestern Law J.* 21 (Summer 1967) 545.

[9]A very well-written study discussing phenomena similar to these in the U.S. House of Rep. Ways and Means Committee; see J. F. Manley, "The House Committee on Ways and Means; Conflict Management in a Congressional Committee," *Amer. Political Science Rev.* 59 (Dec. 1965), 927-939.

[10]The statistics are based on figures prepared by the Grand Jury Div. of the Harris Co. District Attorney's Office in a report to District Attorney Carol Vance.

[11]The usual procedure in Harris County is for the assistant district attorney to present his cases for the day and then to leave the jury room. Then the foreman asks each grand juror which cases he feels should be discussed. With the 177th Grand Jury even if only one of the jurors wished to discuss a particular case, discussion occurred. The interviews suggested that other grand juries follow a similar practice.

[12]An additional explanation of why there is an initial increase followed by a gradual long-term decrease is found in the discussion surrounding Table 4. In brief, the hypothesis is that the grand jury slowly begins to gain confidence and to challenge the work and judgment of the prosecutor—especially on the resolution of certain types of cases. Resenting such challenges, the district attorney then removes these types of cases from subsequent grand jury consideration. Thus, the percentage of cases discussed by the grand jury drops after the first month because many controversial cases considered worthy of discussion are simply removed from the agenda.

[13]Bales, *Interaction Process Analysis,* esp. p. 138.

[14]Percentage of cases on which divided votes occurred for the 177th Grand Jury: (1) victimless sex crimes, 33%; (2) crimes of passion, 6%; (3) drug cases, 6%; (4) theft, 5%; (5) burglary, 4%; (6) robbery, 4%; (7) driving while intoxicated, 4%; and (8) forgery and embezzlement, 0%.

[15]Percentage of grand jurors who cited cases on which their respective grand juries had the largest amount of internal dissension: (1) drug cases, 40%; (2) crimes of passion, 25%; (3) victimless sex crimes, 9%; (4) forgery and embezzlement, 7%; (5) driving while intoxicated, 7%; (6) theft, 5%; (7) burglary, 4%; and (8) robbery, 2%.

[16]Given the average time of five minutes per case, the third claim could not possibly have been the *usual* practice of any of the grand juries.

[17]Disagreement with the district attorney was defined as cases where at least one of the following conditions occurred: the district attorney recommended a true bill and the grand jury voted a no bill; the district attorney sought a no bill and the grand jury brought a true bill; the grand jury indicted for a crime other than the one recommended by the district attorney; the grand jury required the district attorney to collect additional evidence for a particular case before they would consider it.

[18]Cases on which the 177th Grand Jury refused to follow the recommendations of the district attorney: (1) drug cases, 28%; (2) victimless sex crimes, 27%; (3) crimes of passion, 17%; (4) theft, 7%; (5) burglary, 5%; (6) forgery and embezzlement, 2%; (7) robbery, 1%; and (8) driving while intoxicated, 1%.

[19]This evidence is taken from an ongoing

research project on the grand jury selection process conducted by myself and a graduate assistant, Claude Rowland.

[20]*Brooks v. Beto*, 366 F.2d 14 (5th Cir., 1966).

[21]Census Tracts (Houston, Tex.): *Standard Metropolitan Statistical Area* (Washington: U.S. Dept. of Commerce, 1972), pp. 1, 34, 100.

[22]For comparative data on jury composition, see the bibliographic citations in H. Jacob, "Judicial insulation—elections, direct participation, and public attention to the courts in Wisconsin," *Wisconsin Law Rev.* (Summer 1966), pp. 801-819.

[23]This figure is taken from the report at note 10, *supra*.

[24]177th Criminal District Court Grand Jury, *Report of the November 1971 Grand Jury for the 177th Criminal District Court* (Houston, Tex., 1972), p. 1.

[25]Percentage of grand jurors who indicated the length of time required before they claimed to substantially understand the duties, powers, and functions of a grand jury: (1) understood prior to or immediately after 1st session, 22%; (2) understood after 2nd session, 27%; (3) understood after 4th session, 32%; and (4) understood after 6th session or longer, 19%. Median time is somewhat more than the 3rd session.

[26]The statistics in this paragraph are based on figures from the report at note 10, *supra*.

PART II:

IMPRISONMENT, PROBATION, AND PAROLE

14. *In a lengthy preface written for a book on English prisons, George Bernard Shaw captured the essence of prison controversy as it existed in 1922 and as it exists today. In the following excerpt from that preface, Shaw recommends that society must view its actions against criminals as defensive, not as motions to satisfy an emotional need for revenge or as an objective application of the golden rule—"eye for an eye, tooth for a tooth." A vengeful approach, according to Shaw, leads to atrocious prison conditions that intensify rather than placate criminal tendencies; the "eye for an eye" principle can only foster a false sense of puritanical justice based on the fallacious notion that "two blacks make a white."*

If self defense, rather than punishment, is regarded as the prime social motive in the incarceration of lawbreakers, the resolutions to certain central issues become clear. Capital punishment is placed in a proper and rational perspective—"sufficient restraint must be effected not as punishment but as a necessity for public safety" and treatment of "intolerably mischievous human beings" or "hard cases" must not reflect "ethical pretentiousness." The "sentimental vice of vengeance" would be eliminated and, along with it, the spiteful justification of inhumane prison conditions.

According to Shaw, imprisonment must be regarded solely as a social necessity. From this perspective, imprisonment does not necessitate senseless squalor and hence, social guilt reflected by hysterical cries for prison reform is not encouraged.

RECAPITULATION

GEORGE BERNARD SHAW

For the sake of mental convenience, I recapitulate the contentions presented in this preface.

1. Modern imprisonment—That is, imprisonment practiced as a punishment as well as a means of detention, is extremely cruel and mischievous, and therefore extremely wicked. The word extremely is used because our system was pushed to a degree at which prison mortality and prison insanity forced it back to the point at which it is barely endurable, which point may therefore be regarded as the practicable extreme.

2. Although public vindictiveness and public dread are largely responsible for this wickedness, some of the most cruel features of the prison system are not understood by the public, and have not been deliberately invented and contrived for the purpose of increasing the prisoner's torment. The worst of them are (*a*) unsuccessful attempts at reform, (*b*) successful attempts to make the working of the prison cheaper for the State and easier for the officials, or (*c*) accidents of the evolution of the old privately owned detention prison into the new punitive State prison.

3. The prison authorities profess three objects: (*a*) Retribution (a euphemism for vengeance), (*b*) Deterrence (a euphemism for Terrorism), and (*c*) Reform of the prisoner. They achieve the first atrociously. They fail in the second through lack of the necessary certainty of detection and prosecution, partly because their methods are too cruel and mischie-

vous to secure the co-operation of the public, partly because the prosecutor is put to such inconvenience and loss of time that he feels that he is throwing good money after bad, partly because most people desire to avoid an unquestionable family disgrace much more than to secure a very questionable justice, and partly because the proportion of avowedly undetected crimes is high enough to hold out reasonable hopes to the criminal that he will never be called to account. The third is irreconcilable with the first; and the figures of recidivism, and the discovery that the so-called Criminal Type is really a prison type, prove that the process is one of quite uncompensated deterioration.

4. The cardinal vice of the system is the anti-Christian vice of vengeance, or the intentional duplication of malicious injuries in compliance with the expiatory superstition that two blacks made a white. The criminal accepts this, but claims that punishment absolves him if the injuries seem fairly equivalent; and so, when absolution is necessarily denied him, and he is forced back into crime by the refusal to employ him, he feels that he is entitled to revenge this injustice by becoming an enemy of society. No beneficial reform of our treatment of criminals is possible unless and until this essentially sentimental vice of vengeance is unconditionally eradicated.

5. Society claims a right of self-defense, extending to the destruction or restraint of lawbreakers. This right is separable from the right to revenge or punish: it need have no more to do with punishment or revenge than the caging or shooting of a man-eating tiger. It arises from the occurrence of (A) intolerably mischievous human beings, and (B) persons defective in

the self-control needed for free life in modern society, but well behaved and contented under tutelage and discipline. Class A can be painlessly killed or permanently restrained. The requisite tutelage and discipline can be provided for Class B without rancor or insult. The rest can be treated not as criminals but as civil defendants, and made to pay for their depredations

> "Class A [intolerably mischievous human beings] can be painlessly killed or permanently restrained."

in the same manner. At present many persons guilty of conduct much viler than that for which poor men are sent to prison suffer nothing worse than civil actions for damages.

6. The principle to be kept before the minds of the citizens is that as civilized society is a very costly arrangement necessary to their subsistence and security they must justify their share to the cost, and giving no more than their share of trouble, subject to every possible provision by insurance against innocent disability; and that this is a condition precedent to freedom, and might on extreme provocation be enforced to the full extent of removing cases of incurable noxious disability by simply putting an end to their existence.

7. An unconquerable repugnance to resort to killing having led to the abolition of capital punishment in several countries, and to its reservation for specially dangerous or abhorrent crimes in all the others, it is possible that the right to kill may be

renounced by all civilized States. This repugnance may be intensified by the removal of the distinction between sin and infirmity, or, in prison language, between crime and disease, because it leads to the extirpation of the incurable invalid as well as to that of the incurable criminal.

On the other hand, the opposite temperament, which is not squeamish about making short work of hard cases, may be reinforced by the abandonment of ethical pretentiousness, vengeance, malice, and all uncharitableness in the matter, and may become less scrupulous than at present in advocating euthanasia for incurables.

Whichever party may prevail, capital punishment as such is likely to disappear, and with it the earmarking of certain offenses as calling for specially deterrent severities. But it does not follow that lethal treatment of extreme cases will be barred. On the contrary, it may be extended to criminals of all sorts. All that can be said at present is that if it be absolutely barred, sufficient restraint must be effected, not as a punishment but as a necessity for public safety. But there will be no excuse for making it more unpleasant than it need be.

8. In all cases where the detention and restraint are called for, the criminal's right to contact with all the spiritual influences of his day should be respected. Conversation, access to books and pictures and music, unfettered scientific, philosophic, and religious activity, change of scene and occupation, the free formation of friendships and acquaintances, marriage and parentage: in short, all the normal methods of creation and recreation, must be available for criminals as for other persons, partly because deprivation of these things is severely punitive, and partly because it is destructive to the victim, and produces what we call the criminal type, making a cure impossible. Any specific liberty which the criminal's specific defects lead him to abuse will, no doubt, be taken from him; but his right to live must be accepted in the fullest sense, and not, as at present, as merely a right to breathe and circulate his blood. In short, a criminal must be treated, not as a man who has forfeited all normal rights and liberties by the breaking of a single law, but as one who, through some specific weakness or weaknesses is incapable of exercising some specific liberty or liberties.

9. The main difficulty in applying this concept of individual freedom to the criminal arises from the fact that the concept itself is as yet unformed. We do not apply it to children, at home or at school, nor to employees, nor to persons of any class or age who are in the power of other persons. Like Queen Victoria, we conceive Man as being either in authority or as being subject to authority, each person doing only what he is expressly permitted to do, or what the example of the rest of his class encourages him to consider as permitted. The concept of the free man, who does everything he likes and everything he can unless there are express prohibitions to which he is politically a consenting party, is still unusual, and consequently terrifying, in spite of all the individualist pamphlets of the eighteenth and nineteenth centuries. It will be found that those who are most scandalized by the liberties I am claiming for the convict, would be equally scandalized if I claimed them for their own sons.

The conclusion is that imprisonment cannot be fully understood by those who do not understand freedom.

Ayot St. Lawrence,
Dec.-Jan., 1921-22.

15. *John Conrad, in "Corrections and Simple Justice," states that "the ideology of people changing permeates corrections" and also, that "the retributive nature still permeates our culture." People changing people (or trying to) is an embroilment. Assumptions abound, individual perspectives breed confusion, and confusion promotes inappropriate reactions hopelessly enmeshed with dangerous emotions.*

Conrad, in his description of the history of our correctional systems, argues that a rational approach to "correcting" offenders and protecting society has been continually frustrated. Consider the following quotation:

> *Inmates are obsessed with their places in all unfamiliar but constricted work and their hopes for release from it. Staff members are required to give most of their attention to the 'here and now' problems of life in custody, whose relationship to rehabilitation is strained at best.*

Conrad maintains that, to escape the fits and starts of naive altruists or the repressive measure of extreme rationalists (such as Rockefeller and his "draconian laws" for narcotic vendors), "people-changing" requires a recognition that most criminal actions are reactions to the "persistence in social injustices" by society. Once the society has recognized its culpability it must, according to the National Advisory Committee of Standards and Goals (1973), assume responsibility for the problems [it has] generate[d].

The success of community corrections as an alternative to traditional institutional arrangements depends on the quality of interaction between society and the offender. Duffee, in Article 18, stresses the importance of establishing reintegration as a primary correctional goal. Conrad recognizes that so long as society, too, can change, reintegration need not be regarded by the offender as defeat.

CORRECTIONS AND SIMPLE JUSTICE

JOHN P. CONRAD

Until very recently, thoughtful and humane scholars, administrators, and clinicians generally held that it was the business of the prison and other incarcerating facilities to rehabilitate offenders. In addition to a rhetoric of rehabilitation appropriate for the influence of public opinion, this conviction was substantively expressed in the organization of services for offenders. Educators, psychologists and social workers were added to the permanent staff in the contemporary prison.

In the last few years, however, the weight of informed opinion in the United States about correctional rehabilitation has shifted to the negative. Rehabilitation, while still recognized as a meritorious goal, is no longer seen as a practical possibility within our correctional structure by the empirical observer. Nevertheless, the ideology of people-changing permeates corrections. Modern prisons remain committed to treatment; echelons of personnel to carry it out are established on every table of organization. The belief that a prisoner should be a better man as a result of his confinement guides judges in fixing terms and parole boards in reducing them. Rehabilitation continues to be an objective in good standing.

The dissonances produced by this

conflict between opinion and practice are numerous, profound, and destructive of confidence in the criminal justice system. Whether these dissonances can be settled remains to be seen, but, clearly, understanding is critically important to improvement of the situation. In this article I shall explain the change in rehabilitative thought and consider the significance of that change. I shall then review some of the more striking examples of policy departures grounded on rejection of the concept of rehabilitation and conclude with a new conceptualization of the place of corrections in criminal justice. My analysis and conclusions are intended to contribute to the vigorous dialogue which is necessary for the understanding and resolution of any public problem in a democratic society. In the case of corrections, the problem is the attainment of simple justice, a goal which must be achieved if civilized order is to continue.

The Development and Rejection of the Rehabilitative Notion

The idea of rehabilitation is not rooted in antiquity. Until the eighteenth century, charity was the most that any deviant could hope for and much more than most deviants—especially criminals—received. Any history of punishment before that time is an account of grisly and stomach-turning horrors administered by the law to wrong-doers.[1] Our forebears behaved so ferociously for reasons which we can only reconstruct with diffidence. The insecurity of life and property must have played an important part in the evolution of sanctions so disproportionate to harm or the threat of harm, but there was certainly another source of our ancestors' furious response to the criminal: The war they waged against crime was partly a war against Satan. They believed that crime could be ascribed to original sin, that Satan roamed the world seeking the destruction of souls, and that his handiwork could be seen in the will to do wrong. The salvation of the innocent depended on the extirpation of the wicked. It is only in light of belief systems of this kind, varying in detail from culture to culture, that we can explain the Inquisition, the persecution of witches, and the torturing, hanging, drawing, and quartering of common criminals.

The Enlightenment changed all that. If pre-Enlightenment man teetered fearfully on the brink of Hell, desperately condemning sin and sinners in the interest of his own salvation, the philosophies conferred an entirely new hope on him. Rousseau's wonderful vision of man as naturally good relied partly on an interpretation of primitive society which we now dismiss as naive, but the world has never been the same since he offered his alternative.[2] Once relieved of a supernatural burden of evil, man's destiny can be shaped, at least partly, by reason.

Reason created the obligation to change the transgressor instead of damning him or removing him by execution or transportation. The history of corrections, as we now know it, can be interpreted as a series of poorly controlled experiments to see what could be done about changing offenders. It started with incarceration to remove offenders from evil influences which moved them to the commission of crime, a reasonable proposition, given what was known about the conditions which created crime.[3] It is noteworthy that the theoretical basis for expecting benefits from incarceration depended on the perception that the causes of crime might be found in the community rather than in the criminal.

This theory did not survive for long. The actual benefits of incarceration were difficult to identify in support of the expectations of the early American idealists responsible for the original notion. Incarceration was now seen as a satisfactory punishment to administer to the criminal, and if a rationale was needed for it, Jeremy Bentham and the Utilitarians provided it.[4] Punishment would rehabilitate if administered by the "felicific calculus," according to which the proper amount of pain could be administered to discourage the transgressor from continuing his transgressions.

Nineteenth century Americans were finicky about human misery, and they did not like to see it administered intentionally. They responded to the rhetoric of rehabilitation as expressed, for example, in the famous 1870 Declaration of Principles of the American Prison Association.[5] This time, reason provided a new objective, and a new logic to justify it. The prison's purpose was no longer simply to punish the offender, but the prisoner was to be cured of his propensity to crime by religious exhortation, psychological counseling, remedial education, vocational training, or even medical treatment. The Declaration of Principles maintained that some of the causes of crime are to be found in the community. However, while incarcerated, the offender was to be changed for the better lest he be released to offend again. No one seriously advocated that felons should be confined until there was a certainty of their abiding by the law; it was impractical to carry this logic that far.

Gradually, empiricism took control of correctional thought. Its triumph was hastened by the peculiarly available data on recidivism, which was easily obtained and obviously related to questions of program success or failure. Correctional rehabilitation was empirically studied in details ever more refined. In a 1961 paper, Walter Bailey reviewed the evidence available in a hundred studies of correctional treatment and found it wanting in support for the belief that prison programs are related to parole success.[6] A much more massive review, by Lipton, Martinson, and Wilks, still unpublished, was completed in 1969 and reaches the same conclusion.[7] In their impeccably rigorous evaluation of group counseling, Kassebaum, Ward, and Wilner fully substantiate the negative conclusion of their predecessors.[8] In the absence of any strong evidence in favor of the success of rehabilitative programs, it is not possible to continue the justification of policy decisions in corrections on the supposition that such programs achieve rehabilitative objectives.

Paralleling the last twenty years of evaluative research has been much empirically based theoretical work. The classic study of the prison community by Clemmer[9] imposes a structure on observation which, in turn, leads to the theoretical contributions of such writers as Schrag,[10] Sykes,[11] Goffman,[12] and Irwin.[13] Each of these workers brought a different perspective to his analysis, and the methodologies vary fundamentally. However, the picture of the prison which emerges clearly accounts for the unsatisfactory results of all those evaluative studies. The prison is an institution which forces inmates and staff alike to adjust to its requirements. These accommodations are inconsistent with rehabilitation. They are directed toward the present adjustment of the individual to the austerely unnatural conditions in which he finds himself. In some prisons survival becomes a transfixing concern. In any prison, regardless of the hazards to personal safety, the discomforts and irritations of the present occupy the attention of everyone. Inmates are obsessed with their places in an unfamiliar but constricted world and their hopes for release from it. Staff members are required to give most of their attention to the "here and now" problems of life in custody, whose relationship to rehabilitation is strained at best.

Under these conditions, relationships and attitudes in even the most enlightened prison are determined by group responses to official coercion. The ostensible program objectives of rehabilitation may be a high school diploma, a new trade, or increased psychological maturity, but the prevailing attitude towards programs will be determined by group opinions about their value in obtaining favorable consideration for release. Whatever his motivations, man may learn a lot by engaging in a vocational training program. However, the statistical success of such programs in increasing the employability of released inmates is imperceptible. The reasons for this situation are still subject to speculation, but the inference is that few of those involved take the program seriously. The learning process passes the time which must be served and qualifies the individual for the favorable consideration which he desperately seeks. But expectation of a career in a learned vocation does not influence the learner.

The data are not as exhaustive as one would like. Perhaps Glaser's study of the effectiveness of the federal prison system[14] provides the most conclusive picture of the bleak situation. The motivation to enroll in various self-improvement activities for release qualifications is conceded by the author. Neither in Glaser's own study of federal prisoners nor in the studies by others reported by him is there any strong evidence that educational and vocational training are related to post-release success. To this day, we have only anecdotal evidence that any inmate graduates of vocational training programs are successfully placed in careers for which they were trained.

The final word on coercion in the administration of rehabilitation programs may have been pronounced by Etzioni,[15] whose analysis of compliance structures uses the prison as a paradigm of coercion. In Etzioni's formulation, the response to coercion is alienation. He holds that alienation from authority is at its highest when authority uses force to obtain compliance. As force is explicit and to be encountered continuously in the prison, it is obvious that alienation will be universal, although it will take many forms, both active and passive. Indeed, Etzioni hypothesizes that when a prison administration attempts to obtain compliance by other means than coercion it loses stability. Yet it is the very alienation of the prisoner which severely restricts his will to accept the goals of the staff. To choose to be committed to any activity is one of the few choices which cannot be denied the prisoner. For the inmate to accord the staff his volition is an act of enlightened self-interest which exceeds the perspective of most prisoners.

Rehabilitation has been deflated as a goal of correctional custody by empiricism and by sociological theory. Its claims, however, have not been refuted by these forces alone. The findings of research have been paralleled by staff disappointment, scepticism in the media, and administrative policy changes.

It is not possible to document so subjective a change as the loss of confidence in rehabilitation by correctional staff. Indeed, there are still many who continue with program development in the prisons and hope for the best. The establishment in 1969 of the Kennedy Youth Center in Morgantown, West Virginia, represents the persisting faith of the staff and consultants of the Federal Bureau of Prisons. It seems that the Bureau's faith is indomitable. For example, an experimental prison will be built in Butner, North Carolina, to study further the potentiality of treatment in custodial conditions. However, it would be difficult to find a comparable professional investment in institutional treatment. The fervid hopes engendered by the group counseling movement of the late fifties and early sixties have faded into routines and motions.

The part played by journalists in the change of correctional ideology is also hard to evaluate. The contributions of observers so diverse as Jessica Mitford,[16] Ben Bagdikian,[17] Ronald Goldfarb,[18] and Eddie Bunker,[19] have vividly documented the futility of the prison as a rehabilitative agency. The extent to which they have changed public opinion is open to some question, in the absence of a recent poll, but there is a consistent theme in their writing which runs counter to the assumptions of rehabilitation. This theme flourishes without evident response to the contrary.

Administrative policy change has been easy to document. The California Probation Subsidy Act of 1965,[20] a landmark piece of legislation, states that as many offenders as possible should be channeled into probation,

limiting the use of incarceration to cases where the protection of the public requires it. The program has been described in detail elsewhere,[21] but it is firmly based on the proposition that correctional rehabilitation cannot be effectively carried out in conditions of captivity. Whether it can be carried out in the community remains to be seen. As Hood and Sparks have remarked, the research which shows that probation is at least as effective as incarceration "cannot be interpreted as showing that probation is especially effective as a method of treatment."[22]

Nevertheless, the California act has been emulated in several states.[23] It represents a gradual shift which has already emptied some prisons and training schools. The shift has taken a much more abrupt form in Massachusetts, where in March, 1972, all juvenile correctional facilities were closed. The commissioner then responsible, Jerome Miller, acted on the conviction that such facilities do much more harm than good—if they can be said to do any good at all. The attention which the Massachusetts program has drawn because of its almost melodramatic timing has evoked singularly little debate. The local response in Massachusetts has been a fierce controversy, which the program has so far survived, but there has been at least a tacit acceptance throughout the country that the juvenile correctional facility is an institutional arrangement which can and should be terminated.

These academic and public developments portend the collapse of correctional rehabilitation as we have known it for the past twenty-five years. They confront the nation with a continuing need for the prison and no way to make it presentable. The apparatus of education, social casework, and psychiatry at least serve to disguise the oppressive processes required to hold men, women, and children in custody. To rehabilitate is a noble calling; to lock and unlock cages has never been highly regarded. The issue is apparent to many observers, but it is not surprising that we lack a consensus on its resolution.

Impact of Empiricism on Corrections Policy

The Report of the Corrections Task Force of the President's Commission on Law Enforcement and the Administration of Justice in 1967 initiated a series of public considerations of the problems of corrections. Its opening adjuration in the chapter of summary recommendations begins:

> It is clear that the correctional programs of the United States cannot perform their assigned work by mere tinkering with faulty machinery. A substantial upgrading of services and a new orientation of the total enterprise toward integration of offenders into the main stream of community life is needed.[24]

With this blessing a profusion of community-based correctional programs ensued. Furloughs, work-release units, and half-way houses are now common rather than experimental. The use of volunteers is seen as natural and necessary rather than an administrative inconvenience suffered in the interests of public relations. The improvement of the old programs of probation and parole is slow and, in some states, imperceptible, but the Corrections Task Force started a movement which has gained momentum. The growing confidence in corrections in the community is reflected in the decelerated growth of prison populations at a time when crime rates are increasing as never

before. In some states, especially California, the numbers of felons in state prisons has dramatically declined. In many others, including Ohio, Minnesota, and Illinois, the decline in actual institutional populations has been more modest, but that they have declined at all is significant in view of the rise in both populations and rates of crime and delinquency.

These events reflect hundreds of decisions by judges and parole board members. Policy is changing before our eyes. We can see from the data where it seems to be going. We can also see from current official studies that there is much concern about corrections at high executive levels. There is a continuing agreement that something must be done about its apparent ineffectiveness, its wastefulness, and the danger to society presented by the processes of incarceration.

The most prominent of these studies is the massive report of the Corrections Task Force of the National Commission on Criminal Justice Standards and Goals.[25] The Commission's recommendations are exhaustive, but some of them are particularly significant of the great shift which has taken place. Perhaps the greatest achievement of the Commission is its forthright recognition of the community at large as both a breeder of criminal activity and the most logical correctional base. The reasons behind this conclusion include findings that traditional penal institutions tend to compound rather than alleviate the problems they are designed to correct, that most offenders are treated disproportionately to their potential violence and danger, and that imprisonment has a negative rather than positive effect on the offender's ability to reassimilate into the community upon release. On the other hand, the

Commission concluded that community-based programs seem to be capable of providing community protection and by their very nature do not create the environmental problems inherent in the traditional penal institutions. "The move toward community corrections implies that communities must assume responsibility for the problems they generate."[26]

The results of the study find practical expression in recommendations which are stunningly direct. The Commission prescribed that no new juvenile institutions be built and that existing institutions be replaced by local facilities and programs. The suggestions concerning adult corrections were somewhat more cautious: absent a clear finding that no alternative is possible, no new adult institutions should be built either. The point is that the Commission has no confidence in the value of the prison for any purposes other than punishment and incapacitation. The logic carries the Commission to the conclusion that the country has more prisons than it needs and that it should entirely discontinue the incarceration of juvenile offenders.

Obviously, if the Commission's plan is to be carried out, the correctional continuum must heavily stress alternatives to incarceration. Such a continuum must call for communities to increase social service resources to provide for diversion of offenders from criminal justice processing to the greatest extent possible. It must call for a sentencing policy which relies much more explicitly on suspended sentences, fines, court continuances, and various forms of probation in which emphasis is given to the provision of services. Prisons must be reserved for offenders guilty of crimes of violence, and perhaps for other offenders whose crimes are so egre-

gious as to require this level of severity to satisfy the community's desire for retributive justice.

The Commission is not alone in its outspoken demand for change. Compared to the final report of the Wisconsin Citizens' Study Committee on Offender Rehabilitation,[27] the recommendations of the National Advisory Commission are conservative. The Wisconsin report, issued in July, 1972, begins by establishing as "its most fundamental priority the replacement of Wisconsin's existing institutionalized corrections system with a community-based, non-institutional system." The reasons for this admittedly radical proposal are unequivocal. First, "current Wisconsin institutions cannot rehabilitate." Second, "de-institutionalization of Wisconsin's correctional system would, in the long run, save considerable tax dollars." The Committee considered action to "de-institutionalize" the correctional system so urgent that its accomplishment before mid-1975 was recommended. Although the Governor to whom this recommendation was addressed has not adopted it, the significance of such a recommendation from a committee composed of persons drawn from the informed and established professional and business communities is not to be dismissed as an exercise in flighty liberalism. The Wisconsin correctional apparatus has long been admired as an adequately funded, professionally staffed, and rationally organized system, second to none in these respects. If prisons could rehabilitate, some sign of their capabilities to do so should have emerged in that state. This committee looked carefully for such a sign and could find none.

The alternative system recommended for Wisconsin begins with a call for pre-trial diversion of some offenders on the decision of the District Attorney, the use of restitution as an alternative to the full criminal process, and decriminalization of

> fornication, adultery, sexual perversion, lewd behavior, indecent matter and performances, noncommercial gambling, fraud on inn or restaurant keepers, issuance of worthless checks, fraudulent use of credit cards, non-support, the possession, sale and distribution of marijuana, and public drunkenness.[28]

The confirmed addict and the chronic alcoholic are recognized as helplessly infirm persons. The Task Force urged a policy of treatment rather than prosecution, and a program of services rather than incarceration. The recommendations call for the establishment of services which do not now exist in Wisconsin. There is a realistic confrontation with the probable outcome of most services for these gravely handicapped persons: "[T]he committee feels that flexible programming and expectation of failure must be a part of any development of drug treatment programs."[29]

Nevertheless, it is the clear responsibility of the state to provide treatment within a framework in which at least some success can be rationally expected. Even some custodial care will be required for addicts and alcoholics who can be treated in no other way. It is noteworthy, however, that the possibility of providing such custodial care in prison settings is considered only for those addicts who have been guilty of ordinary felonies, and even then such persons are to have the option of treatment in facilities designed for addicts. No consideration was given to the use of correctional facilities for standard treatment for addicts of any kind.

The Wisconsin Task Force saw that their recommendations went several steps beyond the current public consensus. Nobody knows for sure what the limits of public tolerance for change in corrections may be, but even the forthright writers of this report knew that there is a wide gap between a rationally achieved position in these matters and its acceptance by the electorate. This is especially true in the field of narcotics addiction, where lack of accurate information and a plethora of well-meant misinformation, have done so much to distort public opinion. We are so thoroughly committed to the use of the criminal process for the control of social deviance that alternatives are difficult to design with confidence, notwithstanding our knowledge that the criminal justice system is demonstrably ineffective for many kinds of social control. Recognition of the irrationality of this situation does not provide us with obvious remedies. The weakness of this excellent report is that its recommendations can be readily dismissed by the administrator as impractical, even though the present system is itself shown to be thoroughly impractical on the basis of its results.

The Wisconsin study of corrections provides a startling example of the dissatisfaction evoked by an apparently advanced correctional program when dispassionately studied by citizens concerned with the claims of justice and rationality. In Ohio, another Citizens' Task Force on Corrections reported to the governor on the state of the corrections system, but in this case, the Task Force was confronted by one of the most decrepit correctional programs in the country. Generations of pound-foolish fiscal maladministration had produced a situation in which underpaid, poorly supervised staff worked in slovenly, malodorous prisons filled to the bursting point with idle prisoners. The atmosphere thus created had exploded more than once, convincing even the most fiscally conservative persons that something had to be done. The response was the construction of a large new prison in the most remote area in the state. It was obsolete at the time of its design and will probably be a burden to distort the criminal justice system of Ohio for centuries to come.

The *Report of the Ohio Citizens' Task Force on Corrections*[30] was written in the context of a perceived need for "de-institutionalization." Concerned with bringing about some organizational coherence in an agency which conspicuously lacked this basic element, it devotes much time and space to recommendations for the creation of an effective management structure, an equitable personnel policy, a Training Academy, and a Division of Planning and Research. However, the Task Force stresses at the outset of its report that even if all its recommendations were to be immediately implemented, "the public would not be protected one iota more."[31] The report emphatically asserts:

> We must cease depending on institutionalization as an adequate response to the law offender and protection of the public. Instead, we *must* develop a system of community-based alternatives to institutionalization.... The emphasis of the future must be on alternatives to incarceration. The rule, duty, and obligation of this Task Force is to communicate this vital conclusion to the public.[32]

Since the publication of this report in December, 1971, the Division of Correction has been transformed into an adequately staffed Department of Rehabilitation and Correction. An administrative group is at work on the development of an adaptation of the California Probation Subsidy Act as the most likely strategy for the creation of a sufficient range of community-based alternatives to incarceration. The new penitentiary at Lucasville has been opened. In spite of its preposterous location far from the cities from which its inmates come, it at least has made possible a decision to demolish the infamous old prison at Columbus. The Ohio Youth Commission, charged with the maintenance of a correctional program as well, has re-organized to make its preventive program more than nominal. The de-institutionalization of Ohio corrections has not been accomplished, nor will it be accomplished soon, but a structure of administrative planning, research, and evaluative management has been created on the basis of which rational change can be expected. Already the state's confined population has declined by ten percent, in spite of a steadily increasing rate of commitments. Drift and expediency were the villainous influences identified by the Citizens' Task Force; they have been replaced by policies which require rational decision-making. The transformation is not fool-proof, but it will at least discourage fools from rushing in.

Faced with a rapid expansion of its population and the unique problems brought about by its isolation from the rest of the country, Hawaii has drawn on the resources of the National Clearinghouse for Criminal Justice Planning and Architecture to Develop a Correctional Master Plan.[33] The plan explicitly credits the state with a more adequate delivery of correctional services than is available in many states. However, it does not go far enough. It retains a significant emphasis on traditional institutional-ization which "is probably the most expensive response and also the least effective that a criminal justice system can make in dealing with criminal behavior."[34] Cited as support for the ineffectiveness of such institutional-ization are the increased crime rate and high recidivism.

The approach adopted by the Hawaii planners borrows from the concept of the National Clearinghouse and repre-sents the best current example of a fully developed correctional program based on the Clearinghouse guide-lines. To summarize the work of the Clearinghouse in an article such as this is a daunting task; the published *Guidelines*[35] constitute a weighty volume addressed to the whole span of correctional issues. However, the core ideas are simple and identifiable. First, the planning of correctional systems will eliminate the costly waste incurred by needless building of security housing. Second, com-munity-based alternatives to incarcer-ation can afford both protection for the community and effective reinstate-ment services for the vast majority of offenders. Third, the safe assignment of offenders to correctional services requires a process of differential classification, preferably in an "Intake Service Center." Fourth, for the control of dangerous offenders a "Community Correctional Center" should be incorporated in the system with full provision for maximum custody. Throughout the conceptual development of the Clearinghouse *Guidelines* there is the tacit assump-tion that environmental influences are the most accessible points of inter-vention as to any offender and the diagnostic task is to identify those influences which can be brought to bear on his resocialization. Most social science students of criminal

justice issues will recognize these assumptions as hypothetical at best, but their humane and rational intent is obvious. Clearly, an urgent task for research is the evaluation of the consequences of their implementation under such circumstances of full acceptance as the state of Hawaii has accorded.

The momentum of the traditional correctional policies will not be suddenly halted. Regardless of the enjoinders of the Law Enforcement Assistance Administration and of the recommendations of Citizens' Com-missions across the country, more jails will be built, and many offenders will occupy their cells who might just as well be enrolled in an appropriate community program. Neither the staff,

---

"The informed opinion that co-erced rehabilitation is an impractical ob-jective is equally welcome to human liberals and fiscal conservatives."

---

the agencies, nor the sentencing policies are fully enough developed to allow for an immediate implementa-tion of the enlightened recommenda-tions of the Task Force Reports. In a world in which the costs of incarcer-ation have reached annual per capita costs which far exceed average citizen incomes, the future of incarceration must be constrained by a policy of rigorous selectivity. The informed opinion that coerced rehabilitation is an impractical objective is equally welcome to humane liberals and fiscal conservatives. The task of research is to collect the information which will support the strategy of change.

The Demobilization of Corrections

Where will the momentum of change in corrections lead the criminal justice system? In so emotionally charged a set of issues as surrounds the disposition of convicted offenders, it is futile to predict the probable course of events. Criminologists have known for a long time that the execution of murderers cannot be shown to deter murder, but the retributive motive still permeates our culture, and it is not at all certain that the abolition of capital punishment is permanent. Hatred of the criminal and fear of his actions have nothing to do with reasoned plans to protect ourselves from him or to change his behavior. In a period in which crime has assumed the quality of obsessive concern in our society, the wonder is that so many are able to accept the dispassionate view of the offender which characterizes the recommendations of the numerous study commissions working on the renovation of the correctional system. The threat of an irrationally repressive policy is still a real one. The recent demand by Governor Rockefeller for draconian laws to imprison for life the vendor of narcotics will at least serve as a reminder how tenuous may be our hold on rational correctional concepts. Nevertheless, this portent and others like it can be offset by the widespread belief that rational change is possible and desirable. Some encouragement however, may be taken in the support of this position by a broad spectrum of political opinion. The concern for correctional change is not confined to the various liberal shades.

We should specify the structural changes in the criminal justice system which the new correctional ideology implies. Much of the rhetoric of skepticism challenges us to justify the retention of any part of the present correctional system. We are told that the criminal justice system is nothing more than an instrument for the regulation of the poor, and that therefore the interests of justice would be best served by its abolition. This kind of effervescence serves to discredit the motives and good sense of the correctional reform movement, which draws on the evidence of social research to reach conclusions which both establish the obsolescence of the present system and indicate fruitful directions for its renovation. It is time that we considered where these directions will take us.

First, although we do not know how the prison can be converted into a rehabilitative institution, it will have to be retained for the protection of society from some violent and dangerous offenders from whom no alternative means of protection exist. These prisons must be small. They must provide for the long-term prisoner in ways which support psychological stability and his integrity as a person. These objectives require that he should have latitude for choice, that he should have a sense of society's concern for his welfare, and that his life should be restricted as little as possible given the purposes to be achieved in restricting him at all.

The retention of the prison for the containment of the dangerous offender assumes that he can be identified. This assumption is open to attack. The inference that all offenders who have been guilty of major violence will present continuing hazards to the public is refuted by the consistently low rates of recidivism of released murderers. Therefore, we are reduced to predicting a hazard of future danger from the determination of a pattern of repetitive violence. Many authorities on criminal justice will be dissatisfied with the potential for abuse in this kind of prediction.[36] Acknowledging the validity of this criticism, I can only respond that the confidence which a changing system of social control must maintain will rapidly erode if dangerous and predatory offenders are released from prison to resume the behavior for which they were confined in the first place. Until a more satisfactory basis for their identification can be found, we shall have to tolerate some injustice in order to avoid the greater injustices of needlessly confining the obviously harmless. Social science must persist in the improvement of our power to identify the dangerous offender. The quality of justice is heavily dependent on the increase of knowledge in this age when vengeance is being replaced with reconciliation.

The remainder of the correctional panoply is a dubious asset to justice. We have established probation and parole, halfway houses, work-release programs, group homes, and community correctional centers in an effort to create alternatives to incarceration. The effort has largely succeeded; informed observers have been convinced, and policy has changed sufficiently to reduce the rate of commitment to prison in most of the jurisdictions of the country. As humanitarian reforms, these alternatives were essential. They still are. But, there is little evidence to show that these programs are really more effective than the prisons they replace. They are certainly no worse.

But the point is to *improve* the effectiveness of the criminal justice system. It must be made possible for

the offender to choose a lawabiding life and to act on that choice. Offenders must be seen as people with personal problems of great difficulty. They are now provided with second-rate services, if they receive services at all. It is incumbent upon a society which creates much of its crime burden from persistence in social injustice to make available services which can extricate criminals from criminal careers. In most communities these services exist. The Massachusetts experiment of last year in large part consisted of an effort to bring to the offender the regular community services which are available to ordinary citizens, rather than select the offender for special correctional versions of these services. The latter do not assure effective assistance. Instead, they assure that the help offenders receive will have some stigma attached, and that treatment will be affected by the persistence of the myth that criminality itself is a condition to be treated.

Courts, as the administrators of justice, should induce service agencies of all kinds to make their services accessible. The court thus becomes a referral agency, opening doors by its authority, perhaps even by the purchase of services, but not by coercion or the implication that the freedom of the offender depends on his obtaining benefits from services rendered. This is a model of service delivery which will be difficult to learn and even more difficult to live with. There will always be an inclination to draw an invidious conclusion from the offender's inability to persevere in a program intended for his benefit, but it is an important step in itself to make it possible for offenders to choose the services. Those who can choose but reject them anyway will not benefit from compulsion.

If services can be made more effective by projecting offenders into the mainstream of community activity instead of keeping them in a correctional backwater, the surveillance of these services can also be improved by transferring that responsibility to the police. No one is served by the pretense that probation and parole officers possess qualifications for the discharge of this function. Law enforcement duties should be performed by the police, who are trained for the task and organized to do it. To expect that probation and parole officers can accomplish anything in this respect that could not be better done by the police is to compound confusion with unreality.[37]

There are two functions now discharged by probation and parole officers which cannot be easily transferred. The decisions related to the sentence, its imposition, its terms, its completion and revocation cannot be made without essential information systematically collected. The reports which probation officers make to the court and the parole officers make to the parole boards are services to the court which should be carried out by officials under the control of the court.

The information collected by this officer of the court (his functions are so much more specific than those of the present probation officer that we might accurately designate him the Information Officer) will be essential for the service referrals which the court should make. In small courts, information and referral could well be carried out by the same officer; there may be advantages in differentiating the functions in large courts. These residual responsibilities must be maintained, but their discharge will hardly call for the large and many-layered staffs which are to be found in present day probation and parole departments.

There remains the question of sanctions to be imposed on offenders. Less severity but more certainty in punishment will better serve the public protection. The victims of crime should receive restitution from the offender to the limit that restitution is practical. The graduated use of fines, relating them to the offender's resources, has been successfully used in Sweden. An English study, reported by Hood and Sparks,[38] indicates that for property crimes, at least, the fine may well be the most effective sanction. Suspended sentences have not been definitively evaluated as to their effect on recidivism. The tolerance of the sytem for probation and parole services in which contact does not take place after adjudication suggests that we can safely rely on the suspended sentence for a substantial proportion of offenders. Where there is reason to believe that surveillance is necessary, provision for regular police contacts could be made to assure that reliable control is maintained.

Such a system would limit the use of incarceration to pre-trial detention of some exceptional defendants, and post-trial detention of only the most dangerous offenders. It would provide protection where it is needed, service where it is desired by the offender himself, and control in the measure that the circumstances of the community and the offender require it. The victim would no longer have to comfort himself with the knowledge that the law had taken its course toward retribution; he would now receive restitution from the offender or compensation from the public funds as the situation might require.

The system would be adjustable by feedback. Increased control would be obtained by increased use of the more severe sanctions where the data on crime rates called for it. This system would be retributive, but the nature of the retribution would be the minimum required by measured experience rather than the ancient demands made by hatred and custom. Where reconciliation can be achieved, it will be eased, and where control is required it will be exercised, but the claims of simple justice will be essential elements of policy.

Justice can only be approached, never fully achieved. However, unless it is indeed the first virtue of the public institutions which administer it, none of the other virtues these institutions may possess will matter. The claims of simple justice are not satisfied merely by the administration of due process, but by the operation of the

"Justice can only be approached, never fully achieved."

whole system by methods which restrict liberty only to the degree necessary for public purposes, but nevertheless assure that these restrictions are effective. We are far from such a system now. The removal of the assumptions which the belief in rehabilitation has engendered will make possible a system which will be more modest in aims, more rational in its means, and more just in its disposition.

Notes

[1]See, e.g., H. Barnes, The Story of Punishment (1930); G. Ives, A History of Penal Methods (1970).

[2]See J. Rousseau, An Inquiry Into the Nature of the Social Contract (1791).

[3]See D. Rothman, The Discovery of the Asylum (1972), in which the author traces the origins of this hypothesis, its consequences, and the influences it has exerted long since it was disconfirmed.

[4]See J. Bentham, An Introduction to the Principles of Morals and Legislation (rev. ed. 1823).

[5]See Transactions of the National Congress on Penitentiary and Reformatory Discipline, Prison Association of New York, 26th Annual Report (1870).

[6]Bailey, "An Evaluation of 100 Studies of Correctional Outcomes," In The Sociology of Punishment and Correction, N. Johnston, L. Savitz & M. Wolfgang eds. (2d ed., 1970), p. 733.

[7]This work is summarized in R. Martinson, "Correctional Treatment: An Empirical Assessment," 1972 (available in photocopied typescript from The Academy for Contemporary Problems, Columbus, O.).

[8]G. Kassebaum, D. Ward & D. Wilner, Prison Treatment and Parole Survival (1971).

[9]D. Clemmer, The Prison Community (1958).

[10]Schrag, "Leadership Among Prison Inmates," Amer. Sociological Rev. 19 (1954) 37.

[11]G. Sykes, The Society of Captives (1958).

[12]E. Goffman, Asylums (1961).

[13]J. Irwin, The Felon (1970).

[14]See D. Glaser, The Effectiveness of a Prison and Parole System (1964), pp. 260-84.

[15]See A. Etzioni, The Active Society (1968), pp. 370-75. See also A. Etzioni, A Comparative Analysis of Complex Organizations (1961), pp. 12-22.

[16]Mitford, "Kind and Usual Punishment in California," The Atlantic Monthly (March, 1971), p. 45, in B. Atkins & H. Glick, Prisons, Protest and Politics (1972), p. 151.

[17]B. Bagdikian & L. Dade, The Shame of the Prisons (1972).

[18]Goldfarb & Singer, "Redressing Prisoners' Grievances," Geo. Wash. Law Rev. 39 (1970) 175.

[19]Bunker, "War Behind Walls," Harper's Magazine (Feb. 1972), p. 39. See also E. Bunker, No Beast So Fierce (1972).

[20]CAL. WELF & INST. CODE § 1820 et seq. (West 1972).

[21]See R. Smith, A Quiet Revolution (1972). See also Keldgord et al., Coordinated California Corrections: The System (1971) (known as The Keldgord Report). See also L. Kuehn, "Probation Subsidy and the Toleration of Crime," (paper presented at the Criminology Session of the Ann. Meeting of the Amer. Sociological Assn., New Orleans, La., Aug., 1972).

[22]R. Hood & R. Sparks, Key Issues in Criminology 187-88 (1970), pp. 187-88.

[23]See, e.g., NEV. REV. STAT. § 213.220 et seq. (1971); WASH. REV. CODE ANN. § 13.06.010 et seq. (1962). The state of Ohio has legislation under study which would approach the California model. At the time of this writing [1973], the California model is the most advanced in concept and implementation.

[24]President's Commission on Law Enforcement and Administration of Justice, Task Force

Report: Corrections (1967), p. 105.

[25]*Ibid.*, esp. intro. ch. 1, summary of findings & final ch. 18, Priorities and Implementation.

[26]National Advisory Commission on Criminal Justice Standards and Goals, *Working Papers C-3* (1973).

[27]Wisconsin Council on Criminal Justice, *Final Report to the Governor of the Citizen's Study Committee on Offender Rehabilitation* (1972).

[28]*Ibid.*, p. 50.

[29]*Ibid.*, p. 77.

[30]Ohio Citizens' Task Force on Corrections, *Final Report to Governor John J. Gilligan* (1971).

[31]*Ibid.*, at A-8.

[32]*Ibid.*, at A-8, A-9 (emphasis in original).

[33]*See* State Law Enforcement and Juvenile Delinquency Planning Agency, *Correctional Master Plan* (1973), p. 26.

[34]*Ibid.*

[35]F. Moyer, E. Flynn, F. Powers & M. Plautz, *Guidelines for the Planning and Design of Regional and Community Correctional Centers for Adults* (1971). See esp. Section D, Planning Concepts.

[36]*See, e.g.,* von Hirsch, "Prediction of Criminal Conduct and Preventive Confinement of Convicted Persons," Buffalo Law Rev. 21 (1972) 717.

[37]*See* E. Studt, *Surveillance and Service in Parole: A Report of the Parole Action Study* (1972), pp. 70-96.

[38]Hood & Sparks, note 22 *supra,* pp. 188-89.

16. *If the police task is complicated and hindered by preconceived notions of its social purpose, corrections suffer doubly. In the study of criminal justice agencies, there is no other concept that is as highly questioned as "justice." Nevertheless, the courts must administer it and correctional institutions must reflect it. Prisons must appear equitable while robbing men and women of their freedom.*

This contradiction has been the cause of controversy since the beginning of our prison system. However, it can no longer be regarded lightly or discarded as an embarrassing contradiction that, for some reason, persists. Instead, it must be understood that the philosophic necessity to appear just and the practical necessity to temporarily remove deviants from society have warped attempts to realistically understand, evaluate and change our correctional system.

Instead of being involved in abstract controversy, the "New Realists" in corrections* are placing an emphasis on the practical necessities of society rather than the philosophic and emotional consequences of imprisonment. They recognize the need to discard those ideologies that, regardless of their humanistic overtones, are not adaptable to the realities of crime, criminals, and punishment.

Fogel, in the following essay,** by describing the pathetic position of prison guards, reveals the tragic, yet almost ludicrous consequences of misguided and chronically superficial attempts to "better" our prison system. In this essay, we are given a picture of the prison guard, an indispensable administrator of justice who is unconscionably manipulated by administrative policies that vacillate between fitful thrusts of altruism and hard-nosed, self-serving pragma-tism. The situation that is described here provides thoughtful framework for the other essays in this part.

*According to Federal Bureau Prisons Director Norma Carlson, the new trends in correctional evaluations are indicative of a "New Realism."

**Adapted from David Fogel "...*WE ARE THE LIVING PROOF*..." Cincinnati: Anderson, 1975

ON GUARDING PRISONS

DAVID FOGEL

There is no dearth of literature on the inmate. Academicians, for the last generation, have been fascinated with the discovery of inmate types, cultures and, more recently, inmate political groups. Particular focus has centered on *sub rosa* inmate organizations, argot roles, the organization of life in total institutions, and inmate-staff conflicts resulting from the peculiar social organization of a prison. There have been studies of the conflicting roles guards have to play and several on the treatment-versus-custody orientation issue. However, precious little is known about the guard himself—other than through questionnaires. We do not even have a very good composite picture of the guard. The President's Crime Commission (1967), the Joint Correctional Manpower Commission (1969), and the National Advisory Commission on Criminal Justice Standards and Goals (1973) all recommended ways to improve management styles and skills and recruit better personnel, but none really probed with enough depth to understand and thereby know what to improve. All called for more better-trained and higher paid guards, but none spoke of the basic question of how the guard sees himself, how he develops his view of the prison world in which he must contain and manage men against their will. There is a tacit assumption in the literature that guard improvement is a function of his infinite maleability, if only management could figure out the right mold. There are some problems with such a formulation.

Our hazy picture of the guard comes from sociologists and convicts. Convicts simply write more books than guards. Convicts also write more (and better) books than wardens. The latter, usually upon retirement, produce complacent, self-congratulatory collections of reminiscences. Only a few guards have written books after they have left the prison. Convicts' books are better because the selection process for becoming a convict draws upon a more representative group (that includes gifted writers) than guards under civil service and political procedures of selection. Turnover is very high among guards in a prison, who do their "time" in eight-hour shifts; convicts are there full-time. Convicts, with a fairly uncomplicated mission—freedom and "working the system" until freedom comes—understand the prison better than do guards. This is not meant in denigration of the guard but rather as a beginning examination of his status.

Although the individual guard turnover is great (with the rate of 102% of new guards at Stateville, Illinois, in 1973), the role is a fixed one. The guard is a bearer of stability, fixity and the status quo. He is rewarded for prowess in uncovering situations that will upset routine and regularity. Upward mobility is a function of order. Evaluations made of the guard by superiors are heavily weighted in favor of doing the same thing repetitively well. He becomes a master of orderliness. His routine makes him a static entity. If he looks in one direction, he sees a few of his colleagues promoted, while if he looks toward the convict, he sees a very different phenomenon occurring.

Convicts are *expected* to change, to learn, to grow—morally, spiritually, academically, vocationally, emotionally and socially—or even if they regress, it is *expected*. It is no surprise to a guard to find an inmate acting badly; that is why the inmate is in prison. But the guard is *expected* to be a paragon of the honest controlled man. Guards are *supposed* to reflect (ultimately to a parole board) progressive *change* in convicts' behavior. If the guard is *static*, the convict is *dynamic*. The convict is *expected* to become something different, hopefully something better. Even where prisons are programmatically impoverished, guards do not fail to notice that convicts write prose, poetry, plays and occasionally saleable movie-scripts, and that it is possible in craft shops for convicts to produce paintings, leather works, sculpture and other works of art providing incomes that can run in multiples of a guard's wage. Nor is it unnoticed by guards that inmates are provided with vocational shops, staff, and expensive machinery and equipment for self-improvement. If, as has been repeatedly shown, parole preparation and release may be hazardous trips for the convict, these also represent *movement* from one status to another. The guard watches this from a *fixed* position. Guards watch convicts become certified mechanics, office machinery technicians, draftsmen, high school graduates, and even college graduates—all elusive goals for guards. Even if the training most convicts receive has little meaning in relation to recidivism, and this seems to be the case, the convicts are still recipients of much expensive attention. Convicts communicate this phenomenon to guards by making invidious comparisons between themselves and the guards, using their former status or their *anticipated* one as examples. Nor does society reward the occupation of guarding others honorifically or financially. Parents rarely if ever project guarding as a first choice profession for their children. There is little cultural pride attached to being a prison guard.

The Evolution of the Guards' Role

Guards can be better understood by our study of the organization of the prison and their expected work roles rather than by studying guard characteristics individual by individual.[1] We will trace how these expectations affected the guards and produced their contemporary view of their role. Warders, turnkeys or guards, as correctional officers and counselors were called in the old days, were hard to find. Lewis states: "Often the prison had to rely upon men who had been thrown out of work elsewhere and were willing to accept jobs at the penitentiary temporarily until they could find something better. In addition, staff positions were subject to political pressures."[2]

In 1823, an ex-convict, writing about his experience in Newgate, reveals that it was hard to get capable guards at $500 a year. This was especially true because the guard had to remain inside the stockade almost as constantly as the prisoner, being permitted to visit with his family or friends only once or twice a month.[3]

The guard had a clearer task in the early days. All he needed was a whip or a steel-tipped cane (later a rifle) to administer a lock-step, silent system

of prisoner behavior management. His mission was unambiguous: "no escapes, order and silence." This sufficed until the mid to late nineteenth century when a slow erosion of the uncomplicated mission began. The only complication to that point was the convicts' desire for freedom, but that was expected and indeed formed the basis for the uncomplicated mission—and escape-proof order.

It was the Lynds-Cray-Wiltse mentality which set the historical dimensions of the guards' role. These men did not come to their ideas about prison governance (and hence the role of the keeper) accidentally. It was calculated. Nor did they shy away from implementation. Wiltse of Sing-Sing proclaimed: "The best prison is that which the inmates find worst."[4] Presumably, Wiltse's guard force was to make sure his prison was the worst. Lynds and Cray borrowed from the military to march (lock-step) inmates and inflict corporal punishment for the slightest infraction. In so doing, guards had to perform their jobs using a military model, complete with uniforms and weaponry. Enforcing silence upon inmates was never totally successful, but it had an effect upon guards who had to be constantly vigilant. Guards watched for facially expressive communications and patrolled cellblocks barefooted seeking violators of the no-talking rule. When violators were identified, wardens ordered flogging. Quite aside from the brutality of the use of the whip on convicts, guards were being debased first by having to crawl silently around ranges to report conversation and then by having to learn how to use a whip on violators. There was no training program for the use of the lash in early New York prisons but almost "...every officer in the prison, it seemed, had taken a hand in administering the stripes."[5] In Auburn, throughout the year of 1845, there was a flogging every two days for conversation-related offenses.[6]

In the beginning, guards were to consider their charges "wicked and depraved, capable of every atrocity, and ever plotting some means of violence." Menninger still refers to prison life as "a perpetual cold war which at times warms up. . . ." Early newspaper accounts reported that "knives, in some form, are common with convicts, and edged tools in almost every shop are in their hands (1828)."[7] Constant frisks and searches had to be undertaken to reduce the number of homemade weapons available to convicts. Other forms of contraband also found their way into the prison and had to be watched for: beer, liquor, newspapers, letters, fresh fruit, etc. Guards were now given the impossible task of keeping the prison hermitically sealed. With the nexus of cash or other favors still binding the keeper and the kept, guards themselves early became involved in smuggling goods in short supply into the prison and therefore had to watch out for each other. Nor were early prison administrators content with the difficult task of merely ordering compliance of the convicts' public behavior. Masturbation was found by one investigating committee (1847) to be ". . .the besetting sin of all prisons. . . . Its existence is very marked at Auburn, and is doubtless one exciting cause of much of the insanity which has prevailed there."[8]

Except for the 1830-1850 period when the guard was simply told to be perversely vigilant, we find double-messages constantly given him by administrators. Thomas Eddy, the Quaker who was so instrumental in abolishing capital punishment for all but a few crimes at the end of the eighteenth century, is the man who warned of inmates "ever plotting some means of violence." At the same time, however, he also advised that no two inmates were alike and therefore, should not be treated alike, thereby further complicating the guards' role.[9] Following the New York (Sing-Sing) terror period, the guards watched a bewildering array of reformative programs and personnel enter the prison. Price Chenault said (1939):

> Chaplains and other religious enthusiasts were equally certain that they held the key to unlock the door to reformation. In turn have come the industrialist, the educator, the psychologist, the psychiatrist, and the case worker. . . . The claims of all these groups have been exaggerated; their expectations have presented a confused picture to the administrator.[10]

But it was not the administrator who was confused, it was the guard. The administrator brought these disciplines in at a time when the whole issue of whether to continue penitentiaries was in question. The reformative programs were to replace force in maintaining order. The pen was to substitute for the whip. The promise of early release for good conduct under the indeterminate sentence was now available. McKendrick, perhaps the most lucid custodian in correctional history makes this point (1951):

> In this sense, discipline is a central objective in the aims of the administrator and his rehabilitative staff. . . .
> Perhaps the most significant thing about prison discipline from a historical point of view is the tendency toward the mitigation of severe punishments as the evidences of reformative influences are increased in the prison community. Corporal punishments. . .have been

abolished in many places.... *When prisoners know that a record of all infractions of rules will be submitted to the parole board considering their release, they recognize that strong evidences of failure to adjust within the prison community may be interpreted as sound reasons for withholding their release.*[11]

The guards also noticed that the reformative personnel worked 9 a.m. to 5 p.m. Monday through Friday, and were secure in their offices and chapels. Whenever the rhetoric of rehabilitation or reformation escalated, the guards' basic mission was further compromised. Again, McKendrick analyzes the problem:

With each approach to the problem of correctional treatment, the job of the custodian becomes more complex. Each new service that enters the field requires the development of new attitudes, new thoughts and often new duties for the custodial staff. It was a far simpler task to provide security when one resident chaplain and one physician were the only non-uniformed employees than it is today with the addition of teachers, physicians, psychiatrists, psychologists, representatives of various religious denominations, Veterans, Aloholics Anonymous representatives, all a part of the paraphernalia of reform. The liberalization of recreation, correspondence, and visiting privileges has complicated the picture.[12]

The guards were increasingly bewildered. Nobody had prepared them to speak to, much less to relate to, college educated professionals who often spoke a mysterious jargon. The guards withdrew to their familiar tasks. If the disparity of purpose involved in securing "the offender against escape at the same time that he is trained for responsibility and freedom" was not apparent to others, it was apparent to the guards. Tappan (1951) continues:[13]

Abstract ideal objectives are strenuously pursued—at the level of talk—but action betrays the gap when methods are employed that are quite inappropriate to the avowed ends.... At best, [the guard]... is often impelled by the principle of least effort to do the job routinely, with a minimum of mental exertion or of disturbance. In this he is frequently encouraged by his superiors and the public through their preference for a quietly moribund correctional system.[14]

Custody vs. Rehabilitation

Accomplished by eminent scholars, the "Theoretical Studies in Social Organization of the Prisons" (1960) pointed out the folly of trying to maximize the aims of custody and treatment simultaneously under the same roof, behind the same wall.[15] Their statement was clearly a pessimistic view despite the disclaimer that they did not want others to see the work as a "criticism of the existing penal system, but rather as an analysis of its current operations and structure, which may contribute to the eventual improvement of our institutions."[16] No bright new vistas were proposed. The message left—at least for the guards—was extremely discouraging.

Studies which followed were in the same mold. They rediscovered dilemmas confronting prison administrators and suggested different patterns of management[17] or projected new theories for corrections based upon classification of types of prisoners. The basic problem of the prison's *raison d'etre*, to provide custody, which was always crystal clear to the warden, was obscured by the researchers. Attempts to democratize administrative styles or to integrate inmate culture with the guards' focal concerns related to securing custody were like two ships passing in the night. One influential researcher (1961), found that the guard was alienated because of the unilateral flow of information (he being at the uninvolved bottom end of the hierarchy); that guards possessed only an "illusion" of unlimited authority; that autonomy of the official is a fiction; and that inmates, who might be classified as pro-, anti- and psuedo-social were (not surprisingly) more influenced by values built up over a lifetime than they were by their new-found participative patterns as prison inmates.[18] Another researcher (1968), found guards were cooperative, opportunistic or alienated, apparently not unlike the inmates.[19]

Guards, however, did not read this literature, nor did many of their superiors. They were listening to another, earlier drum beat, again from McKendrick (1951):

> The prison is a totalitarian community. The prison is a community in which the most significant values of the governed, the values of freedom, are limited in the interest of the state....
>
> Conflict between the agencies of reform and custodial forces exists, (when)...members of the professional staff fail to recognize the essentially totalitarian structure of the prison community....
>
> The pattern of custody is the oldest and first essential element of confinement. It is as much a part of the prison environment as the presence of inmates. All of the relationships in the prison community take place within the atmosphere of custody, and treatment processes cannot take place apart from it....
>
> For centuries, prisons have been constructed with a single objective, that of security. In a sense, each new prison was an experiment in construction. Whenever an escape occurred, some effort was made to strengthen the physical plant. A wall was constructed, more windows were barred, or perhaps a new

position was created and a guard delegated to eliminate the weak point. The modern prison plant has developed as a result of earlier failures and, expensive as it may be, the modern walled prison is sufficiently secure to prevent escape, provided that neither the personnel nor the procedures of operation are in themselves defective.[20]

Ramsey Clark blamed the current (1971) plight of the guard on the prison environment itself.[21] This is not inconsistent with the view taken here that guards did indeed become the products of their moral and physical (work) environment. If we want to fully appreciate the position of the guard it is instructive to examine what the official and self-proclaimed professional leadership have said the purpose of the prison, hence the role of the guard, to be.

The American Correctional Association (1960) told custody officers the first responsibility of the prison is the "secure custody and control of prisoners." But this is not too helpful since the ACA in other places said that rehabilitation is the first purpose of the prison. The largest department of corrections in the nation informed its guards (1971):

> Remember, CUSTODY is always first in order of importance.... Constant vigilance is the price of efficient custody.... Never show the slightest uncertainty as to the course of your action. You must be a leader in the strongest sense of the word; must know and show your authority.... Do not fraternize with any inmate or group of inmates. IT COULD COST YOU YOUR JOB.[22]

Whatever else was being published in the journals about new breakthroughs, or at best detentes between custody and treatment staffs, the guard in his confusion invariably focused on the micro-world of the cell block.

Prisoners in maximum-security prisons have much time and very little to do. They can afford to spend long hours in patient watching to find any weakness in the behavior of their custodians. They are quick to learn a guard's habits, his interests, hobbies, likes, and dislikes. Every item of information thus acquired may be useful at some future time. Some inmates watch carefully every time a door is unlocked to see whether or not the key is left exposed. They are quick to note every change of assignment and the manner in which each employee carries out his job....

Constant vigilance and alertness are essential preventives against escape from the housing units. Guards must react to unfamiliar sounds, strange odors, and the unusual behavior of any inmate. The guards' time is spent largely in the monotonous patrolling of galleries and in counting the inmate population.

Searching cells should never become a routine or carelessly performed task. Favorite hiding places for contraband are toilets and washbowls, brooms, floor coverings, bed legs, soap, ventilators, innocent-looking pieces of cardboard, and mattresses....

The most important process in the administration of custody is the count.... When counts are made it should be determined that the prisoner is not only present but that he is alive and in suitable condition to fulfill his assignment.[23]

From some rehabilitators, the guard heard that things were getting better. (Loveland, 1951)

One of the major contributions of an effective classification program is better personnel and inmate morale. Aside from bringing all services and personnel together through a cooperative approach to institutional and individual problems, classification gives the custodial officer higher status and a more vital, interesting job. He is no longer just a guard. He has an important job to perform in the training and treatment program.[24]

But Menninger was probably closer to the truth when he observed that the prisoner was being "herded about by men half afraid and half contemptuous of him, toward whom all offenders early learn to present a steadfast attitude of hostility."[25]

Herman Schwartz, who since Attica has become one of the foremost correctional law scholar-activists, simply sees guards as frightened, hostile, rural types who are basically conservative. He did hedge a bit, saying that the following picture might be overdrawn.

These people usually have no understanding or sympathy for these strange urban groups, with their unfamiliar and often 'immoral' life-styles, with their demands and their resentments. Racial prejudice is often present, for the white backlash is particularly powerful among such rural types....

Such frightened and hostile people are sentenced to prison as guards for 20-year or more terms—or as long as it takes to get a retirement pension—and are thrown into the most dangerous and frightening kind of encounters with these militant and resentful minorities. They are seen by the prisoners and often see themselves as policemen; they are often called that by the prisoners and their blue uniforms, para-military organization, billy clubs and the like reinforce that perception. In their unions' utterances and elsewhere, the guards often express a kinship and solidarity with law enforcement which is reciprocated: the Buffalo police force and its newspaper, for example, explicitly affirmed their solidarity with the Attica guards.[26]

George Jackson, in his famous "A Letter from Soledad Prison," picks up the themes of fear, unpredictability, and constant tension of the guard's world.

Since the guard controls the gate and may call on the organized violence of his and other government forces on up to the U.S. Airborne Army, it may seem odd for him to feel insecure. This is the case, however, in fact (and I speak here as objectively as is possible—I never underestimate the intelligence of the people), it is a matter of fact that the guard is less psychologically secure than the man he has trapped. He is more defensive, counter-active, 'hostile,' than his victim. Although he does control the greater violence he still feels that he can never relax. This is understandable when you consider that he knows how offending and disgusting his actions are. He knows that a man can die in seconds and although he does have help they are almost always too far away to save him from a determined attacker. He knows he is one of 40 men whose function is to suppress thousands and, although he can bring into play a superior arm, any one of the thousands streaming past him on normal errands could be armed with a crude but lethal knife, club, zip gun with silencer. Among the men he is commissioned to watch are probably hundreds of schizophrenic-reaction cases. He knows this and he is trying to remember them all or watch all directions. And he is also aware that he looks a great deal like all the rest of the guards, meaning he must also bear their guilt.[27]

Professional Prison Literature

In order to fully understand what the leaders of corrections intended, we surveyed their national publication known as the *Jail Association Journal* (from 1939-1940), then the *Prison World* (from 1941 to 1954) and since July 1954 as the *American Journal of Corrections,* the official organ of the American Correctional Association. We examined the journals in ten-year intervals beginning with the 1941-42 issues. These issues were chosen partly because momentous events* occurred in those years and we were interested in the profession's responses. Further, we were interested in recurring themes, stresses placed on certain aspects of practice and the development of new ideas.

In the early issues (1941-42), one could find a "guest" editorial by a sheriff; a parole board member; a governor; a president of the American Prison Association (predecessor to the ACA); a federal warden; commissioners of corrections from New York City and Alabama; Stanford Bates, head of the New York State Board of Parole; and Francis Biddle, the U.S. Attorney General. They respectively discussed running a sanitary jail; preparing convicts for parole; the high hopes for California's indeterminate sentence; the need to educate the public about corrections; the lack of good training programs for women; the impact of the war on prisons; military drills and the manufacturing of sand bags (anti-incendiary mats); and such themes as: prison is the last chance for convicts to change bad habits; parole should be used to maximize manpower in the war effort; the prisoners must help in the war industries or through induction in the army.

The editors also reserved a regular space called "Spotlighting—Our Editorial Comment" for more outspoken comment. Beginning in March 1941, the editors came out against whipping prisoners because it was inconsistent with the rehabilitative ideal. In July - August 1941, Morris Rudensky,† editor of *The Atlantian,* made his debut, noting that a humble prisoner could get an article published in the *Prison World* and praising the "new spirit" of cooperation between prison personnel and convicts. In the next issue Rudensky, deploring the murder of a warden, warned convicts that they could not "murder their way to freedom." In this same issue Dr. J.D. Wilson, an associate editor, lauds the contribution of psychiatry to penology, concluding:

> Crazy and criminal both begin with the same letter so they have that much in common at least. And, on second thought, penologist and psychiatrist, also both commence with the same letter—which might be considered as another reason for thinking that it is just as much a crime to be crazy as it is crazy to be a criminal.

In 1947, the publication which was then the *Prison World* developed a "Corrections Officers Training Section" column under the editorship of Dr. Walter Wallace, Warden of Wallkill State Prison. In successive issues from 1947 to 1951, when it lapsed, the column was primarily concerned with "how-to-do-it." It begins with such custodial concerns as how to inspect a train or supervise a workgang "because we believe that good custody is basically essential to whatever else may be done in the correctional institution." A guard tells "How to Get Along with the Sergeant," averring that obedience is mandatory, "bite your tongue in face of an unwise order" and "familiarity with superiors breaks down morale." The next issues move on to "How to Search a Cell," "How to Search the Person of an Inmate," "The Prison Hospital" (with trade tips about assuring the inmate's ingestion of medicine through the use of flashlights after placing the medicine in the inmate's mouth yourself), also checking the bathrooms "where degenerates get together," "How to Handle Custody Problems in the Kitchen" (followed with a question which readers might think about: "Should inmates be permitted to talk while at meals?"), "How to Transport Prisoners," "How to Make Reports." In 1949, the column turned to "How to

Promote the Institutions' Sanitation Program," "How the Custodial Officer May Assist the Chaplain," "How to Avoid Fraternizing with Inmates" (by maintaining an insurmountable wall between the inmate and all prison employees), "How to Organize an Institutional Staff to Function in Locating Hideouts Within a Maximum Security Prison," and "How to Patrol a Gallery at Night." In 1950, an issue was devoted to women's prisons and following a series of "how-to" questions, answers were found for the following issues: beautifying the institution, receiving new inmates, supervising a workgang, censoring mail, using a log-book, "how to keep prisoners' laundry straight," and how to deal with visitors. If guards didn't worry enought about routine day-to-day matters, a chief medical officer let them know that it was his:

> firm conviction that the great majority of delinquents present more than the mild psychoneurotic symptoms, and that their psychoneuroses are of considerable importance in producing their delinquent behavior.... Two emotional processes prominent in psychoneurotics are anxiety and hostility. Our present means of detaining offenders certainly does not reduce these emotions but, instead, reinforces them.... The great majority of inmates are mentally, emotionally or socially 'sick'.

Having taken time out for a sprinkling of Freud, we return to the more pedestrian problems (still in 1950), "How to Avoid a Miscount" in which the editor states, "when an officer makes a wrong count, he ought to be regarded by his superiors to ascertain if he is feeble-minded, suffering from a certain nervous breakdown, in need of a literacy test, ill, drunk or taking dope." We also see articles on the guard as a counselor needing to show inmates "sympathetic interest" and a column in using "Community Resources in Pre-release Programs" noting that it is not unusual to see a colored, a Mexican and a white man seated together trying to solve problems!

In 1951, after a wave of self-mutilations in southern state prisons, Dr. Rupert Koeninger (a psychologist) published, "What About Self-Mutilations?" describing the problem and most frequent types of mutilation— severing of the Achilles tendon and inducing infections through introducing lye into razor cuts. In May-June, 1951, a vitriolic attack is made by Louis Messolonghites upon the book, *My Six Convicts.* In the next issue, the guard is introduced to a new idea by Albert C. Wagner "Inmate Participation in Correctional Institutions" in which he calls for less censorship, honor groups, lowering security, respect for inmates, and inmate councils. By the May-June, 1952 issue, a wave of riots had swept the nation. The editorial calmed its readers proclaiming only "A relatively few prisoners in comparatively few prisons...participated, that there is a general unrest in the world and that the riots may have a constructive effect in awakening the public's interest in prisons." The November-December issue gave the annual conference report which contained nothing reflecting the historic riots earlier that Spring.

In 1954, the *Prison World* became the *American Journal of Corrections,* and later the "Training Section" column got a new editor, Walter Dunbar,* then associate warden of San Quentin. The first columns now turned to "How to Handle Prisoners' Mail," "Policies and Standards of Inmate Clothing," "Prison Discipline" and the "Components of Supervision." A few years later, the column told the guard that "the days of the illiterate, two-fisted type of prison guard were over." In his place, the new officer would receive training in the proper use of firearms, security equipment *and* good relationships with the public, fellow officers and the (unexplained) philosophy of rehabilitation, followed by a compulsory program in self-defense, firing on the range and the "Fundamentals of Revolver Shooting."

In 1960, with America beginning to experience the civil rights explosion, we return to the *Journal* to see what was occupying the minds of the leaders of corrections. Beginning in January, 1961, Sanger Powers, Director of the Wisconsin Department of Corrections and President of the ACA, wrote advocating a therapeutic atmosphere for juvenile corrections, described a new construction program in his state and emphasized the need for correctional curriculum in schools of social work. The achievements and challenges of Prison Industries (a dying institution) was extolled by James Curran of Maryland. James V. Bennett, Director of the Federal Bureau of Prisons, gave "A Penal Administrator's View of the Polygraph." Ralph Murdy of the Baltimore Criminal Justice Commission published his "Islam Incarcerated"—the only mention of racial issue in three years. Murdy, speaking of Black Muslims, concluded:

> This organization, then, is led by a man capable of drawing a fanatical following.... while there is certainly a potential danger [of Muslims taking matters into their own hands], this writer believes the continued close watchfulness of the FBI and local enforcement is sufficient to contain it.

The next two years' contributions concern particular types of therapies for types of inmates and an exposition of "success" stories from across the nation and abroad: "Psychological Needs of Women in a Correctional Institution," "The Aged Inmate," "The 'Difficult' Prisoner," and "Group Psychotherapy and the Criminal—An Introduction to Reality," which sweepingly finds "emotional infancy and the morbid fear of reality...fundamental characteristics of the criminal in this or any age." "Facts About Diabetic Inmates" and "Teaching Machines and Programmed Learning" found their way into Rikers Island in November, 1962, and in the same issue "Introductory Handicraft for the Segregated" was offered by the Hobby Craft Director of the Michigan Reformatory. These issues also took us to such exotic places as the "Tochigi Women's Prison, Japan," "Penology in Belgium and France," "Canada's Parole System," and "Penology in Sweden and Denmark." Also, we learned Sweden conducted a "Successful Fight Against Juvenile Delinquency." Closer to home "California Takes Men to the Mountains," "The Ohio Correctional Story," "Adventures in Rehabilitation" (by an architect), "Progress in New Mexico's Penal System," a "Decade of Changes in West Virginia," "The Georgia Penitentiary System" and "Adult Correction in Washington State." In the early 1960s, some academicians of note for the first time published articles in the *Journal:* Donald E. J. MacNamara on capital punishment; Alfred C. Schnur on research; Clarence Schrag on the malintegration of treatment and custody services in a prison. In addition, Peter O. Lejins became the ACA president.

A decade later in 1971, we find the main thrust into drugs, juvenile delinquency, reform in Washington and Florida, collective violence, the new

ABA commitment to corrections, the prisoners' right to medical treatment, W. Clement Stone's "Positive Mental Attitude" programs, a report on the revision of the ACA's Correctional Standards and, in the issue following Attica, the "Politicalization of Prisoners," about which the editor notes "the social separation of staff and inmates increases prisoner acceptance of anti-staff values." A final issue examined was January, 1974, in which it seems we were starting the cycle over; a sheriff writes of "Diverting Idle Hands, An Ideal Now Underway in Harris County Jail" (through art, band, religion and work programs). Currently, most of the *Journal* is usually devoted to advertising, firearms, hardware, radio equipment and the latest security devices including Folger Adams' ubiquitous newest "fool proof" lock. By 1974 it was necessary to have an index for advertisers.

We have gone into this in such length because the ACA's publication is a reasonable index of leading thinking, and one can plausibly extrapolate what guards would be exposed to in their work environments by superiors who subscribed to the publication.*

The American Correctional Association

The ACA membership is currently about 10,000. The National Commission on Causes and Prevention of Violence (1965) estimated the total correctional work force at more than 121,000, with 80% of them custody-related personnel.[28] The ACA believes that 80% of its membership (belonging to the $6.00 per year Regular Category) are mainly guards or other lower echelon practitioners, but its membership director could not identify custody staff as a separate entity. We can therefore estimate that of the 100,000 working guards less than 10% belong to ACA (the figure for state prison personnel is probably less than 5%). We can liberally estimate the ACA guard membership at 3-4,000. However, annual conference attendance and leadership positions are reserved for top echelon. ACA estimates (conservatively) 60% of the annual conference participants to be top management and supervisory types. Line guards up through captains are infrequently found on national committees. However, in 1972 the association took great pains to make its 44-member national board reflect the diversity of correctional practice. The by-laws now assure the election of two line officers from both juvenile and adult correctional institutions and of four at-large members. Of these four, one must be black, one Spanish speaking and one Indian.

Wardens' Association

There is only one other publication which has a specific, albeit limited, custody personnel audience. It is called "The Grapevine." Some six years old, it is the official organ of the American Association of Wardens and Superintendents. It is the field's best example of jingo press. Uncritical acclaim goes to wardens of all stripes, and critical scorn is poured on convicts, radical lawyers, reformers and the like. It very infrequently publishes any comment. It makes its points by reproducing articles and editorials from the daily press everywhere in the nation, judicial findings and letters to various editors. The 1973 editor of "The Grapevine," who presumably also writes the pithy commentaries, was G. Norton Jameson, Warden of the South Dakota State Prison. A few examples will convey the flavor of this xeroxed publication.

From southern Illinois, a guard's letter to the editor, in part, is reprinted (Vol. 5, No. 4):

> Editor, the Southern Illinoisan:
> I can tell by reading your editorials you are a Republican-oriented paper and also anti-establishment. It is disgusting to people like myself that work for a living....
> I also work at a prison. You don't like this either. You preach prison reform. You write about police brutality....
> I would like to know and am sure a lot of people who read your paper would too—have you ever worked behind the walls of a prison or have you ever ridden in a police car. Both jobs take a lot of abuse from do-gooders like you....
> You downgrade prison officials and guards. We are just people going to work, just like you. Not one prison guard put a man in prison and we can't get them out. We just do our job....
> I am writing this letter because I am fed up with this bull that you put about inmates being angels and guards being idiots.
> I am sure more people would be interested in your paper if you did write both sides. You see I have worked at Menard for 10 years and am proud to be a part of the establishment.
> I hope you put this in your paper.
> Lennie Hill
> Chester

Another issue contains a reprint of James J. Kilpatrick's attack on the National Advisory Commission on Criminal Justice Standards and Goals Report on Correctional Reform (*Washington Star*, no date). Finally, there is an editorial comment by Warden Jameson after a very long reprint of a U.S. District Court finding (erroneously referred to as a Supreme Court decision) in Southern Texas favorable to Director George Beto of the Texas Department of Corrections (in 1970).

I think you will agree that the foregoing decision is long overdue. But let's look further—this case indicates exceptional care in its preparation—my hat, and yours, should be off to Dr. Beto, his staff and the lawyers who so carefully presented the facts for their side. It should be kept in mind that the Supreme Court has only those facts that are presented in the trial court upon which to base a decision. If you let the inmates beat you to the punch and fail to present your case, you can expect little else from the high court than what you've been getting.

To their credit, most wardens with whom the author has contact disown "The Grapevine," are ashamed of it and rarely keep back issues for anyone to see—but it is the *official* publication of the Wardens' Association.

The Association has about 130 members out of a potential of nearly five times that number. The new president is Vernon Housewright of Vienna, Illinois, who has a dramatically different world-view of corrections than Jameson's. The Association, or at least its publication, is expected to break with its parochial past under its new leadership.

Administrators' Organization

The Association of State Correctional Administrators (ASCA) is the adult prison system administrators' professional organization. It admits larger city (Chicago, New York, Philadelphia), federal, District of Columbia and Canadian penal executives into membership. There is also an "associate" category for retired well-known state, federal and armed service correctional administrators. Recently, and largely in response to Attica, the ASCA published "Unified Correctional Policies and Procedures." It is a relatively forward-looking document which federal judges increasingly consult in mediating disputes between the keeper and the kept. The ASCA membership turns over rapidly because top administrators are swept in and out of office following gubernatorial elections. It is not uncommon for 25% of the under 70 membership to turn over every two years. There is also turnover of a different type. In a limited personnel market, an administrator could represent one state in one year and another the following year. Ellis MacDougall represented South Carolina, Connecticut and Georgia before retirement. (This writer represented two states before political influence, but it has not yet put into action what it sometimes toys with—the hiring of an executive director and becoming a forceful national lobby for correctional change.)

Organized Labor

Custody officer unions have yet to make their mark. Collective bargaining is a relatively new phenomenon for public workers and is even more novel for most guards. The field is divided between the American Federation of State, County and Municipal Employees (AFSME), the Teamsters Union, a variety of state employee associations and occasionally independent unions (which have generally become disaffected from the others). Being subject to a tight para-military style of work, uniforms and the unquestioning following of orders (even unreasonable ones while biting your tongue) does not prepare one well for union participation. Union programs, at the moment, are narrowly drawn to conditions of work, insurance, wages, seniority and job security. Getting a contract is first on their present agendas. Among custody workers, there is as yet no large-scale concern for correctional innovation. Even within AFSME, locals reflect widely different concerns throughout the nation. The National AFL-CIO (under its Community Service Division) sponsors a Labor-National Council on Crime and Delinquency (NCCD) Participation program which has a broad concern for criminal justice modernization. Under this program, organized labor is playing an increasingly important role in bringing about change. Unfettered from narrow AFSME ("local") concerns, the AFL-CIO-NCCD ("cosmopolitans") come at problems with broader concerns.

The Ethnography of Guarding

One other line of study needs examination before we can make a statement about the emergent guard. There are very few ethnographic studies of the Guard. T.C. Esselstyn studied the off-duty behavior of a small sample of correction personnel in California (1966). Addressing the paucity of information about them he states: "It is as though everyone believed that the processes of social interaction and the emerging social systems do not occur among correctional workers, if they do, they have no significance to the correctional field."[29] Of the thirty-one respondents, which included some guards, county and federal probation workers, Esselstyn says: "Privately, they socialize frequently and spend much of the time in this rich setting for conversation, interaction and the weaving of social bonds."[30] He summarizes frequency of contacts as follows:

> He visits his co-workers; they visit him; and now and then, they go off for a big night together. These social contacts last anywhere from an hour to half a day or night or even more, and on average occupy from two to three hours in a typical week. This is

not, then, momentary socializing.

> It occurs frequently, is widespread throughout the sample, and lasts a long while. When it happens, the conversations almost invariably turn to some phase of correction, often for as long as 20 per cent or more of any interval given over to informal social contact.[31]

In response to a question eliciting the origins of their "ideas about corrections," of the 31, 16 were mildly to greatly influenced by off-duty contact with fellow workers, 5 by clients, and 10 reported the mixed influences of journals, departmental directives or by off-duty contacts with correctional workers.[32] Some of the areas of greatest influence occurring during these contacts were in (1) morale, job satisfaction and sense of belonging; (2) exchange of views about their agencies; and (3) clarifying difficult or conflicting policy issues.[33] Esselstyn was very modest in his conclusions because of the methodological shortcomings of the study, but he did pose some long-range research projects: (1) a study of dropouts and their self-concept (dropouts from correctional jobs may have not developed the self-concept and growth which off-duty contacts seem to contribute to those who stay); and (2) a study of informal socialization patterns focusing on language (interaction is primarily through technical language which is a mix of "prison argot and jive, underworld and street-corner slang" and serves to fence out strangers while simultaneously speeding communication between in-group members and further strengthening bonds.[34]

The most extensive and promising of ethnographic studies is *Prison Guard*, by James B. Jacobs and Harold G. Retsky.* Like Esselstyn's work, 31 guards at Joliet, Illinois were respondents to formal interviews.

Jacobs and Retsky first document role was incompatability:

> It is not surprising that contradictory organizational goals have caused considerable conflict in organizational micro-units like the role of the guard. Under the role prescriptions dictated by the rehabilitative ideal, the guard is to relax and to act spontaneously. Inmates are to be understood, not blamed, and formal disciplinary mechanisms should be triggered as infrequently as possible. These are vague directives.
>
> ...The rehabilitative ideal has no clear directives for the administration of a large scale people processing institution. In order to carry out primary tasks and to manage large numbers of men and materials bureaucratic organization and impersonal treatment are necessary. Furthermore, to distinguish between inmates on the basis of psychological needs leaves the non-professional open to charges of gross bias, discrimination and injustice.[35]

Guards caught in the crossfire of contradictory directives retreat to the good-old-days (iron discipline) of less complexity. Guards are not fearful of reprimands for failure to "meaningfully" communicate with convicts. However, laxness leading to an incident of violence or escape could likely cost him his job; hence he follows, not the Tappan course of "least effort" (guards are not lazy); rather, he

"Guards caught in the crossfire of contradictory directives retreat to the good old days (iron discipline) of less complexity."

follows the McKendrick course of eternal vigilance. In the process, any pretense about rehabilitation fades.

Career development for the guard, Jacobs and Retsky find, is a peculiarly aimless one. Not unlike the early days of the nineteenth century (as Lewis earlier pointed out), the prospective guard is usually coming off a period of unemployment elsewhere.

> Well they had this piece in the paper, see I'm from Hamilton County; that's about 300 miles south of here. And they was wanting guards. I knew several fellows used to work here from down there at the time. The dust—the corn dust—I'm allergic to it and the lint offa cattle. So there's this piece to go to Vermont [an Illinois town] to take a civil service examination.
>
> So I just drove up there that day and I took that civil service examination and in about 3 weeks, they called me up to the Menard Penitentiary.[36]

Despite a fairly good wage at Stateville, it had over 100% of new guard turnover in 1973. The guard's prestige is low. "Guards who we interviewed indicated that even friends do not know what to make of the common belief that prison guards are sadistic and brutal."[37] Like Esselstyn, they found guards withdrawing to themselves; but, unlike Esselstyn's California correctional personnel who did so under circumstances of high morale, Stateville guards clustered because of stigmatization. It was despair—not hope—which brought them together.

> Being a prison guard is a dead end. To date no career ladders have been built to reward those guards who have shown particular promise on the job. The skills necessary for guarding are particularly limited to this occupation. While the guard may hope to be promoted through the ranks to sergeant, lieutenant and

captain (and even to warden) these decisions are often made early in the guard's career. Without an outside sponsor or an immediate acceptance into the ruling clique the guard will have to wait many years for his promotion to sergeant, if indeed he is ever promoted at all.[38]

Further proof that the degradation of the prison routine negatively affects both the keeper and the kept is vividly portrayed in this study. Higher echelon guards assume that contraband smuggling is being conducted by lower echelon guards. Since the former hold power over the latter, they treat them as guards themselves are taught to treat convicts. Guards are "shaken down" or "inspected" on assignment to see that they are working and, as in the case of inmates, receive "tickets" for infractions. Peer level guards (and, not infrequently, convicts also) are encouraged to write reports on guards. Once these are written, as per convict treatment, guards appear before disciplinary tribunals, but, unlike some convicts, apparently without the prospect of due process safeguards.

I was disciplined once because I took a shoeshine in the barber shop and which only takes about 6 minutes. There was a sign in the shop which had fallen down forbidding this. But I did not see it. A captain spotted me and wrote me up, which was only his job and for which I hold no grudge, but I do feel he could have warned me that he was writing me up. I had no knowledge this had happened until I got a letter two weeks later telling me I had to go before the review board. They gave me three days off without pay. I think I was dealt with harshly. One man shouldn't take food from you.[39]

Jacobs and Retsky analyze the guard's work-world, the division of labor in a prison, the work areas, the cell block, the dependence they develop upon inmates, the security concerns of the tower and the gate (the two ways out), the upper echelon (sergeants, lieutenants and captains), and present a final section on "The Guard's World." It is a world of fear of the unanticipated. While the guard may not carry a weapon (except on the tower), inmates are commonly armed with homemade but lethal weapons.

Tension continually looms over the prison threatening to explode into assault or even riot. This is drilled into the recruit during his first training classes. The guard's manual stresses the need for vigilance and alertness lest the unexpected take one unaware. Rule after rule in this handbook deals with use of force, emergency measures and admonishments for protective and defensive actions. Not only is the new guard exposed to the word of mouth stories of fellow students and training officers, but at the prison he may immediately be exposed to situations which confirm his worst fears. 'When I arrived, I was almost immediately assigned to 'B' house which contained a gallery known as 3-gallery lock up. The inmates here had been under constant lock and key for almost a year. As a result of this they were acting like animals and their verbal abuse scared the shit out of me. I decided then and there to turn in my resignation but was talked out of it by my supervising officer.'[40]

Stereotypic images of inmates abound in the guard's world. The study discovers the upper echelon staff (in Goffman's terms, the "tradition bearers") using language to describe inmates which is reminiscent of that used by Eddy, Wiltse and Lynds over 150 years ago. The members of the upper echelon are the ideologists of the system. The younger guards still frequently identify with inmates. There may be obvious answers to account for the difference. In other professions one might see older workers become "case hardened" and, after much thankless effort, turn to frustration with a distrust of their unappreciative clientele. But it may also be, as the authors suggest, related to the fact that newer guards are from similar socio-economic (and most recently ethnic) backgrounds as the convict. Guards are increasingly chosen from high-reported crime areas, not from the less-reported white suburban areas: One of these newer guards said:

> I often put myself in the inmate's position. If I were locked up and the door was locked up and my only contact with authorities would be the officer walking by, it would be frustrating if I couldn't get him to listen to the problems I have. There is nothing worse than being in need of something and not being able to supply it yourself and having the man who can supply it ignore you. This almost makes me explode inside.[41]

Both the treaters and the custodians end up juvenilizing the convict, from apparently different motivations. The keeper makes the inmate dependent through routines of counts, medicine, sick call, communication outside the cellhouse, etc. The treater already believes the convict to be a social, genetic or psychological problem, thereby withdrawing volition from the convict's makeup and in effect simultaneously removing his manhood. The positivist reaches this conclusion through concern for the wayward-individual-patient and the guard through what Jacobs and Retsky found to be efforts "calculated to reduce the inmate to a child."[42]

Interestingly, the closeness, and perhaps the danger in acting otherwise, reduces overt racism in guards —at least in the work situation.

> ...Guards do not openly indicate racist attitudes. Whatever prejudices may exist are kept to one's self. This is in sharp contrast to studies of the police which have found an abundance of openly stated racist comments. Even in informal discussions, we have not heard guards refer to Black inmates as 'niggers' or in other racist terms. We suspect that much of what has been explained as racist attitudes toward inmates in the literature stems from the organizationally sponsored conflict between guards and inmates.

In a prison like Stateville, where Blacks constitute 80% of the inmate population, racism may be a dead letter. There are too few whites to make white/black distinctions significant. The guards come to distinguish instead between the good and the bad inmates among the Blacks.[43]

Reflections of a Pseudo-Guard

In 1974, Stanley griffith, a member of the author's staff (Illinois Law Enforcement Commission) and an attorney, registered in Illinois' first Correctional Officer Training Academy class along with the upper echelon staffs of several of the state's prisons.[44] Having gained their confidence, he was accepted as "one of them" in the formal and informal "off-duty" sessions. Griffith found that the officers welcomed the opportunity for training but had special problems. They had been so long uninvolved and neglected that a considerable period of time was taken up in simply letting them talk about accumulated problems. Lack of involvement feeds on itself. It alienates, making feelings of isolation difficult to overcome even when a forum for involvement is finally provided. The officers lacking facile verbal and writing skills are first easily embarrassed, then made hostile by clerical and professional staff who communicate these shortcomings.

There seemed to be a noticable decline in morale and spirit at breakfast. There was little, if any, breakfast conversation. When I returned to the lounge, I came into the midst of an agitated group of participants. Apparently one of the Academy secretaries had been overheard belittling the Academy participant evaluations which she has been assigned to type. The comment reflected on the poor writing ability of the participants. This was viewed with tremendous anger because throughout the earlier parts of the week Burns [a staff trainer] had bent over backwards to reassure everyone that participants could rely on his not revealing what was discussed to anyone. (E.g., when videotapes of roleplaying had been used one officer was asked to apply the eraser to the tape.) Anonymity and confidence were ultimately important to free flowing participation. Words can barely describe the hurt, anger, embarrassment and sense of betrayal that pervaded the rest of the morning. However, since no trainer was around to intercept the problem, to reassure the participants, the mood continued into the classroom.[45]

The micro-world of the prison is the guard's world. He does not conceptualize it as well as the professional, but the professional, in his hasty anxiety to introduce program (and since he is not a part of that world), does not accurately conceptualize the problem facing the guard. The professional, encountering the guard's need for an orderly world, recasts the guard's hesitancy into resistance.

A part of the Academy training concerned itself with drug abuse in the prison. The Illinois Drug Abuse Program (IDAP) sent staff to teach the guards about drugs.

[An IDAP Trainer] then proclaimed that they were going to be coming around to visit the institutions to talk to correctional staff about a drug counseling program IDAP plans

to run in the institution. He said this is where a real need exists and said that the reason for speaking to guards was to allay their suspicions about what it was they were doing with groups of inmates. At about that point one participant piped up: 'It ain't gonna work.' 'What do you mean.' [A Trainer asked.] . . . Well, the officer tried to explain that the institutions have so many programs which are underutilized already largely because staff is short, space is hard to come by, and because no one ever really plans out how new programs impinge on security, staff's problems of inmate transport, feeding, residence, work assignments and a dozen other little things that need to be adjusted to get an inmate to a program. . . . [The IDAP Trainers] replied—oblivious to what the officer had said—that the guard didn't understand inmates, that IDAP counselors could because [some of them] . . . were exoffenders, and that by allowing IDAP counselors to work with inmates the guard's job would be easier because inmate tensions would be reduced. At that point the battle lines were drawn until the program drew to a close. . . . The speakers preached and did not listen.

The information regarding drug abuse was useful and interesting, but the approach seemed overly alarmist and deficient in the area of actual, practical advice as to how to deal with the problem. It seemed as though this talk was aimed at suburbanites who needed to have their complacency and ignorance knocked out of them—they just had the wrong speech or the wrong audience. The speakers seemed to lay heavy emphasis on their superior ability to communicate, and yet they just couldn't seem to hear what the officers were trying to say about dropping another program into the prison without adequate coordination with the current requirements of the institution.[46]

Another area of guarding which assaults the guards' sense of integrity is the lack of clarity of working rules. The guard force merely looks like a military force, but discretion and accompanying confusion reign nearly supreme. It is hard for a guard to know what will be rewarded.

> The group complained that there were no available standards and that officers were left on their own to decide the difference between major and minor infractions—the absence of disciplinary standards impedes consistent application...
>
> The participants complained of faulty communications. They frequently get word of events through inmates. The Stateville group commented favorably on the Warden's staff meetings, but at [another prison] ... the officers complain they haven't seen a warden for six months.
>
> The officers who routinely work the visitor's gates complained that there are inconsistent standards on visitors and that they are constantly being end-runned by counselors. This touched off a tirade against counselors. First of all, they never write tickets properly. Second, they get little or no orientation to the institution. Third, they have no appreciation of the considerations affecting security. Several officers suggested that all counselors should be broken in by six months' duty as a guard. Furthermore, counselors are never around when you really need them and can never be reached....[47]

Griffith's findings support the contention that the confusion felt by the line worker is a built-in problem in prisons. It is not an Illinois problem. It emerges from a prison work environment which makes contradictory claims about its mission and permits several disciplines to independently "do their thing." Griffith also shows that the guards' focal concern cannot expand to encompass inmate treatment until their more ethnocentric ones are met: safety, accident insurance, legal liabilities, a grievance procedure, more training, involvement in implementing new programs (before they are started), rationalization of rank, job titles, work assignments and correlated pay grades, disability pay, retirement, etc.

Brodsky has suggested a vehicle for responding to the guards' need to be heard in the form of a "bill of rights." Not legal rights—rather organizational and interpersonal ones. Speaking to article I of his program he states:

> There are perspectives and experiences correctional officers have to contribute from their direct contact with the offenders. These perspectives represent important information sources upon which relevant decisions should be made.
>
> ...it is uncomfortable to be swept along in a process over which one has no control.... Correctional officers should serve on boards, committees, and decision-making structures at all levels within penal institutions.... Correctional officers should have a representative body who would meet with warden candidates and at the least would submit advisory recommendations ... a logical implication is that the same privilege should be allocated to inmates. Thus almost all boards and committees in prisons and all decision making—including warden selection—should have inmate participation and representation.[48]

His full "bill of rights," intended to help produce objectivity, pride, status and skill in the guard contains a self-explanatory six-point program.

1. A Piece of the Action.
2. Clearly Defined Roles and Loyalties.
3. Education and Training Relevant to Job Activities and Career Development.
4. Differential Assignments Related to Skills and Abilities.
5. Informed Behavioral Science Consultation on Managing People.

6. The Development of Professionalism.[49]

The fate of the keeper has always been linked to that of the kept. In colonial days, when the criminal-sinner was being detained and worked, the keeper was called upon to merely watch him. With the advent of the humanitarian reduction of death penalties, the elimination of mutilations, and the accompanying rhetoric of reformation, the guard began a long journey of role obfuscation. The humanitarians did not deliver humanity to convicts.

"The fate of the keeper has always been linked to the kept."

Quite to the contrary, the convict was brutalized, and in this calculated schema the guard was brutalized by having to administer the program. Under the tutelage of the Lynds and Crays, and in the process of debasing the convict, the guard himself was debased. Putting a whip in a man's hand with an eye toward reformation was the first mistake. Lynds was not confused—he had no pretentions about reformation—but after he was swept out of office the guard was still holding the whip, cellular confinement was still the order of the day, and reformation remained the rhetoric.

The guard's role under the least complicated circumstances is unique, with no outside counterpart. Cressey has likened it to its closest model— the slave overseer.[50] Over the years many disciplines entered the prison to ply their trades, but they only compli-cated the role of the guard. Warden Casseles of Sing-Sing prison captured

this plight well when he said (1971):

First psychiatry had the answer, then education was the answer, now it's environment—that made the prisoner the way he is? We're no longer trying to force a prisoner into a particular mold, so we have no criteria any more for running a prison. The only criterion is to keep it trouble free.

But maybe it's trouble free because the lid is on tight, who knows? You don't know when to join them or what side to take—and the nature of everything today is taking sides. The same thing that happened in Attica could happen to me....[51]

Wherever prisons were built, men came to work at them but not usually as a first choice. The prison was close, sometimes the only industry around, and sometimes it was sought out by the unemployed. Workers came to it, donned a uniform and were alternately told that their role with prisoners was to keep, whip, counsel, treat, handle from a distance, get close, understand, but to shoot them if necessary. The leaders in the field did not serve the guards well; the literature was confusing, and, while administrators ordered, they did not involve guards. Guards were paid poorly, given low status and worked under hazardous conditions at hours out of tune with their culture. Politi-cians used them for votes, support, campaign funds and, opportunisti-cally, to obtain more severe criminal sentences. And each time the guard agreed and took another step in the direction of the radical right, the net result was to heat up his own work environment with more desperate convicts in the cellhouse who were facing longer sentences with less hope. While reformers blamed guards for the miseries of the prison, profes-sionals disdained them. Today's prison guard is the product of bewildering confusion. His education and ethos leave him poorly equipped to deal with his circumstance. He is disaffected, alienated and survives as a fossil in the anachronistic fortress prison. Winston Churchill said, with some relevance in this case, "We shape our buildings and then our buildings shape us." The guard has always been linked in a shared fate with the convict. They have both come from the same socio-economic group. They became victims of society's ambivalence in relation to crime and its treatment. In their mutual anger, the keeper and kept have only occasionally caught glimmers of their common nemesis—the caging of one set of human beings by another. Jackson once caught that glimmer.

> But the days and months that a guard has to spend on the ground (sometimes locked in a wing or cell-block with no gun guard) are what destroy anything at all that was good, healthy, or social about him before. Fear begets fear. And we come out with two groups of schizoids, one guarding the other. The spiral extends outward and up.[52]

Vienna, Illinois

It is nearly an 800 mile round trip for a Chicago visitor to see an inmate of the Vienna Correctional Facility close to the Illinois-Kentucky border. Opened in 1971, the new facility appears to be a suburban community at first sight. Cellblocks are neighborhoods, cells are rooms, the big yard is a town square, the chapel is a church, there are workshops and shopping areas, a barber, gymnasium, music facility, and a spacious school, library and gymnasium—each of these are separate detached facilities. The rooms all have locks, but the inmates (residents) have the keys. The academic program boasts 32 courses (day and night), but only 168 of the 300

students are convicts, the others are townspeople who come on campus as fellow students. Nearby Shawnee Community College furnishes the faculty. At least half of the convict population is black while only two families in the town are black. Vienna also represents the "rural types" Schwartz described as conservative, racist and backlashers. The difference here is the condition of confinement and therefore the definition of the situation. Vienna has the full range of offenders from swindlers to murderers. But they are defined as safe, and are treated as aspiring humans. They respond, given the normal range of problems with 450 people in a congregate living situation, within the tolerable range of acceptability.

There are no cellblocks to break out of, no walls to climb or towers to shoot from. If a convict leaves, the countryside is not alarmed by what the *Chicago Daily News* recently described as "Killer Cons"; rather, they are "walk aways." In nine years, out of an aggregate of 2,500 men, 23 have left illegally. Vienna has been riot-free since it opened. The town and area are engaged with Vienna in an educational and economic symbiotic relationship. While Stateville, 350 miles to the north has a 102% new staff turnover rate, Vienna has a prospective staff waiting list of 1400 people!

The prisoners operate a multi-county radio-dispatched emergency ambulance service. It has already saved lives of area residents injured in accidents in remote locations of the vast rural expanse it services. In 1974, about 35 women prisoners moved to Vienna, making it one of the largest co-educational correctional facilities in the nation.

But it was not always that way. Under a previous administration in the early 1960s, Illinois had embarked upon a program to build a "minimum security" complex. The original design called for three-story four-winged facilities (nine of them), with central control furnished from a master bullet-proof unit in the middle of an X-shaped unit. The central unit was actually an internal fortress which could rake its four protruding wings with unobstructed fire power.[53] The author visited the only such unit built of the nine projected. It stands at the edge of Vienna's main facility. The leading Republican legislator in the area apologetically explained, pointing to the old facility, "well, that was billyclub Ragen's [former Corrections Director] idea of minimum custody. We didn't like it." What he apparently meant to convey was that the town felt safer with an actual minimum custody facility where there was very little danger of fire power being brought to bear on anyone. It is not at all clear from previous experiences with "urban-types," who are presumably more "sensitive" to ethnic differences, that they would tolerate such a minimal grade of custody in their neighborhoods.

If the facility has a humanizing effect on the convicts and "rural-type" citizens, it had an equally salubrious effect on guards. A study finding that both guards and convicts are humanized in this kind of work environment is the only spark of optimism one can locate in the history of guarding.[54] It corroborates the axiom that we come to believe and act in accord with the conditions under which we are socially structured.

Notes

[1]D.R. Cressey, "Prison Organizations," in James March, ed., *Handbook of Organizations* (Chicago: Rand McNally, 1965), pp. 1023-1070.
[2]W. David Lewis, *From Newgate to Dannemora* (Ithaca, N.Y.: Cornell Univ. Press, 1965), p. 60.
[3]*Ibid.*, p. 38.
[4]*Ibid.*, p. 142.
[5]*Ibid.*, p. 150.
[6]*Ibid.*, p. 133.
[7]*Ibid.*, p. 131.
[8]*Ibid.*
[9]*Ibid.*, p. 31.
[10]P. Chenault, "Education," in Paul W. Tappan, ed., *Contemporary Correction* (New York: McGraw-Hill Book Co., Inc., 1951), p. 254.
[11]C. McKendrick, "Custody and Discipline," in Tappan, *supra* note 10, p. 167.
[12]*Ibid.*, pp. 162-163.
[13]Tappan, *supra* note 10, p. 3.
[14]*Ibid.*, p. 4.
[15]*Theoretical Studies in Social Organization of the Prison*, SSRC (New York: Holt, Rinehart & Co., 1960).
[16]*Ibid.*, p. 4.
[17]Robert M. Carter, Daniel Glaser, & Leslie T. Wilkins, *Correctional Institutions* (New York: J.B. Lippincott Co., 1972).
[18]C. Schrag, "Some Foundations for a Theory of Corrections," In Carter et al., *supra* note 17, pp. 149-172.
[19]T. P. Wilson, "Patterns of Management and Adaptations to Organizational Roles: A Study of Prison Inmates," in Carter et al., *supra* note 17, pp. 248-262.
[20]McKendrick, *supra* note 11, pp. 159-160.
[21]R. Clark, "Prisons: Factories of Crime," in Burton M. Atkins & Henry R. Glick, eds., *Prisons, Protest, and Politics* (Englewood Cliffs, N.J.: Prentice-Hall, Inc., 1972), p. 18.
*McKendrick quoted no less than Roberto Michels for justification: "Authority can neither arise nor be preserved without the establishment and the maintenance of distance between those who command and those who obey..." (*Encyclopedia of the Social Sciences*, Vol. II, p. 320)
But there were other ways in which even the military model might have been invoked, for example:"...It is possible to impart instruction and to give commands in such manner and such a tone of voice to inspire in the soldier no feeling but an intense desire to obey, while the opposite manner and tone of voice cannot fail to excite strong resentment and a desire to disobey.... He who feels the respect which is due to others cannot fail to inspire in them regard for himself, while he who feels, and hence manifests, disrespect toward others, especially his inferiors, cannot fail to inspire hatred against himself." (Major General John M. Schofield, speaking to the Cadets at West Point, August 11, 1879.)
[22]J. Mitford, "Kind and Usual Punishment in California," in Atkins & Glick, *supra* note 21, p. 157.
[23]McKendrick, *supra* note 11, pp. 161-166.
[24]Loveland, "Classification in the Prison System," in Tappan, *supra* note 10, p. 102.
[25]K. Menninger, "The Crime of Punishment,"

in Atkins & Glick, *supra* n. 21, p. 49.

[26]Annual Chief Justice Earl Warren Conference sponsored by the Roscoe Pound-American Trial Lawyers Foundation, *A Program for Prison Reform* (June 9-10, 1972), p. 50.

[27]G. Jackson, *The Village Voice*, (September 10, 1970), as cited in Leonard Orland, *Justice, Punishment, and Treatment: The Correctional Process* (New York: The Free Press, div. MacMillan Pub. Co., Inc., 1973), p. 131.

*World War II; the increasing entry of rehabilitative services; the wave of prison riots in the early 1950s; the human rights explosion of the 1960s; the burgeoning of correctional case law; Attica and several lesser-known but major disturbances; the politicization of prisoner demands; the development of community-based corrections; and the reports of several National Commissions on Violence, on Crime, on Standards and Goals in Criminal Justice.

†Morris, better known as "Red," Rudensky was editor of the Federal Atlanta Penitentiary's inmate newspaper and a well-known writer.

*He subsequently became. . .heavily involved in Attica as Deputy to Commissioner Oswald of New York State.

*Another unexplored vehical would be the annual conferences of ACA.

[28]Orland, *supra* note 27, p. 139.

[29]T.C. Esselstyn, "The Social System of Correctional Workers," *Crime and Delinquency* (Apr. 1966), p. 117.

[30]*Ibid.*, pp. 118-119.

[31]*Ibid.*, p. 119.

[32]*Ibid.*

[33]*Ibid.*, p. 120.

[34]*Ibid.*, pp. 121-122.

*Retsky, at this writing a correctional counselor at Stateville Penitentiary, Joliet, Ill. is one of the few former guards to publish seriously. Jacobs is on the faculty of Cornell University.

[35]B. Jacobs & G. Retsky, "Prison Guard," *Urban Life and Culture*, vol. 4, no. 1 (Apr. 1975) 7-8.

[36]*Ibid.*, p. 9.

[37]*Ibid.*, p. 10.

[38]*Ibid.*, pp. 10-11.

[39]*Ibid.*, p. 12.

[40]*Ibid.*, pp. 22-23.

[41]*Ibid.*, p. 23.

[42]*Ibid.*, p. 25.

[43]*Ibid.*, pp. 26-27.

[44]Stanley Griffith, "A Training Experience as a Pseudo-Guard" (unpubl., 50 pp. plus apps., 1974).

[45]*Ibid.*, p. 34.

[46]*Ibid.*, pp. 37-39.

[47]*Ibid.*, pp. 25-26.

[48]S.L. Brodsky, Ph.D., "A Bill of Rights for the Correctional Officer," *Federal Probation* (June 1974), p. 38.

[49]*Ibid.*, pp. 38-40.

[50]Edwin H. Sutherland & Donald R. Cressey, *Criminology* 9th ed. (Philadelphia: J.B. Lippincott Co., 1974), p. 515.

[51]S. V. Roberts, "Prisons Feel a Mood of Protest," in Atkins & Glick, *supra* note 21, p. 104.

[52]Jackson, *supra* note 27, pp. 131-132.

[53]William G. Nagel, *The New Red Barn: A Critical Look at the Modern American Prison*, (New York: Walker & Co., 1973), p. 69.

[54]Arthur L. Paddock & James D. McMillin, "Final Report Vienna Staff Training Project" mimeo., 18 pp. plus 11 tables (So. Ill. Univ., Carbondale, June 30, 1972).

17. *The preceding articles in this part delineate the many difficulties faced by an increasingly anachronistic correctional system. The root of these organizational problems lies in the basic misconception that criminals can be restrained and "cured" at the same time. This misconception has been the cause, according to Fogel and other critics of the correctional system, of prison riots, staff and administrative disillusionment, and public denouncements of the most obvious arm of our criminal justice system.*

In the following two articles, the consequences spawned by organizational confusion are carefully examined. Piliavin discusses the lack of consensus among correctional workers and indicates that because the organization's goals are not clear, specific job tasks "lack validation." The result is that each group suspects the credibility of other groups in the organization. A polarized working environment is the unfortunate outcome. The "professional" correctional workers, the prison psychologist, the educator, and other treatment-oriented groups, are wont to attribute their suspicions to the lack of education among the "custodians." Hence, the prison guard, as described in Fogel's piece, is blamed not because he is a pawn in a game of mutable ideology but because he is constrained to perform the most obvious and basic of all prison duties. The "professionals," middle managers, and administrators, on the other hand, are considered, by prison guards, Piliavin says, as "ivory towerish" and overly idealistic. This misunderstanding of roles creates an especially volatile occupational environment. Consider the following quote: quote:

The view that the origins of the conflicts lie in the psychological defects of the workers further obstructs the resolution of conflict because of its obvious demeaning implications.

Although Piliavin is not quite clear as to what is meant by "treatment" and its relation to the now discredited idea of rehabilitation, his recommendation that there be a "considerable—even total—overlap [of worker' roles]" is not only adaptable to present systems of incarceration but may be considered a primary function of future correctional alternatives. Piliavin's ideas provide a useful foundation for Duffee's argument (Article 18).

THE REDUCTION OF CUSTODIAN-PROFESSIONAL CONFLICT IN CORRECTIONAL INSTITUTIONS

IRVING PILIAVIN

Although the term "staff conflict" has many meanings, its current usage usually refers to the disagreement, lack of cooperation, and personal dislike existing between members of two or more identifiable divisions within an organization. Within correctional settings, for example, it usually means the problems of relationship between educational and counseling personnel or between custodial and education personnel rather than problems of relationship among members within each of these groups.

The concern regarding this conflict stems from the belief that staff disagreement and lack of cooperation vitiate the efficient working of an organization. Disunity among staff causes work slowdowns, fragmentation of planning, high turnover, and, in service organizations such as the correctional institution, the reduction in effectiveness of treatment programs.

The negative potential of staff conflict within the correctional institution has been underscored in the past decade with the increased acceptance of milieu treatment. Formerly it was believed that only the therapist reached the "basic" self of an inmate and influenced his change and that the actions of other workers toward the inmate had little influence on the therapist's achievements. With this conception, staff conflict was important only insofar as it resulted in the inmate's becoming emotionally inaccessible to the therapist. Futhermore, communication between therapists and other workers was not given great emphasis, at least by the therapists, since the treatment interview was believed to be the only worthwhile way to learn about the person to be treated.

Today it is believed, more or less firmly, that each staff member within the institution has a potentially important role to play in the directed change of inmates. This view stresses first that cooperation and coordination of institutional workers are essential for successful programing. Second, because each worker may have different and pertinent knowledge about particular inmates, open and frequent communication among personnel is vital. Third, since workers must present a consistent front and be immune from divisive endeavors by inmates, mutual respect and support are required.[1]

Much has been done by institutional administrators to attain these goals. Among efforts in this direction have been the provision of opportunities for formal and informal communication among workers whose functions are in need of integration, in-service training of staff, provision of outside educational opportunities to personnel, and designation of previously ancillary workers as members of "the treatment team." What achievements can we expect from these various endeavors? In general, it seems probable that we can expect little—certainly far less than we might hope. In the remainder of this paper I shall try to substantiate this assertion and to suggest more efficacious, though perhaps more difficult, approaches to mitigation of staff conflict. My remarks will be confined to the conflict that most frequently attracts attention, the one between custodial personnel and those responsible for what has been termed therapeutic or casework counseling. These latter workers will be referred to, for convenience, as professionals, treatment workers, or clinicians.

The Bases for Staff Conflict

Let us begin by delineating broadly the basic causes of staff conflicts. Conflict can arise when workers lack the education and training, or both, necessary to carry out adequately their organization roles. Specifically, when the performance of these workers reduces the efficiency of other personnel, the resulting inadequacy leads to mutual dissatisfaction, resentment, and criticism.

Conflict also stems, in part, from the workers' lack of emotional attributes necessary for the type of work to which they are assigned. In correctional work, for example, requisites for the successful worker might well include flexibility, self-confidence, ability to exercise authority, perceptiveness, and concern for the welfare of others. Insofar as workers lacking these traits are assigned tasks which are to be coordinated with those assigned to other employees, dissatisfaction on the part of the latter and consequent conflict can be expected.

A third source of conflict is the difference in goal and task priorities resulting from different responsibilities and problems. The influence of workers' roles on their relationship has been observed in studies of industrial plants,[2] commercial enterprises,[3] government bureaucracies,[4] and mental hospitals,[5] as well as in correctional institutions,[6] where the structural basis for conflict derives from the two basic responsibilities—custody and treatment. Custodial workers are concerned with maintaining control and this concern is reflected in their priorities of action in a given situation as well as in the considerations they express in planning and supervising inmates' activities. On the other hand, treatment personnel tend to be concerned with mitigating the psychological or interpersonal problems of inmates. Conflict engendered by these different priorities is exacerbated because custodial and treatment workers, by virtue of their different responsibilities, are also frequently confronted in a different manner by inmates. These workers thus develop different conceptions of the inmates and each staff group becomes convinced of the correctness of its view and derides that of the other.[7]

It is important to note that among the workers themselves the first two of these causes of conflict draw more attention than the third. Particularly in service organizations, it seems, staff members are wont to see their interpersonal disputes as resulting from the qualities of individuals rather than from their differing functional roles in the organizations which employ them. Thus, in the correctional institution we find social workers, psychologists, and psychiatrists remarking that custodial workers with whom they have had disagreement are rigid, authoritarian, immature, or inadequate. True, on occasion some professionals acknowledge that custodial workers have difficult, conflicting, and thankless tasks, and, at times, such concession may even lead to the recognition that the organization role of custodial workers may limit their ability to coordinate their operations with other staff. More frequently, research suggests, such concession leads to observations about the inherent problems that characterize the individuals who would undertake such roles.[8] This element of human fallibility in explaining staff conflict shows itself in the custodial workers' view of professionals as "ivory towerish," "impractical," and "smug." While the textbook knowledge of professional workers is granted, it is claimed that their lack of experience in the day-to-day care of institution inmates nullifies any contribution they might otherwise make to those providing such care.[9] The view that the origins of the conflicts lie in the psychological defects of the workers further obstructs the resolution of conflict because of its obvious demeaning implications.

Traditional Approaches

It seems likely that measures successful in industry and commerce, such as in-service training, opening communication channels among workers, and making staff previously regarded as ancillary a part of the therapeutic team will have only a limited effect in reducing strained relations among custodial and professional workers because of certain features unique in correctional institutions. The impact of these features can be better appreciated by comparing the correctional agency and the commercial organization. In a commercial enterprise, as a rule, organizational goals (according to Simon, producing the greatest net money return) are well articulated,[10] and the tasks of workers, particularly those in lower positions, are relatively standardized.[11] Secondly, the appropriateness of the tasks assigned to workers has been demonstrated,[12] and the contribution made by various workers to the achievement of the organization's output can be asserted.[13] Thirdly, workers' claims to expertise are usually granted on the basis of their demonstrated accomplishments or their membership in a profession or vocation with demonstrated competence. These conditions aid control of staff conflict in several ways. The recognition of some workers as authorities because of their expertise minimizes disruptive challenges to their decisions. The demonstration of the appropriateness of assigned subgoals and of methods for their achievement guarantees considerable agreement in workers' expectations of one another. Furthermore, in such organizations the availability of evaluative devices to administrators restrains disruptive relations among workers and permits decisions to be made if such disruptions "go too far." In either case, the potential of any conflict to impair the operation of an organization is reduced.

Within correctional institutions, however, these conflict-controlling characteristics are not present. Even if treatment goals are shared among workers, their implications for performance have usually not been empirically demonstrated. Nor are there procedures for assessing the contributions of staff members to the rehabilitation of inmates. In addition, the content and timing of workers' operations (with the exception of custodial duties) have not been well articulated, and claims to treatment expertise by professionals, such as psychiatrists, psychologists, and social workers, have had little empirical support.[14] These conditions increase the probability of conflict within the correctional institution in at least three ways. Because of the ambiguity and lack of programing which inhere in treatment roles, it is very difficult for workers to meet one another's expectations in the handling of inmates. Since few criteria, except perhaps humanitarian ones, are available to determine the validity of workers' definitions of their roles, little other than the threat of administrative sanction can assure compliance when differences in role conception arise. Finally, administrative demands themselves, insofar as they concern the carrying out of treatment responsibilities, must be rather loose because of the inability to evaluate the contribution of workers' performances to the achievement of rehabilitation goals.

These barriers to coordinating and controlling workers' performance in the correctional institution permit staff members to "go their own way"—that is, to attend to their particular obligations without having to be concerned about integrating their work with others. In effect, staff effort is highly segmented. In addition, in-service training of "untrained" workers, inclusion of nonprofessionals in the treatment team, and expansion of communication links among staff may not suffice to reduce this conflict. Precepts underlying treatment tasks as presented in staff-training sessions frequently gain only limited acceptance because they lack validation. Communication among workers may be only partly useful in settling disputes because little basis exists for evaluating the authority of disputants' complaints and solutions. When the nonprofessional is included in the treatment team and does communicate more closely with his colleagues, it is possible that this particular device for minimizing conflict may, in fact, increase it. This anomalous consequence derives from two considerations. First, communication between workers often brings to the fore differences in their status. For example, the professionals may play down or ignore the views of nonprofessionals in making program decisions, a move which may result in the nonprofessionals' withdrawal from participation in such decisions and their alienation from the professionals. Second, in the effort to resolve differences through communication, workers come to learn even more about their mutual activities. Insofar as this additional knowledge fails to mitigate disputes, the possibility cannot be discounted that it may make workers even more knowledgeable about one another's limitations, thus furthering the probability of conflict between them.[15]

A Basis for Mitigating Conflict

If the usual procedures for mitigating staff conflict are of only limited utility in the correctional institution, what measures might be taken to resolve this problem? Zald has suggested that the size of institutions be limited and that all organizational aims other than those concerned with treatment and rehabilitation be mini-

mized.[16] Presumably, the latter course would reduce the probability of goal conflict among workers, while the intimacy resulting from the former would make it possible for workers to develop strong positive personal bonds—sufficiently strong to withstand the possible divisive effects of their differing organization roles.

However, the impracticality of Zald's suggestion within most correctional institutions is readily apparent. Few of these settings are limited in size and the possibility of their developing a pure treatment orientation is highly unlikely. Does this imply that there are no means by which conflict among staff within these organizations can be mitigated? Not necessarily. Such mitigation can be achieved if the current organizational form of correctional institutions is altered in some drastic ways. The basic precondition which must be met is that a common goal and operational framework exist among personnel. One tactic that seems well suited for the achievement of this aim consists of enlarging the scope of the organizational roles assigned to custodial and treatment workers so that their functions overlap. The assumption here is that the more they share organizational tasks and problems, the more likely they will be to share perspectives. That established perspectives will be altered by changing workers' roles was graphically demonstrated by Lieberman[17] and his colleagues in a study of workers employed in an industrial plant. It has also been suggested in a recent investigation of the value orientations of custodial personnel in two California prisons.[18] Three groups of custodians were relevant to the research. One group consisted of custodial officers at what would probably be considered a treatment-oriented institution, and a second group was employed in a so-called custodial prison. The third group of custodians was distinguished by the fact that these workers engaged in group counseling of inmates in addition to their normal duties.[19] Members of the three groups were compared in relation to three different attitudes: their perception of the relative importance of treatment programs, their beliefs on the appropriate balance between treatment and control emphases in institutional programs, and the degree of trust they felt toward inmates. In all of these areas, the workers in group counseling voiced attitudes and values closer to those reflected by professional workers than did the other custodians. Furthermore, group counselors were far more "professionally oriented" than their peers in the custodial setting who were interested in becoming group counselors but had not yet done so. This strongly suggests that the differences found were not merely the result of self-selection processes, and that alteration of custodians' assigned duties can change their perceptions of appropriate organizational aims and task priorities. Whether the converse is true—that is, whether the value orientation of professionals will develop more in accord with that of custodians through alteration of the professional's job—has received no adequate demonstration.

Expansion of workers' responsibilities as suggested above, however, raises some serious problems: (1) What basis is there for assuming that custodial personnel can engage satisfactorily in the tasks of treatment personnel or vice versa? (2) Will the conflict inherent in the two functions —control and treatment—be so great as to immobilize workers attempting to discharge both responsibilities? (3)

What limits should be placed on the expansion of workers' roles?

Custodians Capacity for Treatment

The question of the relative competence of custodians to handle responsibilities heretofore reserved for professionals can be discussed only tentatively, because of the virtual nonexistence of empirical study in this area. So basic a matter as that concerning the abilities of professionally trained psychologists, social workers, and psychiatrists in their own field of treatment has been given almost no investigation.

Even if we were to grant that professional training does provide workers with some competence to dispense treatment, the fact remains that the great majority of persons occupying professional positions in correctional agencies are without such specialized training. They are college graduates whose education reflects an enormous range of intellectual concerns. On what grounds can these workers be said to be better prepared to perform treatment functions than workers without college preparation? It might be argued that some college graduates have been exposed to courses concerned more or less directly with the treatment and prevention of crime. It might also be said that the holder of a college degree has intelligence, curiosity, and a nondoctrinaire commitment to the current way of doing things—qualities necessary for the adequate performance of treatment tasks. While this latter point may be true, it is necessary to recognize that many workers without college degrees also have these attributes. Furthermore, in-service training could provide these personnel (as well as many college-educated staff members) with whatever knowledge is deemed necessary for treatment of offenders. Given proper selection criteria and training programs, there is no demonstrable basis for the assumption that correctional employees without a college education would necessarily perform treatment tasks less adequately than their more highly educated co-workers.

The question of whether professionals can perform custodial tasks is less difficult. Since custodial jobs require no specialized training other than that given within agencies themselves, professionals are as well prepared for this work as present-day custodians. While it might also be argued that treatment personnel do not have the personality attributes necessary for performing custodial tasks, there is no evidence to support this contention. Indeed, Redl and Wineman's account of Pioneer House indicates that professionals can make good custodians, at least in institutions for juvenile offenders.[20] The difficulty may be that many professionals would refuse these tasks regardless of their capabilities to perform them.

Incompatibility of Functions

Some students have suggested that both treatment and control responsibilities cannot be performed by one worker. Cressey, for example, puts the dilemma of the custodian who is responsible in some sense for treatment as follows:

> The custodians ... must "use discretion" and somehow behave both custodially and therapeutically. Yet ... they cannot be given explicit criteria on which to base this discretion. If they enforce the rules, they risk being diagnosed as "rigid" and "just a guard" because such enforcement interferes with individualized treatment. But if their failure to enforce rules creates a threat to institutional security, orderliness, or maintenance, they are not "doing their job."[21]

The consequence of this dilemma, says Cressey, is that the guard simply relaxes; his approach to his job becomes essentially laissez-faire and his performance suffers not only as a custodian but as a treatment worker.

> Because the guard has been granted freedom to use discretion in handling inmates and is not "backed" by an impersonal official hierarchy with demands that custodial rules be routinely administered, when he behaves punitively the inmates, like the front-office workers, are likely to attribute his behavior to personal vindictiveness or maladjustment.... Relaxation by guards, then, is stimulated by an undercurrent of fear, as well as by treatment considerations.[22]

Undeniably, staff who attempt to discharge both custodial and treatment tasks will encounter conflict. Cressey's pessimistic statement of the problem, however, appears to be overdrawn. Organization studies and analyses repeatedly demonstrate that conflict of one sort or another inheres in all but the most routine of organizational roles. The redeveloper is expected to provide new housing in accord with the needs of the poor and the expectations of the wealthy; the automobile designer is expected to develop safe cars which meet popular tastes; and the correctional administrator is expected to get better results and minimize expenditures. Each is confronted with incompatible demands in that maximum achievement of one aim may seriously vitiate the achievement of others. The solution to their dilemmas is not to cast out all but compatible responsibilities. Rather, they forego maximal achievement of a given aim for its optimal achievement in keeping with the demands of other goals. Such compromise is almost routine within the complex organization.[23]

Furthermore, in spite of Cressey's analysis, studies of correctional institutions have failed to find that the custodial worker is, in fact, compromised to the point of inaction if he is given treatment responsibilities. The experience at Highfields, for example, suggests that if both responsibilities are assigned to one organizational position, treatment functions can be performed without vitiating custodial concerns.[24] Furthermore, in the study of prison guards cited above, few custodians who were engaged in providing treatment believed their treatment and custodial roles to be irreconcilable, and none indicated that control was no longer a matter for their concern.[25] Thus, while we might grant Cressey's point that custodians who are given treatment tasks will thereby encounter problems, there is little empirical or theoretical reason to believe these problems will be incapacitating. In fact, it has been argued that custodial and control concerns are in many ways mutually beneficial in dealing with offenders.[26]

Limitations on Role Expansion

As implied in the preceding discussion, some limited overlapping of workers' roles has been employed in a number of correctional institutions. Although the basic distinction between custody and treatment workers has been retained, I do not know of any evidence to indicate that it is useful. This is not to suggest that all workers must be assigned equally integrated responsibilities. Obviously some positions lend themselves more to a treatment or custodial emphasis

> "...but would insure that personnel do not form 'in-group—versus 'out-group' perspectives."

than do others. And while assignment to these positions should be based on competence, this does not imply the necessity for horizontal specialization. Rather, all custodial-treatment personnel could belong to the same hierarchy, with each having at least some treatment responsibilities. This structure not only would provide greater opportunity to develop common job-related values among workers, but would ensure that personnel do not form "in group" versus "out group" perspectives.

Conclusion

In brief, the basic argument of this paper is that staff conflict within correctional institutions—in particular that between custodians and treatment personnel—is not likely to be mitigated by close communication, in-service training, the development of working teams, and other procedures used with some success in other types of organization. The inability to specify criteria for goal achievement and to determine treatment roles detracts from the effectiveness of these traditionally used procedures in the correctional institution. It has been suggested that a possible effective tactic in reducing staff conflict might be the expansion of workers' roles to the point where there is considerable—even total—overlap.

This move, which is equivalent to a reduction in the division of labor, it is suggested, may serve to develop more congruent goals and role expectations among staff members, thus reducing the grounds for much current controversy.

Admittedly such a move may itself create problems. The capacity of workers to fulfill new tasks and their ability to handle incongruent responsibilities are questionable. So, too, is the willingness of workers, particularly professionals, to undertake new responsibilities which they may previously have denigrated. However, the experience of other organizations, including mental hospitals, indicates that these problems are not insoluble. Organizational change is never simple or easy. And for the correctional institution, frequently viewed in its present form as an anachronism,[27] the question is whether the pains of change are worth its achievements.

> "...a parochial viewpoint and mutual disrespect is inimical to organization success..."

Only trial can provide an answer to this query.

This discussion does not advocate the total elimination of controversy among personnel. Disputes among workers who regard one another as competent and as sharing the same goals contribute to the validity of organizational programs. However, conflict which indicates a parochial viewpoint and mutual disrespect among personnel is inimical to organization success,[28] and it is with the latter conflict that the procedures proposed here are concerned.

Notes

[1] Maxwell Jones, *The Therapeutic Community* (New York: Basic Books, 1953).

[2] Alvin Gouldner, *Patterns of Industrial Bureaucracy* (Glencoe: The Free Press, 1954); S. Lieberman, "The Effects of Changes in Roles on the Attitudes of Role Occupants," *Human Relations* (Aug. 1956), pp. 385-402.

[3] William F. Whyte, *Human Relations in the Restaurant Industry* (New York: McGraw Hill, 1948).

[4] Peter M. Blau, *The dynamics of Bureaucracy* (Chicago: Univ. of Chicago Press, 1955); Philip Selznick, *TVA and the Grass Roots* (Berkeley & Los Angeles: Univ. of Calif. Press, 1953).

[5] Alfred Stanton & Morris Schwartz, *The Mental Hospital* (New York: Basic Books, 1954); William Caudill, *The Psychiatric Hospital as a Small Society* (Cambridge: Harvard Univ. Press, 1958).

[6] I. Piliavin, "Conflict between Cottage Parents and Caseworkers," *Social Service Rev.* (Mar. 1963), pp. 17-25; M. W. Zald, "Power Balance and Staff Conflict in Correctional Institutions," *Administrative Science Quart.* (June 1962), pp. 22-49; G. H. Weber, "Conflicts between Professional and Nonprofessional Persons in Institutional Delinquency Treatment," *J. Crim. Law, Criminology & Police Science* (May-June 1957), pp. 26-43.

[7] R. A. Cohen, "Some Relations between Staff Tensions and the Psychotherapeutic Process," in *The Patient and the Mental Hospital,* Milton Greenblatt, Daniel J. Levinson & Richard H. Williams, eds. (New York: The Free Press, 1957), pp. 301-08.

[8] Weber, *supra* note 6; Irving Piliavin "An Investigation of Conflict between Cottage Parents and Other Staff in Juvenile Correctional Institutions" (unpubl. doctoral diss. Columbia Univ. School of Social Work, 1961).

[9] Weber, *supra* note 6, p. 28.

[10] "This goal is relatively easily measured and thus can serve as a criterion for assessing the adequacy of workers' operations." Herbert A. Simon, *Administrative Behavior* (New York: Macmillan, 1958), pp. 172-73.

[11] Peter Blau, *Bureaucracy in Modern Society* (New York: Random House, 1956), p. 18.

[12] *Ibid.* p. 32.

[13] James G. March and Herbert A. Simon, *Organizations* (New York: John Wiley, 1958), p. 145.

[14] J. W. Eaton, "A Scientific Basis for Helping," *Amer. Social Work,* Alfred J. Kahn, ed. (New York: Columbia Univ. Press, 1959), pp. 270-92; H. Alt & H. Grossbard, "Professional Issues in the Institutional Treatment of Delinquent Children," *Amer. J. Orthopsychiatry*

(April 1949), pp. 279-94.

[15]Piliavin, *supra* note 6.

[16]Zald, *supra* note 6.

[17]Lieberman, *supra* note 2.

[18]Barbara Francisco et al., "Attitudes and Role Perceptions of Correctional Officers: A Comparative Study" (unpubl. master's thesis, School of Social Welfare, Univ. of Calif., Berkeley, 1961), ch. IV, p. 19.

[19]For detailed discussion concerning the nature of this counseling service see Norman Fenton, *An Introduction to Group Counseling in State Correctional Service* (Sacramento: State of Calif. Dept. of Corrections, 1957).

[20]Fritz Redl & David Wineman, *The Aggressive Child* (New York: The Free Press, 1957), p. 310.

[21]Donald R. Cressey, "Limitations on Organization of Treatment in the Modern Prison," *Theoretical Studies in Social Organization of the Prison* (New York: Social Science Research Council, 1960), p. 107.

[22]*Ibid.*, p. 108.

[23]Simon, *supra* note 10, pp. 20-44.

[24]Lloyd W. McCorkle, Albert Elias & F. Lovell Bixby, *The Highfields Story* (New York: Henry Holt, 1957).

[25]Francisco, *supra* note 18, p. 19.

[26]E. Studt, "Worker-Client Authority Relationships in Social Work," *Social Work* (Jan. 1959), pp. 18-28.

[27]Marshall Clinard, *Sociology of Deviant Behavior* (New York: Rinehart, 1960), pp. 510-18.

[28]Lewis A. Coser, *The Functions of Social Conflict* (New York: The Free Press, 1956).

18. *Fogel directs his criticism toward rehabilitative policies that have preoccupied prison reformists for years—reformists who have asked "Why not do these criminals some good while they're sitting in prisons twiddling their thumbs?" Fogel, in his condemnation of this seemingly benevolent approach, indirectly asks "what is 'good'?" "What happens when prisoners refuse to have 'good' done to them?" and finally "what happens when the prisoner who has had 'good' done to him is proven to be a chronic recidivist who inadvertantly is thumbing his nose in the confused do-gooders' faces?" Rehabilitation, then, according to Fogel and his contemporaries is an ineffective correctional goal. Its failure as a general correctional goal indicates a need to reassess the actual possibilities and limitations of "humane punishment."*

Although there is an obvious need to be practical in a new approach to prison planning and administration, Duffee, in the next article, suggests that a careful study of correctional policy and its relationship to managerial style, and overall organizational character can be psychologically beneficial for the entire correctional community. He states, "[A policy of Reintegration has as its goal]... returning changed offenders to the changed community" and that this goal can be achieved by "harmonious social interactions."

Duffee's discussion includes a cursory introduction to the four major correctional policies—Reformation, Rehabilitation and Restraint [Reintegration]. He implies that Reintegration is the only policy that allows inmates and correctional personnel a semblance of dignity behind prison walls. "It is this policy (Reintegration) that attempts to change the interactions among inmates and staff rather than change something within inmates."

Duffee claims that "human beings prefer healthy or harmonious climates to unhealthy ones," and that the environment is "the accumulation over time of [human interaction]...." Interaction is dependent on an exchange rather than a one-sided situation where inmates are mere recipients of force, or misguided educational attempts, or both. Significantly, this interaction also depends on the ability to coordinate a definite correctional policy with managerial style. Once the policy is clear and polarization between staff and inmates is minimized by a mutual recognition of specific correctional and social goals, the term "humane punishment" may no longer be regarded as oxymoronic.

ORGANIZATIONAL CLIMATE

DAVID DUFFEE

The situation we are concerned with in this study is not the external visible prison nor is it "what it feels like to be an inmate," or "what it feels like to be an officer." Our situation is the social interactions among all correctional people, including managers, as they are affected by managerial strategies.

One definition of this situation has been called the "character" of the organization.[1] This was one attempt to explicate the felt differences between the internal atmospheres of different juvenile institutions. Trying to raise to a rational level the reasons for these usually intuitive and emotional assessments of institutions was difficult. The argument was made that, analogous to individuals, organizations may have a "character" which is an overall effect of the organization upon any particular observer or participant. The major variables influencing character are relationships with the environment, organizational goals, staff-staff relations, and staff-inmate relations.

A similar description of the organizational situation is given by Street, Vinter, and Perrow. They speak not of character but of organizational "climate."[2] They suggest that each institution has a unique climate, while each institution may not have unique goals or unique executive strategies for the implementation of goals.[3]

The climate is not only the result of executive action, but also of staff and inmate responses to executive directives, action initiated by staff or inmates, and executive responses to these actions. The climate might be called the total effect of living and working within the organization. It is important to distinguish the concept of climate from any particular activity or set of activities (such as a managerial style) because the climate is the accumulation over time of these activities and is thus a variable in its own right.

The claim that an organizational climate is "unique" will be modified as the study of climate progresses. In order to treat climate as a variable, it obviously must become known as having a set of values that can be specified.[4]

One attempt to quantify the organizational climate variable has been Rudolph Moos' work with the "environmental press" of an institution.

According to Moos, the analysis and prediction of behavior has too often emphasized personality factors and too infrequently studied the environmental factors that affect behavior. Recent psychological

studies, particularly concerning institutional behavior

> all...strongly indicate the importance of the setting and the person's interaction with the setting in accounting for the behavioral variance [and] suggest that systematic assessment of environments might greatly increase the accuracy of behavioral predictions.[5]

In other words, Moos saw the importance of measuring the ways in which the social environment of an institution may press an individual toward certain kinds of perceptions and certain kinds of behaviors. He was concerned that correctional officials too frequently consider that inmate behavior is explained in terms of the individual's psychological characteristics. He made the counter-suggestion that much behavior in a prison may be socially induced by pressures that affect all organizational members.

> "The seemingly unwieldy and unyielding prison organization can be changed."

The existence of such an environmental press toward particular kinds of human interaction would be crucial to the formulation of correctional policy. Reform, Rehabilitation, and Reintegration [Restraint][6] policies all seek to change inmate behavior in one way or another. Either the behavior is a direct target of change, or alterations in behavior are treated as indications of variation in an internal change-target such as an "attitude." Since the correctional goal is implemented through policy and managerial style, or through structuring the internal situation in certain ways, that situation of structured interaction is the medium in which plans for inmates unfold and also the medium in which inmate reactions take place and are observed. A measurement of a consensus from organizational members about such a medium or climate would support the policy of Reintegration as a correctional goal, since it is this policy that attempts to change the interactions among inmates and staff rather than change something within inmates. In contrast, Reform and Rehabilitation policies that focus on internal attitudes or conditions rather than on interconnections between people would be less viable alternatives to the extent that the environment is a determinant of behavior.

This kind of consideration is beyond the scope of this study. We are not presently concerned with the consequences of particular climates, although this is obviously an important problem for future investigations. Presently, we want to study climate as a consequence of the two major aspects of the managerial role—style and policy.

Climate as the Integrating Concept in the Study of Prisons as Organizations

If the social climate is really a variable of cumulative interactions in an organization, then this environment should differ as the interaction patterns differ. In particular, we would expect that the environment should press toward social health or harmony when style and policy indicate managerial concern for organizational congruence, and the environment should press toward social ill health and discord when style and policy indicate managerial lack of concern for congruence in organizational life.

For example, if an institution had a managerial policy of Reintegration and a managerial style that stressed team management, the climate should be relatively healthy. In this particular situation, managerial style indicates simultaneous concern for goals of organizational members and goals of the organization itself, while the policy of Reintegration indicates a simultaneous concern for offenders and community. At the opposite extreme, an institution with a managerial style that demands task accomplishment with little regard for socio-psychological variables and a policy of Restraint should be relatively unhealthy.

Both of these combinations of policy and style are effective. That is, the style complements the policy. Both pairs are examples of "congruent" or consistant style and policy but only the first example should produce a healthy organizational climate because a policy of Reintegration and an accomodating managerial style indicates, on the part of the manager, a *conscious* use of the tendency of organizational members to achieve congruence.

The organizational climate is *not* a desired end product of the prison organization; it is only a means to that end. Some prison goals require a healthy climate while some other prison goals require an unhealthy one; the goal in the first example is, by definition, returning changed offenders to the changed community. The organizational environment or the medium in which that goal is achieved is one of harmonious social interactions. The goal in the second example is, by definition, maintaining the organization for its own sake, or holding offenders out of an unchanging society. The social climate or organizational medium in which that goal is effected is one of discord and disharmony even though the policy of restraint is satisfied.

Human beings prefer healthy or harmonious climates to unhealthy ones. Or, stating this idea in terms of its managerial implications, it is more difficult to maintain an unhealthy social climate as a means to an end than it will be to maintain a healthy social climate as a means to an end.

An integrated organization, or one with a healthy climate, increases the probability of achieving organizational goals while the fragmented organization, or one with an unhealthy climate, decreases the probability of achieving goals. The integrated organization would possess the characteristics of a learning system. It would be able to change its internal structure in order to achieve goals. The fragmented organization would, in the long run, seem to be an unstable system. It would not be able to change its structure in order to achieve its goals.

Perceptions about organizational integration can be affected. The

seemingly unwieldy and unyielding prison organization can be changed. The internal social situation will vary as management alters goals and changes the way in which it relates to lower levels of the organization. A healthy social climate would be possible when management is democratic, not autocratic; when it involves people in decision-making rather than treating them like means to an end. Altering the patterns of management in a prison is a large undertaking, but it can be more optimistically addressed if we realize that prison organizations are quite different internally, and it may well be that the recognition of major differences will eventually allow us to change the internal climate so that goals that are now commonly espoused by correctional executives, legislatures, and the public alike can be achieved. Key variables in bringing about change would begin with managerial policy and managerial style, which, taken together, apparently explain to a great degree the internal differences between correctional organizations.

Notes

[1] M. Zald, "The Correctional Institution for Juvenile Offenders: An Analysis of Organizational 'Character,' " in Lawrence Hazelrigg, ed. *Prison Within Society* (Garden City: Doubleday, 1969), pp. 229-246.

[2] David Street, Robert Vinter & Charles Perrow, *Organization for Treatment* (New York: Free Press, 1966), see, e.g., pp. 26-39.

[3] *Ibid.*, pp. 21-22.

[4] See the discussion in Leslie Wilkins, *Evaluation of Penal Measures* (New York: Random House, 1969), pp. 25-26, on the resolution of the argument of "uniqueness" and measurement.

[5] Rudolph Moos, "The Assessment of the Social Climates of Correctional Institutions," *Journal Research in Crime & Delinquency*, 5, no. 2 (July 1968), p. 175.

[6] For the sake of expedience, these four correctional policies have been assigned the labels of Reintegration, Rehabilitation, Reform, and Restraint. These labels are a shorthand reminder of the frame of reference and change strategy associated with each.

Restraint is the policy with low concern about the community and low concern for organizational participants. There is no change strategy involved. Correction in this mode is a holding action or warehousing of inmates.

Reform is the policy with low concern for the participants and high concern for the community. The change strategy is one of compliance; people are molded into different behavior reactions according to a well-established set of rules with rewards and punishments freely administered.

Rehabilitation is the policy with high concern for participants and low concern for the community. The change strategy is one of identification; people change through a manipulation of intrapersonal and interpersonal relationships.

Reintegration is the policy with high concern for participants and high concern for the community. The change strategy is internalization; people change as they discover and test alternate behavior patterns congruent with their values and beliefs.

19.

The somberness of it. Its slow and yet searing psychic force! The obvious terror and depression—constant and unshakeable of those who, in spite of all their courage or their fears, their bravado or their real indifference (there were even those) were still compelled to think and wait. For now, in connection with this. . . prison life he was in constant psychic, if not physical, contact with twenty other convicted characters of varying temperaments and nationalities each of whom, like himself, had responded to some heat or lust or misery of his nature or his circumstances.

Theodore Dreiser
An American Tragedy

The predicament described above was, until 1841, the only lawful outcome of any trial in which an offender was found to be guilty of a crime. It would have been the fate of James Vayle, a drunken derelict, who in 1841 was sentenced by the Boston Municipal Court to its House of Corrections. Such was justice; Vayle was clearly guilty of his crime. But John Augustus, a wealthy cobbler, a "do-gooder," persuaded the court to release Vayle in his custody. Vayle, whose appearance and attitude changed notably while in the care of Augustus, was rehabilitated by the cobbler. Society was protected; Vayle, as a result of his probation, was changed and freed.

Probation became institutionalized in Massachusetts in 1878. Parole, an earlier concept with its roots in the indentured servitude of the seventeenth and eighteenth centuries, was institutionalized by New York in 1876. Thus, both procedures—probation and parole—are little more than a century old and, as Imlay and Reid point out in article 20, "cannot be represented as a linear course of development or evolution but rather as a continuing experiment."

This experiment, the idea of changing the offender who "had responded" —not of his free will but because of some social determinate—"to some heat or lust or misery of his nature or his circumstances," is grounded in the philosophy of determinism. Determinism, applied to criminal behavior, states that an offender behaves not of his own volition, but because of causes over which he has little or no control. Thus, he is not fully responsible for his actions and cannot be punished as though he were. The hypothesis of the experiment, then, is that by altering the causes behind the offender's actions, the offender will be free to act differently (and presumably in a lawful way) in the future. The experiment continues today in various forms: probation, parole, community corrections, diversion, and halfway houses, for example.

David Dressler, in the first article of this section, argues that the "companion services" of probation and parole are not markedly different in character; nor is the probationer significantly unlike the parolee. The probationer is assumed to be a "good risk" and therefore not in need of institutional correction. The parolee has been incarcerated (presumably because he was not a good risk) and may have been "hardened" by the experience. But "case records show that a great many. . . probationers have had a prior institutional experience. Moreover, we cannot hold that all correctional institutions invariably have a destructive effect upon every inmate." Thus, the problems of administering probation are likely to be similar to the difficulties encountered in administering parole.

Although probation and parole are

administered similarly, certain issues pertaining to the parole process, such as the use by parole boards of unchecked discretion when choosing to parole or not to parole an offender (thereby allowing the board to lengthen sentences prescribed by the court) coupled with high rates of recidivism which seem to discredit the parole process, have caused some states to scrap their parole systems altogether. Determinate sentencing, which has been adopted by some of these states, may soon eliminate the need for parole altogether.

Thus, the remainder of this section is devoted primarily to discussions of probation. In that most considerations pertaining to probation parallel, as Dressler points out, similar considerations in the parole process, the discreet reader may apply what he reads about probation to related topics in parole.

PROBATION AND PAROLE: COMPANION SERVICES

DAVID DRESSLER

Having examined the historical and philosophical backgrounds of probation and parole, we may now inquire more closely into the nature of these services. What *are* probation and parole?

Let us approach an answer by first making clear what they are *not*, for there is much confusion in the matter. Public and press are prone to think that anyone with a criminal record must *ipso facto* be a probationer or parolee.

An individual may be fined for his offense and set at liberty. He is not a probationer. Neither is the person who receives a suspended sentence with no stipulation for supervision. Sentences may be suspended without the imposition of a probation term.

The prisoner pardoned by a governor is the beneficiary of executive clemency, not parole. Another inmate may be serving a definite sentence. He will do it all, minus such "good time" as the statute provides. He comes out, not by action of a parole board, but by mandatory features of law.

A man or woman serving an indeterminate sentence may be denied parole when eligible and required to serve the full maximum of his or her term. That person would leave the institution, not as a parolee, but as a free person, released by law and not by action of a parole authority.

And, of course, many people who come to public attention because they commit crimes were once on probation or parole, but finished their terms and were discharged. They were not under supervision when they got into further difficulties and they cannot properly be classed as probationers or parolees.

Obviously, a probationer is an offender placed in his status by a court. A parolee is one who left a correctional institution by action of a parole board. Both court and parole agency had other legal alternatives available.

Each individual concerned is a probationer or parolee so long as his supervision period has not expired or been terminated by revocation.

Differences and Similarities

The essential difference between the two programs is that the parolee has served part of his term in a correctional establishment and will do the balance or some part of it outside, while the probationer does all his time in the community, with no prior incarceration for the offense.

Some persons in the field believe there is another difference. The parolee, they assert, is likely to be more hardened and embittered than the probationer, hence less responsive to treatment. He has, after all, served in an institution.

The present writer feels there is so little contrast between a probationer and a parolee that practically anything said about one supervisory service may with equal validity be asserted about the other. Case records reveal that a great many juvenile and adult probationers *have* had a prior institutional experience. Moreover, we cannot hold that all correctional institutions invariably have a destructive effect upon every inmate. Further, it is conceivable that a probationer who was never in an institution may yet be as resistant to the authority of society as a parolee who has served a long term.

For example, here is an excerpt from a tape recording of an interview by the author with a young man, then seventeen, a juvenile by the laws of his state. Member of a street gang, Roy was in constant trouble with the law. However, he never served a reformatory term. He did have a brief probation period, for drunken driving, without a license, in a stolen car, in the course of which he ran into a dwelling, seriously injuring the occupant.

Q: You've been to Juvenile Court, haven't you?

A: Oh, yeah! A few times. The only thing I don't go for is Juvenile Court. I don't like that for the birds. You can't say anything to defend yourself. All they say is, this petition filed against you on such and such a day, it says you done such and such a thing. Well, we're gonna hold you for so long. Or, I'm gonna send you to the ref, or something. There's nobody to defend you, nothing like that. It just says you did it, you're gonna go away. For Chrissake! Them Juvenile Court judges, they don't know a goddamn thing, just want to get it over with. Bang! Just shove them poor kids in the can!

Q: How about cops?

A: Aw! They start giving you a bad time the minute they get that badge. Rookie cops, they just get on the force and they want to be sergeant right away. Yeah. There's a lot of cops that give you a rough time. They would haul you in for everything. Like if they see you with a can of beer, they don't say, "Well, as long as you're only drinking beer, well, go ahead." If I was a cop I'd rather see a kid sitting around with a can of beer than I would with a marijuana cigarette, something like that. Cops!

Q: Your friend Carl, his father is worth millions. How come he pals around with you guys?

A: Because he's regular, he ain't chicken, he wants to be around decent guys, not some jerk that's gonna stay home and toast marshmallows. He knows we take to him.

Q: Why do you take to him?

A: What I mean, this Carl, where his father could buy him a whole new car if he wanted one, when he wants hub caps, he don't go out and buy them. He goes out and steals them, off some car parked at night.

Q: The rest of you expect that of him? Is that what you mean?

A: No. He expects it of himself. Because he wants to be like other fellows. It would be like Bing Crosby. He's got a name for being rich. He surely wouldn't run around in ragged dungarees, in a Model A. He'd live up to the name that he's got money.

Q: Carl has money. Why doesn't he live up to his name by buying his hub caps instead of stealing them?

A: Because he wants to live up to the gang, like you or me would.

Q: Has everybody got a right to hold on to his own property?

A: Sure. I think so.

Q: Then why do some people steal that property?

A: I don't know. I don't know what the hell they want to do that for.

Q: But you've done it.

A: Yeah.

Q: Well? You know it's wrong but you do it. Why?

A: Everybody else is gonna do it, you might as well do it, too. [Roy and his gang stood by as some teen-agers cut and stabbed a boy with razors and knives, tied him to a car bumper and rammed him into a stone fence, bashing in his skull and killing him.]

Q: Do you think a gang is ever justified in killing a fellow?

A: Oh, yeah! I do.

Q: Under what circumstances?

A: When a guy can't keep his mouth shut about something that's really dangerous.

Q: I see. Any other time when it's O.K. to kill a guy?

A: Yeah. I'd justify myself in killing a cop that got smart. Well, yeah! I might not get away with it, but I'd sure try like held if he got smart.

Q: Roy, you've been given advice by your folks on staying out of trouble. Mr.____, down in the Juvenile Detail, has tried to help

you. You don't have anything nice to say about him, and mighty little, for that matter, about your folks, except maybe your father. You don't like cops, you don't like judges. You didn't like your probation officer. Now, all these people wanted to see you stay out of trouble. You've got no use for them?

A: It ain't that. All I want is they should keep their nose out. There ain't a one of them that knows what I want. Nobody can tell you what you want to do except yourself. I level with my Dad most of the time, because he don't tell me what to do. These cops and things, they been reading books about crime that was written by college professors. What the hell do them college professors know about us kids?

This young man has demonstrated that he means what he says. He has committed rape, robbery, burglary, assault, and other offenses. Police believe he probably is guilty of at least one murder. He is inured to antisocial acts. He fulminates against law enforcement officers. Yet he has never been in a correctional institution.

The point is that many probationers, although of course not all, are tough, antisocial in their attitudes. So are some, but not all, parolees. Some probationers are tougher than parolees and vice versa. The differential may or may not be a prison or reformatory experience. "Parolees and probationers are people. Each one is conditioned by his particular make-up, experiences, and response to environment."[1]

A probation caseload is not likely to be of markedly different character from a parole load. The service needs will be very much the same, as will the techniques for meeting those needs.

Casework? Law Enforcement?

All right. Probation and parole are basically alike. What are they? Casework? Law enforcement? Both? Neither? You can start a heated argument on this wherever correctional workers gather.

Some say probation and parole are casework services, one kind of social work practice and altogether divorced from law enforcement.[2] Others would as vehemently vouchsafe that these are law enforcement functions exclusively and caseworkers should be kept away with an eleven-foot pole. Another segment of opinion maintains that probation and parole are casework *and* law enforcement, one coming into play when the other is no longer effective. And still another group would declare: "A plague o' all your houses! We're not social workers and we aren't policemen. We are a highly specialized and unique practice, different from any other concerned with human relations."

Then, too, there are those who insist this is a service calling for no specialization whatever. Probation and parole are unrelated to any discipline or practice that relies upon the scientific approach, according to proponents of this viewpoint. They are just plain common sense with no frills attached. The less science and "red tape," the better. Anyone with a good heart, or a big stick, depending upon the speaker, can do probation and parole work.

Where lies reality?

In terms of actual practice, everywhere. Somewhere, in some jurisdiction, we find each point of view translated into practice.

But what can we reasonably assert probation and parole ought to be? The author expresses his personal opinion here, reminding the reader that many responsible correctional workers would not share his views.

Probation and parole are social work. *Social work*, not exclusively *casework*. Social work encompasses the several fields of group work, casework, and community organization. Casework plays the greatest part in treatment in correctional settings, but group work and community welfare organization have their role too.

Like all of social work, probation and parole adapt generic principles to their specific objectives and functions. A public assistance agency is a casework organization, but some of its approaches and emphases differ from those in a private family service agency, which also practices casework. A community center is a group work agency, but some of its operations are unlike those found in a settlement house, another group work undertaking. Probation and parole make their adaptations, utilizing whatever is of value anywhere in all the fields of social work.

With regard to the law enforcement *vs.* social work argument, it seems to this writer we need make no choice, in correctional work. We require both. We cannot divorce ourselves from the enforcement function, and it ill behooves us to derogate it. Courts and parole boards are charged with select-

> "We cannot divorce ourselves from the enforcement function, and it ill behooves us to derogate it."

ing for treatment only those calculated to be reasonably safe risks. Probation and parole officers take an oath of office as peace officers. The legislative intent is obvious here. Officers are enjoined to protect the community.

The writer disagrees with those who asseverate that probation and parole are neither law enforcement nor social work, but something uniquely special.[3] He rejects the proposition that probation and parole require no more than common sense, while cheerfully agreeing that common sense is one ingredient essential to practically any undertaking. It tells me my plumbing leaks. But it takes a plumber's skill *and* common sense to fix it. The human being is infinitely more complex than a water faucet. He requires a highly specialized and expertly trained practitioner to help him with his multifarious personal problems. That person must have common sense. But common sense without professional skill can work to the detriment of the individual seeking help.

This, then, is the bias of the author, a bias to be found throughout the volume. The author's thesis is: probation and parole work is social work, with law enforcement and other adaptations. It has borrowed much from the generic social work field. It has done some lending, too. Caseworkers have learned a great deal from probation and parole concerning the constructive meaning and use of authority, to cite one illustration.

Casework is a process seeking to bring about redirection of human behavior. That is why it is suited to the aims of the correctional field.

It will be a long time before the field is staffed completely, or almost completely, by trained social workers. Meantime, acceptable compromises must be made. Many workers trained

> "...*common sense is one ingredient essential to practically any undertaking. It tells me my plumbing leaks.*"

in psychology, sociology, and other disciplines are performing effectively. There is no attempt to assert that *only* the trained social worker has made a contribution to the field. Rather, the argument is that, in recruiting from among thousands of candidates, the agency does best when it strikes out for professional social workers. It will thereby gain a small proportion who, by temperament, are unfit for the work, despite education in it. And it will lose a few who, though not educated in social work, would make splendid officers. But all in all, recruitment methods being crude at best, setting the standard of social work background should yield optimum results.

The Twofold Function

Probation and parole officers have a twofole function. The Federal Probation Officers Association has endorsed a statement on professional standards which includes this assertion: "The primary objective of probation and parole is the protection of society through the rehabilitation of the offender."[4] Here is the end result of the twofold function. the probation and parole officer is charged with a double responsibility: protecting society and aiding the offender. But there is no dichotomy here.

In the community protection role, these services have two obligations: to offer freedom and aid only to those not likely to assault society again; and to supervise them while treating them. Not every offender is fit for unrestricted liberty. Therefore, the court or parole board thinks first of community protection in those cases; it will not turn an offender back to the community when he is an unsafe risk. As for those it does release, it will treat, but be constantly on guard against, potential recidivists.

But—and this is why social work treatment and law enforcement functions are not discrete elements—it will be noted we strive to help bring about social readjustment of offenders while remaining alert to signs of reversion to crime or delinquency. We protect society at the same time that we treat the offender. If we must choose at a given moment, we will accomplish the first by removing someone from the community. But fundamentally, the best community protection lies in so helping those who have offended that they no longer want to offend and no longer do violate the law. In this case, the two-fold function brings one end result. In the sense of the statement of the Federal Probation Officers Association, protection of society is achieved through the rehabiliation of offenders.

Probation and parole, then, are casework services, in public agencies for the most part, that seek to select effectively from among offenders those who shall be offered the opportunities inherent in the programs. Practitioners of these services want to aid men and women, girls and boys, who need help in stabilizing themselves. They also try to assist and protect society and the probationer or parolee by bringing the two into mutual accommodation.

What, finally, are probation and parole? They are services designed to benefit society and the individual who is maladjusted in society. They are social work and law enforcement, not mutually exclusive and acting unilaterally, but cooperating and intertwined throughout.

Notes

[1] Dressler, *Probation and Parole,* pp. 14-15.

[2] We shall be discussing social casework later on, but so we may have the same point of reference, let us for the present use this definition, to be found in Helen Harris Perlman, *Social Casework, a Problem-solving Process* (Chicago: Univ. of Chicago Press, 1957), p. 4: "Social casework is a process used by certain human welfare agencies to help individuals to cope more effectively with their problems in social functioning."

[3] For interesting discussion on this, see T.C. Esselstyn, "Trends in Social Work toward Corrections," *Federal Probation,* 21, no. 2 (1957), 30-33; and Ben S. Meeker, "Social Work and the Correctional Field," *Federal Probation,* 21 no. 3 (1957), 32-42.

[4] "Professional Standards Endorsed by the Federal Probation Officers Association," *Federal Probation,* 21 no. 1 (1957), 48.

20. *The probation officer begins his association with an offender before sentencing takes place. It is his duty to prepare a probation report to advise the sentencing judge that one or another form of correction is most appropriate both to the rehabiliatative needs of the offender and for the benefit of society. It is assumed that sentencing is, foremost, a prescription for processes which will aid both offender and community and, although the assumption has been disputed in several articles found in this volume, the prescriptive nature of sentencing is significant to the probation process.*

Imlay and Reid, in the following article, suggest that sentencing should be based predominantly upon the probation officer's pre-sentence report. To do so, however, tends to undermine the exemplary function of laws which were made for political, rather than social, motives. Thus, the probation officer must counter various political acts which restrict the "science" of sentencing and the experiment of rehabilitation through probation in the name of equality and uniformity.

THE PROBATION OFFICER, SENTENCING, AND THE WINGS OF CHANGE

CARL H. IMLAY and ELSIE L. REID

The first half century of the Federal Probation System cannot be represented as a linear course of development or evolution but rather as a continuing experiment. From the probation concept's seminal beginnings in Massachusetts in 1878, the movement spread throughout the States over the following decades. The subsequent adoption of probation by Federal Courts as an alternative to sentences of imprisonment was hardly precipitous. True, Federal judges had conceived, as an alternative to imprisonment, the custom of indefinitely suspending sentences as a method of conditional release, but in 1916 that practice was disapproved by the Supreme Court in Ex parte *United States.*[1] However, the Court, in dictum, planted the seed for the great experiment by suggesting "probation legislation or such other means as the legislative mind may devise"[2] as a method of expanding the scope of judicial solutions to punishment.

As Merrill A. Smith has pointed out, adoption of a Federal Probation System was long aborning.[3] The first bill which would have established a Federal Probation System was unsuccessfully introduced in 1909. Between 1916 and 1925, probation legislation was introduced futilely in Congress almost every year. Such legislation was routinely opposed by the Department of Justice (which then administered the affairs of the Judiciary) but derived support from some judicial proponents and from the National Probation Association (now the National Council on Crime and Delinquency). From a rather anemic beginning (only five paid officers were appointed between 1925 and 1930), it has increased in size and function to its present proportions. Its transfer from the Bureau of Prisons to the Administrative Office of the United States Courts in 1940 at least symbolically identified Federal probation as part of the judicial establishment, and its officers as an integral part of the courts they serve (despite several later efforts in the 1960's to return the service to the Department of Justice).

While the functional relationship of the probation system with the Department of Justice survives with respect to parole supervision, [4] the role of the service as an independent arm of the court itself has become more sharply defined in respect to probation.[5] Federal Rule of Criminal Procedure 32 details the probation officer's duty of making a presentence investigation and report to the court before the imposition of sentence.[6] The more enlightened legal commentators have, over the years, become increasingly insistent that the judges utilize the presentence report in their sentencing procedures.[7]

Also, though neither spelled out in any rule or statute, the senior probation officer increasingly is functioning for many judges as a confidential advisor on sentencing alternatives and as a correctional expert. This less-talked-about aspect of the probation officer's role, albeit not universal, is an important step toward sharing the responsibility for sentencing at the interpersonal level. More often than not, Federal judges are nominated on the basis of successful careers in civil rather than criminal law and thus do not bring to the bench any special expertise in corrections. Moreover, sentencing is basically a scientific prognosis, not a judicial decision, and the intervention of the social scientist in the sentencing process is a healthy change which should be encouraged and expanded. The value of the probation officer's role as sentencing advisor increases as the impetus for speed in trial and sentence is accelerated by the Speedy Trial Act,[8] by a sharp increase in new criminal case filings,[9] and by the fact that there are too few Federal district judges to meet the current caseloads.[10] Now that Congress has increased the numbers

of probation officers,[11] we can look forward perhaps to their greater participation in the sentencing process.

The probation officer, moreover, exerts a leavening influence on the law. His basic orientation is and should be toward the scientific theory of rehabilitation of the judicial offender, whereas the law attempts through statutory penalties to deal evenly with whole classes of offenders. This clash

> *"The probation officer...exerts a leavening influence on the law. His basic orientation is and should be toward the scientific theory of rehabilitation..."*

of social philosophies which has played a role in correctional debate over the last 50 years is significant as a matter of history and as a continuing phenomenon today.

These and other challenges to a scientific approach to sentencing are hereinafter discussed.

Resistance to Rehabilitation as a Legal Objective

The probation system did not autogenously emerge like mushrooms after a rain. Rather it was the result of a slow change of viewpoint in theories of crime and punishment, and the product of the emerging social sciences in the first half of this century. It orginated as part of the antithetical reaction to the older theories of retributive punishment, and in response to the newer premise that a person's actions are socially determined rather than the result of "free will." Determinism assumes that a person has only a limited range of free will and that his social actions for the most part automatically resulted from external causes.

The theory of social determinism was indeed a product of the developing disciplines of social psychology and sociology and the assumption of those sciences that antisocial behavior results primarily from a breakdown in the individuals relationships and interactions with his society rather than from any inherent evil tendencies. A corollary of this assumption is that the logical social response to crime and punishment should be to attempt to reinstate the errant individual as a functioning unit of his society rather than further to isolate and detach him.

However, the notion of rehabilitation finds countervailing influences in the law itself which in its primary emphasis on maximum prison terms in defining each enumerated crime, still assumes that punishment should serve as a social dissuader rather than as a method of individual rehabilitation.

The law moreover is founded on morality, and its remedies have been traditionally looked upon by its high priests, not as tools of social engineering, but as retribution for moral derelictions. Frank D. Day has been quoted as follows:

> Modern psychiatry to the contrary, the criminal law is grounded upon the theory that, in the absence of special conditions of (duress, compulsion, *et cetera*), individuals are free to exercise a choice between possible courses of conduct and hence are morally responsible. Thus it is moral guilt that the law stresses.[12]

The law moreover abhors social relativism. It deals with clear-cut categorizations such as guilty-not guilty, negligent-not negligent, sane-insane, and so forth. The notion that, in the process of sentencing, two criminals committing the same crime should be dealt with differently because of a more favorable social adjustment prognosis given the one over the other, runs afoul the grain of traditional legal thinking. Judges spend much of their judicial time considering various applications of the equal protection of the law principle and are uncomfortable in applying the law as it relates to sentencing on a differential basis. Based on the retributive or exemplary theories of punishment, all sentences should be equalized. Based on the theory of rehabiltation, all should be individually devised so as to insure that those who are most likely to reassimilate should have the lighter sentences or probation. An example of the interplay of these two inconsistencies in sentencing philosophy is found in the statute establishing Federal sentencing institutes,[13] which are established "[i]n the interest of uniformity in sentencing procedures."[14] The same statute, however, adjures the participants to determine, among other things, "the importance of psychiatric, emotional, sociological and physiological factors involved in crime and their bearing upon sentences."[15]

Uniformity in sentencing is antithetical to the scientific notion of individualized rehabilitation. One authority describes the scientific approach as follows:

> For any strictly scientific probation program, the personality of the offender, the situations and general social aspects of the case rather than the offense itself should determine those eligible for probationary treatment.[16]

The Supreme Court itself in 1949 announced in *Williams v. People of New York:*

> Retribution is no longer the dominant objective of the criminal law. Reformation and rehabilitation of offenders have become the important goals of criminal jurisprudence.[17]

Notwithstanding this policy, the critical public cannot, however, readily comprehend a system of punishment which treats one offender differently than another. We are all familiar with the invectives directed at judges as being soft on crime or as being oblivious to the protection of public safety. The press makes much of the white collar criminal who is given a lenient sentence or one disparate to that given some other garden-variety offender. The public demand is for equality of punishment for any given offense and a strict application of the "eye for an eye and a tooth for a tooth" principle. Retributive punishment is still a dominant public objective.

One of the more enlightened approaches to probation is contained in minimum standards proposed by the American Bar Association which provide that probation should be the sentence in a criminal case, unless (1) confinement is necessary to protect the public from further criminal activity by the defendant, (2) the offender is in need of correctional treatment which can be most effectively provided if he is confined, or (3) it would unduly deprecate the seriousness of the offense if a sentence of probation were granted.[18] This approach at least places the primary emphasis on the rehabilitative remedy, while recognizing in the third proviso that in our system of punishment, the exemplary aspect of sentencing is also a consideration. Indeed, common sense dictates such recognition since laws derive from Congress, which in turn, is frequently motivated to act after some particularly heinous example of a crime has been brought to public attention. In fact, the politics of criminal legislation are such that *laws are enacted to punish,* not to rehabilitate. A congressman's constituents would not be greatly enthralled by his sponsorship of a law defining criminal conduct, which, in describing the applicable penalty, followed the example of the ABA standards making probation the primary process of disposition. On the contrary, political credit is often gained by emphasizing stiff maximum penalties, a fact evidenced by our Federal criminal statutes which are studded with exaggerated forms of penalties. Perhaps it is for this reason that sentencing alternatives and penalties should not be a part of statutory definitions of crimes but should, as in the proposed Federal criminal code,[19] be separately stated in another chapter of the code.

In sum, our experience over the last 50 years convinces that the scientific approach to sentencing must vie with the differing demands of society as written into our laws. Our law-making procedure virtually insures that sentencing provisions will emphasize the exemplary, rather than the rehabilitative goals of sentencing. It is for this reason that probation officers must have a suasive role in the sentencing process to offset the vocal demands that punishment should fit the crime, rather than the individual.

The Trend of Decisions

One generalization as to the trend of court decisions is the evolving requirement that sentencing and dispositional hearings be more formalized and adversarial in nature. These cases recognize, on the one hand, a policy favoring the individualization of the process of imposing sentence so that with flexible administration and in the exercise of broad discretion "careful, humane and comprehensive consideration to the particular situation of each offender"[20] be given. On the other hand, recent cases have interposed restraints upon that "broad discretion," to safeguard against arbitrariness, through the promulgation of due process procedural restrictions upon the sentencing process.[21] The effect has been to depersonalize and make uniform sentencing in the effort to avoid capriciousness. The advent of adversarial disposition may augur a confined role for the probation officer as a sentencing advisor.

An example of the shift from the relatively unstructured to the more formal dispositional process is early seen in the Supreme Court decision, In re *Gault*,[22] dealing with the area of juvenile delinquency. Ostensibly, the Supreme Court in *Gault* referred only to the adjudicatory stage of a delinquency proceeding when it held that a juvenile whose liberty is at stake is entitled to the following rights: (1) notice of the charges; (2) right to counsel; (3) right of confrontation and cross-examination; (4) privilege against self-incrimination; (5) right to a transcript of the proceedings; and (6) right to appellate review.[23]   In fact what *Gault* accomplishes is the division into two distinct phases of what previously had been an informal proceeding that blended factfinding and disposition into one. The prior emphasis had been not so much on the guilt of the juvenile but upon what was best for him. Yet, in essence *Gault* requires that guilt first be ascertained before "punishment" is assessed rather than that the focus be on what is best for a child irrespective

of guilt *per se.* Moreover, the nature of the rights enumerated in *Gault* necessitate a truly adversarial type of proceeding.

A similar, though less drastic trend toward the "legalization" of sentencing procedures, is visible upon comparison of two Supreme Court decisions. In 1949, the Supreme Court recognized in *Williams v. People of New York*,[24] That the function of sentencing is not a simple task but rather a complex undertaking necessitating the judicial exercise of discretion to fit a punishment to the offender. In order to best exercise that broad discretion, the Court held that a judge needed the fullest information possible regarding the offender. Consequently, it was proper for the judge to read and rely upon presentence reports, albeit unsworn, of the probation officials investigating the record and circumstances of the offender.[25] In 1972, however, the Supreme Court held that there was a limit to the quality of information available to the judge at the time of sentencing. In *United States v. Tucker*,[26] the Court ruled that it was reversible error for a sentencing judge to credit an offender's previous criminal convictions in imposing sentence when those convictions were obtained unconstitutionally, that is without either the assistance of counsel or an effective waiver thereof[27] Exemplified by this case is a policy of allowing a convicted offender to challenge the information upon which a judge relies in sentencing, in order to check "misinformed discretion." The type of challenge and the production of evidence to contradict allegedly false information may serve to transform an informal proceeding into an adversary one.

In the area of probation, the same trend toward increasing "legalization" of the sentencing function can be seen in other cases emanating from the Supreme Court. For example, whereas formerly the Supreme Court had articulated the premise that a probationer is entitled to fair treatment "and is not to be made the victim of whim or caprice,"[28] it was not until the last several years that the Court put forth concrete measures to circumscribe the way in which a probationer is to be treated at varying stages of his sentencing experience.[29]

At one time, the availability of probation was deemed entirely a legislative act of grace, a matter of favor and not of right.[30] Being such, it was not something guaranteed to a defendant for whom the denial or revocation of probation would afford any remedy.[31] As a result, the Supreme Court held in 1935 that a trial court must obey only legislative requirements, not constitutional ones, in administering a probation revocation.[32]

First, however, in the case of *Mempa v. Rhay*[33] which required that counsel be appointed for a felony offender in a probation revocation proceeding in which sentencing previously deferred was to be imposed,[34] the Supreme Court began to impose constitutional limitations in the probationary process. Finally, in 1973, the Court, reversing the stance taken in 1935, held in *Gagnon v. Scarpelli*[35] that, as a matter of constitutional law, certain procedural safeguards must be accorded a probationer at a revocation proceeding.[36] Among the rights guaranteed by *Gagnon* was that of a bifurcated proceeding—an initial hearing at the time of arrest and detention to determine if probable cause exists to believe that the probationer has committed a probation violation, and, if so, a more comprehensive hearing prior to the final revocation decision. At both stages the probationer must receive notice of the charges, an opportunity to appear and present evidence, a conditional right to confront and cross-examine witnesses, a right to an independent factfinder, and a right to a written report of the hearing.[37]

These identical rights had earlier been applied to the administrative process of parole revocation in the landmark case of *Morrissey v. Brewer*.[38] *Morrissey* interjected into the heretofore unbridled discretion of parole hearing examiners, in matters of revocation, the procedural rights enumerated above. These due process guarantees have the effect of legalizing, in the adversary nature of the word, the administrative process of assessing whether revocation is advisable and/or justified.

The impact of *Gagnon and Morrissey* is to formalize the former, relatively unstructured process in which the disposition of a convicted offender was in issue. The application of procedural safeguards is designed to have little effect on the substantive dispositional decision except to promote that it be a reasoned, and not arbitrary, one. The practical result may be, however, that informal flexibility is lost by the transformation to an adversary proceeding. Further, judges and parole examiners will be compelled to articulate their reasons for revocation to evidence that their decision was a rational one. The tendency may then be to compare the disposition imposed in one case to that imposed under similar circumstances in other cases for equivalent crimes. By doing so, the objective of individualized sentencing will be sacrificed in the effort to prevent capricious action.

The significance of this case law is its revelation of a movement to subject the sentencing process to judicial review and legal standards. Perhaps the cases reflect a disenchantment with correctional methods now utilized. But they do indicate clearly a trend toward more formalized adversarial dispositional processes. Such processes may further tend to unify sentencing dispositions, running contrary to the notion of individualized sentencing in the pursuit of rehabilitation. Essentially, in an effort to avert arbitrary action with regard to individuals for the wrong reasons or for no reason at all, the Supreme Court has chosen to prescribe certain procedural guarantees which may detract from personalized sentencing undertaken for the motive of rehabilitation. Furthermore, the recommendations and presentations of probation officers at various stages of the sentencing process will be increasingly subject to challenge.

Future Trends in Sentencing

There are at least four recent events which could affect materially the sentencing process in general and, in particular, the future role of the probation officer in sentencing. These four developments are: (1) the passage of the Speedy Trial Act of 1974;[39] (2) the recent adoption of Federal Rule of Criminal Procedure 11 as it relates to plea negotiations;[40] (3) the enactment of the new Rule 32 as it governs disclosure to the defendant of the presentence report;[41] and (4) the proposed adoption of legislation requiring appellate review of sentencing.[42]

The Speedy Trial Act of 1974.

The Speedy Trial Act does not itself place any special restrictions on the period which may elapse between trial and sentencing. For the time being, that matter has been left to the local plans adopted by each district court pursuant to Rule 50(b) of the Rules of Criminal Procedure which does require that a time limit be specified from trial to sentencing. The Speedy Trial Act is directly concerned only with the periods from arrest to indictment, indictment to arraignment, and arraignment to trial.

The inevitable effect, however, of expediting the trial schedules of criminal cases will be to increase the court's burdens with respect to sentencing, at least in the initial stages of the speedy trial program when there will be some "catching up" involved in meeting case deadlines. Just as Parkinson's law declares that effort will expand to meet the limits of the time allowed, so also is the obverse true, that effort will contract as the time allotted for the project decreases. So it is with the judge. The time a judge is allowed to spend in reflection and study with respect to a particular sentencing situation is finite. The more he is forced to yield his attention to "speeding up" trials, the less attention he will be able to devote to the sentencing process.

In this respect, a judicial mind must not be satisfied with pulling a sentence out of the figurative magician's hat. Sentencing is a scientific prognosis based on a congeries of considerations, including not only the individual offender's nexus of familial, societal and economic relationships, his past record, and his psychological and physical health, but also including the availability of treatment facilities or support systems to meet that offender's needs.

If we are entering an era when judges will be forced to devote less time to meditation on sentences, it may become more necessary than ever that the probation officer retain an advisory role with reference to sen-

> *"...a judicial mind must not be satisfied with pulling a sentence out of the figurative magician's hat."*

tencing, that he not be discouraged from imparting advice directly to the sentencing judge, and that to an even greater extent, he be trained in sentencing and correctional alternatives.[43] This suggested role raises the question as to whether such a confidential relationship between judge and probation officer can be maintained in the face of the new requirements of Rule 32.[44]

Rule 32(c)(3)(A) places a maximum emphasis on access by the defendant to the presentence report and on a defendant's right to meaningful allocution as to all information considered by the court in imposing sentence.[45] There is, however, no necessary inconsistency in applying Rule 32 so as to give the defendant access, within the limits of the rule, to all empirical data that go into the presentence report, and simultaneously in allowing the probation officer, as an officer to the court, to continue to function as a sentencing consultant. Rule 32 does not attempt to impose any *ex parte* rule on probation officers but seeks only to insure that all relevant factual data are included in the presentence report and made known to the defendant.

Plea negotiations—Rule 11

The practice of plea bargaining, by which defendants contract with prosecutors to cop pleas for less serious crimes in order to avoid full-scale trials on multiple charges and the possibility of more severe penalties if convicted,[46] has had an impact on the notion of sentencing as a function of rehabilitation. The role of the probation officer as a sentencing advisor wanes in importance when a judge is faced with a recommended sentence which may have a little to do with the offenders outlook for rehabilitation.[47]

Rule 11 of the recently amended Rules of Criminal Procedure will have a major impact on the probation service in the realm of plea bargaining Rule 11(e) requires that, prior to the taking of a negotiated plea, the court will either order a presentence report or explain on the record why this step is not being followed.[48] Rule 32, as recently amended, also permits the court to consider a presentence report before determining whether to accept a negotiated plea.[49] These rules evince a concession to the notion that sentencing is a scientific process rather than a public auction. They make plea bargaining more acceptable, provided that the probation officer's report is fully considered and that the election by the judge of the plea bargaining process does not allow administrative convenience to outweigh scientific and individualized sentencing considerations.

While plea bargaining as a judicial tool is certainly not new, its formalization under new Rule 11 including the explicit requirement of Rule 11(e) (2) that the procedure be recorded, will undoubtedly create a continuing and spirited debate between court administrators, on the one hand, who see the courts as bogged down in a quagmire of stagnant cases, and social scientists, on the other, who perceive no curative solutions in bartered sentencing. Plea bargaining is assuredly not an ideal sentencing device, and can only be rationalized on the basis that for the indefinite future, we are faced with too many cases for too few judges. Perhaps in the next 50 years some solution will be found. In the meanwhile, we can only hope that the sentencing judge will give critical weight to presentence reports before accepting a negotiated plea and sentence.

The disclosure requirements of Rule 32

For a considerable period of time, the Federal district courts have been moving toward routine disclosure of the presentence report. That fact, taken together with the fact that some rather broad exceptions to disclosure are written into the new Rule 32,[50] lessens the impact of the recent rule amendment on the sentencing system. There are certain advantages to report disclosure including enhancement of the quality of reporting and avoidance of factual error. These are the prophylactic values in disclosure, but disclosure may also encourage judges to demand higher standards than would be acceptable if viewing of the report were restricted. Disclosure also results in increased fairness to counsel in meeting his obligations in sentencing procedures.[51]

The real problem would arise if the proposed criminal code, S. 1,[52] were enacted. If appellate review of sentences were adopted as S. 1 provides in §§ 3725 and 3726, the record on review would consist of the sentencing proceeding's transcript and the presentence report. It seems inevitable that the emphasis in preparing such a report would then shift from an intelligent effort to give the sentencing judge an accurate sentencing profile of the defendant, to an effort to satisfy the latest circuit court decision as to what constitutes essential data

or whether the report is complete, or ambiguous on some point, or whether the sentencing judge was, in relying on the report, justified in giving the sentence imposed. Moreover, the judge will be obligated to explain on the record what he relied upon and what he did not in the presentence report.

On the assumption that appellate combing of the written sentencing record is inevitable, so will be the standardization of presentence reports to meet the various criteria of intent that will necessarily be imposed by appellate judges. These judges, not having any direct interpersonal contact with the defendant, will focus on the one written record that was available to the sentencing judge. A cosmetic attempt to doctor these reports to satisfy appellate courts, rather than to fulfill the needs of sentencing judges for candid background data on defendants, may wholly defeat the present value of the probation officers' sentencing investigations. It remains to be seen whether this possibility will result if appellate review of sentencing is instituted.

Appellate review of sentences

In the preceding discussion, several problems involved in the proposed institution of appellate review of sentencing have been mentioned. There are some additional repercussions such a system might have on the relationship of the probation officer to the sentencing process. Moreover, appellate review has as one of its premises the formulation of a rational sentencing policy which may detract from an emphasis on individualized sentencing.

In 1968, the American Bar Association endorsed a model for appellate review of sentences[53] with four basic goals: (1) the correction of grossly excessive sentences; (2) the promotion of rational sentencing; (3) the inducement of respect for the judicial system; and (4) the opportunity to focus on what, in many cases, is the real matter in dispute.[54]

One of the expected advantages of this review is to contribute to an offender's rehabilitation by enhancing his belief that the system is fair and not subject to the unchecked caprice of one official.

S. 1, the newly proposed Federal criminal code[55] provides, as previously indicated, for appellate review of sentencing. This proposal would require a Federal appellate court to determine, for a sentence other than a death sentence, whether it is clearly unreasonable as a function of the following factors, among others: "(A) the nature and circumstances of the offense and the history and characteristics of the defendant; (B) the purposes of sentencing required to be considered by Part III [Sentencing section] of this title; (C) the opportunity of the district court to observe the defendant."

In reviewing death sentences[56] the appellate court must consider if: "(1) the procedures employed in the sentencing hearing were contrary to law; and (2) the findings under section 2402 [Death Sentence provision] were clearly erroneous, having regard for the opportunity of the jury, or if there was no jury, the district court, to observe the defendant."

One of the immediate effects on the probation officer of the provision for appellate review of sentencing is the possibility that an appellate court may find that a sentencing record is so incomplete as to require remand. In such an event the sentencing judge might be well advised to order a further sentencing report to complete the record, or to update certain information if a lengthy period had elapsed since the time of original sentencing.

Certainly appellate review will generate case law articulating standards with which the probation officer will have to be acquainted in order to perform his own role. As sentencing procedures become more and more legalistic and technical, the demands on the probation officer, whose training is grounded in the social sciences, become even more challenging. Given appellate review, the question tends to shift from a prognostic evaluation of the defendant, based on his own peculiar background, to an estimation of whether the sentence imposed comports with, or whether the sentencing judge adequately considered, the holding in *United States v. John Doe.* That kind of inquiry requires that both the sentencing judge and the probation officer be familiar with the facts in John Doe's case, as well as the rule therein promulgated on the basis of those facts, and that they engage in a sort of color-matching of cases.

Finally, appellate review of sentencing enhances the likelihood that a type of equality in sentencing will evolve. The wide discretion allotted those responsible for sentencing in the range of alternatives available to them and of the length of imprisonment which may be imposed has led to fears that "sentence-makers" may on occasion act irrationally, not necessarily evilly, but all the same unfairly.[57] One motive for subjecting such decisions to review is to preclude arbitrary action. Also appellate review of sentencing assumes a merit in sentencing uniformity *per se.* It commits the review decision to circuit courts, not to look solely for arbitrary action, but apparently to make a comparative evaluation of the merits of a sentence in the same way an appellate panel would review any other trial finding. The inquiry of appellate judges will naturally focus on whether the sentence before them for review is inconsistent with that in another reported decision but not on whether it represents a rational judgment based on the peculiarities of an individual offender and his own socio-economic relationships. This difference in emphasis returns us to the debate as to whether punishment is to be primarily exemplary and uniform, or rehabilitative and individualistic. If the latter objective is pursued, appellate review of sentences will be essentially an effort to review a scientific prognostication based on technical data only partially reflected in the record. Any such evaluation by a trial judge would however, also include other factors such as face-to-face encounters, credibility assessments, recidivism factors, availability of treatment facilities, and other diagnostic type data which may not be fully explained in each written presentence report or sentencing transcript. Uniformity in sentencing would, of course, thereby be promoted by appellate review of sentences, in derogation of the notion of individualized sentencing.

Conclusion

The role of the probation officer in the sentencing process has never been fully defined. He came on the scene to fill a recognized void in supervising a probation program, and later his role was expanded to include the investigatory function in the sentencing procedure. He has been caught in the eclectic debate over whether the primary goal in sentencing is rehabilitative and individualistic, or exemplary and uniform. It is his function as a social scientist to promote the former,

even when popular passions run high toward punitive remedies. He must promote elasticity in the face of a more rigid juridical approach to sentencing.

The trend of decisions has been more and more to formalize sentencing and revocation procedures, thus changing the probation officer's role from an objective judicial advisor to a participant in an adversary proceeding. This "legalization" of the sentencing function, moreover, is proceeding apace. New procedures generated by the Speedy Trial Act plus a drastic increase in criminal cases will give the judge less time for contemplative justice in sentencing. It remains to be seen whether the judge will succumb to the temptation of routine plea bargaining as a primary method of termination or will rely to a greater extent on the probation officer as a sentencing consultant.

New rules allowing defendants greater access to presentence reports will, to an increasing extent, bring the probation officer into a defensive posture in the sentencing procedure. The recent encouragement given to plea bargaining may, if the probation officer is not a key participant in negotiated sentences, undermine his scientific approach to sentencing in deference to judicial expediency. Appellate review of sentencing, which looms on the legislative horizon, could further dilute his approach to individualized treatment in favor of the creation of a system of case precedents which will promote sentencing uniformity.

Like Ebenezer Scrooge looking at the ghost of Christmas future, we can only hope that in the next 50 years, our somewhat schizophrenic approach to the sentencing process can be resolved. It will not be enough to arouse the public about increasing crime rates and the necessity for more effective crime detection so long as there are no adequate rehabilitative facilities available and the prisons and jails now existing continue as Dickensian criminal indoctrination and training grounds. If our judges can, at most, achieve through the sentencing process only a "warehousing" of offenders, insulating them from the public for a time, and if, in fact, no "treatment" is available to such persons, society plays a sad charade. We need to direct our attention to "corrections" in the true sense of the word and, to meet that objective, Congress must provide the facilities. We need community rehabilitation centers, halfway houses and a variety of other support systems. We need extensive research into recidivism patterns so that we can more adequately assess probation possibilities. Today, admittedly, this seems like the dream of a novitiate seeking the true way to nirvana.

More importantly, we must decide what our goals are in respect to sentencing. Is sentencing a problem that lies with the social sciences as a matter of individual evaluation and prediction, or is it a problem amenable to uniform application and administration, like the law of the Medes and the Persians, to classes of criminals and crimes? Is there an important role for the probation officer as a sentencing consultant, or will the defendant's future be wholly relegated to the legalistic decisional process? These are questions increasingly ripe for resolution.

Notes

[1]242 U.S. 27 (1916).

[2]*Id.* at 52.

[3]M. Smith, *As a Matter of Fact...An Introduction to Federal Probation* (Federal Judicial Center, 1973), pp. 6-7. *See also* Master, "Legislative Background of the Federal Probation Act," *Federal Probation* (June 1950); Bates, "The Establishment and Early Years of the Federal Probation System," *Federal Probation* (June 1950).

[4]18 U.S.C. §§ 3655, 4164 (1970).

[5]18 U.S.C. § 3651, *et seq.; id.* §§ 5008, 5019, 5020; FED.R.CRIM.P. 32(c), (e), (f).

[6]Effective Dec. 1, 1975, Rule 32(c) is amended to make more explicit the circumstances under which a presentence report may be waived, the defendant or his counsel may read portions or all of the presentence investigation, and the defendant may rebut alleged factual inaccuracies in the report. P.L. 94-64, § 3(33) (Aug. 1, 1975).

[7]*See* American Bar Association, *Standards Relating to Probation*, app. 12 (appr. 1970).

[8]The Speedy Trial Act of 1974, P.L. 93-619, 88 Stat. 2076 (Jan. 3, 1975).

[9]*See* Administrative Office of the United States Courts, *1975 Semi-annual Report of the Director*, p. 9.

[10]Annual Report on the State of the Judiciary, Warren E. Burger, Chief Justice, American Bar Association, Mid-Winter Meeting, Feb. 23, 1975; Address by President Gerald Ford, Sixth Circuit Judicial Conference, July 13, 1975.

[11]Meeker, "The Federal Probation System: The Second 25 Years," *Federal Probation* (June 1975).

[12]Barnes, "Evolutionary Implications of Legalized Punishment," *Criminal Justice Monograph*, vol. 5, no. 3 (Institute of Contemporary Corrections and the Behavioral Sciences, 1974), p. 18.

[13]28 U.S.C. § 334 (1970).

[14]*Id.* at § 334(a).

[15]*Id.*

[16]M. Elliot & F. Merrill, *Social Disorganization* (rev. ed., Harper & Bros. Publishers), pp. 962-63.

[17]337 U.S. 241, 248 (1949). *See also Pennsylvania v. Ashe,* 302 U.S. 51, 55 (1937).

[18]ABA, *Standards Relating to Probation,* § 1.3(a) (appr. 1970). *See also* W. Erickson, "The ABA Standards for Criminal Justice," *Criminal Defense Techniques,* app. 12. Probation (cipes, ed. 1972).

[19]S. 1, 94th Cong., 1st Sess., a bill to codify, revise, and reform title 18 of the United States Code. Part II of S. 1 defines criminal offenses while Part III prescribes sentencing alternatives.

[20]*Burns v. United States,* 287 U.S. 216, 220 (1932) (probation). *See also Williams v. New York,* 337 U.S. 241, 248-50 (1949) (initial sentencing); *Roberts v. United States,* 320 U.S. 264, 272 (1943) (probation).

[21]*See e.g., Gagnon v. Scarpelli,* 411 U.S. 778 (1973) (probation revocation); *Morrissey v. Brewer,* 409 U.S. 471 (1972) (parole revocation); *United States v. Tucker,* 404 U.S. 443 (1972) (imposition of sentence); *Mempa v. Rhay,* 389

U.S. 128 (1967) (imposition of sentence earlier suspended during probation); *In re Gault,* 387 U.S. 1 (1967) (disposition in juvenile delinquency proceedings).

²²387 U.S. 1 (1967).

²³*Id.* at 31-59; *see* Imlay, "The Federal Juvenile Delinquency Act and the Gault Decision," *Federal Probation,* 33 (Sept. 1969), 18.

²⁴337 U.S. 241 (1949).

²⁵*Id.* at 249-51.

²⁶*Tucker, supra* note 21.

²⁷*Id.* at 447-49.

²⁸*Burns, supra,* 287 U.S. at 223.

²⁹*Gagnon, supra; Morrissey, supra; Mempa, supra.* (note 21).

³⁰*Escoe v. Zerbst,* 295 U.S. 490, 492 (1935); *Burns, supra,* 287 U.S. at 220.

³¹The denial of probation is still, apparently, a matter of judicial discretion, reviewable only to the extent of ensuring that the application for probation has been considered and the denial not wholly arbitrary. *See United States v. Hayward,* 471 F.2d 388, 391 (7th Cir. 1972); *Whitfield v. United States,* 401 F.2d 480, 482 (9th Cir. 1958), *cert. denied,* 393 U.S. 1026 (1969); *cf. Scarpa v. United States Bd. of Parole,* 477 F.2d 278, 280 (5th Cir. 1973) (en banc) (denial of parole).

³²*Escoe, supra,* 295 U.S. at 493-94 (*ex parte* revocation improper in light of congressional requirement of judicial hearing).

³³389 U.S. 128 (1967).

³⁴*Id.* at 133-37.

³⁵411 U.S. 778 (1973).

³⁶*Id.* at 781-82.

³⁷*Id.*

³⁸*Morrissey, supra,* note 21. Neither of these cases held that counsel must be furnished to one in danger of having his conditional liberty revoked. *Gagnon* did, however, hold that although a state need not constitutionally furnish counsel in all cases it should do so on a case-by-case basis where the aid of counsel is likely to be efficacious. 411 U.S. at 786-91. Federal legislation does provide for counsel as of right in probation revocation, 18 U.S.C. § 3006A(b), and by discretion in parole revocation, 18 U.S.C. § 3006A(g).

³⁹*See* note 8 *supra.*

⁴⁰*See* P.L. 94-64, § 3(6), (7), effective December 1, 1975.

⁴¹*See* note 6 *supra.*

⁴²*See* note 19 *supra;* S. 1 at §§ 3725, 3726.

⁴³*See* Czajkoski, "Expanding the Quasi-Judicial Role of the Probation Officer," *Federal Probation* (Sept. 1973).

⁴⁴*See* note 6 *supra.*

⁴⁵This rule provides: "Before imposing sentence the court shall upon request permit the defendant, or his counsel if he is so represented, to read the report of the presentence investigation exclusive of any recommendation as to sentence, but not to the extent that in the opinion of the court the report contains diagnostic opinion which might seriously disrupt a program of rehabilitation, sources of information obtained upon a promise of confidentiality, or any other information which, if disclosed, might result in harm, physical or otherwise, to the defendant or other persons; and the court shall afford the defendant or his counsel an opportunity to comment thereon and, at the discretion of the court, to introduce testimony or other information relating to any alleged factual inaccuracy contained in the presentence report."

⁴⁶*See Santobello v. New York,* 404 U.S. 257 (1971).

⁴⁷*See* Dean, "The Illegitimacy of Plea Bargaining," *Federal Probation* (Sept. 1974); Czajkoski, *supra* note 43.

⁴⁸Rule 11 (e) provides:

"(1) IN GENERAL.—The attorney for the government and the attorney for the defendant or the defendant when acting pro se may engage in discussions with a view toward reaching an agreement that, upon the entering of a plea of guilty or nolo contendere to a charged offense or to a lesser or related offense, the attorney for the government will do any of the following:

"(A) move for dismissal of other charges; or

"(B) make a recommendation, or agree not to oppose the defendant's request, for a particular sentence, with the understanding that such recommendation or request shall not be binding upon the court; or

"(C) agree that a specific sentence is the appropriate disposition of the case.

"The court shall not participate in any such discussions.

"(2) NOTICE OF SUCH AGREEMENT.—If a plea agreement has been reached by the parties, the court shall, on the record, require the disclosure of the agreement in open court or, on a showing of good cause, in camera, at the time the plea is offered. Thereupon the court may accept or reject the agreement, or may defer its decision as to the acceptance or rejection until there has been an opportunity to consider the presentence report."

⁴⁹FED.R.CRIM.P. 32(c)(1), effective Dec. 1, 1975. This practice formerly would have been impossible. *See Gregg v. United States,* 394 U.S. 489, 492 (1969).

⁵⁰*See* note 45 *supra.*

⁵¹*See United States v. Malcolm,* 432 F.2d 809, 818-19 (2nd Cir. 1970).

⁵²*See* note 19 *supra.*

⁵³ABA, *Standards Relating to Appellate Review of Sentencing* (appr. 1968).

⁵⁴*Id.,* Introduction pp. 2-3.

⁵⁵*See* note 19 *supra;* S. 1 at §§ 3725, 3726.

⁵⁶S. 1, §§ 2401, 2402. The desire to reinstitute the death penalty in the wake of *Furman v. Georgia,* 408 U.S. 238 (1972), exhibits a societal recognition on the part of some that rehabilitation is not always feasible or desirable. *See Capital Punishment,* J. McCafferty, ed. (1973).

⁵⁷Presumably, for this reason, appellate review of sentences has, to some extent, already been accomplished in a *de facto* manner. See Note, "The United States Courts of Appeals: 1973-1974 Term Criminal Law and Procedure." *Georgia Law J.* 63 (1974), 572-77.

21. *Probation, although it can be seen as a continuing experiment in* humane *crime control, must also serve to protect the community from criminal behavior in such a way that the probationer is as nearly harmless as the offender behind bars. Experimentation, regardless of its probable outcomes, has always been regarded unfavorably by society: consider the public reaction to Galileo's toying with the universe. Experiments and innovations which are potentially harmful are typically viewed in worse light; thus, each probation officer, if he is dedicated to the ultimate success of his method, must to some extent parrot the Hypocratic Oath of the medical profession by saying "If I can do no good (for the probationer) at least I shall do no harm (to the community)."*

Most probation officers are trained as social scientists. Those whose goals reflect a practical application of their science will be disposed more toward doing good through rehabilitation of an offender (but only if he is a "good risk") than toward preventing disorder. The latter goal must often be pursued through law enforcement methods which, as Laningham et al. show in the following article, are often considered inappropriate tasks by an overwhelming percentage of probation officers. This reluctance, coupled with the hesitancy of probation officers to manipulate the probationer's environment or to enforce any code of conduct which would be based upon the prevailing values of the community (55% of the officers surveyed by Laningham et al. considered it inappropriate to order a probationer "who has acquired an auto with no liability insurance to purchase such insurance even though not required by law) may lead to the inability of the probation officer to help the probationer or to protect society.

Thus, the experiment, though it cannot be seen as a failure by any means, is constructed such that its success is in no way guaranteed.

HOW ADULT PROBATION OFFICERS VIEW THEIR JOB RESPONSIBILITIES

DALE E. VAN LANINGHAM, MERLIN TABER, and RITA DIMANTS

When two ro more probation officers come together, the result is often a heated discussion on how their job responsibilities should be handled. For the probation officer is faced daily with dozens of situations in which he is forced to make a choice among possible responses.

From a sociological viewpoint, the problem of choosing consistent ways of response is relevant to the concept of "role." A role may be defined as a unique combination of certain customary ways of responding to recurrent situations—this unique combination being known and expected by others who deal with persons in this role, as well as by the persons who occupy the role.

The role of the probation officer is a relatively new one in our society, and may be viewed in terms of certain more familiar role models. The probationer may see the probation officer as a "policeman," while the judge may view him as an "investigator." The probation officer himself may be striving to be a "big brother" or possibly a "therapist" to the probationer.

A number of "role prescriptions" or "role recipes" have been offered for the probation officer by authorities on the subject. This study[1] was carried out to discover how adult probation officers *themselves* see their role, to explore the differences in their viewpoints, and to learn in what areas agreement might exist. The results, while confirming the expected but disturbing lack of agreement among probation officers, showed surprising agreement in certain areas.

A secondary purpose was to learn some of the characteristics of persons currently working as adult probation officers.

Method

Several hundred adult probation officers were asked to judge the *degree of appropriateness* to their jobs of a number of specific tasks which are known to be performed by at least some probation officers. The respondent was instructed to rate each of these tasks as though he were being required to do it. The categories from which to choose were "very appropriate," "somewhat appropriate," "middle" (or "undecided"), "somewhat inappropriate," and "very inappropriate."

The list of specific tasks was developed in order to make the concept of "role" concrete for research purposes. The first step in designing the questionnaire was to define the role or "job responsibilities" of the probation officer in terms of seven functions, each in turn being represented by a number of "tasks" or specific examples of behavioral responses to a situation.[2] To test the validity of the classification, we asked three experts to assign each task to one of the seven functions and also to judge whether the tasks were, in fact, performed by probation officers. In addition, the reliability of the responses to the items was assessed by the test-retest method performed with a group of people having probation experience. As a result of these procedures, ambiguous and unrealiable items were discarded, and some of the items were clarified. A revised list of fifty-two tasks was organized into the questionnaire form—seven tasks for each function and three unclassified ones.

In addition to rating the fifty-two tasks, the respondents were asked a few questions to determine their age, sex, education, and careers.

The questionnaires were distributed by mail to 417 adult probation officers in selected probation services differing by region, urbanization, and level of education among the staff. The interest of probation officers and probation administrators in this subject is reflected in the high rate—85 per cent—of returns.

Characteristics

The characteristics of the adult probation officers in this study were much the same as the characteristics of workers with adult offenders revealed in a 1960 national survey.[3] While random sampling was not used, the similarity between the two groups indicated that a representative cross-section of adult probation officers had been secured.

Of the 355 responding probation officers, 90 per cent were male. The median age was thirty-six years. Seventy per cent were in the age range of twenty-five to forty-five. Only 5 per cent had no college education, and 88 per cent had received bachelor's degrees. Sixty-two per cent had attended graduate school, and 16 per cent had received master's degrees.

About one-half of the master's degrees were in social work, 14 per cent in sociology, 11 per cent in correctional administration, 5 per cent each in psychology, education, and other social sciences, and 14 per cent in miscellaneous areas.

Sociology was the main subject of undergraduate study, 28 per cent of those who had attended college having chosen it as their major subject.

Social work was the subject most frequently chosen for graduate study. Thirty-five per cent of those who had attended graduate school had studied social work for their major subject. Other relatively popular major subjects at both undergraduate and graduate levels were psychology, education, criminology, police and correctional administration, and various other social sciences. This notable variety of major subjects and the failure of any one to predominate suggests a lack of agreement among probation officers on the appropriate educational preparation for their work.

Thirty-five per cent of the probation officers had worked previously in welfare agencies other than correctional services; 20 per cent had worked previously as juvenile probation or parole officers; 15 per cent had worked in law enforcement agencies.

Overall agreement

For purposes of analysis the five categories of appropriateness were telescoped into three categories— appropriate, middle (undecided), and inappropriate. *Agreement as to the appropriateness of a task, for this study, was agreement by 67 per cent or more of the probation officers on one of these three categories.* Of the fifty-two tasks in the questionnaire, the probation officers were, on this basis, able to agree on the appropriateness or inappropriateness of less than 60 per cent. Approval was given to only thirty of the fifty-two tasks, or 58 per cent of the total.

An example of the wide disagreement that existed on some of the tasks is seen in the response to the statement: "The probation officer orders the probationer to pay his bills." Forty-five per cent considered this appropriate, 31 per cent regarded it as inappropriate, and 25 per cent were in the middle category.

Inability of persons in the same profession to agree on the appropriateness of 42 per cent of tasks in that profession seems surprising. However, examination of responses after grouping of the *tasks* into *functions* reveals a high level of agreement in regard to certain of the *functions*.

The tasks are shown in Tables 1-8, grouped according to their function, with the most highly approved at the head.[4] In the questionnaire the tasks were not so grouped, and no mention was made of the function title.

Referral function

Numerous authorities, such as Dressler and Hardman,[5] have indicated that the probation officer has the function of referring the probationer to other resources in the community for help which the officer or his own agency cannot provide. This function was considered by probation officers as the most appropriate to their work. There was agreement that all seven of the referral tasks in Table 1 were appropriate for an adult probation officer.

The referral task most highly endorsed was that of referring a physically impaired probationer to Vocational Rehabilitation. Ninety-nine per cent of the probation officers

TABLE 1

REFERRAL TASKS	% Appropriate	% Inappropriate
1. Refers the probationer, who is unable to continue his trade because of a physical impairment, to Vocational Rehabilitation.	99	.3
2. Refers the probationer to the state employment office for vocational counseling.	96	2
3. Refers the probationer to a marital counseling resource regarding marital problems.	94	2
4. Refers the probationer to a psychiatric resource for the treatment of homosexuality.	91	4
5. Refers the probationer to the welfare office for financial assistance.	89	3
6. Refers the fundless probationer to a legal resource, known to consider the client's income, for advice regarding a civil suit.	80	9
7. Refers the probationer to a child guidance resource for help with his six-year-old son's bed wetting.	72	10

regarded this as appropriate.

Even the lowest ranked of the referral tasks—referring the probationer to a child guidance resource for help with his six-year-old son's bed wetting—was considered appropriate by 72 per cent of the probation officers.

It appears from these figures that the probationer may expect help from his probation officer in being referred to the proper community resource for assistance with a problem.

Advice and guidance

The advice and guidance function involved providing fairly direct advice or guidance for day-to-day living. In devising tasks to represent this function, we differentiated them from more sophisticated psychological techniques. Like the referral function, the advice and guidance function was highly endorsed as an appropriate job responsibility. There was agreement among the probation officers that six of the seven tasks in this function were appropriate. The first choice in this group—explaining to the probationer the disadvantages in continuing his association with certain known "police characters"—was approved by 96 per cent of the probation officers. (See Table 2.)

The only task in this function on

TABLE 2

ADVICE AND GUIDANCE TASKS	% Appropriate	% Inappropriate
1. Explains to the probationer the disadvantages in continuing his association with certain known "police characters."	96	1
2. Discusses with the probationer the advantages of good grooming and appropriate behavior when applying for a job.	93	1
3. Explains to the probationer who has purchased an auto with no liability insurance the reasons for securing such insurance.	93	2
4. Suggests to the probationer certain activities for his free time.	87	3
5. Helps the probationer to plan a budget.	85	4
6. Considers with the probationer the type of education to pursue.	80	3
7. Explains to the probationer the contents of divorce papers served on the probationer at his wife's initiative.	62	18

which the probation officers did not agree was No. 7: "[The probation officer] explains to the probationer the contents of divorce papers served on the probationer at his wife's initiative." However, even this task was marked as appropriate by 62 per cent, and 20 per cent marked it in the middle category.

Court consultant

The function of court consultant calls for interpreting to the court the social and personal factors concerning the client, knowledge essential in making a decision. The probation officers agreed (see Table 3) that six out of the seven court consultant tasks were appropriate for them. Task No. 1, in which the probation officer, through the presentence investigation, informs the court of the environmental conditions which contributed to the offender's crime, was approved by 98 per cent of the officers.

The only court consultant task upon which the probation officers failed to achieve the required agreement was No. 7: "[The probation officer] informs the court that the condition of probation requiring the probationer to abstain totally from the use of intoxicants no longer appears necessary." While 44 per cent of the probation officers rated this as appro-

TABLE 3

Court Consultant Tasks	% Appropriate	% Inappropriate
1. Through the presentence investigation, informs the court of the environmental conditions which contributed to the offense.	98	1
2. Contacts the court to recommend that the probationer who has made a successful adjustment without close supervision be allowed to move out of state in order to advance his vocation.	97	1
3. Through the presentence investigation, informs the court of community resources applicable to the offender's rehabilitation.	95	1
4. Takes the initiative to advise the court that the probationer has made a good adjustment and would benefit from early probation dismissal.	94	1
5. Recommends to the court that the ordered amount of restitution be reduced to a sum more appropriate to the probationer's situation.	69	20
6. Recommends that the court consider revocation of probation for the probationer whose attitudes, lack of cooperation, and minimal adjustment indicate that another offense is imminent.	67	21
7. Informs the court that the condition of probation requiring the probationer to abstain totally from the use of intoxicants no longer appears necessary.	44	35

priate, 35 per cent considered it inappropriate, and 21 per cent seemed undecided.

Generally, it appears that the function of court consultant is well established among adult probation officers as an appropriate job responsibility.

Psychotherapy

The function of psychotherapy is differentiated from the function of

TABLE 4

Psychotherapy Tasks	% Appropriate	% Inappropriate
1. Helps the probationer understand why he is unduly suspicious of people.	77	9
2. Helps the probationer understand why he takes unnecessary chances which frequently endanger his life.	76	11
3. Helps the probationer understand why he is an alcoholic.	70	15
4. Helps the probationer understand why he has constant anxiety with no apparent cause.	63	17
5. Helps the probationer understand his unconscious reasons for shoplifting.	59	21
6. Provides regular counseling to the probationer and his spouse regarding their marital problems.	56	24
7. Counsels the probationer to help him understand why he is a homosexual.	55	28

advice and guidance in that it utilizes techniques based largely on psychological orientation and is concerned with deep-seated emotional problems.

The probation officers reached agreement on the appropriateness for their work of only three of the psychotherapy tasks in the questionnaire (Table 4). The range in approval for these tasks was from 77 to 70 per cent.

Although approximately two-thirds of the probation officers did not agree that the other four tasks were appropriate to their work, substantial numbers of them did give approval to these tasks. For example, 56 per cent

considered it appropriate to provide regular marital counseling to the probationer and his spouse, while 24 per cent considered it inappropriate. Even the psychotherapy task least approved—helping the probationer understand why he is a homosexual—was regarded as an appropriate job by 55 per cent of the probation officers, with 28 per cent marking it as inappropriate.

Although the type or length of education did not seem to affect to a great extent the way probation officers viewed the appropriateness of performing psychotherapy, these tasks did gain somewhat more approval from those who had studied social work on a graduate level than from the total group.

Law enforcement

The law enforcement function is defined as the use of police, detective, or surveillance techniques to apprehend the probationer who violates the law or his probation conditions, or to detect such violations.

The probation officers in this study approved only two of the seven law enforcement tasks as appropriate.

(See Table 5.) These were: checking with Alcoholics Anonymous to see whether a probationer has been attending as ordered (regarded as appropriate by 83 per cent) and checking court calendars and newspapers to see whether a probationer has appeared in court without the probation officer's knowledge regarded as appropriate by 72 per cent).

Figures in Table 5 show that the remaining five tasks evoked wide divergences of opinion among adult probation officers as to their law enforcement responsibilities. The law

TABLE 5

LAW ENFORCEMENT TASKS	% Appropriate	% Inappropriate
1. Checks with Alcoholics Anonymous to see whether the probationer has been attending as ordered by the court.	83	9
2. Checks court calendars and court columns in newspapers to find out whether the probationer has appeared in court without probation officer's knowledge.	72	13
3. Collaborates with the sheriff or police to trap the probationer who has absconded.	62	21
4. Makes surprise home visits to see whether the probationer is violating his conditions of probation.	43	32
5. Contacts the probationer's employer to see whether any conditions of probation have been violated.	30	49
6. Checks into taverns to see whether the probationer is violating his probation by drinking.	25	52
7. Questions the probationer's neighbors to see whether any conditions of probation have been violated.	16	65

enforcement task considered least appropriate by the probation officers was questioning a probationer's neighbors to see whether any conditions of probation have been violated. Sixty-five per cent designated this as inappropriate, yet 16 per cent checked it as appropriate.

Environmental manipulation

The function of environmental manipulation can be described as the attempt to influence directly the persons and organizations important in the probationer's adjustment. Wallace characterizes these activities as "concrete services," such as "helping someone get a job, be readmitted to school, find a place to live, or establish eligibility for welfare, medical treatment, etc."[6] Wallace points out that many probationers need such services more than they need sympathetic insight into their problems.

Only one manipulative task under this function in the study—talking to a loan company to help ease financial pressure on the probationer—was

TABLE 6

Environmental Manipulative Tasks	% Appropriate	% Inappropriate
1. Talks to the loan company to help ease the financial pressure on the probationer.	67	14
2. Tries to find suitable living arrangements for the probationer.	63	15
3. Attempts to persuade the employer to keep the probationer on the job.	57	17
4. Arranges for the diabetic probationer to have proper diet when he has continually demonstrated an inability to manage this himself.	57	24
5. Arranges for the probationer to be given a restricted driver's license, good for work only, even though his regular driver's license is suspended.	52	29
6. Attempts to persuade the welfare office to provide the probationer with financial assistance.	44	37
7. Uses his car to accompany an unmotivated probationer with a poor work history in search of employment.	29	58

approved among the probation officers as appropriate (see Table 6), and even this one received only the minimal 67 per cent endorsement.

The responses for a few of the six other tasks may illustrate the lack of agreement about the function of environmental manipulation. Sixty-three per cent of the probation officers considered it appropriate to their work to help a probationer find suitable living arrangements, but 15 per cent regarded this as inappropriate. Forty-four per cent rated attempting "to persuade the welfare office to provide the probationer with financial assistance" as appropriate, but 37 per cent marked it as inappropriate. The probation officer's use of his own car to take a probationer with a poor motivation and work history in search of employment was regarded as appropriate by 29 per cent of the probation officers, but inappropriate by 58 per cent.

The tasks constituting environmental manipulation seem to have in common the requirement that the officer take an active part in doing something for the probationer as opposed to giving advice or attempting psychotherapy. Fear of creating dependency, fear of being used by the probationer, and the burden of heavy caseloads possibly explain why probation officers do not regard environmental manipulation as appropriate. No inquiries about the caseloads were made in the questionnaire.

Conduct establishment and enforcement

During the course of the study, it became apparent that some tasks often performed by probation officers did not seem to fit into the traditional functions found in books and articles. These were tasks such as ordering the probationer to pay his bills, to purchase liability insurance for his car, or to change his manner of dress. In other words, it seemed that some probation officers used their authority to attempt to control behavior which was not illegal but of which they disapproved. For the study, this function was named "conduct establishment and enforcement." It is defined as the use of the officer's

> "...some probation officers used their authority to attempt to control behavior which was not illegal but of which they disapproved."

authority to attempt to coerce the probationer into behaving in accordance with the prevailing value system of the community, as interpreted by the probation officer, or into behaving in ways the probation officer considers to have a rehabilitating influence.

The probation officers did not agree that any one of these seven tasks was appropriate; they did, however, agree that two of these tasks were *inappropriate* (see Table 7). Eighty-five per cent of the probation officers considered it inappropriate to order a probationer to attend church, and only 5 per cent regarded this as appropriate. Eighty-four per cent considered it inappropriate to order a probationer to marry his pregnant girl friend, and only 4 per cent thought this was appropriate.

While there was no agreement to either approve or reject the remaining five tasks, there was, as in the law enforcement function, a wide range of

TABLE 7

Conduct Establishment & Enforcement Tasks	% Appropriate	% Inappropriate
1. Orders the probationer not to hang around poolrooms.	43	28
2. Orders the probationer to pay his bills.	45	31
3. Orders the probationer not to wear a "duck-tail" haircut.	32	46
4. Orders the probationer who has acquired an auto with no liability insurance to purchase such insurance even though not required by law.	34	55
5. Orders the probationer to attend Alcoholics Anonymous meetings although attendance was not stipulated in the conditions of probation.	24	57
6. Orders the probationer to attend church.	5	85
7. Orders the probationer to marry his pregnant girl friend.	4	84

responses. Substantial numbers of probation officers did indicate that they regarded it as appropriate to coerce the probationer to behave in a "proper manner." For example, 43 per cent considered it appropriate to order a probationer not to frequent pool rooms, while 28 per cent did not consider this appropriate. Thirty-two per cent thought it appropriate for them to order a probationer not to wear a "duck-tail" haircut, but 46 per cent thought such an order to be inappropriate. Thirty-four per cent approved the task of ordering a probationer to purchase liability insurance for his auto, but 55 per cent considered such an order inappropriate.

Unclassified tasks

The remaining three tasks were not grouped under any of the seven functions. Responses to inquiries about them are shown in Table 8.

Conclusion

This study confirmed the observations of many students of the field of probation: that there is a lack of agreement about the job of a probation officer and about the type of preparation and training required for the field. The study, however, also indicated the specific functions, or types of tasks, where there is general agreement.

Three functions or main aspects of a probation officer's job were generally approved by the adult probation officers in the study—referring probationers to appropriate community resources for help, providing probationers with fairly direct advice and guidance for day-to-day living, and acting as social consultant to the court.

Despite this large area of agreement there are several other functions—psychotherapy, for example—well-established in the literature and in practice, about which probation officers are unable to agree.

Interestingly enough, there was considerable disagreement among the probation officers as to the appropriateness of their law enforcement function, although the lay public often pictures the probation officer as primarily a law enforcer.

Failure of the probation officers to rate environmental manipulation as an appropriate task should cause concern. Unless the probation officer is willing to take an active part in doing something along these lines for the probationer, the best of advice and guidance may fall on deaf ears.

> *"...the best of advice and guidance may fall on deaf ears."*

Attempts to force the probationer to avoid disapproved but not illegal behavior was the least approved function. However, substantial minorities approved some of these tasks. Perhaps the organizers of probation services need to examine their policies and the practice of their officers regarding such "conduct enforcement." Outside the narrowly defined scope of the court order, to what extent should a probationer be subjected to the particular moral standards of his probation officer?

If the general public, the judges, or the probationers themselves were questioned, presumably there would be even greater disagreement about the role of the adult probation officer. This lack of consensus has several possible consequences: the probation officer experiences conflicting and

TABLE 8

UNCLASSIFIED TASKS	% Appropriate	% Inappropriate
1. Reminds the probationer of the consequences of violating the conditions of probation.	91	2
2. Discusses with the probationer the help that may come from a religious faith.	72	12
3. Strikes the probationer when he is disrespectful.	1	99

incompatible demands; the general public does not know how to evaluate the results of probation work; and, most important of all, the probationer does not know what to expect on assignment to a probation officer.

Notes

[1]Special acknowledgment is given to Alan Christiansen, probation supervisor, Iowa State Board of Control, who served as special advisor to the study.

[2]Especially helpful analyses of the probation officer's job were David Dressler, *Practice and Theory of Probation and Parole* (New York: Columbia Univ. Press, 1959), pp. 151-65; D. G. Hardman, "The Function of the Probation Officer," *Federal Probation* (Sept. 1960), pp. 3-10; Charles L. Newman, *Sourcebook on Probation, Parole and Pardons* (Springfield, Ill.: Charles C. Thomas, 1958), pp. 109-73.

[3]National Social Welfare Assembly, "Salaries and Working Conditions of Social Welfare Manpower in 1960."

[4]The figures for each task shown in the tables do not total 100% since the middle category has been omitted.

[5]*Supra* note 2.

[6]J.A. Wallace, "A Fresh Look at Old Probation Standards," *Crime and Delinquency* (Apr. 1964), p. 126.

22. *The probation officer is charged with the dual tasks of reintegrating the probationer into society and, at the same time, protecting society from any errors of judgment or strategy that may result in criminal behavior during the reintegration process. Because the two tasks are to some degree contradictory, the officer must choose either to:*

1. Turn his full attention to the rehabilitative task, hoping that the community will be protected concomitantly (these officers, according to Tomaino in the following article, seem to say, "Probationers will want to keep the rules once they get an insight into themselves. The P.O. should be supportive, warm, and non-judgmental in his relations with them");

2. Spend the bulk of his time checking up on the probationer functioning as little more than a specialized policeman; ("Probationers will keep the rules only if you take a hard line, exert very close supervision, and stay completely objective in your relations with them");

3. Strike a middle ground which, while lacking the clout of fanaticism which is inherent in the above methods, will allow the probation officer to accomplish "humane but realistic treatment of offenders."

Laningham et al. conclude that the current middle ground is by no means balanced. Officers tend to resist those duties which require law enforcement tactics. Louis Tomaino, in "The Five Faces of Probation," uses Blake and Mouton's "Managerial Grid" to quantitatively graph both the extreme methods listed above, and various forms of the third possibility wherein lie the only truly effective means of probation.

THE FIVE FACES OF PROBATION

LOUIS TOMAINO

In seeking to meet the challenge of crime and delinquency, the modern probation officer finds himself caught up in a peculiar double bind. He must serve the needs of his probationers, on one hand, and the needs of the community, on the other. This two-sided facet of the probation officer's function is a result of evolutionary changes in both the conception and scope of probation. It represents corrections' attempt to discover the most effective means of accomplishing humane but realistic treatment of offenders.

The law mandates that probationers should be "helped" to overcome or neutralize their antisocial behaviors. At the same time probation is aimed at "protecting" the community from those same overt behaviors. The dilemma which this poses is well known to probation officers who must put this dual task into some manageable perspective in their work. Too often, the training of correctional personnel shows features of choosing one goal over the other. Depending on whether one's orientation comes from psychology, sociology, criminology, social work, counseling, etc., probation styles tend to treat the dual goals as somewhat mutually exclusive.

Out of this duality here emerges what may be termed the "five faces of probation." this is taken to mean that probation officers manifest certain strategies, approaches, or styles of "probationing" which reflect their degrees of concern for meeting the stated goals of help and protection. Each of these styles "shows it's face" to the probationer and starts the interaction which leads to five differential outcomes in probation officer-probationer relationships.

This set of relationships can be examined and clarified where viewed in terms of a Probation Grid. The grid concept stems from Blake and Mouton's[1] well-known "Managerial Grid" used so successfully by them for training managerial personnel. Such a construction has been applied to other content areas like decisionmaking, change, and leadership. This article proposes to explicate a Probation Grid stemming directly from the probation objectives of helping individuals and protecting the community.

These objectives will be expressed as the probation officer's concern for effective *control* over his client's illegal behaviors, and, the probation officer's concern for satisfactory *rehabilitation* of his probationer. These concerns, for analytical purposes, are seen as being independent of each other, though in practice, probation officers may impose a relationship on them which manifests the five faces of probation. Therefore in the grid model, the two dimensions are oriented at right angles to each other. The horizontal axis of the Probation Grid represents the goal of control experienced by officers, and the vertical axis reflects his concern for rehabilitation of the probationer.

This article is interested in the degree to which a probation officer is concerned about the two grid dimensions. Therefore, as in the Blake-Mouton grid, each axis is scaled from 1 to 9 in order to reflect degree of concern. The value 1 denotes low or minimal "concern for" while 9 symbolizes high or maximal "concern for" By arranging the concerns at right angles to each other and by providing a scalar arrangement the probation faces of probation officers can be assessed from the frame of reference which they bring to the relationship between the concerns. "Concern for" is not a static term rooted only in the officer's attitude. What is significant is how that officer is concerned about control, or about rehabilitation or about how these concerns fuse.

The Probation Grid is presented in Figure 1. Three faces of probation and the grid assume that concerns for control and rehabilitation are in basic conflict with each other and are mutually exclusive. The officer who has this frame of reference finds himself choosing one concern over the other, but not both, as his probation focus. The probation faces which result from this forced choice, reading in grid fashion (right and up) are the 9/1, 1/9, and 1/1. Each of these faces will be evaluated according to it's primary characteristics in probation counseling.

Control is defined as a condition in which the probationer is under close behavioral surveillance by his probation officer and is not violating probation rules. Rehabilitation is defined as a condition obtained when the probationer is not violating his probation rules, is not under close surveillance, and apparently has internalized some prosocial behaviors.

The lower right-hand corner of the grid represents a maximal concern for control and a minimal concern for rehabilitation. This frame of reference is based on the assumption that probationers will respond only when they have to, under coercive surveil-

FIGURE 1
THE PROBATION GRID

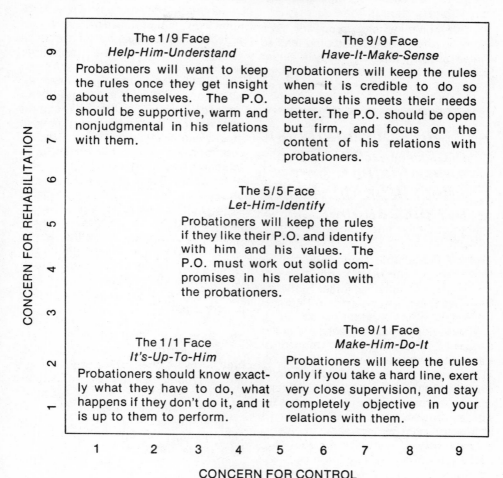

CONCERN FOR REHABILITATION

The 1/9 Face
Help-Him-Understand

Probationers will want to keep the rules once they get insight about themselves. The P.O. should be supportive, warm and nonjudgmental in his relations with them.

The 9/9 Face
Have-It-Make-Sense

Probationers will keep the rules when it is credible to do so because this meets their needs better. The P.O. should be open but firm, and focus on the content of his relations with probationers.

The 5/5 Face
Let-Him-Identify

Probationers will keep the rules if they like their P.O. and identify with him and his values. The P.O. must work out solid compromises in his relations with the probationers.

The 1/1 Face
It's-Up-To-Him

Probationers should know exactly what they have to do, what happens if they don't do it, and it is up to them to perform.

The 9/1 Face
Make-Him-Do-It

Probationers will keep the rules only if you take a hard line, exert very close supervision, and stay completely objective in your relations with them.

CONCERN FOR CONTROL

lance with swift penalties when they do not conform. It is not suggested that P.O.'s with a 9/1 face have no interest in their clients but rather that this interest becomes manifested only under rigid control variables. The 9/1 officer sincerely believes that probationers need a strict leader who governs their otherwise hedonistic tendencies.

A 9/1 officer believes that control is rehabilitation and that his most crucial obligation is to protect community interests via strict limits placed on his clients. If the community is properly protected a kind of *fait accompli* effect is produced in the probationer whose illegal behaviors are blocked through control. Such a system of enforced cooperation induces clients to accept probationary conditions without having to internalize them. Interaction between probation officer and probationer tends to be formal, official, and largely a question of "one upsmanship" on the side of the P.O.

This one-dimension probation face may be effective. It could also lead to false security that a client is under control when, in fact, his compliance is only superficial. Kelman[2] has

> ## "If the community is properly protected a kind of fait accompli effect is produced in the probationer..."

demonstrated that conformity behavior which occurs under conditions of high power remains intact only so long as there is surveillance. Removal of close monitoring results in a decrease of conformity behavior and a return to more prepotent modes of acting which may well be antisocial. Combined with the hostility and resentment which a 9/1 probation face often produces in others, this approach represents an unstable form of behavior management.

The P.O.'s 9/1 face says to the probationer, "I expect you to keep these probationary conditions. I'll do what I can to help you but you will have to 'toe the mark' and there is no room for error."

The 1/9 face

The 1/9 face is designated by the upper left hand grid position which indicates high probation officer concern for rehabilitating his probationer and small concern for controlling him. In this approach the P.O.'s overriding motivation is based on the assumption that individuals are basically good and will seek appropriate, legal behaviors once they are helped to understand themselves. This self-knowledge will promote growth, foster prosocial attitudes, and terminate in satisfactory observance of probationary rules.

The 9/1 face is rejected as constituting an effort by the community to impose its own values of correct behavior on the probationer. This is seen as antithetical to the free choice condition needed if the client is to foster his own adaptation to the orders of the court. The face projected to the probationer in this framework is a warm, supportive, and nonjudgmental countenance. The probation officer tends to emerge primarily as a therapist who facilitates insight on the client's part. He learns to form a close relationship with the probationer and refines a repertoire of clinical skills aimed at rehabilitation.

Unlike the 9/1, a 1/9 face produces probationary supervision under conditions of freedom, mutuality, and a high level of client decision-making. The psychodynamics of individual probationers emerge as more potent than the social determinants of crime or delinquency. This also poses a dilemma for probation officers. A 1/9 face lends itself to manipulation, a perception that it is permissive and there is some likelihood of being "conned."

The P.O's 1/9 face says to the probationer, "I hope that you will understand the need for these probationary conditions. I will support you in every way I can and help you make your own decisions in a way that you will find contentment and not feel threatened by me."

The 1/1 face

The lower-left grid location refers to

probation officers who manifest minimal concerns for both control and rehabilitation. In this face, probationers are thought of as autogenous and, therefore, will change or fail to do so as a result of their own motivation. No conscious or systematic probation strategy will be effective because circumstances, spontaneous occurrences, and genetic chance are the important variables. If individual probationer tendencies for illegal behaviors are in conflict with external probationary attempts to alter them, the probation officer must set up a situation to evaluate what happens. His role is to appraise and advise his client about failure to conform, keep the court informed on the probationer's observance of the rules, and operate as an observer of progress rather than initiator of behavioral change.

Considerable energy is invested into the logistics of probation. Records are well-maintained, reports are current, and probationer contacts are regular. However, the limited affective involvement with clients, and a mechanical approach to probation leaves this officer with no dynamic probation face. It should be noted that such an outcome is not necessarily due to the officer's personality. A 1/1 probation program or administration might well promote status quo values which frustrate aggressive probation officers who then revert to "reporting" procedures as a way to fill the role assigned in their work.

The P.O.'s 1/1 face says to his probationer, "I'm sure you understand these conditions of probation. It's up to you to stick to them. No one can do it for you. If you need me be sure to contact me."

The 5/5 face

In the grid center is found the 5/5 probation officer who proceeds on the assumption that both control and rehabilitation are necessary but that full concern cannot be given to both. This face demonstrates a belief that probationers need leadership; they have not benefited from sound identification figures in the past; in fact, their very alignment with deviant models probably induced their earliest extra-legal actions. Individuals have strong needs for positive affiliations with others and probation officers provide this opportunity for probationers.

The 5/5 face must have and display the personal, psychological, social, and culturally valued qualities which probationers can learn to assume. The probation officer works hard at gaining trust and respect by demonstrating a "regular guy" face which can be trusted to understand the "real" problems encountered by probationers. tioners.

A positive relationship between P.O. and client has always been central to good probation but not necessarily with the view of maintaining the personal charisma of the officer. In the 5/5 face, this likeableness becomes crucial. If the probationer likes his probation officer and attempts therefore, to pleas him, then

"If the probationer likes his probation officer and attempts ...to please him, then the likelihood of his breaking court orders is less."

the likelihood of his breaking court orders is less. By implication, this helps to secure some control while also helping the individual probationer to alter some of his antisocial predispositions.

Some work completed in recent years by attraction theory psychologists suggests that 5/5 face holds promising components for the P.O.-probationer relationship. Aronson,[3] for example, thinks that increasing rewards and punishments from a person have more impact on his attractiveness than constant, invariant rewards and punishments. For the P.O. who must so often "start from scratch" with his probationer, Aronson's mini-theory seems to be significant for developing 5/5 attractiveness in his work.

The P.O.'s 5/5 face suggests to probationer that "you and I will work together in keeping these probation rules. I know how you must be feeling and thinking and if you stick with me you can make it."

The 9/9 face

By orienting the concern for control and the concern for rehabilitation at right angles to each other, it is possible to clarify probation faces reflected to individuals who are on probation. The countenances postulated so far indicate an orientation toward an incompatibility of the dual concerns. This dichotomization has bedeviled corrections for decades.

The 9/9 face seeks to integrate concerns for control and rehabilitation. A 9/9 P.O. brings full concern for both dimensions of the grid at the same time. This means he creates conditions which help a probationer help himself but limited by the reality of probationary conditions. This means that he stresses goals rather than personality traits of his probationer. These traits are treated as important but not necessarily in cause and effect fashion. Instead, the probationer is helped to select from goals calculated to meet his needs more effectively within a legal framework. The 9/9 face organizes legitimate choices and through a collaborative relationship induces the client to act in accord with prosocial expectations.

Underlying a 9/9 face is the notion that probationers are more likely to exert control over themselves and become rehabilitated when they can internalize what is expected of them.

> Internalization can be said to occur when an individual accepts influence because the content of the induced behavior—the ideas and actions of which it is composed—is intrinsically rewarding.[4]

Put another way, it may be said that clients change when it makes sense to do so because there is some kind of "pay off." Their needs are met in better fashion. In the 9/1 face probationers tend to see resentment or fear; in a 1/9 face they are inclined to see chances to manipulate their P.O.; in a 1/1 face, probationers may read apathy; in a 5/5 profile a tenuous balance of charisma shows up. The 9/9 face projects credibility and says to the probationer "let's put our heads together, take a look at what needs to be done now; we may be able to go about doing it and determine the best way of finishing a realistic probation program."

It seems reasonable to assert that probation officers reflect all of these faces with various probationers under different circumstances. Each carries with it a different set of probable outcomes. This article suggests that a basic 9/9 face is more likely to give equitable attention to concerns for both control and rehabilitation. If true, we may hypothesize that this set of conditions is most likely to meet the needs of both probationers and community.

Notes

[1] Robert Blake & Jane Mouton, *The Managerial Grid* (Houston: Gulf Publishing Co., 1964).
[2] H.C. Kelman, "Compliance, Identification, and Internalization: Three Processes of Attitude Change," *Journal of Conflict Resolution, 2* (1958), 51-60.
[3] E. Aronson, "Who Likes Whom and Why," *Psych. Today* (Aug. 1970), pp. 48-50, 74.
[4] Kelman, *supra* note 2, p. 54.

23. *Incarceration, as seen in Part II of this volume, can serve three functions: it isolates an offender, thus obviating any further harm which he may do to the community; it can be used retributively both as a means of settling the debt which the offender "owes" society and as an example for potential offenders; and it can provide a controlled environment in which the offender can be rehabilitated. Typically, a prison sentence serves all three functions, though not in equal amounts. The prison walls are a reasonably effective isolator and, although recent court decisions and trends in prison management have caused the proponents of punishment to rally behind cries of laxity, the deprivation of the offender's freedom is, in a democratic state, an indisputable form of retribution. The rehabilitative function of incarceration, however, has been attacked by the school of thought which says "it can't work and look—it doesn't," and by those who say "it can work, although it doesn't seem to be working." The former claim that the offender cannot be rehabilitated, while the latter assert that the ills of rehabilitation are inherent in the prison setting and are not fundamental to the rehabilitation idea.*

Thus, at the same time that many rehabilitative innovations (such as parole) are floundering, probation flourishes. The offender who is a "good risk" is offered a period of time during which his freedom is mildly curtailed by the restrictions of probation and during which he may be changed for the good of society. The proponents of probation argue that an offender can be more successfully reintegrated into society if he is, in fact, a part of that society and not removed to an institutional setting.

Yet, as was shown in the preceding articles, the rehabilitative function of probation is, to a degree, hampered by the reluctance on the part of probation officers to properly balance the rehabilitative function against a law enforcement function.

Irving Reichert, in the concluding article of this part, addresses an equally important impediment to the probation process: numbers. Probation officers must handle so many cases at once that, according to one report, cited in the following article, "probation...supervision typically consist[s] of a ten to fifteen minute interview once or twice a month...." The probation officer who works under such conditions, even though he may assume what Tomaino would call a 9/9 face, would have only seven and one-half minutes in which to be concerned about the probationer's rehabilitation and another seven and one-half minutes during which he can conrol. And though a two-minute phone call to the right agency may, in fact, work wonders, the problem of too little time in which to change too many people remains.

WHY PROBATION FAILS

IRVING F. REICHERT, JR.

Formal probation for adults is a costly and frequently meaningless function. The courts' expectations of adult probation services and supervision are unrealistically broad, and the caseloads borne by probation officers are impossibly heavy.

According to one leading report,

>...the probation or parole officer's first duty is to "keep track" of

his cases and see... that they stay out of trouble; that they maintain regular employment or stay in school; that they not drink or use narcotics. Often he has little time for these functions. If this were the whole of the job, it would still not be easy to accomplish in most jurisdictions. But in fact, probation and parole supervisors aim at much more...An officer is expected to offer counseling and guidance and to help in getting a job or in straightening out family difficulties. In practice, he is almost always too pressed to do this well...Probation and parole supervision typically consist of a *ten to fifteen minute interview once or twice a month....* (emphasis added in original article)[1]

Though the foregoing was written in 1967, it is not outdated. It still appears to present a reasonably accurate picture of the work that is going on in most adult probation departments.[2] It is time to restructure our courts' overburdened and ineffective probation policies.

After a defendant is found guilty, the court has a limited number of sentencing alternatives. The judge may sentence the person to the state prison or the county jail, depending upon the seriousness of the offense. A jail sentence may be given for a certain period of time without probation attached or may be imposed as a condition of granting probation.

The judge may place the person on *formal* probation (i.e., reporting to and under supervision by the probation department), setting certain probationary conditions with which the defendant must comply; or he may place the person on *summary* probation, which means that he need not report to the probation department but is subject to sentencing by the court for his original offense should he get into further trouble during the probationary period.

The judge may merely impose a fine, which must be paid either immediately or over a period of time. Frequently the court orders such payments to be made to the probation department to insure compliance.

These are the alternatives primarily available to the courts, although there are some variations, such as requiring a person, as a condition of either formal or summary probation, to spend a certain number of hours in "voluntary" employment projects of benefit to the community. Discussion of such alternatives is not necessary for the purpose of this article.

What we are concerned with here is the type of probation order issued by the court. We begin with the premise that the court has determined that a straight jail or prison sentence is not warranted by the circumstances of the offense. On the other hand, the court feels that the person cannot possibly be released without some sort of sanction imposed, and therefore turns to probation.

There are a number of reasons why the court may determine that a defendant should be placed on formal rather than summary probation. While on formal probation, the defendant will receive at least some degree of supervision and control. This may give the community a little more security and protection than if the defendant were placed on summary probation. The defendant may also receive medical or psychological treatment or counseling which may be helpful and may provide an additional safeguard to the community.

The court may feel that the defendant needs some kind of punishment that is not as stringent as prison or jail but is more punitive than summary probation as it is generally used. There is less chance of the public accusing the court of laxity if the defendant is placed on formal rather than summary probation. Also, formal probation may serve as some sort of deterrent to the defendant or to others who hear about the case.

A realistic look at the actual operation of an adult probation department forces us to confront some very uncomfortable facts which to a great extent offset the intended benefits of formal probation.

Caseloads are so high that there can be no effective supervision, little if any provision of useful services to the defendant and no reasonable protection to the community. The 1974 Annual Report of the Santa Clara County Adult Probation Department shows that the average supervision caseload is 150 per deputy. In the Alcoholic Supervision Unit the caseload is 220 per deputy. These figures are more meaningful when considered with the following:

• The Report of the President's Commission on Law Enforcement and Administration of Justice (1967) recommended supervisory caseloads of 35 (p. 167). This is approximately the same figure used by other organizations that have studied probation.

• A memorandum dated August 6, 1975, from an administrative analyst in the Santa Clara County Executive's Office to the Chief Adult Probation Officer, entitled *Increased Workload or Reduction in Level of Service,* states that the Adult Probation Department faces "a workload crisis in 1975-76." The analysis, based on time and motion studies, shows that the actual number of hours worked by a probation officer (exclusive of vacation, sick leave, etc.) is 150.8 per month. The projected caseload per deputy per month for 1975-76 ranges from 138 to 285.7 for the Alcoholic Supervision Unit.

• Several probation officers in the department estimate that a probation officer spends over 70 per cent of his time in paper work required by law and departmental policy. An operations analysis of the Adult Probation Department recently made by the County Executive's Office shows even more startling figures: actual contact (face-to-face or by telephone) between probation officers and probationers accounts for less than 10 per cent of probation officers' time. With caseloads of 175, the average number of times a probation officer sees a client is .66 times per month, or less than eight times a year.

On the other hand, there is little if any reliable research showing that probation officers with lower caseloads are able to achieve better results than those with higher caseloads. In fact, *A Review of Accumulated Research in the California Youth Authority* (May, 1974) includes a "Parole Research Project" conducted from 1959 to 1961 that was designed to see whether reduced caseloads resulted in improved parole performance. The finding was "that wards in reduced caseloads performed no better than those on regular caseloads." A number of similar studies have reached much the same conclusion.[3]

Another shortcoming of formal probation is that probation officers often lack qualifications to deal with many problems confronting their clients. Furthermore, it is doubtful whether any training is known or available that can help them. Several factors make this so. One is that, unfortunately, we know very little about the basic causes of criminal behavior, rehabilitation, predictability of behavior, and similar matters. Another is that the defendant's current predicament can be attributed to numerous factors: poverty, ghetto living conditions, a bad family situation, the values of the group from which he comes or with whom he associates, an inferior education, or a myriad of other societal and economic factors. These are situations about which the best of probation officers can frequently do little or nothing. What they *can* provide may only be in the form of temporary, stop-gap measures. In some cases (though this is dubious) professionals with higher levels of training (e.g., psychiatrists or psychologists) might achieve better results, but even if this were possible the costs would appear to be prohibitive.

Additionally, the increased use of lay volunteers by probation departments throughout the country and the success claims attributed to the "one-to-one" relationship with an untrained layman "who cares" suggest

that professional training and expertise found in the best of our probation

---

"We know very little about the basic causes of criminal behavior. . ."

---

officers may be unnecessary or superfluous.

It is also possible that in most cases, the mere threat of jail for violating reasonable court-imposed conditions of probation is as effective a deterrent to the defendant, and as "rehabilitative" a force, as the "services and supervision" given by the

FIGURE 1
PROBATION PRESENTENCE REPORT

It is recommended that the defendant be placed on:

☐ formal probation
☐ summary probation

If summary probation is recommended, complete the following:

☐ It is recommended that the defendant be placed on summary probation and be instructed by the court to comply with the following conditions: (list conditions)
☐ It is recommended that the defendant be placed on summary probation with no conditions other than the court's admonition that further criminal acts committed during the probationary period may result in a jail sentence.

☐ It is recommended that the defendant be placed on summary probation and pay a fine of $____ and/or restitution in the amount of $____. This can be handled by a cashier in our office. If payment is not made, the court will be advised and a bench warrant will be requested.
☐ The defendant needs the following services: (list)
These can be provided by one or more of the following agencies, which have agreed to accept the defendant at a cost which is stated after the name of the agency:
The defendant agrees to follow the instructions of the agency (agencies) and has been informed that failure to do so may result in revocation of his probation and a

FIGURE 1 (Continued)

possible jail sentence. The agency (agencies) agrees(s) to notify ☐ the clerk of the court ☐ the appropriate person in our office should the defendant fail to follow his prescribed program. The person in our office who will be so notified is _____.

If formal probation is recommended, complete the following:

☐ It is recommended that the defendant be placed on formal probation so that he can receive the following services or supervision which he cannot receive on summary probation: (list services)

The above services:
☐ are only available through the Adult Probation Department.
☐ are available through community agencies, but these agencies ☐ will accept referrals only through Probation, not directly from the court; ☐ refuse for policy reasons to report to the court if the defendant fails to follow the prescribed program; ☐ are more expensive than similar services offered by the Adult Probation Department; ☐ are too crowded to accept the defendant until (approximate date). (list agencies that provide services needed and the name of the person called.); ☐ are available in the Adult Probation Department. Probation Officer (name) has been contacted. His/her current caseload is ____ supervisory cases and ____ presentence investigations per

month, and he/she can give this case the attention it requires.

This probation officer is qualified to handle this case. He/she estimates that this case will require approximately ____ hours per month in personal contact with the defendant and ____ hours per month in paper work. In the event that the probation officer's caseload increases or that the defendant's problems demand more time than expected, so that the probation officer cannot give proper attention to the defendant, he/she will immediately notify the court of the change of circumstance. If it later appears that the defendant no longer needs formal probation services, and that summary probation will suffice, the probation officer will notify the court and recommend that such action be taken.

The planned supervision of this defendant will include the following procedures:
____ Number of visits per month at home or place of employment. (____ hours per month)
____ Number of office visits per month by defendant. (____ hours per month)
____ Other (describe)____
The estimated department cost per month of the proposed program of formal probation is $____.
The defendant is able to pay $____ per month toward the cost of such services. ☐ He/she agrees to do so. ☐ He/she is unwilling to do so.

probation officer. At this time I know of no data that contradict this hypothesis.

Finally, formal probation results in higher costs to the taxpayer than summary probation, and the advantages of using the former in many cases are not apparent.

A Proposed Probation Policy

I propose a more realistic, more effective, and less costly utilization of probation department services. Formal probation should be used only when the adult probation department can show that its services are necessary, that they are available, and that its staff is able to provide services or supervision which appear to be of sufficient benefit to warrant the costs involved. Research on what types of effective services probation officers can provide is sorely needed. It may be that probation departments should primarily serve as conduits to other agencies that specialize in drug abuse problems, alcoholism, mental illness, vocational training, etc.

If a probationer is not referred to a community agency, the department should be required to show either 1) that there is no agency that can provide the necessary services, or 2) that the department can provide the same services at a lower cost.

To those who say that such burden of proof cannot be met because of the lack of supporting research, because of the inability to predict results with any degree of certainty, or because of our present lack of knowledge in this area, I would respond that since the cost of government is soaring to heights unbearable to the taxpayers, no governmental services should be provided unless their benefits and value can be reasonably predicted or demonstrated.

In a large number of cases, the results the court wishes to achieve—or can realistically hope to achieve—can be accomplished just as effectively and at much lower cost by placing the defendant on summary probation. And if the court will specify that the defendant is not to be assigned to an ordinary caseload but is merely to pay restitution or fines to a cashier or clerk in that department, the resources of the department may

> *"...no governmental services should be provided unless their benefits and value can be reasonably predicted..."*

be employed to much greater advantage. The morale of probation officers will certainly improve if they are relieved of responsibility for matters in which they feel that no action on their part is necessary or helpful; officers will be able to spend more time on cases where services or supervision really are necessary; caseloads will be more manageable; and the costs to taxpayers will be substantially reduced, with a possible concurrent increase in financial benefits to the community.

The collecting of these restitutions and fines can be handled by the court clerk, by a designated clerk or cashier in the probation department, or by a central court collection agency. Thus, the probation department might be involved in summary probation cases, but only to the extent that it would hire, at a savings, a person who needs neither the training nor the expertise of a probation officer.

Under summary probation, defendants can be referred *directly* to community agencies rather than going through formal probation. Compliance and non-compliance with the court's order and progress reports by the referral agency can be made either to the clerk of the court or to a probation officer assigned to that court, who can take whatever steps are appropriate.

If the courts' policy concerning the uses of summary and formal probation is changed along the lines suggested here, and the courts think more in terms of summary than formal probation, undoubtedly many more imaginative ideas will occur to the judges. The emphasis, however, should always be on using formal probation sparingly, only when the interests of the community or of the defendant require it and the reasonably foreseeable benefits justify the cost and use of professional manpower.

In each case, before formal probation is invoked by the courts a specific plan should be presented as part of the presentence report. This plan should state both the nature of the defendant's problem and the services and supervision that can be assured by the department—services that will offer either a strong possibility of benefit to the defendant or increased protection to the community by *effective* supervision, or both. If a satisfactory plan cannot be furnished to the court, what justification is there for further swelling the probation caseloads and subjecting the taxpayers to the increased expense of a meaningless service?

A cover sheet should accompany each presentence report. The actual sheet will take more detailed planning than the one presented here. However, Figure One suggests a possible format.

Impact

What would the impact be on the present staffing of the Adult Probation Department if this policy were carried out? Would the jobs and futures of probation officers be affected?

Probation officers should not fear but should welcome the adoption of such a policy. First, diminishing the flow of referrals to the Probation Department will reduce caseloads and enable officers to do a better job on the cases that they are handling. Second, an immediate, careful screening of present caseloads, using the criteria suggested here, will cut caseloads to a more manageable level.

There should be, under the proposed plan, one or more probation officers without formal caseloads. I envision the courts placing people on summary probation *without* any reporting requirements, but urging them to call the probation department for assistance if they should need any type of help. Assistance should be readily available to those who *seek* such counsel.

This plan would accomplish several objectives. It would reduce caseloads and enable better work to be done. It would save taxpayers money and at the same time improve the quality of service. It would raise the morale of probation officers by enabling them to do a more professional, conscientious job. And it would screen present and future cases to eliminate those in which no real service can be performed. It would be of significant value to judges, probation workers, persons on probation and the community.

Notes

[1] *The Challenge of Crime in a Free Society*, A report by the President's Commission on Law Enforcement and Administration of Justice (U.S. Gov. Print. Off. 1967) p. 165.

[2] Although references and data cited in this article pertain primarily to the Adult Probation Dept. in Santa Clara Co., Calif., conversations with leading probation authorities as well as general reading in the field confirms that the problems dealt with in this article are far more universal than unique.

[3] *Corrections Magazine* (May/June 1975) reports that a Jan. 1975 study of the probation subsidy program in California showed no difference in recidivism between the special caseloads (averaging about 30) and regular probation caseloads (numbering from 75 to more than 100). Allen Breed, director of the Calif. Youth Authority, is quoted as saying, "The question of why special supervision and regular probation are no different is really beyond me. It could mean that it doesn't really help to intervene in people's lives." The article states that the study provided for the possibility that those in special caseloads were caught in illegal behavior more often than those on regular probation. "That isn't an explanation," said "a discouraged Breed" (p. 23).